M

ʌ

THE POETRY OF EMILY DICKINSON

BOOK II.

EMBLEM II.

Pfalm 69.15.

My Bark's already wreck'd! O timely save
The wretched Suppliant from a Watry Grave

The illustration above and that on page 273 were photographed from Emily Dickinson's edition of Francis Quarles's *Emblems, Divine and Moral,* now in the collection of the Houghton Library of Harvard University.

The Poetry of Emily Dickinson

BY

RUTH MILLER

WESLEYAN UNIVERSITY PRESS

Middletown, Connecticut

To my husband
Irving Kriesberg

Contents

Acknowledgments

I WISH TO EXPRESS MY GRATITUDE TO THOSE WHO HAVE ENCOURAGED and aided me: Maxwell Geismar, Professor William M. Gibson, Professor Alfred Kazin, Professor Ilse D. Lind, Professor Henry Bamford Parkes. I owe a special debt to Professor Richard B. Sewall for his gallant sharing of facts and sources, as well as his wise admonishments that saved me from many an error. I cherish the memory of my conversation with Mrs. Millicent Todd Bingham, who welcomes all who are engaged with the poetry of Emily Dickinson. The generous support of the Yaddo Foundation at Saratoga Springs and the Projects, Grants and Research Committee of the Graduate School, State University of New York at Stony Brook, enabled me to devote myself totally to the completion of my work.

I acknowledge too the courtesy and valuable assistance of the librarians in charge of the special collections of Emily Dickinson materials: Miss Carolyn E. Jakeman, the Houghton Library, Harvard University; C. T. Laugher, the Frost Library, Amherst College; Charles R. Green, the Jones Library, Amherst; Miss Gladys K. E. MacKenzie, Archivist for the Todd Collection at the Sterling Library, Yale University. I had easy access to the files of the *Springfield Daily Republican,* the *Hampshire Gazette,* and the *Hampshire and Franklin Express* at the Forbes Library at Northampton, and the City Library Association at Springfield. The active interest of the library staff of the Melville Library at my own institution, State University of New York at Stony Brook, secured for my prolonged use the invaluable Lexicon, the 1847 edition of Webster's Dictionary.

I am grateful also to the several publishers who have granted me permission to reprint materials from works under their control, and to the members of their staffs who handled the complex details of my requests—most particularly, Mrs. Helen Lane of Harper & Row; Miss June D. Pagett, Mr. David Horne, and Mr. Thomas J. Wilson of Harvard University Press; Miss Barbara E. Amidon of Houghton Mifflin; and Miss Kathleen Brooks and Mr. J. Randall Williams of Little, Brown. Detailed credits for these borrowings are given elsewhere in this volume.

My colleagues in the department of English, particularly Professor Herbert Weisinger, were helplessly tolerant of my defection from all but Emily Dickinson business. The greatest tolerance of all came from my family, who I believe have at last forgiven me for requiring them to listen.

But the consistent intolerance of my friend, Dr. Elizabeth Coleman, requires me to say publicly: Your sharp red pencil and your sharp tongue made my task far more difficult than it otherwise would have been—and all the better for that.

Roslyn, Long Island   RUTH MILLER
January, 1968

THE POETRY OF EMILY DICKINSON

CHAPTER ONE

The First Publication

TODO AND HIGGINSON

Myths are the institutions of the mind. They have an organic life of their own; they remain alive despite fact and reason, despite evidence and proof. Bored by the commonplace, we dream of broken hearts and undying loyalties; gnawed by materialism and expedience, we relish the extraordinary, we are bewitched by the exotic, we dream of dedication to ethereal abstractions. The mythic Emily Dickinson was a shy primitive, a recluse whose retirement from the active world was due to an act of renunciation of an unattainable lover. The poet Emily Dickinson does not fit the woman of this myth. The poems she left to the world, the best evidence we have today, are the speculations and contemplations, the queries and outbursts of a tough-minded, independent woman whose self-doubt and timidities were a mask. She was a woman who allayed her despair at the world's rejection of her as a poet by composing hymns to herself and hymns to God. Emily Dickinson knew the sacrifice she was making, knew why, and was willing to gamble on an imitation of Christ for the sake of a victory like His—immortality.

When she died in 1886 only close relatives, a few friends and acquaintances had received her poems. She had renounced all hope of publication in her lifetime as early as 1862. Her own disavowal appears in her third letter to Thomas Higginson: "I smile when you suggest that I delay 'to publish'—that being foreign to my thought, as Firmament to Fin—"[1] Many biographers of the poet have taken this to be an expression of her agreement with Higginson that she was not yet ready. Yet there follows in this same letter her explanation of why she smiles: "If fame belonged to me, I could not escape her—if she did not, the longest day would pass me on the chase." This does not mean she does not wish to publish. It means the matter is out of her hands.

Between 1858 and 1862 Emily Dickinson had besieged her friend Samuel Bowles, editor of the *Springfield Republican,* with poems and with pleas on their behalf but failed to move him.[2] Now in 1862 she applied to Thomas Higginson, critic and essayist, associated with the *Atlantic Monthly,* and his response, though more delicate, served as a confirmation of Bowles' opinion: Higginson would be willing to correspond with her, but he could not in conscience advise her to publish.[3]

Thus she had made two major efforts to achieve status in her lifetime as a professional poet—to achieve the success that publication would signify. Despite her present failure and a despair which almost engulfed her, Emily Dickinson remained unshaken in her assessment of herself as a great poet. She merely renounced hope. She seems even to have cherished this renunciation of the larger world as a kind of price she must pay for her ultimate success. She could not easily dismiss the fact of her failure but she withstood it, withstood the misery that preyed on her spirit. Her disavowal, like her pose as the pupil of Higginson, became a mask to wear in public.

In the privacy of her room she strove for immortality as a poet in the only way left open to her: she practiced her craft with scrupulous commitment, seeking out the exact word, creating the precise metaphor, experimenting with meter and rhyme and syntax and line length. She refined a meticulous form that was to become a unique style, a poetic manner altogether at home in the twentieth century. She refined her thoughts and feelings about herself in a transient world, experimenting with ideas and attitudes, speculating about Nature and Time and Heaven, until she arrived at a synthesis of belief that could not have comforted the heart or illuminated the mind of her contemporaries.

We have evidence of her tough-minded healing faith; it resides in the poetry itself, in the subject matter and the form. Emily Dickinson records how she grew more patient as she crystallized her belief in Christ's saving grace, and therefore in the safety of her soul. Inside her sober world, the belief in her personal redemption became intricately interwoven with the belief in the ultimate immortality of herself as a poet. And she set about to prepare the way for the saving of her poems. She read and reread them: she scrutinized them for the meaningful image, she contemplated their subliminal ideas, and when she received some intuition of a structuring principle she selected and organized them into larger constructs of disparate but finished parts. She transcribed her choices carefully onto sheets of fine white paper, sewed the four or five pages together, tied the twine into a knot, and placed these fascicles one by one by one away to await the time when fame should arrive to capture them.

Toward the end of her life she had the satisfaction of beholding a witness of her glad tidings. Helen Hunt Jackson was valiant in her efforts to persuade the poet to alter her decision to seek no public hearing for her work:

> You are a great poet—and it is a wrong to the day you live in, that you will not sing aloud. When you are what men call dead, you will be sorry you were so stingy. [October, 1875]

> You say you find great pleasure in reading my verses. Let somebody somewhere whom you do not know have the same pleasure in reading yours; [1876]

> It is a cruel wrong to your "day and generation" that you will not give them light.—If such a thing should happen as that I should outlive you, I wish you would make me your literary legatee & executor. Surely, after you are what is called "dead," you will be willing that the poor ghosts you have left behind, should be cheered and pleased by your verses, will you not?—You ought to be. [September, 1884] [4]

Mrs. Jackson succeeded in placing one of Emily Dickinson's poems, "Success," in an anthology, *A Masque of Poets,* in 1878. Out of this there grew a correspondence between the poet and Thomas Niles, the publisher of this anthology, later editor of Roberts Brothers. He wrote to her in April, 1882:

> H. H. once told me that she wished you could be induced to publish a volume of poems. I should not want to say how highly she praised them, but to such an extent that I wish also that you could.[5]

In April, 1883, Niles returned Emily Dickinson's gift of a copy of Currer, Ellis and Acton Bell's *Poems,* with this statement:

> If I may presume to say so, I will take instead a M.S. collection of your poems, that is, if you want to give them to the world through the medium of a publisher.[6]

Emily Dickinson responded to Niles' interest by sending poems, first two, then one, and then a sampling of three. His reaction was favorable. But now the delay to publish was not to be a matter for anyone's choosing. In March of 1883 Judge Lord, the poet's beloved friend, suffered a stroke; her eight-year-old nephew Gilbert died in October; Judge Lord died in March of 1884; Emily Dickinson suffered a nervous breakdown in June, 1884; Helen Junt Jackson died in August, 1885, and the poet's death occurred on May 15, 1886.

But the ebon box was there. Inside lay 39 threaded fascicles (811 poems), 4 unthreaded fascicles (72 poems), and 8 packets of loose manuscripts (240 poems). Several hundred scraps of verse and worksheet drafts had also been carefully preserved.

Lavinia Dickinson denied any awareness of the extent to which her sister Emily had devoted herself to poetry. And yet the two sisters lived all their lives together, side by side, in the same house—Lavinia caring for her pets, Emily for her flowers—sharing the chores between them, sharing friends and gossip. Lavinia may even have thought of herself as the shield of her sister, protecting her from any undesirable intrusions, keeping the world at a safe distance. But it may have been Lavinia who learned the lesson of resilience and courage from Emily. It was Lavinia, in fact, who suffered from a thwarted love, as Professor R. B. Sewall has so conclusively demonstrated in his recent discovery and publication of the Lyman letters.[7] That both sisters withdrew more and more from active participation in the world outside is not proof that they withdrew from each other.

If one examines those "scraps" on which Emily Dickinson jotted down verses as they came into her head, one sees they are written on the blank side of grocery lists, envelopes, recipes, bills, programs, flyers, old letters, and so on. These scraps, carefully filed in the Special Collections Room of the Frost Library at Amherst College, reveal not chaos, not haphazardness, not carelessness, but frugality and care. Nothing in the household was wasted. Wastepaper was salvaged and used. When Emily Dickinson examined her worksheets and found a poem to her taste, she copied it carefully onto a better piece of paper. She would rework the draft ultimately into a fair copy, which she then placed into a packet of loose sheets to await the time when it could be fitted into a fascicle. If the scraps were not used yet—they might one day be. Hence they remained. Surely this kind of jotting and starts and hasty alteration does not seem to be a maneuver of secrecy. It is much simpler, though not as romantic, to imagine an ordinary kitchen, with each sister going about the routine of ordinary household activities, interrupted from time to time when one sister stops what she has been doing and takes up a reclaimed scrap of paper on which she writes a dangerously fleeting metaphor. There would be time enough to retire upstairs to work over what had been written down during the course of the day.

No. Lavinia knew, as did her sister-in-law Susan, as did her brother Austin, as did eventually the warm and affectionate friend of Lavinia and Austin and Emily—Mabel Loomis Todd—that the house sheltered a poet,[8] a poet who had no doubts whatever about her capacity for verse or her chances of success:

> To undertake is to achieve
> Be Undertaking blent
> With fortitude of obstacle
> And toward encouragement
>
> That fine Suspicion, Natures must
> Permitted to revere
> Departed Standards and the few
> Criterion Sources here [9]

This poem was sent to Higginson in 1865 and is itself an artful disguise of her attitude toward her mentor. Emily Dickinson tells him that to undertake the writing of poetry such as hers is already an achievement. Especially is this true if the undertaking, this effort, this taking on the task, be blended with two strong barriers to success: one, the fortitude of the obstacle itself (it is a hard thing to write a good poem) and two, if the only encouragement one has is suspicion from critics [Natures] who of course must be suspicious if all they permit themselves to admire [revere] are old poets who established the traditional forms [Departed Standards] or those few successful contemporary poets [Criterion Sources] who are assumed to be the criterion of good poetry.

It was this mentor, this Suspicious Nature, Higginson, to whom Lavinia wrote, to prevail upon him to undertake the task of editing the manuscripts. His refusal is no surprise. Yes, he had been in correspondence many years with the poet about her poetry; yes, he had visited her twice and had indeed come to Amherst to attend her funeral; but he was unwilling to wade through so much illegible and indeterminate material. Moreover, he doubted that he could find enough good poems to constitute a volume.

Lavinia ignored the second part of this reply and pressed Mrs. Todd to assist her in dealing with the first objection. Mrs. Todd's deep friendship for Austin Dickinson would have won her consent even had she not felt genuine love for the poetry. The story of how Lavinia Dickinson and Mabel Loomis Todd transferred an unknown poet and a unique poetry from a small bedroom in Amherst out into the world, where she was to win her place as a major poet exerting influences on subsequent generations of young writers, is a singular episode of American literary history.

The manuscripts in the fascicles left by the poet were clean, without variants for the most part, easy to decipher. It was their original, wholly unconventional poetic style that proved a stumbling block to the first editors. And so the knots of the little booklets were untied, the gatherings dispersed, the poems subjected to the taste and choice of Lavinia and Mrs. Todd, treated as entities in themselves. They did not think to let Emily Dickinson's choice guide them. It was Mabel Todd who was given the task to select and determine what might be the best form among poems the poet had not finalized. Mrs. Todd had to decide upon the most appropriate word from among the variants Emily Dickinson put down for herself on the margins of her paper or below the text. She had to choose an entire stanza when the poet left alternative versions. This problem might have been eliminated had Mrs. Todd confined herself to fair copies, clean, without variants, of which there were hundreds. But she desired to woo, first the conventional taste of Higginson, and after him, that of the public. Higginson's name was needed to lend an air of dignity to the enterprise. He had refused to engage in that first labor; he must now be convinced by poems of high quality, not rare originality. Mrs. Todd chose poems that would lend themselves to her purpose. Fair copy or worksheet draft was less important. Even when fair copies were used, regularization of the verse was insisted upon.

A note in her journal, dated November 30, 1890, reveals that Mrs. Todd also wished to satisfy her own sense of good form:

At the same time, their carelessness of form exasperated me. I could always find the gist & meaning, and I admired her strange words and ways of using them, but the simplest laws of verse-making she ignored, and what she called rhymes grated on me. But she could not hide her wonderful power, and I knew she had genius.[10]

Mrs. Todd thought herself a well-educated person, sensitive to the qualities of great literature. She had written short stories and articles and had been trained in music and art. She had no compunctions about the changes she made. Colloquialisms were removed, syntax was altered, words substituted to effect a proper rhyme, punctuation corrected, underlining removed, capital letters eliminated, line-length fixed, and irregular stanzas reconstructed into orderly quatrains. It worked. Higginson joined the enterprise.

He played his part reluctantly at first, remaining detached except for external details. It was his idea to arrange the poems of the forthcoming volume according to themes. His four categories of "Life," "Love," "Nature," "Time and Eternity," were familiar and comfortable. That Emily Dickinson herself believed in no such distinctions, that to her the relationship between life and nature and eternity was a seamless one, was not understood by the first editors.[11] Although the poet had supplied titles to only five of her poems, Higginson decided to provide each with one in order to clarify its meaning. It is doubtful that his choices did much to illuminate the poems: "Astra Castra," "Rouge Gagne!" or "By the Sea," or "The Wind." His efforts to secure a publisher were desultory. It was Mabel Todd who brought the manuscript to Roberts Brothers, the house they hoped would honor Thomas Niles' early interest. But Niles, too, was cautious and conventional. He asked Arlo Bates, a writer of fiction and verse, to appraise the manuscript. Higginson was so intimidated by Bates' adverse critical comments he sent the poems back to Mrs. Todd and requested her to revise them further "with these criticisms and then return to me."

Arlo Bates had been outraged by the technical imperfections, by the violations of meter and rhythm and rhyme. A comparison of the fair copy and the edited version of the following stanzas reveals how she polished the verse in order to satisfy such objections:

[the fair copy]

> How they will tell the Story —
> When Winter shake the Door —
> Till the Children urge —
> But the Forty —
> Did they — come back no more?

Then a softness—suffuse the Story—
And a silence—the Teller's eye—
And the Children—no further question—
And only the Sea—reply—

[the edited version]

How they will tell the shipwreck
    When winter shakes the door,
Till the children ask, "But the forty?
    Did they come back no more?"

Then a silence suffuses the story
    And a softness the teller's eye,
And the children no further question;
    And only the waves reply.

Higginson was no less troubled by the unusual style of the poems than he had always been. In his preface to the *Poems, First Series* he acknowledges the "Unconventional utterance of daring thoughts," warns that the verses are set "in a seemingly whimsical or even rugged frame," but suggests that to the sympathetic reader they will seem "like poetry torn up by the roots, with rain and dew and earth still clinging to them." He admits "we catch glimpses of a lyric strain, sustained perhaps but for a line or two at a time and making the reader regret its sudden cessation" but praises the grasp and the insight, the gift of vivid imagination of the poet.

Perhaps it was to offset the strange mannerisms of the poetry that he chose to speak at length of the strange mannerisms of the poet:

A recluse by temperament and habit, literally spending years without setting her foot beyond the doorstep, and many more years during which her walks were strictly limited to her father's grounds, she habitually concealed her mind, like her person, from all but a very few friends; and it was with great difficulty that she was persuaded to print, during her lifetime, three or four poems. . . . I saw her but twice face to face, and brought away the impression of something as unique and remote as Undine or Mignon or Thekla.[12]

Mabel Todd's faith in the poetry was more firm. An old friend of her family was William Dean Howells; she brought some of the manuscripts to him and Howells offered to write about the poems for *Harper's*

Magazine. Mrs. Todd communicated Howells' enthusiasm to Higginson, but he replied cautiously: "What you say about Howells is interesting, but he is a dangerous friend, often praising so whimsically, . . . that his praise rouses opposition as much as sympathy. . . . Do not trust too much in Howells' prediction of a sale." [13]

It is no surprise to us, now, to read that Howells predicted a great sale for the volume of poems, for it is a fact of our literary history that he recognized and encouraged and often sponsored young poets and novelists who were eventually to take their place among our most significant writers. It was his controversial reputation as a critic that worried Higginson, for Howells consistently championed the reading of Continental literature during a time of remarkable provincialism in our culture. Today we credit Howells with the broadening of American taste in literature, but in his generation he frequently antagonized, even outraged, critics who disagreed with his taste and judgment. His direct hand in the poetic history of Emily Dickinson was in large part responsible for the controversy that greeted the first publication.

Howells went himself to the publisher Thomas Niles, a month before publication date, November 12, to secure an advance copy of the poems. His famous review of *Poems, First Series,* written for *Harper's,* had just the effect on public opinion that Higginson feared. Curiosity or acclaim was intensified by the review of so important a critic as Howells. Whether a reviewer responded amiably or with vitriolic condemnation to the poetry of Emily Dickinson, he usually began with a quotation from the Howells article. But the following letter from Higginson to Mrs. Todd, written November 12, 1890, shows how we were placed more practically in Howells' debt:

> I am distressed exceedingly to find that among E.D.'s countless letters there are poems as good as any we printed—one on the Blue Jay . . . one on the Humming Bird . . . etc. This shows we *must* have another volume by and by & this must include prose from her letters, often quite as marvellous as her poetry. Howells is doing missionary work in private & that lovely child Mildred [Howells] selected as her chief favorite, today in talking with me *your* favorite about the two who died & talked between the tombs. . . .[14]

Higginson thus came to believe in the value of the poetry itself, well before the volume was published, before any adverse criticism might have intimidated him. He began immediately to cooperate with Mrs. Todd in the preparation of a second volume of poems.

Moreover, Howells was exactly right in his prediction. Between November 12 and December 27, 1890, *Poems, First Series,* had to be reprinted twice. In 1891 a fourth, a fifth, and a sixth edition sold out. A "Deluxe Edition" found a ready market. In the next year the poems were through their eleventh printing. All hesitation dissolved; a new volume needed to be published quickly before public interest cooled. The editors began to work at top speed, Mrs. Todd copying and selecting, Higginson organizing, titling, and advising.

The great success of the *Poems* had brought communications from far and near, many of them from friends and relatives of Emily Dickinson. Proud now of their relationship to her, they came forward with manuscripts sent them by the poet. Perez Cowan wrote to Mrs. Todd:

> Miss D. was a highly valued cousin of mine. During my college course at Amherst (1862–1866) one of her poems on the Sunset was given me, which I have greatly enjoyed, and which I was sorry not to find in the first volume of her poems. Thinking that possibly it may not have been brought to your attention, I refer to it, with the hope that it may appear in the volume soon to be published.[15]

Higginson was approached by Fanny Norcross:

> I am impelled to send to you my cousin's poem on the Mushroom . . . and also this gem about a Spider.
>
> I remember that you said you had not seen the first, and as I was reading it to a friend yesterday, I was so much impressed with its weirdness and originality, that I felt you ought to see it at once.[16]

He quickly wrote to Mrs. Todd: "I send a real *trouvaille* & assume yr. consent to putting in both poems. . . . But what can 'fleeter than a tare' mean. Tear?" This was the poem in question:

> The Mushroom is the Elf of Plants—
> At Evening, it is not—
> At Morning, in a Truffled Hut
> It stop upon a Spot
>
> As if it tarried always
> And yet it's whole Career
> Is shorter than a Snake's Delay
> And fleeter than a Tare—

Mrs. Todd accepted the spider poem for a reason that seems humorous today: "The spider poem is fine. I have one or two more about spiders, so perhaps this had better go in, also." But her interpretation of the questionable word "tare" reveals that she better understood its meaning than did Higginson:

> I think "fleeter than a *tare*" is what she meant. Tares are supposed to grow very fast—faster than wheat or anything else useful; but the mushroom comes quicker yet—"fleeter" as she says, and lives an even shorter time. Might it not mean this?

Mrs. Todd need not have speculated; had she referred to Emily Dickinson's Lexicon, which defines "tare" as "A weed that grows among corn" she could have settled the matter.

And when it came to interpreting the meaning of a poem when the words were simple enough and familiar enough, Mrs. Todd again was able to resolve Higginson's confusion. This was the case with the following poem:

> He put the Belt around my life—
> I heard the Buckle snap—
> And turned away, imperial,
> My Lifetime folding up—
> Deliberate, as a Duke would do
> A Kingdom's Title Deed—
> Henceforth, a Dedicated sort—
> A Member of the Cloud.
>
> Yet not too far to come at call—
> And do the little Toils
> That make the Circuit of the Rest—
> And deal occasional smiles
> To lives that stoop to notice mine—
> And kindly ask it in—
> Whose invitation, know you not
> For Whom I must decline?

Higginson is uncertain:

> In "He put the buckle round my life" is it "a member of the cloud," & what does it mean? "a member of the breed" would be intelligible & rhyme.

Mrs. Todd supplies an interpretation that quiets his uneasiness, saves the poem from his good rhyme, and avoids a distorted meaning:

> The line in "He put the belt around my life" does read "A member of the cloud," in the original, and I suppose simply means to express the great loftiness conferred by the love given, which made her "fold up" her lifetime, "henceforth a dedicated sort."

Had she examined the poem in the frame provided by Emily Dickinson, had she looked into Fascicle 14, where the poem lay beside such companion pieces as "I taste a liquor never brewed—" and "I've heard an Organ talk, sometimes—" and "Of all the Sounds despatched abroad," Mrs. Todd could have identified exactly the kind of dedication, the nature of that "Cloud" and the precise source of her "loftiness," not conferred by love but achieved by the poet: she would have understood that Emily Dickinson meant poetry. And she could have verified all this by examining the variant poem, transcribed into this same fascicle, in which the terms are so similar that their recurrence seems to be almost deliberate for the sake of interillumination:

> A solemn thing—it was—I said—
> A Woman—white—to be—
> And wear—if God should count me fit—
> Her blameless mystery—
>
> A timid thing—to drop a life
> Into the mystic well—
> Too plummetless—that it come back—
> Eternity—until—
>
> I pondered how the bliss would look—
> And would it feel as big—
> When I could take it in my hand—
> As hovering—seen—through fog—
>
> And then—the size of this "small" life—
> The Sages—call it small—
> Swelled—like Horizons—in my breast—
> And I sneered—softly—"small"!

The "dedicated sort" of the first poem becomes the "Woman—white" of the variant; the one who wears "Her blameless mystery" is that same

"Member of the Cloud." In the first, the poet folds up her lifetime at God's claiming of her (putting a Belt around her life); in the variant she ponders more the risk, is more timid, for she must "drop" her life into a well so deep it will not come back until Eternity. It is consistent that in the first poem the poet should become imperial after her ritual experience of dedication, for she has been chosen, and she chooses, and so may go on with her mundane tasks knowing well that these only enhance the real task [the Rest]; she need not respond to people who beckon her, for she now belongs to God. And it is consistent that there be an analogue to pride in the variant poem, and that it be humility, for that is exactly what is variant—her attitude toward her commitment. But the poet rights herself and comes out at the same place: her early timidity shifts to a sneer at the Sages who have intimidated her, just as her new bliss grows and grows in her breast. By the time her "small" life swells to "Horizons" she has become the imperial recipient of her "Kingdom's Title Deed." [17]

Had Mrs. Todd studied the poem "He put the Belt around my life—" in its first context, Emily Dickinson's own construct, she might never have untied the booklets and gone picking and choosing her way, assessing the poems "Class C," "Class B," "Class A": good, better and best. But it was the desire of both editors, now immersed in their task of creating a second volume of poems that would please an eager public, convince a recalcitrant public, and lure the stand-off public that remained.

They took care to avoid poems that might cause undue difficulty. When Higginson asked Mrs. Todd "Is not 'The flower must not blame the bee' a little too enigmatical?" she answered "If 'The flower must not blame the bee' seems too enigmatical, let us leave it out." It was eliminated.

So much did they desire to have poems that were more conventional, they did not hesitate to create them when that became necessary. Higginson explains his procedure to Mrs. Todd: "I have combined the two 'Juggler of Day' poems, using the otter's window of course (oriell!!) & making the juggler a woman, as is proper." Mrs. Todd defends her practice to Higginson: "I only put the longer lines [the two first as one] in 'I know that he exists' because it seemed to give a more dignified resonance to the noble words, and because it seemed to show somewhat more of connection between the rather far-apart rhymes." [18]

A note from Mrs. Todd to Higginson shows that even Lavinia, with no pretensions to literary judgment, had a hand in the alterations of the text:

"Pompless no life can pass away" is not my change—Miss Vinnie says it is the right way according to the original—and I am going over there now to verify * * * [The asterisks are Mrs. Todd's to indicate a hiatus of time.] She cannot find the original, but she is sure "Pompless no life," etc., is right, and wants it so.

Mrs. Todd's journal records that she was frequently "at work with Vinnie" and read to her all the poems they were intending to use, in the hope of enlightening comments; but there is no record that any were received.[19]

The accelerating efforts of Mabel Todd and T. W. Higginson to hurry to press a new volume were dominated, then, by purposes extraneous to the poetry. Primarily they worked with a fixed and pervasive conception of public taste. And the best answer, after all, to the charge that rankled most—that Emily Dickinson was inept, simply unskilled in the craft—was to publish poems that looked like and sounded like conventional poetry. They gave to her lines the "grace of smoothness" and refined the "harsh exterior"; they sought out lyrics or else they fashioned lyrics they believed would be pleasant.

It was hoped that a more logical, a more obvious organization of the poems within the old framework would make up for what seemed to the critics of that time the illogic and often incoherence of single poems. Higginson's insistence on titles was one device; his grouping the poems of similar subject matter was another:

I hv. put titles to many of the Nature poems, wh. you can *dele*. . . . I hv. put "Mother Nature" first, then the Dawn poems & so through the day—then spring to autumn, mingling in birds, etc., closing with "Summer's Parting."

Mrs. Todd was more exact in her effort to achieve coherence through chronological ordering:

I have changed the order of some of the last "Nature" poems, so that the two on the departure of summer may not come after "November" but before, bringing "November" just before "Snow."

Higginson asked Mrs. Todd to write the preface to the *Second Series*. She was gracious, in her turn, offering to submit the preface to Higginson for his approval before printing. Her note accompanying the manuscript reveals her sense of the complexity of her task: she wished to "answer, point by point, the things said of [Emily Dickinson] by the critics"; [20] she wished to explain the reason for variations in the published text from different versions held by the poet's friends; she hoped to "forestall further spreading of what is not true about her."

In her effort to achieve her first objective, Mrs. Todd seems to have had Howells' review beside her on her writing table. Like Howells, she acknowledges the fact of the critical attack and her defense, and like Howells, she writes: "The very roughness of her own rendering is part of herself, and not lightly to be touched; for it seems in many cases that she intentionally avoided the smoother and more usual rhymes." The words in Howells' review admit and defend in very similar fashion: "Occasionally, the outside of the poem . . . is left so rough, so rude, that the art seems to have faltered. But there is apparent to reflection the fact that the artist meant just this harsh exterior to remain, and that no grace of smoothness could have imparted her intention as it does." [21]

Mrs. Todd seeks to dissuade the critics by explaining that in the very lack of conventional form lies the source of Emily Dickinson's poetic power:

> In Emily Dickinson's exacting hands, the especial, intrinsic fitness of a particular order of words might not be sacrificed to anything virtually extrinsic; and her verses all show a strange cadence of inner rhythmical music. Lines are always daringly constructed, and the "thought-rhyme" appears frequently,—appealing, indeed, to an unrecognized sense more elusive than hearing.

She echoes the words of Howells, who had analyzed the quality of the poetry without apology, tempting the reader with the "intrinsic experience" that awaits him. Howells found the vitality of the poetry in the subtle interplay between the form and the idea, enriched by her music:

> In the stanzas below there is a still, solemn, rapt movement of the thought and music together that is of exquisite charm. . . . the love poems are of the same piercingly introspective cast as those differently named. The same force of imagination is in them. . . . They are [the short poems] each a compassed whole, a sharply finished point, and there is evidence, circumstantial and direct, that the author spared no pains in the perfect expression of her ideals.

Mrs. Todd was obviously influenced by Howells' approach, although she did not carry it so far as did the more practiced critic. Howells certainly fended off all attacks on Emily Dickinson's versifying, her lack of polish, her so-called crudities. But he was bound by no other motive than the desire to exercise his own critical faculties. And his insight enabled him to perceive exactly where Emily Dickinson's skill as a craftsman lay—not in mere originality, but in her deliberate manipulation of the formal elements of verse to render a deeply felt experience. Untroubled by her departure from tradition, he foresaw she would create her own tradition. But his judgment had to wait a long time before it became the starting point of an entirely new approach to her work. At least he was a spur, now, to the immediate publication of a second volume.

Unfortunately his insights into the value of the poetry were dispersed in the confusions and speculations concerning the hidden life of the poet. Mrs. Todd had to contend with this problem that was eventually to become the single major issue—the poet's private life. Her earliest effort to dispel the gossip may be seen in this direct statement taken from her preface to the new volume:

> She had tried society and the world, and found them lacking. She was not an invalid, and she lived in seclusion from no love-disappointment. Her life was the normal blossoming of a nature introspective to a high degree. . . .

But her voice was to be drowned out by her well-intentioned co-editor. At the last moment, to give Emily Dickinson a larger stature, to alter that image of her as a totally withdrawn New England spinster (which Higginson had fostered by initially calling her work "The Poetry of the Portfolio") he asked Mrs. Todd to feature in her preface Emily Dickinson's long friendship with Helen Hunt Jackson (d.1885) who in 1891 was still remembered with respect and admiration:

> I wish you wd. send me that passage in wh. HH. expressed the wish to be E.D.'s literary executor & that you wd. consider the expediency of prefixing it as a sort of motto for the new vol. I shld. like to link their names.

If Higginson intended to turn the attention of the public to the poetry by linking the widely known novelist and the recluse poet at this stage of Emily Dickinson's literary debut, he failed. For this novelist had caused quite a stir with the anonymous publication of her story "Esther Wynn's Love Letters" (*Scribner's,* 1871), a sentimental account of the fruitless passionate attachment between a genteel maiden poet and a married man.[22] The story was included in the anonymous *Saxe Holm's Stories:*

First Series published in 1873. Amherst was deeply excited by an editorial which appeared in the *Springfield Republican,* July 25, 1878, announcing its opinion that the writer was an Amherst woman:

> . . . all these lead us to the conclusion that the author may be a person long shut out from the world and living in a world of her own; that perhaps she is a recluse. . . . We cannot refrain, also, from picturing her robed in white. . . .[23]

The conjecture may have come from Franklin Sanborn, who had very recently received a letter from Emily Dickinson refusing his invitation to contribute to the paper for which he was now writing literary notes.[24] The following week, August 3, 1878, a direct denial had to be made: "We can only say that we happen to know that no person by the name of Dickinson is in any way responsible for the *Saxe Holm Stories.*"[25] But the damage was done. The *Springfield Union* had printed outright "that she answers in private to the honored name of Dickinson." It never retracted.

Doubtless Mrs. Jackson was irritated by the misconstruction. She was herself Esther Wynn and the Master was Higginson, her mentor and her teacher, "the only man to whom & to whose style, I chiefly owe what little I have done in literature."[26] She says further in her letter to a friend, "He is really the only man who can *swear* I wrote them. He read the first three or four [*Saxe Holm's Stories*] page by page, as I wrote them."[27]

Whatever Higginson's motives, however justified his "sense of expedience," as he himself calls it, his deliberate effort to engage the attention of the potential reader with bits of information from the biography shifted the focus to the love-tragedy and undermined Mrs. Todd's attempt to focus on the poetry. Probabably she could do nothing else but agree to remove a portion of her critical discussion and incorporate the "H.H. letter" in its place.

And Higginson was not content with this alone. If it was good publicity to link Helen Hunt Jackson's name with Emily Dickinson, it was better to come directly forth and link his own. Before *Poems, Second Series,* was published, Higginson placed an article in the *Atlantic Monthly* (October, 1891) that featured the letters he had received from Emily Dickinson during their years of correspondence. Ostensibly he wished to draw attention to the quality of her prose; in fact he enhanced those elements of mystery and secrecy surrounding the poet, and raised public interest in her personal tragedy to a peak. He emphasizes the fearful, the awestruck relationship she had with her father, the other-worldly quality of her appearance, the childlike aura surrounding her actions; he describes her manner of speaking as quaint and extravagant. Always the enigmatic nature of the poet is stressed: "The impression undoubtedly made on me was that of an excess of tension and of an abnormal life." [28]

The degree to which all reticence seems to have disintegrated can be seen from this gleeful note sent to Higginson from Lavinia:

> Thank you for giving Emilies wonderful letters to the world. . . . I believe the 2nd volume will be welcomed most eagerly. I'm sure *you* are glad I *insisted* the poems *should* be published. Aren't you?

Even Mrs. Todd was pleased:

> I wanted, first, to congratulate you on the *Atlantic* article, not only on its reading even more entertainingly than in the proof, if possible, but on its great notoriety and popularity, everywhere.[29]

Indeed it was popular and marked a turning point in Mrs. Todd's own conception of her role as a discoverer of a significant body of poetry. She put aside the manuscripts of the poems and turned her full attention to the preparation of a collection of Emily Dickinson's letters. Instead of gathering poems for a third volume of verse, she gathered letters. And her diligent search unearthed hundreds. Now all readers would know, as they had the "right to know something more of this gifted and most interesting woman." So rationalized Mrs. Todd.

When it came to organizing the letters for printing, she decided to group them according to recipients instead of poetic ideas. And she edited the text in a manner that pointed up her many tantalizing deletions, stimulating an interest far out of proportion to what had been removed. She may or may not have been careless of the implications embedded in her preface:

> It was with something almost like dread that I approached the task of arranging these letters, lest the deep revelations of a peculiarly shy inner life. . . .

> . . . the sanctities were not invaded . . .

> In her later years, Emily Dickinson rarely addressed the envelopes: it seemed as if her sensitive nature shrank from the publicity which even her handwriting would undergo. . . .[30]

But the reviewers and the readers, provided with such public admission of temerity by the editor herself, could hardly do less than believe that there was an enigma about Emily Dickinson's retirement, a secret about her life. Everywhere now, it was relevation of the poet that was wanted, not illumination of the poetry. No one remembered that the poet had used both letters and poems to communicate some specific thought or feeling; no one bothered about the fact that in almost every instance a poem accompanied a letter, that there was a significant relationship between the two in the poet's mind. There was no one to examine the letters for the occasion or event or idea that was confirmed in or explained by or commented upon or rendered in the poem. Except for Howells and his original appraisal that the significance of the newly discovered poet lay in the unique quality of her verse, no one seemed interested in the poetry.

Thus did Emily Dickinson fall prey to the cult of secrets that flourished in this period. There was a kind of stylization of anonymity affected by the publishing world—in newspapers, magazines, as well as books—the *Saxe Holm's Stories* being only one manifestation. There was the entire "No-Name Series" of novels published without the name of the author fixed on the title-page. John Hay's *The Bread-Winners* (1884), Henry Adams' *Democracy* (1879), and *Esther* (1884) were all published under an enticing screen of anonymity. The public enjoyed reading the stories and trying to outguess the critics, who for their part joined the game, performing literary analyses of style and subject in order to prove their guess. The volume of verse that Mrs. Jackson edited, *A Masque of Poets,* consisted of poems contributed anonymously—the point being the game of identification. A poem by Emily Dickinson found its way into that book, and the fact that it was ascribed to Emerson was supposed to be a matter of congratulation for the poet. Learning now of the original secrecy surrounding Emily Dickinson's poetry, hearing about hidden manuscripts and the recluse poet, the public immediately fell to speculating on the covert truth they assumed to lie concealed in the verse.[31]

It is refreshing to take note of Howells' consistency. Promised a copy of the *Letters* by Mrs. Todd, he seems noncommittal in his reply:

> I shall be glad of the Emily Dickinson letters, I am sure, when they come, and I thank you for thinking of me. What a rare and strange spirit she was! Any revelations of personality that her letters may make will be most welcome to those who now love her afar.[32]

So far as we know there was no further communication from Howells about the letters.

The unfortunate emphasis on the biography of the poet is significant as a turning point in the poetic history of Emily Dickinson. Although the poetry had been highly profitable to Lavinia Dickinson, no provision had been made for any financial reward to the editors: there is record of only one payment of $100 given Mrs. Todd and Colonel Higginson. But now that the letters were about to be published, expectations were high that there would be a great sale. Austin Dickinson tried to secure a legal agreement from Lavinia that would require her to share equally in money earned with Mrs. Todd, whose sole undertaking it was, since Higginson had withdrawn from all active participation. Austin's interference seemed to cause an estrangement between his sister and Mrs. Todd. As a gesture of good will, indeed to protect her interests, Austin planned to present her with a piece of his land which bordered the Todd property. Before the transfer could be effected he died—quite suddenly—and Mrs. Todd's last partisan was gone. Lavinia did actually sign the document deeding the land according to her brother's instructions; the *Third Series* of poems was in process of being edited by Mrs. Todd. Once the new volume of poems was in print Lavinia sued Mrs. Todd to prevent the exchange of property. All of the excitement of the discovery of Emily Dickinson and her poetry was obscured and finally disintegrated in the scandal of this lawsuit. Lavinia Dickinson won the case. Mrs. Todd closed the lid of her box of manuscripts and ended her association with the poetry.

CHAPTER TWO

Literary Intrigue

WITHIN A YEAR, MISS LAVINIA WAS DEAD, AND ALL HER ESTATE fell into the hands of Susan, the widow of Austin Dickinson. She lived on quietly in the less pleasant house next door, interesting herself more in the literary career of her daughter Martha than in the publishing history of her sister-in-law Emily. Eventually all responsibility for the precious manuscripts settled on young Martha, Emily Dickinson's niece, a woman of culture and sophistication, familiar with members of the literary circles of the time. She had sole access to the poetry, sole legal right to all that had been published, and all, it was supposed, that would eventually be published.

Not until 1914 did any further poems appear. Martha Dickinson (now Mrs. Bianchi) edited *The Single Hound,* consisting only of those poems her mother had received from the poet. She made a great point of using solely the manuscripts sent across the lawn from Emily to Sue, for these seemed to document a deep and abiding friendship between the poet and her sister-in-law. She deliberately ignored the manuscripts carried by Lavinia to Mrs. Todd, those preserved in the fascicles. This meant, of course, that none of the Todd-Higginson changes, none of Emily Dickinson's variants was used. The public was confused; the partisans of the poet were baffled; the dissenters were delighted.

Here began that continuing discrepancy in texts that defied anyone's sustained effort to get at the aesthetic quality of the poetry. Perhaps all that could be done with the poetry at this time was to cite lines of verse as documentation for some hypothesis contrived to interpret the meaning of Emily Dickinson's life.

Martha Gilbert Dickinson Bianchi (as she usually called herself) supplied two such hypotheses—it had become a rather large public. In 1918 Mrs. Bianchi published a novel [1] whose heroine is the last survivor of an austere New England family. The young sensitive musical poetical girl may not marry, may not bear children, because of a taint in her blood, not named insanity as such, but scattered throughout the novel are many hints that it is just that. This taint is specifically identified as deriving from her ancestress who had been a poet, her "Anne Bradstreet connection." We are told that the insanity is the guarded secret of the family:

> It is in New England that a secret is kept to the end. Lives are ruined for it, if need be. It is often a mistaken devotion . . . sacrificing happiness and development without a murmur. . . . "Don't let the neighbors know" is the first and most stubborn commandment.

In 1924 Mrs. Bianchi brought out *The Life and Letters of Emily Dickinson.*[2] In the *Life* a more attractive love-story was featured. Here, for the first time, the renunciation by Emily of the Reverend Charles Wadsworth was recounted, with much embellishment, and the authoritative ring of a niece's testimony.[3]

In the 1890's when sentimentality had prevailed, and romantic secrets excited where poetic style might repel, lovers had been construed, tragic partings hinted at; now an actual passionate attachment had been described and the man identified. This settled nothing, however; it merely pointed the way to new romantic discoveries.

In 1930 two further biographies presented new lovers. Genevieve Taggard brought forward Leonard Humphrey, principal at Amherst Academy during Emily Dickinson's final year there (in 1847). She added for good measure an even more shadowy George Gould, an editor of the Amherst College monthly and a friend of Austin Dickinson.[4] Josephine Pollitt sentimentalized an attachment to Helen Hunt Jackson's second husband, Lieutenant Hunt, the ordnance engineer who accidentally blew himself up.[5] Because of Lieutenant Hunt's early death Miss Pollitt was now able to explain the many love poems lamenting the *death* of the beloved;[6] for her evidence she cited the poet's unusual use of the imagery of guns and cannonballs.[7] In these and in all such biographies the fact that no letters could be found as evidence was freely admitted, but that fact never seemed to cast doubt on the narratives; rather it confirmed them.

Mrs. Todd would have preferred to continue her silence but her daughter, Millicent Todd [Bingham], was eager to take up the quarrel.[8] She finally prevailed upon her mother to enter the arena. How strange it is to contemplate these young women continuing a battle on behalf of their mothers, with the poems of Emily Dickinson falling always into a greater state of hopeless confusion.

Because the biographical distortions seemed more pressing, Mrs. Todd agreed to publish an expanded collection of letters sent by the poet. Luckily she had still in her possession most of those letters she had expurgated or suppressed entirely when preparing her 1894 volume. By releasing now the correspondence of Emily Dickinson and the Clark brothers, friends of the Philadelphia minister, with the careful notation that they had earlier been thought too private to reveal, Mrs. Todd inadvertently reinforced Mrs. Bianchi's legend. These letters were written in 1882 and concern the death of Reverend Wadsworth. No one seemed to notice, or care if they did, that Emily Dickinson asks questions of J. D. Clark that indicate distance rather than intimacy:

> I thought it possible you might tell me if our lost
> one had brother or sister,
>
> were his children near him at the last?
>
> the griefs of which you speak were unknown to me
>
> he never spoke of himself. . . . of his home. . . .[9]

And curiously enough, no letter to either Clark brother is without specific mention of Lavinia who is described as equally solicitous of the elder Clark's well-being. It may have been Lavinia's privacy that was being protected in 1894.

Mrs. Todd did not collate the letters in the new collection with any of the poems that accompanied them. Frequently four or five or more poems were simply printed in sequence, following a lengthy series of letters, almost as if they were intended to enliven the appearance of the text. That there might be a significant interplay between a specific letter and its enclosed poem was not even possible to discern.

The new collection was countered by the immediate appearance of a similar volume from Mrs. Bianchi.[10] She combined further letters with scraps of prose and even more corrupted versions of poems, and joined them all together with personal reminiscences. The only revision Mrs. Bianchi engaged in was to restore the name of her mother "Sue" which she suggests had been deliberately eliminated all those years.

To challenge the implication behind this charge, Millicent Todd Bingham now decided it would be wise to write as full an account as possible of the early association of her mother and Lavinia Dickinson, of Lavinia and Susan, and explain too the effect of family quarrels on the literary history of Emily Dickinson. The poetry must wait still. Her mother's sudden death at the time this task began only spurred Mrs. Bingham on to her goal of vindicating Mrs. Todd. *Ancestors' Brocades: The Literary Debut of Emily Dickinson* [11] is that defense, partisan, to be sure, but careful in its documentation of the exact roles played by her mother and T. W. Higginson in the unfortunate bowdlerization of the text. She makes quite clear her mother's responsibility for the versions of the poems as they were printed. Perhaps she lays too much stress on the chaotic and unfinished state of the manuscripts in order to justify the editing of Mrs. Todd. Today it is possible to examine the manuscripts and to see for oneself that Emily Dickinson left hundreds of poems in a finished state, waiting the printer's lead, not the editor's pencil.

This touchy subject is finally left behind and the story of the lawsuit pervades the rest of the book. There is, it should be added, one interpolation: since Mrs. Bianchi had published yet another volume, *Unpublished Poems of Emily Dickinson,* [12] Mrs. Bingham, with her mother's original transcripts beside her, was able to point out all the errors of omission and distortion committed by Emily Dickinson's niece.

The story of the literary debut is brought to a close with the admonition that all of the poems needed to have a "thorough overhauling" but "such a task cannot be undertaken . . . until all her existing manuscripts have been made available." She could not restore all of the published poems to their original text, but she could make available the manuscripts that still lay in her mother's camphorwood chest. In 1945 Mrs. Bingham edited a new volume of poetry; out of more than six hundred poems, four hundred were entirely new to the public. [13] It is on Thomas Johnson's authority that we know the source of these new poems; he tells us in his preface to the Variorum edition that Mrs. Todd had retained in her possession all those packets numbered 80 through 98, as well as the many loose scraps and worksheets placed in envelopes and numbered 99 through 110. Only the threaded fascicles, 1 through 40, had been returned to Lavinia and passed on subsequently to Mrs. Bianchi. Now Millicent Bingham had inherited from *her* mother these long-hidden manuscripts.

Mrs. Bingham knew to what extent bowdlerization on everyone's part had harmed the poetry. Her guiding principle now was to render the original manuscripts as exactly as it was possible to do. Relieved of the need to cater to public taste, she nevertheless still had to edit the poems. Because many of her new discoveries were primarily the worksheets and the scraps, she had to choose from among the variants placed on these manuscripts by Emily Dickinson. And indeed this problem of choice among alternatives can never be resolved, nor can a definitive text be created for any but the fair copies. So long as the poet did not herself choose, the editor must.

In order to further dissociate her work from all previous publications, Mrs. Bingham changed the organization of the volume of poetry. It was an exceedingly complicated scheme, fostered by her commitment to more specific subject matter. She abandoned the old ordering according to the general categories and chose her titles from among the lines of verse. The format looked strange, but it had a new air of authenticity:

> The Far Theatricals of Day [sunrise, nightfall]
> The Round Year [seasons]
> My Pageantry [gardens]
> Our Little Kinsmen [animals]
> Once a Child [small boys, primarily]
> The Mob Within the Heart [autobiography]
> Italic Faces [actual persons]
> The Infinite Aurora [love rhapsodes]

Following these sections, she placed poems about "Death" and divided them even more intricately:

> The White Exploit [general descriptions]
> The Final Inch [physical aspect of death, usually pertaining to the decease of specific persons]
> The Silver Reticence [personal outcries at the spectacle of death]
> Repealed from Observation [meditations on the great gulf that divides the living from the dead]
> Lids of Steel [the tomb]
> Concluded Lives [detached contemplations]
> Creatures Clad in Miracle [serene affirmations of immortality]

And finally:

> Vital Light [the sources of poetic inspiration]
> That Campaign Inscrutable [renderings of generalized emotion]
> The Ablative Estate [meditations on abstract ideas]

Having given four hundred new poems to an astonished world, Mrs. Bingham took up again her labors to dispel the confusions surrounding the life of the poet. First came *Emily Dickinson: A Revelation.*[14] The revelation consists of a series of letters, conjecturally dated in the late 1870's and early 1880's, written to Judge Otis P. Lord, with whom the poet was unequivocally in love. She documents a genuine and a mutual attachment that was unfortunately severed by the sudden death of Judge Lord on March 13, 1884; she dismisses the spurious attachment, speculating that Susan Dickinson and Martha Bianchi together had invented the Wadsworth legend in order to protect the survivors of Judge Lord, who were also the friends of Susan, from the unwelcome publicity of what seemed to them an "immoral" love affair.

Within the year a second volume took its place beside the *Revelation.* This was *Emily Dickinson's Home.*[15] Long ago, Amy Lowell had expressed the wish to neutralize the effect of *Life and Letters* by Martha Bianchi by writing "a life of Emily Dickinson in which analysis of her relationship to the members of her family would be the central theme." [16] Amy Lowell never fulfilled that plan, but Millicent Todd Bingham did at least supply the materials for such a project. *Home* is a source book for family documents containing letters written by Edward Dickinson and his family, with a connecting narrative designed to illuminate that Amherst household within which Emily Dickinson lived.

With these volumes Mrs. Bingham concluded her major work, satisfied that she had fulfilled an obligation to her mother to publish every manuscript left in her possession relevant to the poetry and the poet. So far as she is concerned the meaning and significance of the poetry rests in other hands.

Mrs. Bianchi, too, had relinquished her hold on relevant materials when she assigned to her associate, Alfred Leete Hampson, all her possessions, all that remained in her household relevant to the Dickinson family. At her death Mr. Hampson sold everything to Gilbert Montague of Springfield, Massachusetts, and thus Mr. Montague was able to present the large though incomplete collection of Dickinson materials, as well as the library of books accumulated by all the Dickinson family, to Harvard University. Emily Dickinson had remained twenty years within a self-imposed, impregnable retirement, writing for herself now, for posterity surely, poems of incredible beauty and power. These very poems did place her finally so much in the public eye that the very shawl she carried, her garnet brooch, her Bible, the pictures on her walls, her quaint old-fashioned piano, and her threaded booklets—all her cherished possessions—were brought to stand forever clean and safe and on permanent public view in a hushed sanctuary of memorabilia and manuscripts, in the Houghton Library of Harvard University.

The curious literary history of the poems of Emily Dickinson is an oddity of American literature: the gradual release of poems of sometimes more and sometimes less authenticity, despite the fact that the poet herself, devoted solely to her career as a poet, patient for her fame but sure, had ready, when fame should arrive to capture her, 39 threaded fascicles, containing 811 poems, revised, winnowed, organized, neat. These she had prepared for the world.[17] But they were received by a world that assumed the right to decide for itself what it would have from her pen. And the world chose poems that proved Emily Dickinson was a tragic sufferer, a Puritan, a Transcendentalist, a social satirist, a Gnostic, a homosexual, a maiden suffering from an Electra complex, and an Existentialist. For biographical interpretation joined with literary historiography and philosophical analysis. Indeed so many tributaries began to flow into the stream that one views this second phase of Emily Dickinson's literary history as a rising flood of interpretations that would eventually smash the poems apart, and hurl the fragments against the stolid rocks of critical determinism.

George F. Whicher, a professor of literature at Amherst College, living within walking distance of the Dickinson homestead at the time when Mrs. Bianchi was busily editing all the papers legally in her possession, pauses over the so-called romantic disaster, and then quite matter-of-factly acknowledges Emily Dickinson's withdrawal from the world. Whicher stresses that the poet withdrew from common society primarily because "she had more poems to write than she could find time to write them in." [18] That she trapped herself in a psychic prison he does not deny, but it is what she did inside that prison that interests him. He discusses her reading, her literary friends, and finally her poetry, devoting a major portion of his critical biography to questions of her themes and her style, as both were products of nineteenth-century American currents that "came to a confluence in her poetry: the Puritan tradition in which she was nurtured; the Yankee or, more broadly, American humor that was just coming out of the ground; [19] and the spiritual unrest, typified by Emerson, which everywhere was melting the frost of custom." Instead of responding to her use of the concrete detail as a device of her poetic style, or as the source of her poetic vitality, he sees that "her emphasis on the small particular truth brings her near to the center of the Puritan tradition in literature."

Henry W. Wells, wide-ranging literary critic with a bent to comparative literature, acknowledges his debt to Whicher and then devotes himself to the poet who "is one of the foremost masters of poetic English since Shakespeare, and in the severe economy of her speech comparable to Dante." [20] His book explores the themes of Emily Dickinson's poetry, as they were her significant challenge to her age, discovering in her religious poems satirical thrusts at orthodoxy (opposed to the Puritan tradition). He probes her relation to institutional society and concludes she is primarily a poet of social protest. "Lenin and she might have been much in agreement as to the actual functioning of organized religion." (p. 89) "With the revolutionary spirit of Jefferson supported by a more seasoned philosophical vision than most thinkers nursed in the eighteenth century commanded, she observed. . . ." and so on. (p. 193)

Richard Chase, a literary historiographer, concerned with the history of ideas, establishes Emily Dickinson's relationship to the writers of her time, Emerson, Whitman, and Melville. He proceeds to examine her ideas but admits she was "incapable of systematic abstract thought." [21] She is a poet without poetic coherence; she is, if anything, a wit, a humorist. Nevertheless Chase engages us in an analysis of particular poems in order to trace out a complex of typical nineteenth-century American attitudes and ideas: her New England Calvinism, her Romanticism, her Transcendentalism, her Stoicism, and finally her Gnosticism, substantiating all he says with quotations from poems and letters. Primarily, Chase is interested in a historical analysis of the poetry, and he seeks to establish a definition of her poetic style not as it is an intrinsic manifestation of the individual Emily Dickinson, but as it is an American manifestation of the European rococo art style.

With the appearance of Rebecca Patterson's book we return to the continuation of biographical interpretation. But it was not the sentimental probing of the earlier period which contented itself with romantic attachments to fine young men or noble and virtuous mentors. In the 1950's and 1960's, sophistication demands guilt and repression, fixations of a different order. Miss Patterson creates an intricate narrative out of her surmise that a hidden guilt-ridden attachment for Catherine Anthon, and an awareness that this was a forbidden love, and—what was worse—that Mrs. Anthon did not respond, caused Emily Dickinson to withdraw from the world.[22]

A similarly formidable psychological inquiry into the sexual fright and neurotic detachment of the poet emerged in the singular analysis of Clark Griffith.[23] He combines value judgments on the art, places Emily Dickinson in the stream of American literature, and at the same time reveals the nature of the traumatic experience: Emily Dickinson dreaded any erotic attachment because she had a complicated attachment to her father. Unable to confront her father, she neurotically tries to remain a child, to make time stand still. To keep change from touching her, she retreats. Having satisfied himself with his psychological inquiry, he moves on. Because she is afraid of Death, she becomes a type of "Post-Romantic child," and therefore fits squarely into the nineteenth-century American literary tradition; from this point of view she becomes kinsman to Herman Melville. And now Griffith is ready to take up the poet's connection with contemporary poetry:

> The truth is that Emily Dickinson was a tragic poet, endowed with great tragic insight, and a great tragic sensibility. Her finest poems have to do with man's lot in a world that is tragically "other" than himself: developing this theme, they anticipate the tragic sense of life as it has been reformulated for our time by Unamuno and the existentialists.[24]

Between 1955 and 1960 three major works, long awaited and highly crucial for the study of the poems, were published. The *Poems of Emily Dickinson* (numbered 1 to 1776) appeared in 1955.[25] *The Letters of Emily Dickinson* (numbered 1 to 1049) appeared in 1958.[26] *The Years and Hours of Emily Dickinson,* a chronological record of the events and a gathering of possibly relevant documents from diaries, letters, newspapers, and magazines appeared in 1960.[27]

Thomas Johnson's devotion to the task of reconstructing the complete text, as nearly faithful to the original manuscripts as it was supposed possible to achieve, was welcomed on the assumption that the lack of such a text had been the primary obstacle to understanding confronting the reader. Were that so, then the problem of disorder and variant printings resolved by the appearance of the Variorum edition would eliminate all disagreement on the level of interpretation of particular poems. But a glance at analyses of "I heard a Fly buzz" made subsequent to the publication of the definitive text shows no such thing.

> I heard a Fly buzz—when I died—
> The Stillness in the Room
> Was like the Stillness in the Air—
> Between the Heaves of Storm—
>
> The Eyes around—had wrung them dry—
> And Breaths were gathering firm
> For that last Onset—when the King
> Be witnessed—in the Room—
>
> I willed my Keepsakes—Signed away
> What portion of me be
> Assignable—and then it was
> There interposed a Fly—
>
> With Blue—uncertain stumbling Buzz—
> Between the light—and me—
> And then the Windows failed—and then
> I could not see to see—

Here is Johnson's own interpretation of the meaning of that fly:

The buzzing fly, so familiar a part of the natural order of persistent household discomforts, is brought in at the last to give the touch of petty irritabilities that are concomittant with living—and indeed—with dying.[28]

And here are several others, all based on the same text:

The dying person does in fact not merely suffer an unwelcome external interruption of an otherwise resolute expectancy, but falls from a higher consciousness, from liberating insight, from faith, into an intensely skeptical mood. . . . To the dying person, the buzzing fly would thus become a timely, untimely reminder of man's final, cadaverous condition and putrefaction.[29] [Gerhard Friedrich, 1955]

I understand that fly to be the last kiss of the world, the last buzz from life. . . . [I] think of the fly not as a distraction taking Emily's thoughts from glory and blocking the divine light . . . but as a last dear sound from the world as the light of consciousness sank from her . . . [John Ciardi, 1956]

The only sound of heavenly music, or of wings taking flight, was the 'Blue—uncertain stumbling Buzz' of a fly that filled her dying ear. Instead of a final vision of the hereafter, this world simply faded from her eyes. . . . To take this poem literally as an attempted inside view of the gradual extinction of consciousness and the beginning of the soul's flight into eternity would be to distort its meaning. [Charles Anderson, 1960]

And what kind of a fly? A fly "with blue, uncertain stumbling buzz"—a blowfly. . . . She was a practical housewife, and every housewife abhors a blowfly. It pollutes everything it touches. Its eggs are maggots. It is as carrion as a buzzard. What we know of Emily Dickinson gives us assurance that just as she would abhor the blowfly she would abhor the deathbed scene. [Caroline Hogue, 1961]

So long as the fly's gyrations can be seen or its noises distract, the poem is positioned in the everyday world of sense. As the fly disappears, sense is ebbing with it. When the fly is gone, the speaker herself has been transported to an ineffable other-world. . . . A more complex possibility is broached when we go on to think of the fly as a feeder upon carrion. This means that, during her last moments alive, the speaker beholds an awful vision of what is to come—glimpses, in the new symbolic activities of the fly, a hint that stink and corruption are death's only legacies. . . . Her image belies any likelihood of immortal life by suggesting that within the precincts of the grave decay will be all and the maggot will take ultimate and absolute dominion. . . . At its most demonic—even as the potential destroyer of dead human flesh—the insect continues to represent life. . . . Emily Dickinson has elected to symbolize life through the ugly annoyance: that she has located in an experience connoting the height of disturbance, discomfort, and nastiness an ideal emblem for the world from which her speaker departs. What the identification of fly with life . . . forces us to see [is] that while death may carry one ineluctably to the fly, still it is no less true that only through death can the fly be escaped. . . . beyond the fly and safely past the *Heaves of Storm,* she has also shut out a world with enough unpleasant features to make the leaving of it an experience that is at least bearable.[30]

Anyone familiar with recent literary criticism that strives to explain the poetry of Emily Dickinson knows that this one example of diverse interpretations of a single poem may be repeated for any number of others. The establishment of a definitive text had resolved nothing so far as her meaning was concerned.

More recently there have arrived scholars content with a more modest kind of insight, content to dwell on the technical devices used by the poet. William Howard concentrates on the vocabulary alone. These are among his discoveries:

much of the high tension of Dickinson's poetry results from the constant juxtaposition of Latin derivatives with words of Anglo-Saxon origin.

The most significant feature of the Amherst poet's use of individual words is the small number of high-frequency words in her poetry.

Another significant characteristic of the Amherst poet's verbal habits is the ratio of adjectives, nouns, and verbs used, which in her case, works out to 5 adjectives, 12 nouns, and 8 verbs per 10 lines.[31]

Howard's objective analysis of the poetry concludes with the discovery that the primary characteristic of Emily Dickinson's choice of words is particularization, that she is never abstract, never symbolic but works within a matrix of the physical world, in tangible reality. Howard is comfortable with the implications of his point of view: those are literal beggars standing before mechanical gates that swing on pearl hinges; they are transformable into literal queens who smile as they receive their proper diadems from splendid little literal cherubs.

Archibald MacLeish has written an essay that concerns itself with the imagery as the most significant part of the vocabulary. He demonstrates that the metaphors appeal to the imagination and not to the senses at all, that her vocabulary is often abstract and generalized and inert but that nevertheless her poems are precise and vivid. At the same time he praises her sense of the "dramatic," the "eventful," her transmitted sense of "urgency." He praises her restraint, her lack of posture and pose. Out of all this he extracts the essence of her "tone" which is "spontaneity." [32]

Edith Perry Stamm contributes a highly specialized discussion of the poetry and punctuation. She is glad to have the restoration of the original punctuation in the Variorum edition, but immediately launches an attack on Johnson for having erred so blatantly in transcribing the angular slants ($/$) as commas, and the reverse slants ($\backslash$) as commas, and for ignoring the placement and elongation of the horizontal dashes, for having treated them as mere signs for a break in thought. Taking for her special tool Noah Porter's *Rhetorical Reader,* published in 1837, used in the Amherst Academy, Miss Stamm explains that Emily Dickinson's punctuation is a system of musical notation to indicate the proper reading voice for line by line of the text. Placed always after a word, the mark indicates a rhetorical inflection:

$—$ = monotone reading with pauses, if coming at the end of a line
$/$ = a rising inflection
$\backslash$ = a falling inflection

When the marks appear above or below the line a change in the pitch of the voice is intended. The capital letters are meant for voice stress, and perhaps most astonishing, the misspellings are intentional, for the sake of a specific sound.[33]

This analysis rests on the assumption that Emily Dickinson was so highly meticulous a craftsman that her handwriting was more deliberate than her choice of words. Whatever the line ultimately was to say, it must be said slowly or in a high-pitched or low-pitched voice.

This kind of discourse is not an aberration of perception. It falls well within a school of analysis that has attained wide respectability. Unfortunately a critical commitment to the object of the poem itself does not protect the poetry from being distorted to fit an extraneous frame of reference. Even so intrinsic a material as the prosody has fallen victim to critical determinism.

It was George Whicher who began that convention of analyzing Emily Dickinson's prosody in terms of her use of the hymn meter. In the "technical details of her poetry she was as native as a blueberry" because she used hymn meters, particularly short and common measure. What relevance such knowledge—even if it were true—has to the elucidation of any of her poems is never made explicit. Thomas Johnson, too, is fascinated by the idea of the hymn meter:

Basically all her poems employ meters derived from English hymnology. They are usually iambic or trochaic, but occasionally dactylic. . . . the measures in which Watts' hymns were composed.[34]

Here is the application which Johnson makes of this type of analysis:

> The metric and rhyme shifts [in "I never told the buried gold"] are many and seem to be deliberate. The first two stanzas, in Common Meter, are followed by a third in Sevens and Sixes. The fourth, beginning in line two, shifts to trochaic Sixes and Fives, with which the poem concludes in stanza five. The rhymes are exact in the first, second, and last stanzas; imperfect in the third, and suspended in the fourth. There are internal exact rhymes in the first and third lines of stanzas one and two. The poem survives in two fair copies and in both she has deliberately arranged the second stanza in five lines.[35]

The poem in question is the following:

> I never told the buried gold
> Upon the hill—that lies—
> I saw the sun—his plunder done
> Crouch low to guard his prize.
>
> He stood as near
> As stood you here—
> A pace had been between—
> Did but a snake bisect the brake
> My life had forfeit been.
>
> That was a wondrous booty—
> I hope twas honest gained.
> Those were the fairest ingots
> That ever kissed the spade!
>
> Whether to keep the secret—
> Whether to reveal—
> Whether as I ponder
> "Kidd" will sudden sail—
>
> Could a shrewd advise me
> We might e'en divide—
> Should a shrewd betray me—
> Atropos decide!

Johnson has nothing more to say of this poem. But it is not enough to declare that the meter and rhyme shift deliberately and neglect to explain why. It serves no purpose to point out the shift from the compressed iambic to the more leisurely expanded meter, and take note of the swing to a reversal of the early iambic to the more hurried trochaic verse without commenting on the function of these shifts as they imitate a development in the experience of the poet. For that is what counts in this poem: the lowering sun is personified as a thief, the effect of the sunset on the hills becomes his booty, and the consequences for *her* as she shifts, as she encounters a phenomenon described as an inadvertent stumbling on a theft, her standing in silent motionless fear (had the snake come creeping by she would have jumped—as who would not—as the form of the quatrain jumps to five lines) and then, her wondering what to do, to tell or to keep silent, realizing that if she hesitates too long the thief may escape, and finally, then, with the immediate danger gone, realizing she can come to no decision. It is that series of moves in the action that is important, the accidental encounter with a thief, to a speculation on the booty (deserving a shift in meter) to a confusion on the poet's part as to what she ought to do (deserving the release from the certainties of rhyme in stanza 4) to a kind of ambivalence for which she settles, that indecisive conclusion yoked to a rhyme and rhythm that is decisive. This conjoining of a concluding well-articulated metrical scheme and rhyme pattern with an ultimate ambivalence of action is the source of vitality in the poem. Such explanation is dispensed with in favor of the naming of the Sevens and Sixes, the Sixes and Fives.

Even Charles Anderson, who has lately taken upon himself the primary task of assessing the poetic achievement of Emily Dickinson and rightly believes her to have been a highly conscious poet for whom every device of style was some instrument for her "strategy," explains the strategy of her prosody in terms of the hymn meter.

> Perhaps the finest stroke of her wit was the choice of Common Hymn Meter as her basic pattern, a point of departure and return. . . . It offered the immediate advantage of novelty, since no poet had ever exploited it fully as a serious verse form. Even its rude simplicity could be turned into a vehicle of surprise by making it carry the burden of novel and intricate ideas. . . . This rudimentary quatrain consisted of iambic lines, of four and three stresses alternately, with only the second and fourth rhyming. As worked out in the measures of Watts, a copy of whose *Christian Psalmody* was readily available in her father's library, there were other stanza forms with richer rhyme schemes, as in the Common Particular

(aabccb), and numerous variations on these, by dropping syllables at the line ends or by reversing the accentual pattern so as to change iambic feet into trochaic . . .[36]

There are no examples given of the application of this kind of analysis to any particular poem, eloquent testimony to its irrelevance.

Even R. H. Pearce, in the midst of an essay "On the Continuity of American Poetry" that argues for the hypothesis that our poetry and history are interwoven and that our poetry often enables us to understand our history, pauses in his description of the "self" in Emily Dickinson's poetry to say:

Above all, it is *her* world, framed by variations on the hymn stanza and seeming-casual rhymes, held together by a variety of subtle internal echoings and parallels, modulated . . . by an improvised kind of punctuation (mostly dashes) —all of which let us sense a quality of vital annotation . . .[37]

It is disconcerting to find Pearce overlooking Emily Dickinson's absolutely unique syntax, structure, diction, and conception of reality as an example of American individualism and resorting instead to Whicher, contenting himself with the conventional identification of her verse as a variation of the hymn meter.

Studies based on the Variorum edition did shift the emphasis. The cult of secrecy has long given way to the community of certainty. Predilections of biographers and critics have replaced the loyalties of relatives and associates and partisans. Nevertheless there is as much controversy today as there has ever been. With the Johnson text in hand it is no longer possible to doubt that this was indeed a great poet but there remains a persistent disagreement on what precisely was great, her ideas or her manner, her suffering or her spirit, her torment or her wisdom. There has been instead a continuing fragmentation of the text by her multiplex interpreters striving to establish her significance—always her significance—to her times, to her place, to her progenitors, to her hymnbook.[38]

Perhaps we who operate in what we are accustomed to respect as the world cannot believe that a poet would speculate on this world, find it distasteful and turn away, not because of neurosis but out of contempt. That within the confines of a garden or a small bedroom a poet may strive to understand time and space, the infinite and finite, immortality and mortality, God and the self.

CHAPTER THREE

"Letter to a Young Contributor"

THE CONVENTIONS OF PUBLIC TASTE WERE NO DOUBT SHARED BY the first editors of Emily Dickinson. But the unprecedented success of the first volume of poetry set a quaint process in motion. In order to take advantage of widespread public interest, a poetry altogether unique was reshaped so that the style might seem more commonplace; the decidedly uneventful life of the poet was distorted in order that the poet might seem altogether unique. Subsequent quarrels between rival factions created a situation in which rival editors increased the disparities in the poems they published until there appeared in fact to be rival texts.

But even when the localisms were restored, substitutes of nouns for pronouns removed, interpolations of better rhyming words eliminated, her own grammatical constructions put back, none of this really made much difference when it came to understanding what the poet was trying to say. There were still, after the printing of the canon—with as exact a reproduction of the manuscripts as possible—as many interpretations as there were again biographers and critics to make them.

Surely it was the gnomic quality of the poetry—the line, the stanza, the poem itself—that generated the sense of elusive meaning and stimulated the scholars, each with his own preferred instrument, to strive to break through the barriers to her meaning.

That this should be the case is perhaps the strangest phenomenon of all, for Emily Dickinson strove all her days to make herself plain. Her poetry was an instrument of direct communication of an immediate experience, a rendering in verse what had not been understood in colloquy or prose exchange with another person, a crystallization of her response to a specific publication or event.

And what is even more significant in this connection is her practice of meditation on her own ideas, her writing variant poems that were further speculations, sharper clarifications, for her own sake, almost as if she were seeking to discover for herself what she believed. Of first importance to her was the nature of the poetic process; therefore she frequently contemplated the craft itself, and explained to whoever would care to know, and to herself, for she soon discovered it was she alone who cared most deeply to know, the source, the subject matter, the value, and the style of her own art.

The puzzling nature of Emily Dickinson's poetry, her meaning and her manner, can be resolved if the poems are subjected to a new kind of scrutiny, one that derives not from her biography or background or the climate of opinion of the nineteenth century, but from an analysis of the metaphors and syntax and context of the works themselves. By context I mean more than the external frame. There is the obvious one of her letters and other writings (poems and prose) that appeared in newspapers and magazines and books. There is the equally important context of the metaphor, the expanding metaphor of the single poem, the variant metaphors that point us in the direction of clusters of related poems. Finally there is the context of the fascicle, the gathering of poems into an organization of related parts, into a unified and discrete structure that satisfied the poet's own sense of interrelationship and interillumination. To read the poems in context, to allow the connotations of her words to spread only so far as her own context allows, to trace her images as they recur in variant poems or letters, to explore her ideas as they reflect other writings to which she was responding, will enable us to cut away much that is conjecture and theory.

We have available two important groups of poems and letters and collateral prose (articles from magazines and newspapers) which enable us to proceed in this way. We know that Emily Dickinson read Higginson's article, "Letter to a Young Contributor," written for the *Atlantic Monthly,* April, 1862; we have her first letter to Higginson and the poems she enclosed with it; we have the letters and further poems of their correspondence during that crucial year, 1862. And we have another reliable cluster of materials—the letters and poems sent to Samuel Bowles. In these two specific and well-documented instances, she made a major effort to convince Higginson and Bowles, both literary men, of her skill as a poet; she strove to tell them about her poetry; she responded in letter and verse to their reply.

These two clusters of material both belong to the period of

1860–1862 when Emily Dickinson was writing with complete self-assurance. During these two years, when she was trying to convince these two judges of the quality of her poetry, she made two distinct appraisals of what was best, choosing poems that were finished lyrics, unequivocal in language and form, and these she transcribed. It is logical therefore to use these poems and these letters to evolve a critical method that is best suited to illuminate the poetry of Emily Dickinson.

How else may we penetrate the mysterious domain into which the poet retreated? After the rebuffs she met with at the hands of both men, after her desire to achieve a public career as a poet was thwarted, after she accepted the judgment of Bowles and Higginson, Emily Dickinson turned inward, she lived on in communication with herself. She engaged in a colloquy with God, struggling with doubt, striving for certainty, making now a major effort to convince herself about immortality, telling Christ about her poetry, listening to the songs of birds, observing the miniscule details of the natural world and interpreting that as her reply. Eventually she became wryly content to remain in the world, tolerant of its inhabitants, satisfied with her present and her ultimate destiny. All this lies carefully preserved in the fascicles.

There is no denying that her sense of what was after all best in her poetry was shaken, and the variants I believe to be a sign of that intimidation. There is that large number of worksheets, with drafts and redrafts of hundreds of verses left in a state of irresolution. But there is also the series of fascicles consisting of carefully copied poems placed together by her own hand. These fascicles are a kind of hand-printing of small volumes of verse, a kind of publication she devised for herself, to confirm for herself her validity as a poet. To verify this we can apply the same method of analysis of metaphor and context, the context then being the poems she placed into the threaded booklets.

Had Emily Dickinson not read "Letter to a Young Contributor," had she not sent its author four poems, Thomas Higginson would have enjoyed a comfortable obscurity as a nineteenth-century social reformer and literary commentator. Today he has a fame that borders on notoriety. Those who admire Emily Dickinson have always reviled Higginson as a fatuous, genteel but wooden Victorian gentleman, ignorant, obtuse, and timid. But it was the poet who chose him. What were her expectations?

She was not ignorant of the quality of his mind. He had been publishing articles in the *Atlantic* since its birth in 1857. The titles of his essays reveal a wide variety of interests but only the essays on nature come near to literary concerns.[1] He was more interested in social issues and historical episodes, a fact which surely did not draw the poet's attention. She might have ignored Higginson, had not complimentary notices of his essays appeared frequently in the "Books, Authors & Art" column of the *Springfield Republican,*[2] a newspaper read daily by members of the Dickinson family. The opinion of either Dr. Holland or Samuel Bowles, both associated with the paper, both good friends of the Dickinsons, was always respected by the poet. That there was interest in the man, prior even to reading the crucial article, is confirmed by an entry in Jay Leyda's *Years and Hours;* he reprints a reply from Bowles to a request from Susan Dickinson for a photograph of Higginson. The entry is dated February, 1862. The article itself was publicized in the "Books" column on March 29, 1862:

> The *Atlantic Monthly* for April is one of the best numbers ever issued. . . . Its leading article, Thomas Wentworth Higginson's "Letter to a Young Contributor," ought to be read by all the would-be authors of the land. . . . It is a test of latent power. Whoever rises from its thorough perusal strengthened and encouraged, may be reasonably certain of ultimate success.

When one reads the article, with its practical advice to would-be poets on matters of style, and its general exposition of the relationship between literature and life, its wise affirmation of the eternality of art, one is immediately struck not by Higginson's obtuseness but by Emily Dickinson's attitude toward him, revealed so clearly in her first letter. She is ironic, not deferential, polite but proud.

The first part of Higginson's "Letter" stipulates the proper manners for contributors to observe. Calling to their attention the fact that editors are human—far from being despots, they are bland and virtuous men—he cautions "Draw near him, therefore, with soft approaches and mild persuasions. . . . His time has some value, if yours has not." Emily Dickinson's letter contains little that is soft and nothing that is mild:

> Are you too deeply occupied to say if my Verse is alive?
> The Mind is so near itself—it cannot see, distinctly—and I have none to ask—
> Should you think it breathed—and had you the leisure to tell me, I should feel quick gratitude—

If I make the mistake—that you dared to tell me—would give me sincerer honor—toward you—

I enclose my name—asking you, if you please—Sir—to tell me what is true?

That you will not betray me—it is needless to ask—since Honor is it's own pawn.[3]

She could resist neither the ironic question nor the sarcastic comment "Are you too deeply occupied" and "had you the leisure to tell me." The phrase "that you dared to tell me" puts the challenge to him more than it solicits guidance.

Higginson derides in the opening paragraph of his article the foolish practice of disguise: "My dear young Cecil Dreemes of literature who superscribe their offered manuscripts with very masculine names in very feminine handwriting . . ." [4] Emily Dickinson did more than disguise her name. She wrote it on a separate card and sealed this in its own small envelope. Her saying emphatically he must not make her communication known is a singular type of reticence. Her father had recently rejected an offer to run for the office of Lieutenant Governor in the state of Massachusetts. The *Springfield Republican* had spoken frequently of the prospective candidacy. Should Higginson fail to connect the names, the business of the separate envelope protecting no pseudonym might even have pointed up the fact that Dickinson was an important name.

But when it came to his rules for proper style in poetry, the poet more than ignored, she deliberately flouted all his strictures by sending four poems that conform to none of his rules. It is true she sends to ask if her verse is alive, if he thinks it breathes, but her four choices were not designed to placate him by seeming to have fulfilled his conventional advice.

One suggestion Higginson had offered young contributors was this: "Such being the majesty of the art you seek to practice, you can at least take time and deliberation before dishonoring it." Emily Dickinson sent three poems written not only quite recently but they may even have been composed in direct response to his article. "I'll tell you how the Sun rose," is almost a reply in verse to this statement in the article:

I have observed, in addressing audiences of children in schools and elsewhere, that there is no fact so grave, no thought so abstract, but you can make it very interesting to the small people, if you will only put in plenty of detail and illustration.

Her description of sunrise and sunset not only has a concreteness and a simplicity that might have charmed "small people," but personifies the sunset itself as children coming home to their gray-robed Dominie.

> I'll tell you how the Sun rose—
> A Ribbon at a time—
> The Steeples swam in Amethyst—
> The news, like Squirrels, ran—
> The Hills untied their Bonnets—
> The Bobolinks—begun—
> Then I said softly to myself—
> "That must have been the Sun"!
> But how he set—I know not—
> There seemed a purple stile
> That little Yellow boys and girls
> Were climbing all the while—
> Till when they reached the other side,
> A Dominie in Gray—
> Put gently up the evening Bars—
> And led the flock away—

Higginson advises contributors to learn patience; he suggests that perhaps the best school for budding writers is a newspaper office where "Nothing is so good to teach the use of materials, and to compel to pungency of style." He points out the need to practice arduously in order to achieve the miraculous in the precision of the instantaneous line, so that "There may be phrases which shall be palaces to dwell in, treasure houses to explore." In the face of that she sends him a poem which reads almost like an ironic commentary on his exhortation:

> We play at Paste—
> Till qualified, for Pearl—
> Then, drop the Paste—
> And deem ourself a fool—
>
> The Shapes—though—were similar—
> And our new Hands
> Learned *Gem*—tactics—
> Practicing *Sands*—

It is possible of course that this poem renders the relationship between life on this earth and afterlife. But there are so many variant poems describing Emily Dickinson's sense of her poetry, and in them gem imagery recurs, the particular analogy of "pearl" and poem recurs, that we may interpret "We play at Paste—" also as a reply to Higginson's statement that poets need to practice their art.[5] Furthermore, the fact that this poem was not found in any fascicle suggests that it was composed in response to the article, for it was often the case that Emily Dickinson did not transcribe poems written for a specific occasion or to enhance or clarify a particular and private communication.[6] In any case, her sending such a poem is scarcely the act of a humble student, as many critics have interpreted Emily Dickinson's writing to Higginson to be, with the significant exception of David T. Porter, who characterizes her attitude as "the diffident surrogate posing in the letters [to Higginson]."[7]

The case of "Safe in their Alabaster Chambers" is even more interesting in this connection. Higginson's exhortation to revise and revise until the object is as near perfect as possible, his citing the example of Balzac's endless labor for the sake of effective composition, may have led the poet to choose "Safe in their Alabaster Chambers," for she had indeed labored over it. In fact, she had not been able to decide finally on a second stanza. The *Republican* had printed that poem six weeks earlier with a second stanza different from that which Higginson received. The newspaper had printed:

The Sleeping

Safe in their alabaster chambers,
Untouched by morning,
  And untouched by noon,
Sleep the meek members of the Resurrection,
  Rafter of satin, and roof of stone.

Light laughs the breeze
In her castle above them,
  Babbles the bee in a stolid ear,
Pipe the sweet birds in ignorant cadences:
  Ah! what sagacity perished here!

She chose to send Higginson this alternate version:

Safe in their Alabaster Chambers—
Untouched by Morning—

And untouched by Noon—
Sleep the meek members of the Resurrection,
Rafter of Satin—and Roof of Stone—

Grand go the Years,
In the Crescent above them—
Worlds scoop their Arcs—
And Firmaments—row—
Diadems—drop—
And Doges—surrender—
Soundless as Dots,
On a Disc of Snow.

Perhaps it was to secure the opinion of a judge other than Samuel Bowles, who had rejected this version despite her own preference.

The variant stanza has interesting connections to her reading in the February issue of the *Atlantic.* Higginson had published there an essay titled "Snow." This sentence is his:

. . . glittering necklaces and wreaths and tiaras of brilliant ice-work cling and trail around its edges, and no regal palace shines with such carcanets of jewels as this winter ball-room.

Would not the writer of such a passage look favorably on her own imagery in that second stanza?

Furthermore, a poem called "Midwinter" had appeared in that same February issue, containing these lines:

The hooded beehive, small and low
Stands like a maiden in the snow;
And the old door-slab is half hid
Under an alabaster lid.

Even Mr. Bowles had liked "Midwinter" enough to reprint it in the *Republican,* although he had rejected her second stanza. Might not Higginson recognize her superior verse? Would he perhaps see she knew how to deal properly with an alabaster lid? With this much evidence we can at least judge that the choice of poems was not haphazard, not without deliberation.

Another piece of advice from Higginson, in his "Letter," cautions that submissions be "agreeable" for the public's sake. Not that he means amusing, he is quick to say, but that there be no "conundrums," nothing "abstruse," the utterances must be "clear and attractive," even "lucid." Emily Dickinson obviously decided to ignore this advice. She had far more lucid and simple poems than those she chose to send, among them "The morns are meeker than they were," or "The Bee is not afraid of me," or "Will there really be a 'Morning'?" The poem she sent, "The nearest Dream recedes—unrealized," was one that Higginson admitted years afterward, in 1891, still baffled him.

Moreover, despite Higginson's caution against improprieties of speech, the poet allowed verse with barbarisms: "And deem ourself a fool," "The Bobolinks—begun," and "There seemed a purple stile." Despite his warnings against yoked words, against using the props of italics and exclamation points, loose ends, straggling things, parentheses and dashes, she allowed verse that violated all these strictures. Higginson asked for "clear terms and close connections." He would not easily find them in "The nearest Dream recedes—unrealized—" where the connection between "The nearest Dream" (and Heaven) to the "June Bee" (and steadfast Honey) is surely not obvious. Nor would he easily discover the connection between "Firmaments row," "Diadems drop," and "Doges surrender" in "Safe in their Alabaster Chambers—" That poets must avoid strings of epithets is another rule Emily Dickinson ignores. She even violated his advice concerning proper diction and the best source for allusions:

> For purposes of illustration and elucidation and even for amplitude of vocabulary, wealth of accumulated materials is essential and whether this wealth be won by reading or experience makes no great difference. . . . books remain the chief quarries.

No poem she sent shows her quarrying from books in his sense; her quarry was nature, her squirrels and bobolinks, her June bee and clover. Her vocabulary had none of the elegance of thought that Higginson counsels.

The poems she chose in the light of his advice to young contributors seem almost to challenge Higginson to tell her she does indeed "make the mistake."

Even had she misunderstood him, she could not have been ignorant of what the *Atlantic Monthly* editors thought was good poetry. Reading month by month what was printed there, she could not have been unaware of the difference between "Midwinter" and a poem she had written about the snow. The published poem reads:

> On turf and curb and bower-roof
> The snow-storm spreads its ivory woof;
> It paves with pearl the garden walk;
> And lovingly round tattered stalk
> And shivering stem its magic weaves
> A mantle fair as lily-leaves.

The lines of her poem read:

> I counted till they danced so
> Their slippers leaped the town,
> And then I took a pencil
> To note the rebels down.
> And then they grew so jolly
> I did resign the prig,
> And ten of my once stately toes
> Are marshalled for a jig!

That same April issue containing the "Letter to a Young Contributor," printed a poem about a soldier that must have made her aware of the unique qualities of her verse:

> *The Volunteer*
>
> "At dawn," he said, "I bid them all farewell,
>   To go where bugles call and rifles gleam."
> And with the restless thought asleep he fell,
>   And glided into dream.
>   . . . .
> Wise youth! By few is glory's wreath attained;
>   But death or late or soon awaiteth all.
> To fight in freedom's cause is something gained,—
>   And nothing lost, to fall.

Surely she herself could distinguish the difference between that and her own:

> Bless God, he went as soldiers,
> His musket on his breast—
> Grant God, he charge the bravest
> Of all the martial blest!

> Please God, might I behold him
> In epauletted white—
> I should not fear the foe then—
> I should not fear the fight!

And she knew that Higginson, the man from whom she was soliciting a good opinion, wrote for this very magazine. What then in the article drew her to Higginson?

If one reads beyond the conventional recommendations, one discovers material there, usually overlooked by critics who find the major part of Higginson's "Letter" irrelevant to their purpose. Higginson describes the true nature of the poet, his function vis à vis society, in such a way that Emily Dickinson must have felt she exactly fulfilled his definition.

In the "Letter" Higginson speculates at length on the relationship between literature and life, an especially acute problem for all poets in 1862. Higginson was committed to social reform as well as to belles-lettres; he was devoted to American Democracy; he was an Abolitionist. And now he was confronted with a great and noble cause: the Civil War. But the chaos of this struggle threatened not only society but all that was best in society, its art and its literature, the very culture itself. Read in this context the address to young authors may be seen as only a frame piece, used by Higginson to exhort American writers not to abandon their sense of proportion in an America torn apart by political and social struggle. These passages are taken from the "Letter:"

> Yesterday I turned from treatises on gunnery to open Milton's Latin poems. . . . And there . . . I came upon a passage as grand as anything in "Paradise Lost,"—his description of Plato's archetypal man, the vast ideal of the human race, eternal, incorrupt, coeval with the stars, dwelling either in the sidereal spaces, or among the Lethean mansions of souls unborn, or pacing the unexplored confines of the habitual globe. . . . Then all these present fascinating trivialities of war and diplomacy ebbed away, like Greece and Rome before them. . . .

> Indeed, it is the same with all contemporary notorieties. In all free governments, especially it is the habit to overrate the *dramatis personae* of the hour. . . . If anything preserves the statesmen of to-day, it will be only because we are coming to a contest of more vital principles, which may better embalm the man.

General Wolfe, on the eve of battle, said of Gray's "Elegy," "Gentlemen, I would rather have written that poem than have taken Quebec." [8]

Higginson says clearly that the pursuits of peace are real; that war is the accident. Despite the apparent immediacy of war, the serene pursuits of art and science will be restored.

Think how Spain and Portugal once divided the globe between them in a treaty, when England was a petty kingdom of illiterate tribes! —and now all Spain is condensed for us into Cervantes.

He declares that Shakespeare's emergence out of the "petty kingdom" is vastly more significant than the ultimate forging of the English nation through violent partisan struggles. Higginson is speaking in April 1862 to an America just so torn apart and it is to *this America* he had something crucial to say, not to young contributors at all. He speaks to all writers, not merely novices, and advises them to be patient of fame, to resist active engagement in day-by-day affairs:

it is this vast, unimpassioned, unconscious tribunal [9] this average judgment of intelligent minds . . . something more undying than senates and more omnipotent than courts, something which rapidly cancels all transitory reputations, and at last becomes the organ of eternal justice and infallibly awards posthumous fame.

Emily Dickinson shared precisely Higginson's sense of the eternality of art. She dissociated herself from any active participation in the Civil War, although there are several poems that indicate she was indeed aware of it.

But there is more than this abstract idea of dedication; she had chosen to lead a life precisely akin to that described by these words in the "Letter":

War or peace, fame or forgetfulness, can bring no real injury to one who has formed the fixed purpose to live nobly day by day. I fancy that in some other realm of existence we may look back with some kind interest on this scene of our earlier life, and say to one another,—"Do you remember yonder planet, where once we went to school?" And whether our elective study here lay chiefly in the fields of action or of thought will matter little to us then. . . . .

Even more to the point is the sentence that directly precedes the passage quoted above:

Who cannot bear a few disappointments, if the vista be so wide that the mute inglorious Miltons of this sphere may in some other sing their Paradise as Found?

It was this portion of the "Letter" that Emily Dickinson believed. These were the precepts she knew she fulfilled remarkably well: patience of fame, victory over suffering, commitment to the field of thought.

The significance of this section for her consciousness may be verified by this poem found in Fascicle 15. It contains the metaphor of the schoolroom as well as the experience of an injury:

> I shall know why—when Time is over—
> And I have ceased to wonder why—
> Christ will explain each separate anguish
> In the fair schoolroom of the sky—
>
> He will tell me what "Peter" promised—
> And I—for wonder at his woe—
> I shall forget the drop of Anguish
> That scalds me now—that scalds me now!

That the image is so closely connected to the metaphor Higginson used is perhaps a clue to the meaning of the "Anguish" of which the poet speaks. Higginson's rejection of her poetry as not ready for publication is well known to have caused the poet anguish.

Of course there is no way to reconstruct the activity of the mind of the poet; all we can do is take notice of at least the presence of a flintstone and remain aware of instances where sparks fell. Here is another example that shows how an idea from this part of the article takes hold of her poetic imagination. Higginson had said:

Literature is attar of roses, one distilled drop from a million blossoms.

This poem was found in Fascicle 11:

> Essential Oils—are wrung—
> The Attar from the Rose
> Be not expressed by Suns—alone—
> It is the gift of Screws—
>
> The General Rose—decay—
> But this—in Lady's Drawer
> Make Summer—When the Lady lie
> In Ceaseless Rosemary—

Not only is there an echo of the metaphor itself, but the idea of this part of the "Letter" pervades the subject matter of the poem. It is the poetry that is in this lady's drawer and it will blossom on and on long after she is dead.[10]

Emily Dickinson believed, as did Higginson, that great poets would enjoy ultimate vindication from the Tribunal of Time. She sent him poems to prove herself just such a poet. By examining the poems she chose from among some three hundred manuscripts already carefully arranged in her threaded booklets, we can discover what she thought would assure her that ultimate fame of which Higginson speaks, a subject matter that was true, a style that was finished and waiting discovery.

She knew her subject matter—her contemplations of immortality, her expositions of death as a link between this life and the afterlife—was serious. That meaning is present in the poetry so often as to constitute a pervasive theme of Emily Dickinson's work.[11] And she knew it was her function, as a poet, to proclaim this truth; the poet was a bard, singing his discoveries, singing spontaneously what his intuition revealed.

And she had a fully developed style in her control for the concrete rendering of her vision of the truth. She needed no guidance as analysis of this poem will demonstrate.

> Safe in their Alabaster Chambers—
> Untouched by Morning—
> And untouched by Noon—
> Sleep the meek members of the Resurrection,
> Rafter of Satin—and Roof of Stone—
>
> Grand go the Years,
> In the Crescent above them—
> Worlds scoop their Arcs—
> And Firmaments—row—
> Diadems—drop—
> And Doges—surrender—
> Soundless as Dots,
> On a Disc of Snow.

While the dead sleep, waiting to rise to the place of Resurrection, the real world continues, in time, in change. The idea is not profound; it is a commonplace enough conception of the relation between the living and the dead. But Emily Dickinson's manner of rendering this theme is not ordinary; she mingles the concrete and abstract, the immobile and mobile, the passive and the vital in a most unexpected fashion.

First, she characterizes the dead, the out-of-this-world. Second, she characterizes the world with an image that particularizes universal space with implied motions through time. Third, she characterizes human actions, but broadly, in terms that signify power and justice. Fourth, she veers back to further characterize the dead, this time in words that contract, are in fact polar to the expanding imagery used to depict the not-dead. We are directed toward the utmost in slightness and effortlessness. It is these dead, no greater in size or power than a snowflake, that nevertheless endure, transfixed and changeless as they are opposed to all the grand motions of the actual world. They sleep (all the intervening lines are a hiatus in the thought) soundless as dots on a disc of snow.

The dead are untouched by the occurrences of this world: outside the tomb natural phenomena continue with the passage of time (morning, noon, years), the passage of planets (worlds scoop their arcs), and the passage of stars (rowing in the firmament); outside the tomb human acts continue with their lapses in power (monarchs and magistrates). We must look close, for there are few words here, but those few have been carefully chosen. The quality of the motion of the passing of solar and sidereal time is delineated by the use of words like "Crescent" and "Arcs" and "row," words that imply half-circles, incomplete and endless, not because time is eternal but time has no arrival, no purpose beyond fulfilling its own horizontal movement.

The same sense of change is present in the description of human events but the direction of the motion is altered to vertical and downward. The Diadems (an ancient sign of royalty) drop; Doges (a more modern image for rule) surrender. The only possibility remaining, upward motion, is reserved (by implication) for the meek members who wait for the Resurrection, for their rising. It is their *inaction* that has purpose, in contrast to the forceful active change but without goal of the non-dead. The poet cannot tell how the dead will rise except to imply that Resurrection will occur without their energy; through analogues the dead are described as waiting without any sound or movement on their part. The dead are in fact likened to the most evanescent, weak, insubstantial object Emily Dickinson can think of, dots of snow composing the crystalline structure of a snowflake. Yet such as these are safe, preserved for the sake of a fixed and stable final goal, ultimately enabled to take a far more distant journey. Snowflakes opposed to the Universe.[12] And it is this all but immaterial, this utterly passive snowflake that characterizes how the meek members wait. Untouched by Morning and Noon (sunlight could so quickly melt a snowflake) they are safe, asleep, abiding without motion or sound, protected by marble and stone, outside time and change until the Resurrection.

The idea of Resurrection is a commonplace subject matter for poetry. Rendering the means of redemption as the trappings of the grave is a conventional device. But the effort to render the miraculous nature of redemption in terms other than a vision is not ordinary. To juxtapose metaphors that render the saved as the most transient, the most perishable, to use a minute snowflake of the soul, and to pit that bead against time and space and all human events is startling, is unique. It was too startling for Higginson. To reverberate his ideas was not enough. To render his thoughts in imagery that juxtaposes the pre-eminently transient with eternity, and then to require him to grasp that it is the insubstantial that is permanent, the passive that has purpose, the fixed and stable abstractions of time and space and place that are after all, the transient, was asking too much of Higginson, of 1862, and perhaps even of the present day.

Was the poet naive? No, she was hopeful and she was helpless. The vitality of this poem and of all her poems depended upon the active participation of her reader. She could not do less than test his sensibility. She could not do otherwise, for she had no other way, no other manner, as analysis of the companion poem, "The nearest Dream recedes— unrealized—" reveals:

> The nearest Dream recedes—unrealized—
> The Heaven we chase,
> Like the June Bee—before the School Boy,
> Invites the Race—
> Stoops—to an easy Clover—
> Dips—evades—teases—deploys—
> Then—to the Royal Clouds
> Lifts his light Pinnace—
> Heedless of the Boy—
> Staring—bewildered—at the mocking sky—
>
> Homesick for steadfast Honey—
> Ah, the Bee flies not
> That brews that rare variety!

Let us check first the 1847 Webster's Dictionary definitions for the words in the opening line, to see if they will point the reader in any special direction:

Near: Intimate; united in close ties of affections; Dear; affecting one's interest or feelings

Dream: in which a person imagines he has a view of real things or transactions; in Scriptures, dreams were sometimes impressions on the minds of sleeping persons, made by divine agency

Recedes: ceded back to its former possessor

Unrealized: not having been made real; in appearance only

Having read the definitions for this single line, we are indeed prepared for what follows. "The Heaven we chase" is not only the most persistent dream we have, it affects us, it may have its source in the divine itself, and it is evanescent. The dream of Heaven filled our imagination just before awaking; it seemed so very real, but as we try to reconstruct what we dreamed, half a moment ago, it is already escaping. The waking mind cannot operate on the fantasies of sleep. We can dream a Heaven that exists but we cannot know with our waking mind, with our intellect, precisely what that Heaven is.

The poet shifts to a more external reality by constructing the analogy of this dream and the June Bee. We are teased by the affective presence of the dream; we try to catch hold and keep it but it defies us as the School Boy is outrun by the Bee; it takes itself back to its source, the sky, as the bee flies off, up and away.

Like the June Bee, the dream of Heaven comes down, close to us as summer clover, but it dips, evades, teases, deploys like a Bee, like that tiny sailboat running before the wind.

Now the poet shifts, or perhaps modulates would be a better term, to a third analogy. The knowledge of Heaven was like any dream. Dreams are as unattainable to us as is a June Bee to a School Boy. Now the wing of that evanescent bee becomes a sail on a boat. As unexpectedly as the dream becomes a Bee, transforms into a boat, and then lifts itself in flight among the Clouds where it is lost, so do we leap from metaphor to metaphor, we too are veritably in motion.

So much for the bee, the dream, and Heaven. What of the other line of this elaborate analogy, the pursuing boy and the dreaming man? A man is like the School Boy, unlearned, naive, without reason or experience to keep him from the chase. As the Bee-Dream increases in its erratic motion, the Boy contracts his movement until he remains standing, staring, bewildered by the mocking sky. By transference, so does the man.

In this poem, too, the reader must create the meaning out of metaphors that are expanding terms of an analogy; he must be ready to join the final three lines to the second line of the first stanza, "The Heaven we chase," in order to experience the poem fully. It is the reader who must recollect it is not a June Bee chased by a School Boy, but the steadfast honey of the realized Heaven that a man desires. The coiled tension is there awaiting his insight; he must release the spring to energize the poem.

What practical advice could Higginson give Emily Dickinson? To the substantive advice, that one must be patient of fame, that there would be an ultimate victory over suffering, that there was, indeed, another sphere in which Paradise might be found, she made reply and she affirmed all that he said, although only she would know it. How did she respond to his verbal axe, his cleaving of life into two, only two spheres, "the fields of action or of thought"? What Emily Dickinson knows of the world of action it is not difficult to surmise. What is her view of the capacity of the mind?

She was no metaphysician, but she understood that corporeal reality may be perceived only by the senses, that no act of intellect may operate on that which is beyond reality. What she longs so much to attain is knowledge of God, of Heaven, of afterlife. But if sense perception is the sole means to knowledge and the nature of God is incorporeal and immaterial, she can never know.[13] The knowledge of God remains inaccessible to mortals. Faith in God, belief that Heaven exists, that Immortality awaits us must be felt by intuition.

A variant poem that states this idea explicitly is this:

> You'll know it—as you know 'tis Noon—
> By Glory—
> As you do the Sun—
> By Glory—
> As you will in Heaven—
> Know God the Father—and the Son.
>
> By intuition, Mightiest Things
> Assert themselves—and not by terms—

"I'm Midnight"—need the Midnight say—
"I'm Sunrise"—Need the Majesty?

Omnipotence—had not a Tongue—
His lisp—is Lightning—and the Sun—
His Conversation—with the Sea—
"How shall you know"?
Consult your Eye!

But intuition is not always satisfying, and less so to a poet bound to concrete reality. In this sense, contradiction is the very center of Emily Dickinson's psyche. There is more to it than the fact that we can find poems in the canon that say opposite things:

This World is not Conclusion.
A Species stands beyond—
Invisible, as Music—
But positive, as Sound—
It beckons, and it baffles—
Philosophy—dont know—
And through a Riddle, at the last—
Sagacity, must go—
To guess it, puzzles scholars—
To gain it, Men have borne
Contempt of Generations
And Crucifixion, shown—
Faith slips—and laughs, and rallies—
Blushes, if any see—
Plucks at a twig of Evidence—
And asks a Vane, the way—
Much Gesture, from the Pulpit—
Strong Hallelujahs roll—
Narcotics cannot still the Tooth
That nibbles at the soul—

. . .

At least—to pray—is left—is left—
Oh Jesus—in the Air—
I know not which thy chamber is—
I'm knocking—everywhere—

Thou settest Earthquake in the South—
And Maelstrom, in the Sea—

> Say, Jesus Christ of Nazareth—
> Hast thou no Arm for Me?

In her perception itself there is contradiction. She always perceives events as real but not fulfilled; she writes again and again of experience as significant missed encounters, disjunctive confrontations. She understands the present well enough, but always longs to know the future. To her the real world stands as proxy for the unreal world. Sometimes the here and now contents her; sometimes the here and now is an excruciating reminder of her deprivation.

This understood, it becomes apparent that the remaining poem sent with her first letter to Higginson is in substance a denial of the capacity of the mind to attain to certainty, to verify truth.

> I'll tell you how the Sun rose—
> A Ribbon at a time—
> The Steeples swam in Amethyst—
> The news, like Squirrels, ran—
> The Hills untied their Bonnets—
> The Bobolinks—begun—
> Then I said softly to myself—
> "That must have been the Sun"!
> But how he set—I know not—
> There seemed a purple stile
> That little Yellow boys and girls
> Were climbing all the while—
> Till when they reached the other side,
> A Dominie in Gray—
> Put gently up the evening Bars—
> And led the flock away—

The poet can tell how the sun rose, but only piecemeal, and by material signs of motion and light and sound: the new light on the steeples, an increasing stir and energy, the uncovering of hilltop foliage, the beginning of the birds' song. By these signs we know. The setting of the sun is less perceptible. Since she can see only real things, from which all action of the universe must be inferred, that which is out of the reach of her vision cannot be described except in metaphor. So she constructs her analogy of the setting sun and a gathering of children led by a Dominie in Gray. There is a quality of calm about that gentle, passive, protective Dominie; there is no sense in this poem of terror of darkness or night.

But there are in the canon many many poems that do convey her fear, her terror, her anger, her bitterness, all of them outcries against mortal limitation. Whether she contemplates a bird or a sunbeam, a visitor or a corpse, she wrestles with her discontent at her limited perception. She strives for knowledge of a different order, but is well aware that all she can know is the material reality, through sense perception, whether acted upon by reason, or not.

Emily Dickinson's struggles to resolve this primary conflict generate tones of feeling that are as varied as the metaphors she finds to render the paradox. Sometimes she accepts the necessity of ignorance with patience, sometimes with irony, sometimes with indignation, sometimes with melancholy, with despair, with resignation. These are of course generalizations, but they can be concretized again and again by reading the poems.[14]

All of them say fairly the same thing, only her feelings change and change again. In this sense the canon of her poetry becomes almost a spectrum of the whole range of emotional response it is possible to experience in the presence of such truths as she has found. These two poems, variants of the same idea, have vastly different feeling tones:

> Just lost, when I was saved!
> Just felt the world go by!
> Just girt me for the onset with Eternity,
> When breath blew back,
> And on the other side
> I heard recede the disappointed tide!
>
> Therefore, as One returned, I feel,
> Odd secrets of the line to tell!
> Some Sailor, skirting foreign shores —
> Some pale Reporter, from the awful doors
> Before the Seal!
>
> Next time, to stay!
> Next time, the things to see
> By Ear unheard,
> Unscrutinized by Eye —
>
> Next time, to tarry,
> While the Ages steal —

Slow tramp the Centuries,
And the Cycles wheel!

. . .

Is Bliss then, such Abyss,
I must not put my foot amiss
For fear I spoil my shoe?

I'd rather suit my foot
Than save my Boot—
For yet to buy another Pair
Is possible,
At any store—

But Bliss, is sold just once.
The Patent lost
None buy it any more—
Say, Foot, decide the point—
The Lady cross, or not?
Verdict for Boot!

In each case the persona of the poem misses her encounter with death but there is a vast difference between the reasons for the retreat. In the first it is the accident of being saved; in the second it is choice. In the first poem there is a kind of dedication on her return to tell those "odd secrets of the line," and there is also a sense that at the next encounter she will make it through and truly perceive what is beyond the Seal. In the second poem there is a dialogue with the self which the lady ostensibly wins, but when the case is put to the foot to proceed—that physical foot—it prefers not, not to be put "amiss," not to spoil its shoe.

Between the seriousness of the first and the irony of the second lies the matter-of-fact declaration of this poem:

Their Hight in Heaven comforts not—
Their Glory—nought to me—
'Twas best imperfect—as it was—
I'm finite—I cant see—

The House of Supposition—
The Glimmering Frontier that
skirts the Acres of Perhaps—
To Me—shows insecure—

The Wealth I had—contented me—
If 'twas a meaner size—
Then I had counted it until
It pleased my narrow Eyes—

Better than larger values—
That show however true—
This timid life of Evidence
Keeps pleading—"I dont know."

Some readers may detect in this poem a wistful tone, but that is still somewhat on the middle segment of the spectrum of emotion. Eventually Emily Dickinson does arrive at a resolution of her doubts and hopes, despairs and whimpers. Then she will express in many a bardic avowal her faith that the unknown will one day be known, the true but nevertheless incorporeal, the real but nevertheless immaterial, is certain and sure and may one day be perceived. The instrument of that perception must remain intuition until eventually, mysteriously, it will one day become fact.

Emily Dickinson requires no counsel from Higginson. Her understanding of the relationship of life and death, of death and afterlife is fixed when she sends her first poems to him. Her understanding of the relationship of sense perception to knowledge, of knowledge to intuition, and of intuition to truth is fixed. The manner in which she renders the interplay is fixed too. She seeks no guidance. She introduces herself and hopes for welcome.

CHAPTER FOUR

Dickinson and Higginson

THAT EMILY DICKINSON DID NOT FAVORABLY IMPRESS T. W. Higginson we know. On April 17 he writes to his own editor, James T. Fields:

> I foresee that "Young Contributors" will send me worse things than ever now. Two such specimens of verse as came yesterday & day before— fortunately *not* to be forwarded for publication!

And on the next day he wrote to his mother:

> I have more wonderful effusions than ever sent me to read with request for advice, which is hard to give. Louise was quite overwhelmed with two which came in two successive days.[1]

Writing many years later, in 1891, when the poems were selling well, and he found himself in the remarkable position of gaining fame as the editor of the "effusions" of his "cracked poetess," Higginson tries to recall what answer he made to Emily Dickinson in 1862:

> It is probable that the adviser sought to gain time a little and find out with what strange creature he was dealing. I remember to have ventured on some criticism which she afterwards called "surgery," and on some questions, part of which she evaded, as will be seen, with a naive skill such as the most experienced and worldly coquette might envy.[2]

A careful reading of the second letter Emily Dickinson sent him in return will suggest what that criticism was, and confirm that she was indeed skilled in the practice of evasion.

> Your kindness claimed earlier gratitude—but I was ill—and write today, from my pillow.
>
> Thank you for the surgery—it was not so painful as I supposed. I bring you others—as you ask—though they might not differ—

While my thought is undressed—I can make the distinction, but when I put them in the Gown—they look alike, and numb.

You asked how old I was? I made no verse—but one or two—until this winter—Sir—

I had a terror—since September—I could tell to none—and so I sing, as the Boy does by the Burying Ground—because I am afraid—You inquire my Books—For Poets—I have Keats—and Mr and Mrs Browning. For Prose—Mr Ruskin—Sir Thomas Browne—and the Revelations. I went to school—but in your manner of the phrase—had no education. When a little Girl, I had a friend, who taught me Immortality—but venturing too near, himself—he never returned—Soon after, my Tutor, died—and for several years, my Lexicon—was my only companion—Then I found one more—but he was not contented I be his scholar—so he left the Land.

You ask of my Companions Hills—Sir—and the Sundown—and a dog—large as myself, that my Father bought me—They are better than beings—because they know—but do not tell—and the noise in the Pool, at Noon—excels my Piano. I have a Brother and Sister—My Mother does not care for thought—and Father, too busy with his Briefs—to notice what we do—He buys me many Books—but begs me not to read them—because he fears they joggle the Mind. They are religious—except me—and address an Eclipse, every morning—whom they call their "Father." But I fear my story fatigues you—I would like to learn—Could you tell me how to grow—or is it unconveyed—like Melody—or witchcraft?

You speak of Mr Whitman—I never read his Book—but was told that he was disgraceful—

I read Miss Prescott's "Circumstance," but it followed me, in the Dark—so I avoided her—

Two Editors of Journals came to my Father's House, this winter—and asked me for my Mind—and when I asked them "Why," they said I was penurious—and they, would use it for the World—

I could not weigh myself—Myself—

My size felt small—to me—I read your Chapters in the Atlantic—and experienced honor for you—I was sure you would not reject a confiding question—

Is this—Sir—what you asked me to tell you? [3]

It is a curious mask that has been assumed by the poet. In this letter there are truths (she had very little formal schooling) and there are actual distortions of the truth. To evade the question of her age she replies as if it were a question of how long she had been writing poetry: "You asked how old I was? I made no verse—but one or two—until this winter." She pretends she is a novice: "Could you tell me how to grow?" "My size felt small to me." The pose is retained when she speaks of the friend who taught her Immortality "When a little Girl." There is no doubt she means Benjamin Newton (1821-1853) with whom she talked of poetry and her own verse before her eighteenth year.[4] She chooses to hide twelve years of devotion to her craft and yet she refers to Immortality when replying to a question about her poetry.

Another example of her distortion of the literal truth occurs in her reference to the two editors who came to her father's house "this winter." They are, of course, her old friends, Dr. Holland and Samuel Bowles. That they wanted her poetry for the world is certainly a conceit, and in fact contradicts her pose as an amateur. But she is writing to Higginson, a literary personage, a frequent contributor to journals who can teach her how to achieve not skill but honor as a poet, who may perhaps be wooed to confirm their judgment; perhaps he too would urge her to give her poetry to the world. It may be that Higginson had inquired "Why do you ask me?" Her response, "I could not weigh myself—Myself—My size felt small—to me," is another contradiction, but it provides her with an opportunity to compliment him. Would he return the favor?

The characterization of herself as a new poet is a pose; her humility is a pretense. What of her disguise as the uneducated girl? Higginson has evidently asked what authors she liked, and suggested that possibly Whitman has influenced her, or Miss Prescott. We know that she read Miss Prescott's "Circumstance," in the May, 1860 *Atlantic Monthly*. Jay Leyda tells us that she had cut out the title of Harriet Prescott's essay, "The Author of 'Charles Auchester'" from the June, 1862 *Atlantic*. But her direct denial that she was acquainted with Whitman is more complex. Long ago there had appeared a disapproving article on Whitman written by the editor of the *Springfield Republican*. The issue of March 24, 1860 carried an editorial denouncing Whitman's "Bardic Symbols" and had singled out the *Atlantic Monthly* for censure for having committed the folly of printing that poem:

> It is a very sad indication of the age we live in, that a new edition of Walt Whitman's poems should be announced by a Boston publisher; we didn't suppose anybody admired them but Emerson, and that fact was the only really bad thing we ever knew of him.[5]

When the book was published the *Springfield Republican* review was unequivocal in its condemnation of the disgraceful poet:

Those who wish to gain some idea of Walt Whitman's rank as a writer, and to meet with favorable specimens of his style, without incurring the perilous risk of failing to skip in his volume the pages that should not be read, will find what they desire in the following, from the *London Saturday Review:* "We are far from saying that he has nothing of the poetical fiber. He is certainly an unredeemed New York rowdy of the lowest stamp. He has obviously no sort of acquaintance with the masters of his art and his studies have been apparently confined to Mr. Tupper,[6] his newspaper and the semi-lyrical rhapsodies of the Boston transcenden- talists. But his taste, now hopelessly perverted, seems to have been naturally delicate, and he has a very vivid imagination. When his pictures happen (as is rarely the case) to be neither befouled with filth nor defaced by vulgarity, they are for the most part strikingly presented. . . ." We conclude with some lines which are more like true poetry than anything else in the volume. They are fished out from the very midst of a sea of foul impurities.[7]

She had indeed discovered he was disgraceful. Some fifty lines of the poetry are reprinted, and what is more to the point, she had read the poetry, as the following images drawn from Whitman's "Bardic Symbols" (published in the *Atlantic,* April 1860 issue) and from Emily Dickinson's poetry make clear. These are from Whitman:

> As I listen to the dirge, the voices of men and women wrecked,
>
> As the ocean so mysterious rolls toward me closer and closer,
>
> I have not once had the least idea who or what I am,
>
> Withdrawn far, mocking me with mock-congratulatory signs and
>   bows,
>
> I, too, have bubbled up, floated the measureless float, and been
>   washed on your shores.
>
> Oh I sing, some day, what you have certainly said to me!
>
> Rustle not up so hoarse and angry against my feet

These are from Emily Dickinson:

> The stray ships—passing—
> Spied a face—
> Upon the waters borne—

With eyes in death—still begging raised—
And hands—beseeching—thrown!

. . .

My River runs to thee—
Blue Sea! Wilt welcome me?
My River waits reply—
Oh Sea—look graciously—

. . .

At last, to be identified!
At last, the lamps upon Thy side
The rest of Life to see!

. . .

The Drop, that wrestles in the Sea—
Forgets her own locality
The Ocean—smiles—at her Conceit

. . .

And He—He followed—close behind—
I felt His Silver Heel
Upon my Ancle—Then my Shoes
Would overflow with Pearl—

Until we met the Solid Town—
No one He seemed to know—
And bowing—with a Mighty look—
At me—The Sea withdrew—

. . .

Just lost, when I was saved!
I heard recede the disappointed tide!

Therefore, as One returned, I feel,
Odd secrets of the line to tell!
Some Sailor, skirting foreign shores—
Some pale Reporter, from the awful doors
Before the Seal!

. . .

Exultation is the going
Of an inland soul to sea,

Past the houses—past the headlands—
Into deep Eternity—

. . .

Oh, could you catch her last Refrain—
Bubble! "forgive"—"Some better"—Bubble!
"Carol for Him—when I am gone"!

These quotations from Emily Dickinson indicate enough of a similarity in the images and perhaps even in the conception to raise doubts about her declaration that she never read Whitman. But it is not Whitman she is being evasive about; it is her own poetic style, her own content, her unique self she is describing. That is the logic of her disavowal of any "education," of her pose as ignorant, of her companionship with the Lexicon. Emily Dickinson can sustain no charge of borrowing or of influences. She states the same thing again, even more explicitly, in a letter to Higginson dated August 1862: "[I] never consciously touch a paint, mixed by another person—" That the truth is a far cry from this declaration, I shall have occasion to demonstrate in Chapter Nine.[8]

Conversely those writers she professes to admire seem not to have left much mark on her verse. They are named because Higginson names them in his article and not because she had any unusual interest in them. Of the five she admits in her letter, Keats, Mr. and Mrs. Browning, Ruskin, Sir Thomas Browne, three were cited by Higginson in his "Letter to a Young Contributor." In discussing the importance of style, he quotes Ruskin, who said:

> . . . it is in the perfection and precision of the instantaneous line that the claim to immortality is made. . . .

Higginson cites Keats as an example of the truly great craftsman:

> [Keats] has left behind him winged wonders of expression which are not surpassed by Shakespeare or by any one else who ever dared touch the English tongue.

When cautioning against mannerisms in poetry, Higginson named Sir Thomas Browne, comparing him to Carlyle, who has been outgrown:

> [the age now] is approaching a mode of writing which unites the smoothness of the eighteenth century with the vital vigor of the seventeenth, so that Sir Thomas Browne . . . seems quite as near to us as Pope or Addison. . . .

Her acknowledgment of these literary influences, then, is not necessarily any more true than her claim that she is a novice. What shapes her response is what Higginson wrote, not what was literally true in her experience.

A more obvious instance of Emily Dickinson's willingness to shape her metaphors to serve the purpose of her rhetoric is that matter of her illness, with which she begins her second letter; it is not a biographical fact but a reference to his critical appraisal of her poems: "Thank you for the surgery—it was not so painful as I supposed." She has left us a poem which speaks of her disappointment at Higginson's judgment in a way that causes us to marvel at her courage to be artful in public:

> There is a Languor of the Life
> More imminent than Pain—
> 'Tis Pain's Successor—When the Soul
> Has suffered all it can—
>
> A Drowsiness—diffuses—
> A Dimness like a Fog
> Envelopes Consciousness—
> As Mists—obliterate a Crag.
>
> The Surgeon—does not blanch—at pain—
> His Habit—is severe—
> But tell him that it ceased to feel—
> The Creature lying there—
>
> And he will tell you—skill is late—
> A Mightier than He—
> Has ministered before Him—
> There's no Vitality

The poem is especially poignant when we realize that she is brooding over her recent pain inflicted by "A Mightier than He—" Higginson, and that was Samuel Bowles. There is in the same threaded booklet 21 another poem, similar in image and tone, likewise sent to no correspondent:

> It knew no Medicine—
> It was not Sickness—then—
> Nor any need of Surgery—
> And therefore—'twas not Pain—

It moved away the Cheeks—
A Dimple at a time—
And left the Profile—plainer—
And in the place of Bloom

It left the little Tint
That never had a Name—
You've seen it on a Cast's face—
Was Paradise—to blame—

If momently ajar—
Temerity—drew near—
And sickened—ever afterward
For Somewhat that it saw?

The variant poems, resting in the fascicles, linked by the metaphors, are the reliable indicators of Emily Dickinson's thoughts and feelings; the prose or verse sent out into the world are the disguises.

One probes this disguise not to betray the poet by unmasking but to enable us to penetrate the meaning of the poetry. Too much disservice has been done the poet by critics who have taken the mask for real, and then proceeded to hunt for identities that lie outside demonstrable fact, verifying their guesses by quoting lines of poetry.

A good example is the hunt generated by the phrase in the letter that suggests a single traumatic experience: "I had a terror—since September—I could tell to none—" That terror has been interpreted again and again as the loss of a lover; there has been disagreement only on his name. And because the poet goes on to say "I sing, as the Boy does by the Burying Ground—" obituary columns for September of that year have been combed by the scholars. Emily Dickinson may have chosen that word, "terror," because of the description that Higginson has given of the common experience of all genuine poets—they must expect to bear disappointments, to suffer. But it is more significant to notice her joining the idea of a "terror" with an explanation of why she writes poetry: I write poetry to ease my fear of death. A letter to Samuel Bowles contains one line which says quite plainly that Emily Dickinson was fearful of death: "That Bareheaded life—under the grass—worries one like a Wasp." She composed numberless poems on the occasion and meaning of death. An interesting example seems to expand the prose statement to Higginson:

> I sing to use the Waiting
> My Bonnet but to tie
> And shut the Door unto my House
> No more to do have I
>
> Till His best step approaching
> We journey to the Day
> And tell each other how We sung
> To Keep the Dark away.

The poem is transcribed into Fascicle 86, a booklet of poems mingling the themes of death and immortality and patience and poetry.[9]

It is relevant that the tutor who had taught her immortality had died, leaving her to sing her uncertainties, alone. But when she goes on immediately thereafter to speak of her "Lexicon" is she not talking further of her education, and not of her personal losses? She does name, just there, another companion who left the land. This companion has been identified as the Reverend Charles Wadsworth, as Major Hunt, as George Gould, as Kate Anthon. Strangely enough, Samuel Bowles, who had sailed for Europe just weeks prior to her writing the letter, who had received so many of her poems and finally published one the month before (with alterations in the text), has been mentioned only once, by Winfield Townley Scott.[10] And yet Bowles, on whom she did look as a companion (many references in her letters call him just that), had left America, and, as will be shown later, had indeed left her education and development as a poet to her, precisely the context in which she mentions the companion.

Would Emily Dickinson have yoked her secret lover and a Lexicon? Would she have in only her second letter to such a man as she knew Higginson to be—a man who had not even praised her poetry, let alone inquired of her lovers—would she have chosen at this moment to reveal, and in so ironic a line, the secret of a traumatic experience, the tragic experience of blighted love, a secret she is said to have nurtured twenty years and more?

Moreover, the paragraph following gives answer to Higginson's personal question concerning her human companions, another sign that her reply earlier was referring to literary companions. Even here she veers around to talk of her poetry, as earlier she had parried the question of her age. "I would like to learn. Could you tell me how to grow—or is it unconveyed—like Melody—or Witchcraft?"

The largest part of this second letter is clearly written in answer to questions about her reading, her education, her friends; her responses are to Higginson's interest in her poetic development. This phrase at the beginning of the letter sounds in fact the keynote that she is replying to criticism of the poetry, and to the specific comment that she did not revise enough:

> While my thought is undressed—I can, make the distinction, but when I put them in the Gown—they look alike, and numb.

At first glance "gown" seems to refer to conventional prosody, traditional rhyme schemes. So it has usually been interpreted with the startling exception of Thomas Johnson, who made a quaint conjecture:

> She then adds: "While my thought is undressed I can make the distinction, but when I put them in the Gown, they look alike and numb." What she means is that when she gathers them in one envelope, to be critically reviewed by a professional judge, she had the usual fright experienced by an actor awaiting his initial cue.[11]

One forgives Johnson much out of gratitude for his labors to produce a definitive text of the poems; but such perception is a disquieting display of the same obtuseness for which he often condemns Higginson.

The thought-dress image ought to be read in context with Higginson's article. When he describes his process of revision he says:

> When I [Higginson] think how slowly my poor thoughts come in, how tardily they connect themselves, what a delicious prolonged perplexity it is to cut and contrive a decent clothing of words for them . . . nay, how many new outfits a single sentence sometimes costs before it is presentable, till it seems at last . . . as if it never could be thoroughly clothed . . .

From this sentence he goes on to speak of the absolute necessity of revision. After having singled out the example of Ariosto's sixteen revisions of a single stanza, it is just here that he recounts the anecdote of Balzac's labor over his manuscript. Her reply using his very metaphor for revision is surely related to a suggestion that she revise, that she work and rework her verses before believing them finished.

But Emily Dickinson's theory of song precludes such revision, for primary to her sense of the nature of her poetry is her awareness of just her spontaneity, with its source in intuition. She defends the spontaneous quality with an image Higginson would (she believed) understand.

There is a poem, in that same Fascicle 86, referred to above, which speaks to this very point:

> Just as He spoke it from his Hands
> This Edifice remain—
> A Turret more, a Turret less
> Dishonor his Design—
>
> According as his skill prefer
> It perish, or endure—
> Content, soe'er, it ornament
> His absent character.

But the best proof that she is talking primarily about her poetry throughout this letter, and that she knows her substance and her manner and is defining it in the correspondence with Higginson, lies with the poems that accompanied the letter, "Of all the Sounds despatched abroad," "There came a Day at Summer's full," and "South Winds jostle them—": three poems that answer at once all Higginson's queries about her companions, her influences, and her teachers, poems that explain why she writes and poems that explain the nature of her craft.

"Of all the Sounds despatched abroad," may be taken for a rendering in verse of this passage in her second letter:

> You ask of my Companions Hills—Sir—and the Sundown . . . and the noise in the Pool, at Noon—excels my piano. . . . They [her family] are religious—except me—and address an Eclipse, every morning—whom they call their "Father". . . .

"There came a Day at Summer's full," attempts to explain precisely the quality of her religious commitment (her God is no Being who blots out the Sun leaving the world in darkness, no Eclipse) and conveys as well her sense of self as isolated. Both poems together avow Emily Dickinson to be a poet who has a grasp of Nature that transcends learning. Her song is like the song of God. Not that God is in her, but strangely enough, that she is of a stature commensurate with God because of her acutely sensitive perception of reality and its transmission in song.[12]

> Of all the Sounds despatched abroad,
> There's not a Charge to me
> Like that old measure in the Boughs—
> That phraseless Melody—

The Wind does—working like a Hand,
Whose fingers Comb the Sky—
Then quiver down—with tufts of Tune—
Permitted Gods, and me—

Inheritance, it is, to us—
Beyond the Art to Earn—
Beyond the trait to take away
By Robber, since the Gain
Is gotten not of fingers—
And inner than the Bone—
Hid golden, for the whole of Days,
And even in the Urn,
I cannot vouch the merry Dust
Do not arise and play
In some odd fashion of it's own,
Some quainter Holiday,
When Winds go round and round in Bands—
And thrum upon the door,
And Birds take places, overhead,
To bear them Orchestra.

I crave Him grace of Summer Boughs,
If such an Outcast be—
Who never heard that fleshless Chant—
Rise—solemn—on the Tree,
As if some Caravan of Sound
Off Deserts, in the Sky,
Had parted Rank,
Then knit, and swept—
In Seamless Company—

"Charge," in *Webster's,* 1847, means "That which is enjoined, committed, intrusted, or delivered to another, implying care, custody . . . or duty to be performed by the person intrusted." And understanding that the word implies an assignment, a commission, a duty or employment, then the word "despatched" is illuminated as well, for if there has been a "charge" it has come from somewhere, which just that word "despatched" implies.

Her song, "melody," has been sent down to her from the sky, with the "old measure in the Boughs" the intermediary. It has been entrusted to her care and is the most important inheritance she receives. In fact, it is not a gift of God; rather such phraseless melody is permitted Gods *and* the poet. Such a shared inheritance has attributes beyond the Art to earn (so much for revision, sir; so much for reading, sir!). Such "Tune" cannot be taken away; it cannot be imitated: "Beyond the trait to take away / by Robber," because it is not a discrete entity, it is not a learned skill, but instinctual, "Is gotten not of fingers— / and inner than the Bone." She cannot say this directly to Higginson, but her metaphor can. She continues the expansion of the nature of her poetry: it is golden, hidden but golden, and despite the fact that her poetry is so exceptionally personal, original, so intrinsic a part of herself, it will outlast her. Golden during her lifetime, "for the whole of Days," it will lie golden "in the Urn," surviving her death.

The word "vouch" means to declare, to affirm; to establish proof; she declares, with a startling sense of prophecy,

> I cannot vouch the merry Dust
> Do not arise and play
> In some odd fashion of it's own,
> Some quainter Holiday,

Although she cannot prove it, these ashes—the poems—will be recomposed, revitalized, will be heard eventually. In the future others will hear them. That same wind will "thrum upon the door," and such singers as I declare myself to be will have taken their places above, to become then the source of phraseless melody for new poets:

> And Birds take places, overhead,
> To bear them [the winds] Orchestra.

The final stanza of this poem takes an interesting turn, altogether in keeping with its function as an explanation in verse of her defense in prose:

> I crave Him grace of Summer Boughs,
> If such an Outcast be—

Among the many definitions for "grace" in the Lexicon there is this relevant one: "Spiritual instruction, improvement, and edification." Let *him* seek instruction, *he* is the Outcast who has never heard such new song as her fleshless chant. And her final metaphor characterizes that chant as spontaneous, as an inextricable blending of sound and sense, a kind of seamless prosody.

An ironic gibe at Higginson's conception of elegance of line lies embedded in that metaphor of her prosody, for she renders her poetry as a veritable caravan of sound that sweeps past him in a great and massive company. So tactful a lesson does she give to *her* presumptuous and inquiring and advising scholar.

How wondrous appears the self-confidence of Emily Dickinson in the poetry; how unfortunate the mask of naiveté and pretense of ignorance in the prose writer, and out of this disparity has come all that confusion of interpretation, not merely of this poem, but of so much of Emily Dickinson's poetry. One may have sympathy for the diffidence of the letter writer when she confronts the literary Mr. Higginson, but one need not believe it of the poet.

"There came a Day at Summer's full" was chosen to go in company with the preceding poem.

> There came a Day at Summer's full,
> Entirely for me —
> I thought that such were for the Saints,
> Where Resurrections — be —
>
> The Sun, as common, went abroad,
> The flowers, accustomed, blew,
> As if no soul the solstice passed
> That maketh all things new —
>
> The time was scarce profaned, by speech —
> The symbol of a word
> Was needless, as at Sacrament,
> The Wardrobe — of our Lord —
>
> Each was to each The Sealed Church,
> Permitted to commune this — time —
> Lest we too awkward show —
> At Supper of the Lamb.
>
> The Hours slid fast — as Hours will,
> Clutched tight, by greedy hands —
> So faces on two Decks, look back,
> Bound to opposing lands —
>
> And so when all the time had leaked,
> Without external sound

Each bound the Other's Crucifix—
We gave no other Bond—

Sufficient troth, that we shall rise—
Deposed—at length, the Grave—
To that new Marriage,
Justified—through Calvaries of Love—

What interplay exists between the two poems? That summer boughs is linked with a day at summer's full is obvious. What more? There is again the image of special significance (or charge) in this day for her, "Entirely for me." And just as that sound came from the sky and was permitted Gods and the poet, so here, she had thought that such days were only reserved for the Saints who were already enjoying Heaven ("Where Resurrections be"). Here she is, on earth, enjoying Heaven.

The poet does not merely record what was abroad that day. She is the perceiver of the meaning of that spectacular, that heaven-like "full" of summer. The Sun just goes about as usual, the flowers are accustomed to such days and just blossom, but she experiences a rebirth, a transition so important, it seems as if her soul had changed its declination and has entered into a new ecliptic. She is made new.

That Emily Dickinson has stated before this belief in Nature—specifically cyclical change, precisely summer—as a guarantor of regeneration, can be confirmed at once by recalling "An altered look about the hills—" Here all the signs of summer (the sounds, the scents, the appearance) are actually linked with the question put by Nicodemus to Jesus, "How can a man be born when he is old? Can he enter the second time into his mother's womb, and be born?" (John 3:4). The poet supplies her own answer:

An altered look about the hills—
A Tyrian light the village fills—
A wider sunrise in the morn—
A deeper twilight on the lawn—
A print of a vermillion foot—
A purple finger on the slope—
A flippant fly upon the pane—
A spider at his trade again—
An added strut in Chanticleer—
A flower expected everywhere—

> An axe shrill singing in the woods—
> Fern odors on untravelled roads—
> All this and more I cannot tell—
> A furtive look you know as well—
> And Nicodemus' Mystery
> Receives it's annual reply!

In the poem sent to Higginson the emphasis is on something beyond sense-perception, for she is concerned here not solely with her art (as was the case with "Of all the Sounds despatched abroad,") but with her meaning, her belief, the subject matter of her art. The perception of the meaning of the summer day is an act of intuition of the soul.

> The time was scarce profaned, by speech—

This has been an internal transformation.[13] Nothing has to be said. It is as if she were present at a genuine communion and the Sacrament could be taken without the conventional symbols relied upon in the conventional church.

The word "wardrobe" must be joined to the opening line, a "Day at Summer's full," rather than to the word that precedes it immediately, "Sacrament"; that expands our perception of its meaning to encompass the whole physical world, all the actual manifestations of the presence of God.

There are many variant poems that render the physical world in exactly the imagery associated with the wardrobe. Consider, for example, the more obvious:

> Ribbons of the Year—
> Multitude Brocade—
> Worn to Nature's Party once
>
> Then, as flung aside
> As a faded Bead
> Or a Wrinkled Pearl—
> Who shall charge the Vanity
> Of the Maker's Girl?

Nature, here, is the daughter of God. A more abstract rendering of this idea appears in the following poem:

> All Circumstances are the Frame
> In which His Face is set—

All Latitudes exist for His
Sufficient Continent —

The Light His Action, and the Dark
The Leisure of His Will —
In Him Existence serve or set
A Force illegible.

That Circumstance is the natural world. It is not the imagery of dress, but the relationship between nature and God is explicit. The following poem combines both:

The Day undressed — Herself —
Her Garter — was of Gold —
Her Petticoat — of Purple plain —
Her Dimities — as old

Exactly — as the World —
And yet the newest Star —
Enrolled upon the Hemisphere
Be wrinkled — much as Her —

Too near to God — to pray —
Too near to Heaven — to fear —
The Lady of the Occident
Retired without a care —

. . . .

The link between a summer day and the idea of a genuine sacrament is made even more explicit in the following poems:

These are the days when Birds come back —
A very few — a Bird or two —
To take a backward look.

. . . .

Oh Sacrament of summer days,
Oh Last Communion in the Haze —
Permit a child to join.

Thy sacred emblems to partake —
Thy consecrated bread to take
And thine immortal wine!

. . .

It will be Summer—eventually.

. . . .

The Wild Rose—redden in the Bog—
The Aster—on the Hill
Her everlasting fashion—set—
And Covenant Gentians—frill—

Till Summer folds her miracle—
As Women—do—their Gown—
Or Priests—adjust the Symbols—
When Sacrament—is done—

The transforming experience of a summer's day is not an unusual subject
for Emily Dickinson. Here are some variants:

A something in a summer's Day
As slow her flambeaux burn away
Which solemnizes me.

A something in a summer's noon—
A depth—an Azure—a perfume—
Transcending extasy.

And still within a summer's night
A something so transporting bright
I clap my hands to see—

. . . .

. . .

I reckon—when I count at all—
First—Poets—Then the Sun—
Then Summer—Then the Heaven of God—
And then—the List is done—

. . . .

. . .

The Heaven vests for Each
In that small Deity
It craved the grace to worship
Some bashful Summer's Day—

. . . .

If the world of nature is the genuine sacrament of God, what is the sacramental offering of the poet? (Recall that Emily Dickinson has linked her stature with that of God.) Or to put it another way, if God gives nature, what does the poet give? A very close reading, paying particular attention to the unusual syntax, recalling the context of this poem to be the letter to Higginson and the companion poem, and relying on the variant poems transcribed into the fascicles for further illumination, we can arrive at an answer: the poet gives her poems.

> The Wardrobe—of our Lord—
>
> Each was to each The Sealed Church,
> Permitted to commune this—time—
> Lest we too awkward show
> At Supper of the Lamb.

Syntax joined Wardrobe with Sacrament and Summer Day; now the word Lord joins to "Each" and "Church." It is the Lord and the poet that combine to make the sealed Church. It is the Lord and the Poet who are permitted to commune. Together they form a private and authentic Church.[14] The Lord and Emily Dickinson are in direct communion so that, having met before, they will not be awkward, when she comes to the real supper.

Poem after poem confirms that this is the vision the poet has of herself—the barefoot singer who will walk on the golden floor, the jasper floor, greeted by God, envied by Angels. But a distinction must be made between God and Christ. As a matter of fact, that "each" is not God, but Jesus. Unless we pause to see this, we will not be prepared for what follows, the image of the Crucifix and the Bond, the metaphor of her poems.

Emily Dickinson has spoken of her relationship to Jesus before. She has pictured herself as the bride, the woman in white, the wife of Jesus. She has said often in verse that He is her guest and her friend. She has said too, and often, that his stay is temporary. An interesting rendering of this bond which is more of a process than a fixed and settled matter occurs in this poem:

> I gave myself to Him—
> And took Himself, for Pay,
> The solemn contract of a Life
> Was ratified, this way—

> The Wealth might disappoint—
> Myself a poorer prove
> Than this great Purchaser suspect,
> The Daily Own—of Love
>
> Depreciate the Vision—
> But till the Merchant buy—
> Still Fable—in the Isles of Spice—
> The subtle Cargoes—lie—
>
> At least—'tis Mutual—Risk—
> Some—found it—Mutual Gain—
> Sweet Debt of Life—Each Night to owe—
> Insolvent—every Noon—

Here it is a contract. The Vision she has of Heaven will have no real value, will remain a fable until the Merchant to whom she gave herself, God, take her; neither will know the value of this mutual bargain until she dies. While she is mortal, her union cannot be other than transient.

So in "There came a Day at Summer's full," the day itself cannot last; the day and the poet are in solar time, and the time has leaked out. She acknowledges their separation in the metaphor of two faces on two Decks looking back, bound to opposing lands (the Lord going to where he must; the summer going to where it must; and she to where she must). Note that this same metaphor of the ship appeared in "I gave myself to Him—" a poem rendering the identical commitment, but permeated with doubt.

Another poem is a variant of this idea of dedication and departure:

> He found my Being—set it up—
> Adjusted it to place—
> Then carved his name—upon it—
> And bade it to the East
>
> Be faithful—in his absence—
> And he would come again—
> With Equipage of Amber—
> That time—to take it Home—

That East signifies Dawn, morning, the rebirth of day, another sign from Nature of ultimate regeneration. In the poet's long quest for certainty, her long struggle with doubt, it was conviction and faith that won out. To recognize "He" as Jesus is the main issue. It is easy to verify that meaning by taking notice of that word "Equipage" and then to recall how often Emily Dickinson describes the experience of death in terms of a caller who arrives in a carriage to transport her "Home." A typical example, using all the metaphors of the chariot, of nature and time, of a bond and silent acquiescence, is this:

> It was a quiet way—
> He asked if I was his—
> I made no answer of the Tongue
> But answer of the Eyes—
> And then He bore me on
> Before this mortal noise
> With swiftness, as of Chariots
> And distance, as of Wheels.
> This World did drop away
> As Acres from the feet
> Of one that leaneth from Balloon
> Upon an Ether street.
> The Gulf behind was not,
> The Continents were new—
> Eternity it was before
> Eternity was due.
> No Seasons were to us—
> It was not Night nor Noon—
> For Sunrise stopped upon the place
> And fastened it in Dawn.

There is really an astonishing consistency in the poems of Emily Dickinson. Time after time she pledges herself to Christ; she pictures herself waiting patiently for Him to claim her, she broods over the trust she has placed in Him; in "There came a Day at Summer's full," she names her part of the bargain:

> Each bound the Other's Crucifix—
> We gave no other Bond—

That the bond of Jesus is the Crucifixion is a conventional symbol; even that men view their suffering as an imitation of Christ is commonplace. The poet has written this way often:

> Jesus! thy Crucifix
> Enable thee to guess
> The smaller size!
>
> Jesus! thy second face
> Mind thee in Paradise
> Of our's!

And a variant of her outcry is familiar:

> One Crucifixion is recorded—only—
> How many be
> Is not affirmed of Mathematics—
> Or History—
>
> One Calvary—exhibited to Stranger—
> As many be
> As Persons—or Peninsulas—
> Gethsemane—
>
> Is but a Province—in the Being's Centre—
> Judea—
> For Journey—or Crusade's Achieving—
> Too near—
>
> Our Lord—indeed—made Compound Witness—
> And yet—
> There's newer—nearer Crucifixion
> Than That—

But that for which she has suffered is by no means an ordinary idea. And it is just here that we will discover the analogue to the sacrament of God, that which the poet has to give. The letter to Higginson has been concerned chiefly with her development as a poet; the first poem has described her song-self. And just as those ashes in the urn, that merry dust, will rise again and play, so here, her crucifix, her bond, is her poems, and so will she depose the grave. There are so many poems that seek to articulate the ideas presented here, one is all but persuaded that this is the pervasive theme of Emily Dickinson's poetry.

> The Martyr Poets—did not tell—
> But wrought their Pang in syllable—

That when their mortal name be numb—
Their mortal fate—encourage Some—
The Martyr Painters—never spoke—
Bequeathing—rather—to their Work—
That when their conscious fingers cease—
Some seek in Art—the Art of Peace—

. . .

I shall keep singing!
Birds will pass me
On their way to Yellower Climes—
Each—with a Robin's expectation—
I—with my Redbreast—
And my Rhymes—

Late—when I take my place in summer—
But—I shall bring a fuller tune—
Vespers—are sweeter than Matins—Signor—
Morning—only the seed of Noon—

. . .

The Poets light but Lamps—
Themselves—go out—
The Wicks they stimulate—
If vital Light

Inhere as do the Suns—
Each Age a Lens
Disseminating their
Circumference—

But perhaps the most poignant synthesis occurs here:

This is a Blossom of the Brain—
A small—italic Seed
Lodged by Design or Happening
The Spirit fructified—

Shy as the Wind of his Chambers
Swift as a Freshet's Tongue
So of the Flower of the Soul
It's process is unknown.

When it is found, a few rejoice
The Wise convey it Home
Carefully cherishing the spot
If other Flower become.

When it is lost, that Day shall be
The Funeral of God,
Upon his Breast, a closing Soul
The Flower of our Lord.

What help could such a poet be presumed to need?

Poor Higginson. He had no Variorum text, no biographies, no aesthetic or psychological systems to arbitrate meaning. Yet critics far more astute than he are still in consistent disagreement about the meaning of this poem, "There came a Day at Summer's full."

Caroline Hogue believes it to be a love poem in which Emily Dickinson bids adieu to Charles Wadsworth forever.[15] Her evidence rests on parallels between the poem and Tennyson's "Love and Duty." How did she fix on Tennyson? A letter written by Emily Dickinson to Mrs. Josiah Holland, in 1883, says that "the Death of the Loved is all moments— now," and quotes from "Love and Duty," "Of Love that never found it's earthly close, what sequel?" The anniversary of Wadsworth's death was approaching, therefore the poet meant Wadsworth, therefore the metaphor of departure is the primary meaning of the poem. Caroline Hogue did not know that in March 1883, Judge Lord had suffered his stroke, from which he did not fully recover. The circumstances of the relationship between Emily Dickinson and Judge Lord were not revealed until 1954 when Mrs. Bingham published *A Revelation*.

William Howard, writing in 1954, disagrees with Caroline Hogue, on the basis of a further reading of the letter to Mrs. Holland. "Love" she continues, "has but one Date—'The first of April.'" Howard says it is Benjamin Newton that was meant; he was the beloved person of the poem construed as elegy; he died on March 24, but the *Springfield Republican* would not have reached the Amherst household until the first week in April; thus for the next thirty years Emily Dickinson laments the death of Newton on April 1.

In 1960, Clark Griffith ignores the 1883 letter but still sees the poem as a sob of blighted love, although he does not care whom the poet has lost. The poem laments "the transience which weakens and destroys all human ties. The theme is deprivation, to be sure." [16]

And yet this poem lay, with its companion piece beside it, in the letter sent to Higginson; numberless variant and illuminating poems lay everywhere in *The Poems of Emily Dickinson*. And Higginson's article, "Letter to a Young Contributor," lay printed, in its entirety, in the *Atlantic Monthly*.

Indeed the whole matter of the poet's earliest approach to Thomas Higginson has been frequently misinterpreted. Critics such as Charles Anderson and Clark Griffith have certainly been alert to the fact of the poet's irony but they have understood this irony to be a strategy, limited in some way, or as a device of protection against a frightening world.

It is true that Anderson does recognize that the correspondence with Higginson was not that of a literary mentor and a naive protégé, that Higginson was simply a foil for her wit, but he believes her correspondence "had begun as a sincere request for counsel." He is sure that the ironic mask was used for withdrawal into an indispensable solitude needed for this "spiritual pioneer." Her wit was the instrument by which she detached herself from a current world that displeased and even repelled her. "She mastered this outer world by renouncing it." [17] Why then she should have been engaged in a "desperate search for literary counsel," I cannot see, but Anderson does not find any contradiction. In fact, the very poems she sent, seeking counsel, are those cited as examples of her wit, her instrument of detachment.

Moreover, Anderson tells us in the first chapter of his book that Emily Dickinson had at the earliest stage of her poetic career already reached a sardonic tolerance of industrializing America, had already renounced both religious hypocrisy and her ineffectual parents; he tells us that she had very early in her life penetrated the sham of ornate Romantic poetry and had even begun to defend the independence of women. If Emily Dickinson fits that image Anderson gives us, then surely she would have penetrated to the core of such a literary man as Higginson; she would not have needed several exchanges of letters to learn that she had not "found the critic she needed but the perfect foil for her wit."

Clark Griffith believes profoundly in the dramatic event that occurred in 1858–1859, her "inner drama," as he calls it. By the time she "addressed her famous appeal to Thomas Wentworth Higginson, the editor of the *Atlantic Monthly*,[18] she had no fewer than four hundred separate poems" on hand. "If her personal behavior was mad—and in some respects it no doubt was—then the madness was at least a productive aberration, very close to genius."[19] Griffith has her "timidly" submitting her poetry, and because it was a "masculine critic [who] failed Emily Dickinson," she was "never able to muster an adequate defense" thereafter.

This conception of the "masculine" drives Griffith into an even more grotesque corner. He assesses the entire Dickinson-Higginson correspondence in this way:

> It will be helpful at this point to mention the two distinct tones of Emily Dickinson's correspondence. When men are addressed, her style is likely to be grand and philosophical and, increasingly over the years, oracular and profound. This would be the case from the "Master letters," through the correspondence with Higginson and Samuel Bowles. . . .[20]

It may not be fair to quote from these letters, since Griffith does not, but ought one to think of fair play when a critic of our own time characterizes Emily Dickinson as neurotic, erotic, laconic, and scared? This is an example of her writing to Bowles:

> I find bright pretext to ask you how you are tonight, and for the health of four more, Elder and Minor "Mary," Sallie and Sam, tenderly to inquire. I hope your cups are full. I hope your vintage is untouched. In such a porcelain life, one likes to be *sure* that all is well, lest one stumble upon one's hopes in a pile of broken crockery.[21]

Here is another written two years later:

> I am much ashamed. I misbehaved tonight. I would like to sit in the dust. I fear I am your little friend no more, but Mrs Jim Crow.
> I am sorry I smiled at women.
> Indeed, I revere holy ones, like Mrs Fry and Miss Nightingale. I will never be giddy again. Pray forgive me now. Respect little Bob o' Lincoln again![22]

And she writes thus to the "Master":

> I am ill, but grieving more that you are ill . . . I would that all I love, should be weak no more. The Violets are by my side, the Robin very near, and "Spring" they say, Who is she—going by the door—
> I wish that I were great, like Mr. Michael Angelo, and could paint for you. You ask me what my flowers said—then they were disobedient. . . .[23]

And here is more of that philosophical, that grand style that is so oracular and profound:

> One drop more from the gash that stains your Daisy's bosom—then would you *believe?* Thomas' faith in Anatomy, was stronger than his faith in faith. God made me—(Sir) Master—I didn't be myself. I don't know how it was done. He built the heart in me—Bye and bye it outgrew me—and like the little mother—with the big child—I got tired holding him.[24]

Griffith has a fixed point of view which derives from his monist idea of reality. It would not matter which poet or what poetry—all would have to fit into his pseudo-Freudian frame of reference.

But Thomas Johnson, the editor who established the reliable text of Emily Dickinson's poetry, and surely must have been deeply immersed in her world, nevertheless consistently misinterprets poems and letters. His summation of the sense of Higginson's article itself is wholly inaccurate, because I suppose he did not bother to read all of it, or if he did, thought most of it irrelevant. He says only this and nothing more about the article:

> It was practical advice for beginners, with emphasis on smoothness of style, and avoidance of prolixity and high-flown language.[25]

Johnson is misinformed about Higginson, but so authentic is his voice we believe him when he tells us that Higginson was "interested in the status of women in general and women writers in particular" and that Emily Dickinson "genuinely admired his writing." We simply dismiss, because Johnson does, the facts that are available to anyone, that the critical time of this correspondence was 1862 when Higginson was preoccupied with the Civil War, and it was not the status of women but the status of Negroes that interested Higginson.[26] He became a champion of women writers in the 1870's, for it was then he met Helen Hunt Jackson, and it was then he married his own young lady poet, Mary Potter Thacher (in 1879). But it is not easy to dismiss passages such as these, for they distort more crucial truths:

> Higginson's impression after he had pondered the "Alabaster" poem was that it lacked form. It was imperfectly rhymed and its metric beat spasmodic . . .

The "Alabaster" poem was sent with the first letter. The question of "spasmodic" was an issue raised in the third letter. Johnson, who established the text of the letters as well as the poetry, simply ignores the second intervening letter and the poems sent with it. He goes on to create a fanciful construction:

> He had suggested that, since her rhymes were imperfect or casually dropped in, she might better give them up entirely. She says that she "could not drop the Bells whose jingling cooled my Tramp." For Higginson a rhyme, or indeed a poem for that matter was something to be produced as you get water from a tap. Emily Dickinson was incapable of an analysis of her techniques. . . . But even if she had been able to explain, she would never have affronted the kindly friend who was willing to respond to her appeal with a sincere if bewildered understanding. Her own certainties are positively implied in two sentences, each written as a separate paragraph. "You think my gait 'spasmodic'—I am in danger—Sir. You think me 'uncontrolled'—I have no Tribunal." [27]

Just why such two statements should indicate her "certainties" I cannot tell, nor does Thomas Johnson explain. But I do find that in a literary history published in 1875, *Victorian Poets,* Edmund Clarence Stedman writes disparagingly of a group of mid-nineteenth-century poets,

> whose outpourings the wits speedily characterized by the epithet "spasmodic." Their work constantly affords examples of the knack of substitution. . . . Its adherents, lacking perception and synthesis, and mistaking the materials of poetry for poetry itself, aimed at the production of quotable passages, and crammed their verse with mixed and conceited imagery, gushing diction, interjections, and that mockery of passion which is but surface deep. . . . With much impressiveness of imagery and extravagant diction . . . it was vicious in style, loose in thought, and devoid of real vigor or beauty. . . . [28]

And I confirm this concrete meaning of the term "spasmodic" by finding an entry in Chambers' *Cyclopaedia,* revised edition:

Spasmodic School
> The name implied an overstrained and unnatural method of sentiment and expression which sometimes grew out of sheer affectation and not seldom sank hopelessly into bathos.

Both Stedman and Chambers speak of *Firmilian,* a parody of the "Spasmodics" published in 1854, as a widely read burlesque of the grandiose style.

When Johnson looks closely at the letters it is to be able to tell us that Emily Dickinson wrote two sentences in two separate paragraphs. The exact meaning of what she says is less significant. And when he turns to the poetry that accompanied the letters he sees no relationship, he does not think of them as a group. And so he treats "We play at Paste" as a separate entity and makes the same swift assessment of her meaning, equally erroneous:

> No language could say more directly that the writer looks back upon the work she produced four or five years ago and finds it trifling.[29]

That Emily Dickinson was to send Higginson within a short time poems that Johnson himself dates as 1858 ("As if I asked a common Alms") and 1860 ("Some keep the Sabbath going to Church") and 1859 ("Success is counted sweetest") stands in direct contradiction to his interpretation of "We play at Paste." Doubtless she would not have sent trifling poems.

But the recent editor is bent on exposing the first editor, and not on illuminating the poetry of Emily Dickinson. Higginson had said that "We play at Paste" "comprises in its eight lines a truth so searching that it seems a condensed summary of the whole experience of a long life." Johnson bursts out:

> The fatuousness of the remark is beside the point. The fact is that he never came to have the slightest concept of what Dickinson's artistic achievement consisted, not even when he timidly sponsored publication. His comment on the other poem is of such a nature as to raise serious doubt whether he even understood it.

A glance at Johnson's interpretation of "Wild Nights" raises doubts about his own understanding of Emily Dickinson's poetry:

> This is also the time when she wrote two love poems that employ sexual imagery with unabashed frankness.

> Wild Nights—Wild Nights!
> Were I with thee
> Wild Nights should be
> our luxury!

Futile—the Winds—
To a Heart in port—
Done with the Compass—
Done with the Chart!

Rowing in Eden—
Ah, the Sea!
Might I but moor—Tonight—
In Thee!

The water imagery is conspicuous . . . but the metrics . . . derives from the mood. The slow regularity of the beginning is speeded up at the end of the second stanza. The third stanza opens with a panting dactyl that slows to a quiet measure, shortened, in the last line, to two feet. The imagery throughout is unmistakably concrete.

This is manifestly erotic poetry. From what experience was she enabled to give these sensations an artistic creation? With what intent did she write the poems? [30]

Johnson answers his own question in this fashion:

Answers to such questions may be hidden, but their concealment cannot prevent the knowledge, that any creation is a true statement of something. She wrote the poems and she transcribed them fair into her packets.

Indeed! "Their concealment cannot prevent the knowledge that any creation is a true statement of something." Whatever that phrase means to Thomas Johnson, it does not explain how this poem can be construed as an allegory of sexual intercourse.

Emily Dickinson has many poems transcribed into her threaded booklets that speak in anguished terms of her desire to be with someone,[31] but her longing is always thwarted by some barrier, some impossibility. The person may be a lost friend, her sister Sue, Samuel Bowles, or Jesus Christ; it is the attribute of the unattainable, the unrealized, that is always present as the resolution of the action of the poem. This poem may have had direct reference to a beloved man, a deeply cherished man, for Emily Dickinson had no lover although she would have welcomed one, but the imagery of the poem does not prove it, for it is as credible that this poem expresses a longing for Jesus. So many poems speak of home as Heaven, the ultimate returning to eternal peace experienced by God's precious creatures, so many poems speak of the Sea as passage to that home, that

"Wild Nights" may be read simply as a variant of the idea of arrival in Heaven.

Emily Dickinson had access to the volume of Quarles' *Divine Emblems* in her father's collection of books. The engraving for Emblem 11 * depicts a scene so akin to that rendered by the poet as to suggest the possibility that she was looking at the picture and composing her own poem for it, just as Quarles himself had done.

This may be confirmed for "Wild Nights" if we examine the words of the poem closely, using the Lexicon definitions instead of those immediate connotations grown familiar and stale. We find a disciplined consistency in her maritime references. The Lexicon prints a derivation of "Wild" that is interesting for its characterization of the persona of this poem: "Saxon, *wealh,* a traveler, foreigner, or pilgrim." Among the many definitions, most are predictable to us—roving, wandering, uncultivated, savage, turbulent, ungoverned, mutable—but if we take note of this definition of "Wild" quoted by Webster from the Maritime Dictionary, "exposed to the wind and sea; as, a wild roadstead [a place where ships may ride at anchor, at some distance from the shore]," then we may see the poem has not erotic imagery but interlaces flexible strands of navigation metaphors.

"Chart" is a marine map used to guide a ship through the dangerous channels as it seeks entrance into its harbor. It is a word that has a terrestrial, an earth-bound, significance.

"Compass" is the "mariner's compass used for directing or ascertaining the course of ships at sea." It "consists of a circular box . . . covered with glass, to prevent the motion of the card from being disturbed by the wind. . . ." "Disturbed by the wind" seems to have stuck in the poet's mind. "Futile—the Winds—/ To a Heart in port—" is her modulation.

"Moor" is "To confine or secure a ship in a particular station, beneath the water. A ship is never said to be *moored* when she rides by a single anchor." Her heart in port is to be free of that torment of pulling through that roadstead where her boat is weighed down by that single anchor, the attachment to life, just outside the harbor. Were she moored in that harbor such wild nights would be unnecessary. Fixed there with the cables and chains of security, placid in Eden, she would not need any chart (no shoals) or any compass (no traveling). She would know where she was and would not be journeying any more. She would be safe. Ah but, before she can do that she must pass through that dangerous Sea.

* See frontispiece.

To verify this paraphrase there is the context of similar metaphors in other poems. Water imagery is conspicuous in "Wild Nights" as it is in more than twenty other poems.[32] The sea is a symbol for the place of transition between life and afterlife, death, as it is here.

> Could live — *did* live —
> Could die — *did* die —
> Could smile upon the whole
> Through faith in one he met not,
> To introduce his soul
>
> . . . .
>
> Such trust had one among us,
> Among us *not* today —
> We who saw the launching
> Never sailed the Bay!
>
>
> . . .
>
>
> Whether my bark went down at sea —
> Whether she met with gales —
> Whether to isles enchanted
> She bent her docile sails —
>
> By what mystic mooring
> She is held today —
> This is the errand of the eye
> Out upon the Bay.

The metaphor of Eden is her symbol for Paradise, true, but it is a Paradise of ultimate fruition, the place that poets finally reach — fame, publication. Arrival in Eden is often her metaphor of the experience of bliss such as only the poet can know. The poem "Wild Nights" is copied on to the same sheet of stationery, back to back, with this poem, which associates Eden with song:

> Why — do they shut Me out of Heaven?
> Did I sing — too loud?
> But — I can say a little "Minor"
> Timid as a Bird!
>
> Would'nt the Angels try me —
> Just — once — more —

Just—see—if I troubled them—
But dont—shut the door!

Oh, if I—were the Gentleman
In the "White Robe"—
And they—were the little Hand—that knocked—
Could—I—forbid?

Other poems in this same Fascicle 8 are lamentations at her rejection as a poet, "The Robin's my criterion for Tune—" and "I shall keep singing!" This one is copied just below "Wild Nights" with a thin line drawn to indicate separation.[33]

I shall keep singing!
Birds will pass me
On their way to Yellower Climes—
Each—with a Robin's expectation—
I—with my Redbreast—
And my Rhymes—

Late—when I take my place in summer—
But—I shall bring a fuller tune—
Vespers—are sweeter than Matins—Signor—
Morning—only the seed of Noon—

In another fascicle, 37, there is this plaintive little poem of patience, one of the many variants on her conception of the meaning of her poetic history.

Come slowly—Eden!
Lips unused to Thee—
Bashful—sip thy Jessamines—
As the fainting Bee—

Reaching late his flower,
Round her chamber hums—
Counts his nectars—
Enters—and is lost in Balms.

Among others in Fascicle 37 are "poet poems" ("The Lamp burns sure—within—" and "Tho' my destiny be Fustian—"), and copied onto the same sheet of paper of "Come slowly—Eden!" is a poem so like "Wild Nights" as to qualify as a variant:

Just lost, when I was saved!
Just felt the world go by!
Just girt me for the onset with Eternity,
When breath blew back,
And on the other side
I heard recede the disappointed tide!

Therefore, as One returned, I feel,
Odd secrets of the line to tell!
Some Sailor, skirting foreign shores—
Some pale Reporter, from the awful doors
Before the Seal!

Next time, to stay!
Next time, the things to see
By Ear unheard,
Unscrutinized by Eye—

Next time, to tarry,
While the Ages steal—
Slow tramp the Centuries,
And the Cycles wheel!

Such relationships provide more reliable clues to Emily Dickinson's meaning than do authorities who speculate on "panting dactyls."

Another poem, written close in time, has the same subject matter and the same imagery; it is in no fascicle, for the poet left it as a scrap, but it is relevant for the insight it offers into the way Emily Dickinson explained to herself why the struggle was necessary.

Did the Harebell loose her girdle
To the lover Bee
Would the Bee the Harebell *hallow*
Much as formerly?

Did the "Paradise"—persuaded—
Yield her moat of pearl—
Would the Eden *be* an Eden,
Or the Earl—an *Earl?*

This importuning poet knows that were Paradise to open to her out of her artful persuasion rather than her intrinsic worth, Eden would no longer be so great an achievement, her Earldom spurious; just as were that bell-shaped flower to open of itself to the importuning bee, her nectar would not be so prized.

In 1862 Emily Dickinson had little choice but to wait, not patiently, but persistently. Higginson's response to her second letter and to the poems sent him was perhaps more complimentary, but he gave her little cause to hope. Conventional gallantries on the one hand, metaphors and cryptic phrases on the other, hid from neither correspondent that what was between them was a poetry so different, so unique, that despite all the explanations and defenses the poet offered, the critic did not understand. His delicate questioning was met with distortions of fact; his tactful criticism was met with irony. The third letter begins:

> Your letter gave no Drunkenness, because I had tasted Rum before — Domingo comes but once — yet I have had few pleasures so deep as your opinion, and if I tried to thank you, my tears would block my tongue —
> My dying Tutor told me that he would like to live till I had been a poet, but Death was much of Mob as I could master — then — And when far afterward — a sudden light on Orchards, or a new fashion in the wind troubled my attention — I felt a palsy, here — the Verses just relieve — [34]

What was intended for compliment she turned aside with hyperbole. Higginson understood the quality of poetry to reside in its craftsmanship; Emily Dickinson believed it resided in the subject matter. This second paragraph is a history of her poetic development, explained as a shift that had occurred in theme. That early tutor would have liked to live long enough to see her become a poet, but she was unable to master versifying because she was beset with the subject matter of Death; she was preoccupied with the meaning of Death. In the next stage of her development, the meaning of Nature became her subject: the sudden light on orchards ("There came a Day at Summer's full,") and the new fashion in the wind ("Of all the sounds despatched abroad,") took her attention.

Instead of striving to understand Death, she was grasped, herself taken, by a force outside herself, "I felt a palsy." This does not mean only fear or trembling, but what her Lexicon describes palsy to be: an abolition of voluntary motion, a slackening of the function of intellect. The verses took their form, not from the conventions of prosody, from no external frame, not out of deliberation, but spontaneously, without control. "The Verses just relieve" must be understood in terms supplied by her Lexicon, which defines "relieve" as "To assist; to support, [to] set off by contrast." Her new subject, intuition of immortality, is derived from her perception of Nature; the rhythm, the rhyme, the imagery, only assists or supports the message. She is a bard, no versifier. She goes on:

> Your second letter surprised me, and for a moment, swung—I had not supposed it. Your first—gave no dishonor, because the True are not ashamed—I thanked you for your justice—but could not drop the Bells whose jingling cooled my Tramp—Perhaps the Balm, seemed better, because you bled me, first.

Dizzied (swung) with the effect of his Rum or praise, she admits she had not believed she would receive it, not after having had his first letter, in which he wondered who her influences had been, what education she had, what religious beliefs she held, why indeed she wrote poetry at all. Higginson has evidently apologized for his harshness; now she reassures him that his adverse criticism had not injured her, for her own sense of herself as a poet tells her she and her poetry are genuine, are honest, are right: "the True—are not ashamed." Far from humble, she mingles herself here with her subject matter and her style. My reaction, she assures him, was to thank you for your efforts to apply the laws of poetry to my case, no doubt a violation of those laws. But I reject your effort to correct my defects in accordance with what you think are the proper rules laid down by critics. They are not my principles of right poetic practice. "I could not drop the Bells whose jingling cooled *my* Tramp." Whatever Higginson may think of her prosody, she knows that her Bells fit her subject matter. Earlier it was "the Verses just relieve"; now the jingling cools the tramp.

How is it a "tramp" needs cooling? Tramp seems at first a word implying a kind of walk, a stroll. But indisputably, she says "drop the Bells whose jingling cooled my Tramp." The tramp is therefore uncool. Surely a mere walk is scarcely characterized as cool or uncool. "Tramp" in the Lexicon is given only half a line, defining it as the synonym for "Tread." Looking up "Tread," we discover it is defined, yes, as walking, but primarily as "Trample." Here then is the source of Emily Dickinson's meaning. "Trample" is to tread upon with pride, contempt, triumph, or scorn. "Trample" is to tread with force or rapidity. Now we are able to put the phrase in its proper context, not merely her subject matter, but her own conception of the meaning of her verse. She is by no means ignorant of her pride, she is well aware of her scorn and her contempt of others, so-called friends, judges, poetical ladies.

But there is more to it. Recall the line in the second letter, "I sing, as the Boy does by the Burying Ground—because I am afraid." That line has been transformed to appear in this third letter as "Death was much of a Mob as I could master." And when she expands it to signify the new fashion in the wind, the new sense she has of Nature's meaning, we begin to perceive another level of meaning. She knows she sings more fiercely, more triumphantly, with greater force because of this tremor of her spirit which needs the cooling application of Poetry itself, not verse, not prosody, but Poetry.

In the context of this first portion of the letter, the next paragraph takes on a new clarity: she is indeed scornful; and she is well aware of her own worth.

> I smile when you suggest that I delay "to publish"—that being foreign to my thought, as Firmament—to Fin—
> If fame belonged to me, I could not escape her—if she did not, the longest day would pass me on the chase—and the approbation of my dog, would forsake me—then—My Barefoot—Rank is better—
> You think my gait "spasmodic"—I am in danger—Sir—
> You think me "uncontrolled"—I have no Tribunal.

The irony of her assertion, "I smile when you suggest that I delay 'to publish'" has already been pointed out; it will be verified when the exchange of letters and poems with Samuel Bowles is described, for between Emily Dickinson and Bowles there was a constant subject, over a much longer period of time: the validity of her poetry and a plea for its publication. From that discussion it will become clear that her use of the word "delay" is a transparent irony—as if she could choose to delay or to hasten publication! What seems at first glance to be a laconic dismissal of the question takes on a new tone when one reads her letter to Higginson with the knowledge of what Emily Dickinson's poetic career has been. Even the idea of the "Barefoot Rank," which enters in here so airily, is a phrase often found in her communications to Bowles, and in private colloquy with herself when she is reassuring herself that she will find fame eventually.

But let us examine now "Barefoot Rank" as it is linked to the next line, "You think my gait 'spasmodic'—I am in danger—Sir." As we have already seen, that word *spasmodic* has been erroneously interpreted as a word associated with the craft of poetry; in the period during which Emily Dickinson wrote, it was a word associated with the subject matter of poetry. There had been a constant barrage of attacks on young lady poets in this period, laughter at their bathos, their sentimentality. If Higginson hints that her gait is spasmodic he is relegating her to that school of poetry accused of banality and affectation. Bowles had written one such attack and published it in the *Springfield Republican* in 1860, under the title of "What Shall We Write?"

> There is another kind of writing only too common, appealing to the sympathies of the reader without recommending itself to his judgment. It may be called the literature of misery. Its writers are chiefly women, gifted women may be, full of thought and feeling and fancy, but poor, lonely and unhappy. Also that suffering is so seldom healthful. It may be a valuable discipline in the end, but for the time being it too often clouds, withers, distorts. It is so difficult to see objects distinctly through a mist of tears. The sketch or poem is usually the writer's photograph in miniature. It reveals a countenance we would gladly brighten, but not by exposing it to the gaze of a worthless world.[35]

That charge of "spasmodic" was an all too familiar valuation of her poetry and it rankled. Bowles' article had been the cause of deep anguish to Emily Dickinson, who took it to refer directly to her and was interpreted by her as an act of treason; long years afterward, she still called it so. Convert the word as she would to an ironic pun on "gait" (I am in danger—Sir") she writhed under the name.

The passage ends with "You think me 'uncontrolled'—I have no Tribunal." This ties everything to the question not of mentor but publication, for that word "Tribunal" is exactly the word Higginson had used in his "Letter to a Young Contributor":

> If one were expecting to be judged by a few scholars only, one might hope somehow to cajole them; but it is this vast, unimpassioned, unconscious tribunal, this average judgment of intelligent minds, which is truly formidable . . . and at last becomes the organ of eternal justice and infallibly awards posthumous fame.

Bowles had said he would certainly not publish this sort of poetic indulgence; Higginson advised her to delay to publish. Indeed she had no Tribunal nor would she have in her lifetime.

The concluding paragraphs of Emily Dickinson's letter have always been understood to be incontestable proof of the poet's humility. But that is because they have been wrenched out of their context.

> Would you have time to be the "friend" you should [seem to] think I need? I have a little shape—it would not crowd your Desk—nor make much Racket as the Mouse, that dents your Galleries—

Emily Dickinson was by no means ignorant of the poets Higginson sponsored, of the poets who were enjoying Tribunals in their lifetime. But she is not the Mouse; it is the Mouse that makes the racket. Ironic again, she promises her noise will be less, far less than the nibblings of the other poets who are making dents in his galleries.

That word "Galleries" signifies a ship (it is the projecting balcony, protruding from the stern) and in fact is itself part of an expanding metaphor:

> If I might bring you what I do—not so frequent to trouble you—and ask you if I told it clear—'twould be control, to me—
> The Sailor cannot see the North—but knows the Needle can—

She will not nibble at the shipboards (which may eventually bring about the ruin of the whole structure); she will sail on the ship, she is the Sailor; he, the Needle. The Needle can guide the ship. She asks him then for steering, for "control" but *she* is sailing. Guidance such as this seems simple enough,

> The "hand you stretch me in the Dark," I put mine in, and turn away—I have no Saxon, now—

but the letter is not yet finished. Finally her established practice asserts itself: she will say in the verse what the prose has not yet said. The poem she includes in this final portion contains a turn of thought that will undermine what has seemed to be her plea:

> As if I asked a common Alms,
> And in my wondering hand
> A Stranger pressed a Kingdom,
> And I, bewildered, stand—
> As if I asked the Orient

Had it for me a Morn —
And it should lift it's purple Dikes,
And shatter me with Dawn!

But, will you be my Preceptor, Mr. Higginson?

Here obviously is a poem fit precisely to this occasion. She is "in the Dark" as the letter says; she asks for light. She is barefoot as the letter says; here she seeks alms. She has swung in the letter; here she stands bewildered. And the quality of an ironic gallantry of her own pervades the letter as well as the poem.

Will he be her friend? Will he let her bring her poems for his control? Should the stranger agree, it will be like pressing a kingdom into the hand of an importuning beggar; should he agree, it will be like the graciousness of the Orient—the East—with its double meaning of the place of wealth and the sky shattering her with dawn.

To be sure, the East by its very nature must and always does bestow the dawn. By the logic of analogy, that stranger will have to bestow a kingdom on this quaint beggar. It is Emily Dickinson's conception of the beggar as someone deserving at least a Kingdom by natural right that is so unique. By "beggar" she means the poet.

There are several poems in the fascicles similar in imagery and in conception to "As if I asked a common Alms." They would probably not have been of much help to Higginson in his effort to understand the kind of poet who was ostensibly offering to place herself under his guidance. But they can illuminate her meaning for us.

What precisely is that Barefoot Rank of which Emily Dickinson speaks in the letter, what that beggar of the poem? There is a poem that uses both the image of the beggar and the action of the dawn.

As Watchers hang upon the East,
As Beggars revel at a feast
By savory Fancy spread —
As brooks in deserts babble sweet
On ear too far for the delight,
Heaven beguiles the tired.

As that same watcher, when the East
Opens the lid of Amethyst
And lets the morning go —

> That Beggar, when an honored Guest,
> Those thirsty lips to flagons pressed,
> Heaven to us, if true.

This poem was sent to Samuel Bowles. The variant poem connects the variant preceptors.

There is a poem which reverberates that phrase of the Barefoot Rank in the third letter to Higginson, and it has a similar conception of a beggar who will be transformed to a royal estate by natural right; it has the same concern with a change, not from night to day but from death to eternal life and from deprivation to ultimate vindication. And this poem is copied into the same fascicle, 83, where "As Watchers hang upon the East," appears.

> In rags mysterious as these
> The shining Courtiers go—
> Vailing the purple, and the plumes—
> Vailing the ermine so.

> Smiling, as they request an alms—
> At some imposing door!
> Smiling when we walk barefoot
> Upon their golden floor!

The poet pictures a scene in Heaven, analogous to her situation on Earth. These Courtiers who enter through the gate of Heaven hide their nobility, shroud their regal plumes and ermine, smiling as they seek entry. So she hides her own sheen behind a mask of humility. They play at asking for alms as she plays at asking for guidance. They enjoy their natural inheritance—to walk on the golden floor of Heaven. And she, knocking at the terrestrial door of the imposing critics, will walk in her natural state, without artifice, barefoot, she will walk, just as she is, on that domain, that golden floor of acceptance that lies behind the barrier. Let Higginson do what he will. She will enter the Heaven she seeks.

Of course Emily Dickinson was not always so comforted. Another poem appears in the same fascicle, using the same image, but the feeling tone has altered.

> Talk with prudence to a Beggar
> Of "Potosi," and the mines!

Reverently, to the Hungry
Of your viands, and your wines!

Cautious, hint to any Captive
You have passed enfranchized feet!
Anecdotes of air in Dungeons
Have sometimes proved deadly sweet!

If that Beggar signifies Emily Dickinson's conception of her status as a
poet, and we remember how frequently her two editors came to visit the
Dickinson house in Amherst, then the poem takes on a bitter tone. She
may have sat amiably enough in the family circle listening to the chitchat
of the magazine and newspaper world, but in the privacy of her room she
sang her truths, lamenting her fate. There is also in this Fascicle:

Success is counted sweetest
By those who ne'er succeed.
To comprehend a nectar
Requires sorest need.

Not one of all the purple Host
Who took the Flag today
Can tell the definition
So clear of Victory

As he defeated—dying—
On whose forbidden ear
The distant strains of triumph
Burst agonized and clear!

The best clue we have to the cause of deprivation is in a companion
poem:

Her breast is fit for pearls,
But I was not a "Diver"—
Her brow is fit for thrones
But I have not a crest.
Her heart is fit for *home*—
I—a Sparrow—build there
Sweet of twigs and twine
My perennial nest.

Here the poet contemplates the muse of poetry, and estimates her own thwarted but still dedicated status. How, though, can we be absolutely certain? By seeking another "beggar" poem in a different Fascicle.

> I met a King this afternoon!
> He had not on a Crown indeed,
> A little Palmleaf Hat was all,
> And he was barefoot, I'm afraid!
>
> But sure I am he Ermine wore
> Beneath his faded Jacket's blue—
> And sure I am, the crest he bore
> Within that Jacket's pocket too!
>
> For 'twas too stately for an Earl—
> A Marquis would not go so grand!
> 'Twas possibly a Czar petite—
> A Pope, or something of that kind!
>
> If I must tell you, of a Horse
> My freckled Monarch held the rein—
> Doubtless an estimable Beast,
> But not at all disposed to run!
>
> And such a wagon! While I live
> Dare I presume to see
> Another such a vehicle
> As then transported me!
>
> Two other ragged Princes
> His royal state partook!
> Doubtless the first excursion
> These sovereigns ever took!
>
> I question if the Royal Coach
> Round which the Footmen wait
> Has the significance, on high,
> Of this Barefoot Estate!

Here surely is that Barefoot Rank. If we hesitate to associate this poem with Emily Dickinson's conception of the unique quality of her poetry, we can pause to verify further. In this fascicle (now it is #4 we are considering) there is that pathetic cry of joy and mingled trepidation that seems almost to have been written when she posted her first letter to Higginson.

> 'Tis so much joy! 'Tis so much joy!
> If I should fail, what poverty!
> And yet, as poor as I,
> Have ventured all upon a throw!
> Have gained! Yes! Hesitated so —
> This side the Victory!
>
> Life is but Life! And Death, but Death!
> Bliss is but Bliss, and Breath but Breath!
> And if indeed I fail,
> At least, to know the worst, is sweet!
> Defeat means nothing *but* Defeat,
> No drearier, can befall!
>
> And if I gain! Oh Gun at Sea!
> Oh Bells, that in the Steeples be!
> At first, repeat it slow!
> For Heaven is a different thing,
> Conjectured, and waked sudden in —
> And might extinguish me!

Emily Dickinson was surely hoping for something. And she copied onto that selfsame sheet of paper,

> At last, to be identified!
> At last, the lamps upon thy side
> The rest of Life to *see!*
>
> Past Midnight! Past the Morning Star!
> Past Sunrise!
> Ah, What leagues there *were*
> Between our feet, and Day!

So important an emblem did Emily Dickinson judge this poem to be, she copied it again for Fascicle 34, a gathering of several "poet poems" among the rest, for example "They shut me up in Prose—" and "This was a Poet—It is That" and "I died for Beauty—but was scarce". There is even a "pearl" poem,

The Malay—took the Pearl—
Not—I—the Earl—
I—feared the Sea—too much
Unsanctified—to touch—

Praying that I might be
Worthy—the Destiny—
The Swarthy fellow swam—
And bore my Jewel—Home—

Home to the Hut! What lot
Had I—the Jewel—got—
Borne on a Dusky Breast—
I had not deemed a Vest
Of Amber—fit—

The Negro never knew
I—wooed it—too—
To gain, or be undone—
Alike to Him—One—

This poem so exactly parallels "Her breast is fit for pearls," we may entertain now a stronger conviction that the imagery of pearl is associated with a poem, the beggar is associated with a poet, and the deprivation, surely, the adverse opinion of both Bowles and Higginson. It seems almost as if the poet recopied her "At last, to be identified!" as an ironic jibe at her own former hopes, which lie wasting in Fascicle 34.

Now we can interpret "I met a King this afternoon!" without hesitation as a dramatic rendering of the nature of her verse. How sure she is of the unique quality of her poetry. How indifferent to the gait of the horse, but not to the Wagon (the carrier, the vehicle for the poetry), for that is distinctive, rich, more significant than any Royal Coach (accepted poetry) driven by a poet comfortable in his public acclaim, followed by his lackeys. And one can enjoy her private assessment of editors, those ragged Princes on their first excursion into such poetry as hers.

Emily Dickinson would lash out against the stupidity of her judges all the rest of her life. Here is an inspiriting outcry of indignation:

To hear an Oriole sing
May be a common thing—
Or only a divine.

It is not of the Bird
Who sings the same, unheard,
As unto Crowd—

The fashion of the Ear
Attireth that it hear
In Dun, or fair—

So whether it be Rune,
Or whether it be none,
Is of within.

The "Tune is in the Tree—"
The Skeptic—showeth me—
"No Sir! In Thee!"

This poem can be read as a variant of her poem sent to Higginson, "Of all the Sounds despatched abroad," except that this has so acid a tone it may have been generated by her earlier rejection by Bowles. In any case it hints at the poet's determination to sing whether heard or not; it comes straight out with her withering declaration that the perception of a song depends on the ability of the listener to hear; his judgment has nothing to do with the song, but with his preconception of what is "Dun, or fair," of what is "Rune [Webster's: poetry or rhymes] or none." That skeptic, Higginson (earlier Bowles), thinks the quality of the verse resides in the versification: "No Sir! In Thee!"

She would seek again and again to reassure herself; she was in dialogue with herself and often raised questions that intimidated her poise and faith, but always she ended by giving herself answers that, poem by poem and year by year, strengthened the fibres of her soul.

I reckon—when I count at all—
First—Poets—Then the Sun—
Then Summer—Then the Heaven of God—
And then—the List is done—

But, looking back—the First so seems
To Comprehend the Whole—
The Others look a needless Show—
So I write—Poets—All—

Their Summer—lasts a Solid Year—
They can afford a Sun
The East—would deem extravagant—
And if the Further Heaven—

Be Beautiful as they prepare
For Those who worship Them—
It is too difficult a Grace—
To justify the Dream—

The first two stanzas would have shocked her preceptor; they say precisely what her poems have said: the meaning of the poetry is just the meaning of Nature and of God. The last two stanzas would have been worse for him; poetry not only speaks of immortality, poetry is itself immortal. Poets. through their poems, last a solid—unbroken—year (transcend time); poets, through their poems, have an external light greater than the sun (transcend nature). And if Heaven be beautiful, it is the poets, through their poetry, who prepare mortals to recognize that beauty, by giving them hints of it in their work.

She affirmed and reaffirmed the impregnability of her poetry; she asserted her immunity to rejection:

The Lamp burns sure—within—
Tho' Serfs—supply the Oil—
It matters not the busy Wick—
At her phosphoric toil!

The Slave—forgets—to fill—
The Lamp—burns golden—on—
Unconscious that the oil is out—
As that the Slave—is gone.

She convinced herself of the need to continue despite all adverse response:

To fill a Gap
Insert the Thing that caused it—
Block it up
With Other—and 'twill yawn the more—
You cannot solder an Abyss
With Air.

She strove to teach herself contentment:

> Alone, I cannot be —
> The Hosts — do visit me —
> Recordless Company —
> Who baffle Key —
>
> They have no Robes, nor Names —
> No Almanacs — nor Climes —
> But general Homes
> Like Gnomes —
>
> Their Coming, may be known
> By Couriers within —
> Their going — is not,
> For they're never gone —

But the rejection of her poetry was no indifferent thing to Emily Dickinson. It was not enough to jab at her critics, to call them stupid, to deny their validity, to make herself immune to their evaluation. During this time she wrote poems picturing herself as dying of despair; she envied the dead who had no burdens; she visualized herself reaching Heaven where her tribulations on Earth would be rewarded with a royal seat. The funereal songs of her rejection toll through the poems of 1862 and ever afterwards she remembered the bitterness of submission. Her isolation was at once comfort and retaliation. Her white election was her personal metaphor of martyrdom. She purified herself and withdrew from a world which was not ready.

How she would have relished the vision of W. D. Howells, taking an interest in Stephen Crane in 1893, sitting down at their first meeting to read aloud her poems to the startlingly young and highly original author of *Maggie*.[36] How she would have relished the spectacle of the Imagists at war on tradition, on convention, on all the dogmas of Victorian poetry. She would surely have smiled at their struggles to justify the elimination of useless connectives, the introduction of concentrated stress, the "invention" of the poetic interval — the pause.[37] How she would have enjoyed reading T. S. Eliot's "Gerontion," with lines echoing her own:

> [Eliot]
> The tiger springs in the new year. Us he devours.
> Think at last

We have not reached conclusion, when I
Stiffen in a rented house.

[E.D.]
This World is not Conclusion.
A Species stands beyond—
Invisible, as Music—
But positive, as Sound—

or Saul Bellow's plaintive cry, "I want, I want," so reminiscent of her own:

"I want"—it pleaded—All it's life—
I want—was chief it said

Eventually she came to believe in her prophecy that her Bird-song would take its place "overhead / To bear [new poets] Orchestra." Eventually it was so.

CHAPTER FIVE

Dickinson and Bowles

WE TURN OUR ATTENTION NOW TO THE RELATIONSHIP BETWEEN Samuel Bowles and Emily Dickinson. I have delayed because it was necessary to establish the validity of a method of reading her poems, first in context with the letters known to have accompanied them, second in context with related articles, correspondence, other poetry, events and occasions, and third in context with their variants, those clusters of poems linked by their metaphors, transcribed into the fascicles where they remained for the poet alone, where they were allowed to express feelings and to render ideas she was unwilling to expose to unfriendly or disapproving or uncomprehending or indifferent eyes.

Emily Dickinson loved Samuel Bowles. I know this sentence has the quality of one of those penknife cuttings on an oak tree. I mean it so. It is exactly what her pen copied with the greatest care onto the fine white stationery with the watermarks and the pin holes and the twine drawn through. She told him so. And that too is on record in the fascicles. She met with him one night, began to speak, but failed, failed to make herself understood, failed to move him or convince him, and when questioned further, failed to articulate another syllable of the matter. She presented herself and was not taken. She offered her poems and they were not taken. And although only she knew what she had meant, she was herself not certain whether she had muffed it or missed it or let the moment pass her by. She was tormented for many years after that with the need to justify her silence, with a need to justify her offer. And in her solitude she began to speak out her endless answer and she created her fantasy of ardent love. But always she writhed under the shame of this double refusal and called it her Calvary.

There were, as I say, two separate issues, Emily Dickinson's offering of love and her offering of poems. And there were two processes of recovery: the first was the way of the woman, the second the way of the poet. Emily Dickinson made her decision to love nonetheless, to remain loyal, devoted, and changeless, until united with her beloved in Heaven. She shut her door and taught herself sufficiency to herself alone. She admitted only one guest inside her private world—Jesus Christ. And she wrote her poems nonetheless. She created for herself worlds of vast dimension out of the minutiae of her own visible reality. She admitted to her writing table the specimens of poetry that her times applauded and proved to herself again and again how much better she could do the job. She taught herself patience, and rested her case before the minister of God: Time.

It will be unpleasant to discover the degree to which Emily Dickinson suffered at the rejection of Samuel Bowles. It may be uncomfortable to realize how much her turning to Christ came out of a private need. It may dismay our sense of balance to see how vulnerable was the woman, and to what mummery she resorted, and yet how invulnerable the poet, how inflexible her judgment about the validity of her poems.

But if we keep before us always that salient truth about Emily Dickinson, that she has now a worldwide reputation, that she has now achieved a status equal to that of our very few writers to whom we assign the first magnitude, and we remind ourselves that this has come about not because of her plaintive tears—we are not making up to her for those years of desolation—but because of the intrinsic beauty of her poems, because of her skill in the craft, because of her astonishing transformation of the banal details of a limited experience into the lyric outcries of the bard, then it may not be unpleasant after all.

In 1858 the friendship between Samuel Bowles and the poet began. Although the Johnson collection prints over thirty letters from Emily Dickinson to Bowles, he ascribes only three to this period. Johnson admits that his dates are always conjectural and doubtless there were more, for Emily Dickinson's own statement in Letter #205 (early April, 1859) implies as much: "I write you frequently, and am much ashamed." Since she had already formed the habit of communicating with her friends in verse, she may have meant the many poems we do in fact know were sent to him: fifty-one are listed in Appendix II Q; others, referred to, are presumed lost.

The following letter, #193, dated August, 1858, speaks with sentiment of their friendship, but in a bantering tone both are said to have enjoyed.

> Summer stopped since you were here. Nobody noticed her—that is, no men and women. Doubtless, the fields are rent by petite anguish, and "mourners go about" the Woods. But this is not for us. Business enough indeed, our stately Resurrection! A special Courtesy, I judge, from what the Clergy say! To the "natural man," Bumblebees would seem an improvement, and a spicing of Birds, but far be it from me, to impugn such majestic tastes. Our Pastor says we are a "Worm." How is that reconciled? "Vain—sinful Worm" is possibly of another species.
>
> Do you think we shall "see God"? Think of "Abraham" strolling with him in genial promenade!

Another letter to Bowles, #205, dated April, 1859, has a more wistful feeling:

> Friends are gems—infrequent. Potosi is a care, Sir. I guard it reverently for I could not afford to be poor now, after affluence.

Her private assessment of their friendship is not so casual as these letters would suggest, for in many of the fascicles there are poems, sent to no one, but using the same imagery of those letters and poems known to have been received by Bowles, and they are more outspoken, more poignant in tone, sorrowful, often angry, and they reveal more of her inner feelings because they are without the usual disguise. Such for example is the case of "Talk with prudence to a Beggar", cited in the preceding chapter, but worth reading again in context with the letter above:

> Talk with prudence to a Beggar
> Of "Potosi," and the mines!
> Reverently, to the Hungry
> Of your viands, and your wines!
>
> Cautious, hint to any Captive
> You have passed enfranchized feet!
> Anecdotes of air in Dungeons
> Have sometimes proved deadly sweet!

What is the justification for linking the two? The parallel images of Potosi is the obvious clue. But notice how even such words as "care" and "reverently" are used again ("care" transposed to "prudence," then to "cautious"). His friendship is a gem in the letter, and she declares she guards it for she cannot afford to be poor, having known the affluence of possession. But in the poem her contemplation takes a decidedly different turn. She is a beggar; she is a captive in a dungeon. And she is less than reverent, indeed she says *he* had better be more reverent, he must stop talking to her, a beggar, about a different kind of affluence, to stop telling her, a hungry deprived person about his food and his wines; be careful, she warns, stop dropping hints to her, a captive, that there are those who are free—such anecdotes may just kill her.

This is a very different relationship from that conveyed in the simple letter.

There is a poem known to have been sent to Bowles that contains a similar plea for friendship, that begs for a mere smile, but the metaphor of poverty changes to one of wealth:

> I Came to buy a smile—today—
> But just a single smile—
> The smallest one upon your face
> Will suit me just as well—
> The one that no one else would miss
> It shone so very small—
> I'm pleading at the "counter"—sir—
> Could you afford to sell—
>
> I've *Diamonds*—on my fingers—
> You know what *Diamonds* are?
> I've Rubies—like the Evening Blood—
> And Topaz—like the star!
> 'Twould be "a Bargain" for a *Jew!*
> *Say*—may I have it—Sir?

The gems, the riches, are her attributes now; those mines of "Potosi" are her mines now, her diamonds, her rubies, her topaz. And Bowles is not so much of a friend, for he is pictured as withholding his smile.

That Emily Dickinson used the metaphor of riches to signify her poems can be documented from the best source—her poems.

> I made slow Riches but my Gain
> Was steady as the Sun

And every Night, it numbered more
Than the preceding One

All Days, I did not earn the same
But my perceiveless Gain
Inferred the less by Growing than
The Sum that it had grown.

. . .

This was a Poet—It is That
Distills amazing sense

. . . .

Of Pictures, the Discloser—
The Poet—it is He—
Entitles Us—by Contrast—
To ceaseless Poverty—

Of Portion—so unconscious—
The Robbing—could not harm—
Himself—to Him—a Fortune—
Exterior—to Time—

. . .

Rich! 'Twas Myself—was rich—
To take the name of Gold—*
And Gold to own—in solid Bars—
The Difference—made me bold—

. . .

'Tis little I—could care for Pearls—
Who own the ample sea—
Or Brooches—when the Emperor—
With Rubies—pelteth me—

Or Gold—who am the Prince of Mines—
Or Diamonds—when have I
A Diadem to fit a Dome—
Continual upon me—

What Emily Dickinson offers this merchant for his smile is her poems,
and although she may change the image from gems to flowers, or to

* to call herself a poet.

brooks appealing to the Sea, always the metaphor of offering is present in the poems she sends to Bowles.

He was not much of a taker. The smile she seeks is publication, or at least praise, and that is withheld from her always, except for two feeble instances, two weak concessions. Bowles simply did not like her poetry.

This early view of herself as a supplicant is lighthearted compared to what is to come. The poems to Bowles form a discrete group of lyrics remarkable for the tone of challenge, pleading, outrage, and downright bitterness; eventually a deep gloom, despair, and suffering overcome her. These poems, sent with cryptic little notes, indicate a changing relationship between Bowles and Emily Dickinson that is far from simple fellowship.

Both Rebecca Patterson, in her book *The Riddle of Emily Dickinson,* and Winfield Townley Scott, in his article "The Errand from My Heart," call attention to a letter said to have been written by Samuel Bowles and sent to that favorite character in all official biographies, the "unidentified recipient":

> You must give if you expect to receive—give happiness, friendship, love, joy, and you will find them floating back to you. Sometimes you will give more than you receive. We all do that in some of our relations, but it is as true a pleasure often to give without return as life can afford us. We must not make bargains with the heart, as we would with the butcher for his meat. Our business is to give what we have to give—what we can get to give. The return we have nothing to do with. It will all come in due time—in this world or another. We shall have our dues. One will not give us what we give them—others will more than we can or do give them—and so the amounts will balance themselves. It is so with my loves and friendships—it is so with everybody's. There is no call for any of us to *humble* ourselves before each other.

We do not know that this letter was intended for Emily Dickinson. Bowles corresponded with Austin Dickinson, with his wife Susan, and with many an affectionate young woman. Indeed there is nothing in this letter to indicate anything more than a straightforward, well-meaning piece of advice, the kind of advice Bowles was to give generously to all the readers of his comments on poetry in the *Springfield Republican,* for he was ever on the side of uncomplicated and sunny optimism.

But there are intriguing echoes of this letter in two poems, one meant for no one, and one sent to Bowles. The first may be her indignant and passionate outburst at Bowles' rather cool and detached "It will all come in due time—in this world or another":

> What if I say I shall not wait!
> What if I burst the fleshly Gate—
> And pass escaped—to thee!
>
> What if I file this Mortal—off—
> See where it hurt me—That's enough—
> And step in Liberty!
>
> They cannot take me—any more!
> Dungeons can call—and Guns implore
> Unmeaning—now—to me—
>
> As laughter—was—an hour ago—
> Or Laces—or a Travelling Show—
> Or who died—yesterday!

We are justified in thinking so, for here is that recurring image of the Dungeon, the longing for liberty, already singled out for notice in the poem quoted above. But we must guard against the conclusion that "thee" refers solely to Bowles, despite the fact that we know there are many poems that describe her ultimate union with a beloved person in Heaven. There are as many poems that project a union with the Lord of Heaven. "Thee" may signify Christ. As her suffering became more difficult to bear, Emily Dickinson strove to equip herself with a more impregnable armor, a belief in immortality, and to ally herself with a more dependable friend, Jesus. Often the quest for love merged with the desire for safety in the all-embracing arms of the Lord, and it is not everywhere possible to distinguish between the two. Some may call this confusion; others may think of it rather as a double frame of reference and hence a means for attaining a larger significance.

The second poem, the one actually sent to Bowles, begins with an image that seems like a direct response to the last line of his letter: "There is no call for any of us to humble ourselves before each other."

> Perhaps you think me stooping
> I'm not ashamed of that
> Christ—stooped until He touched the Grave—
> Do those at Sacrament

> Commemorate Dishonor
> Or love annealed of love
> Until it bend as low as Death
> Redignified, above? [1]

Here is nothing equivocal. Emily Dickinson uses Christ for her defense. She justifies her humble demeanor by a comparison that is mighty proud. She thinks of herself as martyred, not for Christ's sake but as Christ had been. Her suffering is akin to His suffering.

Whether it was she who received Bowles' letter cannot be determined; but Bowles received the poem. What did he make of it? Later, when we come to see the kind of poetry Bowles appreciated, the kind he understood and admired, we will know he could make nothing of it. He must have been fairly uncomfortable, seated in Higginson's boat, when it came to reading the poetry of Emily Dickinson. Puzzled, dismayed but chivalrous, indifferent but not unkind, he did what Higginson did, he put the poems away among his papers, and went on with the work of his world.

It is curious how similar in professional character Samuel Bowles and Thomas Higginson seem to be. Bowles, too, was a spokesman for the liberal cause in the East; at the same time he thought of himself as a literary man, often writing the notices of significant new publications by novelists and poets, historians and philosophers, though his literary editor was for a long time Mrs. Frances H. Cook, "a lady of fine intellectual accomplishments, and a thorough and careful worker." [2] Frequently familiar essays appeared in the *Republican* signed with the initials "S. B." and even here he wrote, as did Higginson, about health, morality, and women.

What sort of a man was Samuel Bowles? What can the poet have expected from her importunities? He had a kind of gayety about him, an exuberance he took no care to hide. The following letter, dated January 16, 1859, was written by Bowles to Austin Dickinson, and reveals the personality of a man who liked to drink and to enjoy the company of beautiful women:

> I fear you are not vigorous enough in your drinks—come down & take a course in ale & whiskey with me. . . . I would that I might see your wife's beautiful friend [Mrs. Turner] but *how* can I? Mrs. Bowles is very liberal in her government: would it be fair to take advantage of it to go 40 miles over [?] railroads to see beauty & grace & wit in that most

enticing of mortal packages, which the elder Weller has so immortally warned all susceptible Samuels against? [3]

Austin's wife's "beautiful friend" was by all accounts an attractive young widow. An old friend of Susan's, she paid several long visits to the house next door to Emily Dickinson. Many years later Kate Turner, now Mrs. Anthon, recalls the "celestial evenings" and the "inextinguishable laughter" of the congenial circle, during the early part of 1859.

Another letter to Austin came from Bowles late in March, 1859:

> My properest remembrances to the ladies of your household, permanent and temporary, & let there be something over for the sister of the other house who never forgets my spiritual longings.[4]

She did indeed have a care for at least her own "spiritual longings," as we know. Certainly the spiritual matters to which Bowles refers with blitheness were eventually to become a deeply serious issue for the poet, and as she thought, between them. When we come to examine the Master letters, which I believe to have been intended for Samuel Bowles, we will discover how complicated her attachment to Bowles became. We will see how the questions of the soul became inextricably interwoven with her desire for love, how her appeals for enlightenment on the meaning of Redemption merged with pleas for acceptance in her own person. We will see how her quest for understanding, her desire to be cherished, mingled with arguments in defense of her poetry. In the early stage of Emily Dickinson's friendship with Samuel Bowles she appealed to him for approbation. Later she defended herself against his indifference, perhaps even his laughter. Finally she turned away.

In her early effort to convince Bowles of the quality of her work (1858–1860) she sent poems that seem to be almost wry in their challenge of his opinion:

> Her breast is fit for pearls,
> But I was not a "Diver" —
> Her brow is fit for thrones
> But I have not a crest.
> Her heart is fit for *home* —
> I — a Sparrow — build there
> Sweet of twigs and twine
> My perennial nest.

. . .

Tho' my destiny be Fustian —
Her's be damask fine —
Tho' she wear a silver apron —
I, a less divine —

Still, my little Gipsey being
I would far prefer,
Still, my little sunburnt bosom
To her Rosier,

For, when Frosts, their punctual fingers
On her forehead lay,
You and I, and Dr. Holland,
Bloom Eternally!

Roses of a steadfast summer
In a steadfast land,
Where no Autumn lifts her pencil —
And no Reapers stand! [5]

Emily Dickinson was not in awe of Samuel Bowles, for all her pretended humility. It is satisfying to see her sending her ironic notes of scorn, sneering at the poets Bowles championed. It is a relief to hear her declare that her poetry will eventually achieve immortal fame. At least it mitigates the whining tone of this poem sent to the presiding editor of a flourishing liberal and literary newspaper:

"They have not chosen me," he said,
"But I have chosen them!"
Brave — Broken hearted statement —
Uttered in Bethlehem!

I could not have told it,
But since *Jesus dared* —
Sovreign! Know a Daisy
Thy dishonor shared! *

Perhaps she already sensed that this man who enjoyed so much having people around him and prided himself on his diverse affiliations and traveled widely, lecturing and writing as he journeyed, also wrote a kind

* Sovreign means Jesus. She, too, has chosen and been rejected.

of journalese, and believed the homily not the epigram, and supported banalities, not the unconventional. Doubtless from where she sat he cut a romantic figure, but what is more to the point, he was a man of influence, one who could place her poems in the public eye. And it seemed to her he did not have very astute perception when it came to literary judgment.

She was right. Bowles frequently did grant space in the columns of his paper to young lady poets. Here is a sampling from the year 1860: poems by Luella Clarke, "Milly the Shepherdess," "Getting the Pony Shod," "The Broken Lilies"; by Miss M. A. Butterfield, "Do Good as Ye Have Opportunity"; by Sarah Shelley Clemmer, "Nora is dying as well as the year"; by Mrs. George P. Marsh, "Sweet was our rest in Arno's lovely vale" (reviewed favorably for her nobility of sentiment, her "simple, unaffected, healthy, humane sentiment . . ."); and more of the kind by Ellen P. Champion, Juliette H. Beach, Nancie A. W. Priest, Julia Gill, Ruth Allen and Mary Carleton. He allowed a cruel parody of Whitman's poetry to appear in the June 16, 1860 *Republican.* On the same page a poem, "Lines on Finding a Dead Young Robin in My Corn Field While Hoeing," written by "The Peasant Bard," was printed without adverse comment; it was no parody.

And this unsigned poem was printed without critical reproof:

> God bless the girls
> Whose golden curls
> Blend with our evening dreams
> They haunt our lives
> Like spirit wives,
> Or—as the naiads haunt the stream.

Leyda's *Years and Hours* has this entry for April 4, 1859:

> Samuel Bowles writes to Collette Loomis, a very young poet in West Springfield: Was I so stupid the other day as not to say to you how much we appreciate your little poetic gems? . . . We place you among our pet contributors; and though my "weakness" is not poetry, I am always charmed with your little compact, thoughtful, mysterious & suggestive poems.[6]

In the following year, when Miss Loomis died, the editor himself sadly undertook the task of writing a memorial column lamenting the untimely departure of this "esteemed fair young poetess."

Emily Dickinson could not have read the letter sent to Miss Loomis, but she had read enough of Collette's poems to know something of Bowles' taste. "Tho' my destiny be Fustian" seems to be a caustic response to the judgment of the editor who not only printed but praised poems such as this:

THE PORTRAIT

written for the Springfield Republican

It had hung for years in the old south room,
　　Where the May afternoons always lingered so,
It had looked from the wall with its quiet eyes,
It had searched the south room with its calm blue eyes,
　　Many and many a year ago.

We hung it with blooming May-day wreaths,
　　And filled the old room with a May-day song;
And we thought that the lips would surely speak —
We almost paused for the lips to speak,
　　And bless the light-hearted, wistful throng.

But our May-days, fleeter than flying birds,
　　Fled over the earth on their silver wings,
And our Junes, so glorious with gold and green,
Passed silently into a world unseen,
　　And they were numbered with by-gone things.

But Time touched the youth of the picture not,
　　The locks were unsought by its silver snow;
As we prayed that we with our locks of gold,
Might live, love, labor and never grow old,
　　Many and many a year ago.

We love to remember the dear old room,
　　And the Mays, and the May-day songs we sung;
We love to look back at the pictured face,
To the earnest face, to the beauteous face,
　　To the radiant face that was always young.

We must all grow old, for time goes on;
　　The flowers will fade that we live among;

But the flowers of feeling their strength impart
To the genial heart, to the tender heart,
  To the gladsome heart that is always young.

And age may whiten the shining locks,
  When the May-day glories of youth depart;
But a beauty brighter than all beside,
Than all that is fleeting and fair beside,
  Is theirs, who are always young at heart.
                    Collette [7]

How even the merest expectation could arise in Emily Dickinson's heart is as mysterious as it is pathetic. She surely knew the difference between her verses and those for which the *Springfield Republican* provided space. One of her favorite pastimes was pitting her skill against the poets whose work she saw in print. This is an example of the kind of transformation she achieved:

A TENDER LAY

(Thursday, July 2, 1857)

Be gentle to the new laid egg,
  For eggs are brilliant things;
They cannot fly until they're hatched,
  And have a pair of wings:
If once you break the tender shell,
  The wrong you can't redress;
The "yolk and white" will all run out,
  And make a dreadful "mess."

Emily Dickinson transcribed her own use of the image of the hatched egg into her own place of publication, Fascicle 92:

What shall I do when the Summer troubles—
What, when the Rose is ripe—
What when the Eggs fly off in Music
From the Maple Keep?

. . . .

And in this same booklet there is another which may be her ironic comment on that long, sentimental, and altogether conventional poem by Collette quoted above, or on Bowles' obituary of Collette herself.

Not all die early, dying young —
Maturity of Fate
Is consummated equally
In Ages, or a Night —

A Hoary Boy, I've known to drop
Whole statured — by the side
Of Junior of Fourscore — 'twas Act
Not Period — that died.

Johnson tells us this poem was sent to Dr. Holland, contributing editor to the *Springfield Republican.* Emily Dickinson certainly was aware of what she had to contend against, and was not unwilling to taunt those editors who praised mediocrity. But it was Bowles' lapse in taste that irritated her more. He commended to his readers Dr. William Allen's *Book of Christian Sonnets* because it had moral value, and he reprinted these exemplary lines:

I praise thee, God of love! for this Day's light,
    Which leads the train of days in this New Year, —
    For months not seeming destin'd to me here,
    But ah instead thereof a darksome night
In the low grave, of all earth's joys the blight.
    I live! and in my thoughts old scenes appear.[8]

But he did more than print the worst sort of poems; he frequently singled them out for specific praise. Bowles saw this poem in the forthcoming issue of *Atlantic Monthly:*

ON A MAGNOLIA FLOWER

Memorial of my former days,
    Magnolia, as I scent thy breath,
And on thy pallid beauty gaze,
    I feel not far from death!

So much hath happened! and so much
    The tomb hath claimed of what was mine!
Thy fragrance moves me with a touch
    As from a hand divine:

So many dead! so many wed!
    Since first, by this Magnolia's tree,

I pressed a gentle hand and said,
   A word no more for me!

Lady, who sendest from the South
   This frail, pale token of the past,
I press the petals, to my mouth,
   And sigh—as 'twere my last.

Oh, love, we live, but many fell!
   The world's a wreck, but we survive! —
Say, rather, still on earth we dwell,
   But gray at thirty-five!

He reprinted it in his newspaper, calling it "genuine and alive," and telling his readers that it "proves the superiority of 'one touch of nature' over the most elaborate touches of art." Bowles filled the columns of his newspaper with sentimental banalities and in his literary reviews urged what he thought was the appropriate reception:

> Now, in the flower season, let us welcome the kindred flowers of poetry and romance, and never idly fancy the time is lost that is spent in their enjoyment. . . . Both [books of poems] are full of human hopes, affections, struggles and conquests, and are written by "the weak who are strong, to wit, women." [9]

Surely all this did have significance for Emily Dickinson. We know she found it ludicrous. She sent poems that challenged Bowles. A letter is extant in which she apologizes for her outright laughter at his taste:

> I am much ashamed. I misbehaved tonight. I would like to sit in the dust. I fear I am your little friend no more, but Mrs Jim Crow.
>   I am sorry I smiled at women.
>   Indeed I revere holy ones, like Mrs Fry and Miss Nightingale. I will never be giddy again. Pray forgive me now. Respect little Bob O Lincoln again! [10]

Despite her smiles, Emily Dickinson did take seriously whatever Bowles said and wrote. Here is a paragraph printed July 1860:

> I.E. THAT IS—The names of girls in these latter days have a decided tendency to terminate in "i.e." Taking up a couple of catalogues of ladies' schools [11] the other day—pleasant reading by the way, these pages are full of the names of school girls! —we found the following angels in it: Essie

and Elsie, and Carrie and Kittie and Katie and Fannie and Annie and Millie . . . . ! Whether the blossoming out of the dear old fashioned names into foreign posies is the result of European tours, or whether Shakespeare is wrong about the sweetness of roses, or whatever it is, we can only exclaim, Y, GIRLS!

S.B.

This was reprinted in the Saturday issue, July 14, 1860. It was then that she too was using "Emilie" as her signature. It was no longer her practice in 1861, except in the instance of one letter to the Norcross sisters. In fact there is no more sign of "Emilie" after a letter sent to Kate Scott (Anthon) dated the summer of 1860.

The following explanation by Richard Chase of the significance of Emily Dickinson's signature is an example of the distortions that occur when scholars search the letters and poems for proof of a preconceived hypothesis, in this case, that the great secret of Emily Dickinson's life was her tragic love affair with Charles Wadsworth. Chase tells us that when her mentor was Ben Newton, and her beloved friend was Charles Wadsworth, she signed herself "Emilie"; after she renounced the love of Charles Wadsworth, in 1862, she changed to "Emily."

> . . . "ie" gave her name a kind of romantic quality, perhaps calling to mind a certain aura of the French or medieval. A certain fairy-tale queenliness may be implied. The new spelling indicates a new self-consciousness. . . . The name "Emilie" indicated that its bearer was different from most of her friends and from her family. It hinted at intellectual emancipation and exciting adventures of the spirit. It suggested an enigmatic complexity of character which expressed itself with insouciance and "harum-scarum" humor but which was equally ready to confess to a sense of loss and renunciation, a growing reluctance to think of leaving home, a new dependence on the affection of friends, a steady contemplation of death, and a longing for immortality.[12]

All this, indeed. From what Bowles has said of "ie" it would seem that restoring "y" would achieve individuality in that period.

Emily Dickinson accepted Bowles' admonishment in the matter of names, but refused for a long time to concede to his taste in poetry. She tried again and again to interest him in her own. We may conjecture the kind of response he made to her effort from this caustic poem she sent him:

> "Faith" is a fine invention
> When Gentlemen can *see* —
> But *Microscopes* are prudent
> In an Emergency.

Always this poem has been cited as evidence of Emily Dickinson's attitude toward science. Her imagery is no doubt derived from that realm of discourse, but how can the poem be so dissociated from the note to which she joined it? The note is cryptic but nevertheless necessary to take account of:

> You spoke of the "East." I have thought about it this winter. Don't you think you and I should be shrewder to take the *Mountain Road?* (Letter #220)

The word "prudent" in the poem and "shrewder" in the letter locks both together.

Perhaps the East is that Eastern Seaboard where magazines were publishing poetry month by month, perhaps Cambridge from where the *Atlantic Monthly* issued, or New York, where *Harper's* was published. When vision is unimpaired, "Faith" is a fine invention. These words seem to be again an answer to the lines in the letter cited earlier in which Bowles assures his correspondent "It will all come in due time—in this world or another. We shall have our dues." But Emily Dickinson is not content with such patience. In fact she has called the situation referred to an "emergency." The object under scrutiny is not obvious; use a microscope to enlarge the material, bring it up into the field of visibility. The perception of no gentlemen-editors, New York or Boston (or Springfield) can be trusted. Publish the poems in the Springfield paper. Print them clear in the small newspaper. Take the mountain road. It is both necessary and wise.

Emily Dickinson may have been ironic. Bowles surely remained indifferent. Eventually her patience and her pose wore out. She began to besiege him with pleas; she became gradually more and more urgent. In a poem sent to him she depicts a great struggle for life that is taking place, one in which a swimmer loses his life in the conflict:

> Two swimmers wrestled on the spar —
> Until the morning sun —
> When One—turned smiling to the land —
> Oh God! the Other One!

The stray ships—passing—
Spied a face—
Upon the waters borne—
With eyes in death—still begging raised—
And hands—beseeching—thrown!

Another, closely related in imagery and in conception as well as in feeling, was also sent to Bowles:

Should you but fail at—Sea—
In sight of me—
Or doomed lie—
Next Sun—to die—
Or rap—at Paradise—unheard
I'd *harass* God
Until he let you in!

This is a far cry from the ironic appeal and it is apparent that no favorable response was forthcoming. Far from it. When Bowles spoke at last it was in the form of an article published over his name in the *Springfield Republican,* and it seemed a rebuke addressed to her alone. This article, "What Should We Write?" assessed her verses as the tearful outpourings of an unhealthy mind.[13] He derides the "literature of misery." He publicly chastizes those poets ("chiefly women,") who cannot "see objects distinctly through a mist of tears," and although he would gladly brighten their countenance it will not be by "exposing it to the gaze of a worthless world."

The mortification of such a reprimand can hardly be underestimated. Her anguish is amply rendered in such poems as "I felt a Funeral, in my Brain," or "I felt a Cleaving in my Mind—" a variant. She did more than write poems. She called Bowles and confronted him. This may be verified from the many lyrics that have as their action a crucial encounter which ends with silence and withdrawal.

But what did she want? Did she call him to come to her in order to defend her unhealthy poems? Did she, under the guise of defending her unhealthy poems, call him to her? There is no way to know. Bowles probably would not guess. He could understand affection but the genuine concern of this poet, her questions of redemption, of salvation, her fears of death, her visions of immortality, always made him uncomfortable. "What?" That he put some such question is revealed by the content of the metaphors of this encounter, varied though they may be, for Emily Dickinson wrote about this experience over and over again, almost as if she were striving to exorcise it from her consciousness: The wind questions the grass, the grass does not reply but bends to the wind; the motion of the moon queries the sea, it does not speak, but leans and adjusts herself to the tide; the heart is questioned and will not reply, but takes a silent pledge of undying fealty.

Silence is a quaint response for one so skilled in the verbal art. And yet we have the evidence that this was Emily Dickinson's answer. She sent this poem to Bowles:

> *"Speech"* — is a prank of *Parliament* —
> *"Tears"* — a trick of the *nerve* —
> But the Heart with the heaviest freight on —
> Does'nt — always — move —

In a private recollection of the encounter she records her hesitation, and again, her silence.

> I could suffice for Him, I knew —
> He — could suffice for Me —
> Yet Hesitating Fractions — Both
> Surveyed Infinity —
>
> "Would I be Whole" He sudden broached —
> My syllable rebelled —
> 'Twas face to face with Nature — forced —
> 'Twas face to face with God —
>
> Withdrew the Sun — to Other Wests —
> Withdrew the furthest Star
> Before Decision — stooped to speech —
> And then — be audibler
>
> The Answer of the Sea unto
> The Motion of the Moon —
> Herself adjust Her Tides — unto —
> Could I — do else — with Mine?

A paraphrase of this poem may seem to reveal what happened. But we know enough about the style of her poetry to recognize the limitations that confront us in our search for any fact. Emily Dickinson's poetry is always highly subjective, almost totally concerned with the self. And yet we cannot learn from this poem what he really said or did, not even why she delayed, why she vacillated, for what interests the poet is never a literal record of an actual event, but a conflict compressed into a transient moment of an experience that may be used for a leap or a swirl up and out and beyond the real world to some realm of infinity and eternality where she can discover her true nature. But even an ostensible description of the encounter between two lovers can be valuable, for it is her conflict that is the starting point, and her experience that forms the narrative, and her conception of the spirit and God that she affirms.

I and he both knew, the poet says, we could be sufficient for each other, but then we considered Infinity and we paused. Both hesitating fractions, reluctant to join to form a whole, paused. The beloved is allowed to speak; he says in effect, you love me, all right, but would I then be the whole object of your love? "Would I be Whole?" The syllable of answer we expect is Yes, for the poem begins with "I could suffice for Him, I knew—" but it, the syllable, the Yes, rebels. For to say Yes, you will be the whole of life to me, will be a denial of an equally beloved Nature. That fraction of Infinity is the natural world, the flowers, the birds, the sunsets, the rain. And if she forces the syllable to emerge nevertheless, if she is able to give up the companion Nature, for him, then the other fraction of Infinity, God, must be denied. Can she give up God? The problem is stated in the first half of the poem; her resolution is presented in the second half.

They seem to have stood there a longish time; the sun went down, the stars passed over, and still no decision.[14] When at last she does speak it is scarcely audible. Note that the word used is "stooped," there is an intrinsic disdain in her reply, if not in her decision. The response is less audible than the answer the Sea makes to the Moon as it crosses the Heavens, since no one hears the surface of the sea rise—it is a phenomenon of Nature, that flood tide and ebbtide. It is a yes and no together; the word "adjust" signifies a movement in either direction, for the moon is not a fixed orb.

From the analogy drawn between her reply and the tide, itself a demonstration of the power and the force of Nature, we may surmise the answer: Emily Dickinson states that her world is united to a larger world, she chooses a union with Nature and God.

A confirmation of her meaning may be found in a variant poem that was sent to Bowles:

> Nature and God—I neither knew
> Yet Both so well knew me
> They startled, like Executors
> Of My identity.
>
> Yet Neither told—that I could learn—
> My Secret as secure
> As Herschel's private interest [15]
> Or Mercury's affair—

The poem is a cooler version but the same terms are present: Nature and God and secrets and silences.

Can we ever know Bowles' reply to the maiden sister of his friend Austin? Transcribed into Fascicle 20 is a poem that was sent to no one, that provides a semblance of his reaction and it is not quite the same used by the poet to generate her startling revelation about herself.

> One Year ago—jots what?
> God—spell the word! I—cant—
> Was't Grace? Not that—
> Was't Glory? That—will do—
> Spell slower—Glory—
>
> Such Anniversary shall be—
> Sometimes—not often—in Eternity—
> When farther Parted, than the Common Wo—
> Look—feed upon each other's faces—so—
> In doubtful meal, if it be possible
> Their Banquet's real—
>
> I tasted—careless—then—
> I did not know the Wine
> Came once a World—Did you?
> Oh, had you told me so—
> This Thirst would blister—easier—now—
> You said it hurt you—most—
> Mine—was an Acorn's Breast—
> And could not know how fondness grew

In Shaggier Vest—
Perhaps—I could'nt—
But, had you looked in—
A Giant—eye to eye with you, had been—
No Acorn—then—

So—Twelve months ago—
We breathed—
Then dropped the Air—
Which bore it best?
Was this—the patientest—
Because it was a Child, you know—
And could not value—Air?

If to be "Elder"—mean most pain—
I'm old enough, today, I'm certain—then—
As old as thee—how soon?
One—Birthday more—or Ten?
Let me—choose!
Ah, Sir, None!

Emily Dickinson again recalls the encounter, and again she is not about to say what happened. "Jots what?" And that syllable that never got spoken, she leaves now to God to say; she cannot. God spells out his attributes: Grace? No, she answers. Was it Glory? Oh yes, that is good—glory. A year ago, then, the poet experienced Glory. But before one's heart leaps with joy for Emily Dickinson's sake, notice she has used a minimizing word, *jots,* a tittle of a mark, indicating an iota. This should alert us to the irony of her speculation.

If it were Glory, how shall we mark its Anniversary? It should be of the sort that occurs in Heaven when two people meet again, having been separated not as is common in petty life, but as happens when two people reunite after death.[16] In that "Common Wo" we just stood there gazing at each other not realizing it was the real thing, the genuine victual of love. Oh if you had only said you know how rare this love was, and told me so (*and told me so*) I would have joined our hesitating fractions, I would have said that Yes; then our parting would have been eased, the thirst would not blister me now for I would then have taken a great draught of you instead of a careless sip, a taste. But you said another thing, you said it hurt you most, that I was but a child and could not understand such fondness as a grown-up knows, I knew nothing of love. But had you really looked at me you would have seen no acorn but the full-fledged tree, not little David but Goliath. I was woman enough. Ah well. We separated. Who stood the pain best? I, because I was a child and did not understand love? Or you because you were so much older and wiser than I? No. I had the greatest pain. And if the degree of pain signifies the degree of maturity, I'm ready now, right now, Today. How soon will I have another chance to prove it? In one year again? In ten more years? If I had my way: None.

None what? No more waiting or no more encounters? What does Emily Dickinson choose? "None" is ambiguous. Read this poem as many times as we may we cannot solve that question, for the poet, with her equivocal word, mocks certainty itself: no more birthdays? no more waiting? right now? never?

Had Emily Dickinson spoken out, that would have been the end of the matter. But her silence at a critical moment preyed on her mind; she could not accept that she had not told him the truth about herself. She sent a poem to Samuel Bowles with this cryptic note attached:

> Here's—what I had to "tell you"—
> You will tell no other?
> Honor—is it's own pawn—
>
> Title divine—is mine!
> The Wife—without the Sign!
> Acute Degree—conferred on me—
> Empress of Calvary!
> Royal—all but the Crown!
> Betrothed—without the swoon
> God sends us Women—
> When you—hold—Garnet to Garnet—*
> Gold—to Gold—
> Born—Bridalled—Shrouded—
> In a Day—
> "My Husband"—women say—
> Stroking the Melody—
> Is *this*—the way?

* hold, as in matching.

Here then is the evidence that she called him to her side in order to defend her poetry. And that he misconstrued her intention and thought she was asking for love. Here too is evidence that she called him to her side and offered love and he laughed at her and when she recovered her equilibrium enough to speak again it was to tell him he had misconceived her. Indeed he would not be whole. The question put during this missed encounter, this sober if not dramatic experience, she answers now with a deflating scorn, with a ringing declaration that her devotion is to God. The emphasis here is more on poetry, on the poet and her affiliation with Christ. Emily Dickinson takes her own title and dissolves the distinction between herself and her poetry, her life-spirit and her bardic song, her martyrdom on behalf of her rejection and Christ's martyrdom in crucifixion; she gives herself redemption as a living soul and immortality as a poet.

Had Emily Dickinson said Yes and Bowles agreed, she would have had her lover and occupied herself from then on with the business of travel and traffic. But he said "What?" to her, and perhaps No, my poor girl, no my dear friend, and although this encounter had for its immediate issue silence, it had for its ultimate fruition that great outpouring of lyrics, those attempts to forget, those recollections of misery that plunged her to such depths of despair she feared madness, those experiments in healing when she begins her passage through all the stages of shock and numbness and languor to arrive at sober isolation, tolerance of deprivation, and finally consecration of herself to God.

We know that she brought the literary side of her case to a new literary arbiter. Higginson's judgment came swiftly; between April 15 and June 7, in 1862, Bowles' opinion of her poetry was confirmed. Together they drove her into that total retreat, into that crisis of sorrow which became a haven for her bruised soul, a parlor that admitted only God, furnished with a writing table, not an altar; pens, pencils, and paper, not candles or incense.

Emily Dickinson miraculously becomes less self-effacing, less humble, more and more self-assured, more and more convinced of her own ultimate triumph. Her agony finally became exasperation, the disgrace became resentment. It was almost as if the experience of suffering recharged her soul. She emerged with a new fortitude, a more vigorous spirit. It was as if that regenerative process she proclaimed to be the primary attribute of nature, she now experienced herself. It is true her sunsets transform to funerals, her meadows become the sod, her freshets and dews change to the sea, but her gems and jewels burnish to a stellar radiance, the songs of birds reverberate as the song of eternal spring, and her little footloose beggars put on the robes of saints and over all there broods the compassionate eye of Jesus.

This poem sent to Samuel Bowles is a good example of the changing tone:

> For this—accepted Breath—
> Through it—compete with Death—
> The fellow cannot touch this Crown—
> By it—my title take—
> Ah, what a royal sake
> To my nescessity—stooped down!
>
> No Wilderness—can be
> Where this attendeth thee—
> No Desert Noon—
> No fear of frost to come
> Haunt the perennial bloom—
> But Certain June!
>
> Get Gabriel—to tell—the royal syllable—
> Get Saints—with new—unsteady tongue—
> To say what trance below
> Most like their glory show—
> Fittest the Crown!

The disappointment is there, but combined with that is a realization of her own validity, a discernment that what fate denies her now, the judgment of eternity will restore.

The antecedent of "This" in line 8 is "Breath," but we must supply the analogue of "Breath": her inspiriting power as a poet. Countless times she renders this life-force as a divine gift, that which sustains her as she dives down into the depths of the sea to wrest a pearl hidden there, a poem. The imagery may change but it does not stray far: the pearl may be another jewel, a ruby, a diamond, topaz, or garnet, but always it is the metaphor of her own riches, her poems, to be placed in the diadem waiting for her on high, her crown, her garland.

In "I met a King this afternoon!" a poem that derives from the first stage of Emily Dickinson's poetic history, that little King is herself, the true poet, disguised, and all the familiar imagery of royalty is used to render the significance of that barefoot estate: the "Crown" is mentioned, though on earth it is only a "little Palmleaf Hat." In "I'm ceded—I've stopped being Their's" she announces she can wait for her "second Rank" where she will leave off being "A half unconscious Queen" and stand "Adequate—Erect" to take her crown. This marks the second stage.

That this crown is waiting for her is the guarantee of Christ: "Ah, what a royal sake / To my nescessity—stooped down!" With an intuition that "it" (her Breath) will enable her to withstand wilderness and death, that "it" (the kind of life she seems to be leading below) is exactly like the glory of sainthood, she is patient that ultimately she will take her title, her crown.

A variant has so much the same imagery it acts almost as an illumination of "For this—accepted Breath":

> The face I carry with me—last—
> When I go out of Time—
> To take my Rank—by—in the West—*
> That face—will just be thine—
>
> I'll hand it to the Angel—
> That—Sir—was my Degree—
> In Kingdoms—you have heard the Raised—
> Refer to—possibly.
>
> He'll take it—scan it—step aside—
> Return—with such a crown
> As Gabriel—never capered at—
> And beg me put it on—
>
> And then—he'll turn me round and round—
> To an admiring sky—
> As one that bore her Master's name—
> Sufficient Royalty!

Of course Emily Dickinson had her pride to reckon with. That sense of her own validity could generate indignation as well as poise; indignation belongs to the first stage of the poetic history:

* "By" signifies that matching process again; she will take the Rank that matches the face she carries with her, the face akin to suffering Christ.

If the foolish, call them *"flowers"* —
Need the wiser, *tell?*
If the Savans "Classify" them
It is just as well!

Those who read the "Revelations"
Must not criticize
Those who read the same Edition —
With beclouded Eyes!

Could we stand with that old "Moses" —
"Canaan" denied —
Scan like him, the stately landscape
On the other side —

Doubtless, we should deem superfluous
Many Sciences,
Not pursued by learned Angels
In scholastic skies!

Low amid that glad Belles lettres
Grant that we may stand,
Stars, amid profound *Galaxies* —
At that grand "Right hand"!

We know whom she meant by "the foolish," having read these words in the *Springfield Republican,* signed by Bowles: "Now in the flower season, let us welcome the kindred flowers of poetry and romance, and never idly fancy the time is lost that is spent in their enjoyment."

And she could become harsh with herself, scold herself for hanging her head:

To hang our head — ostensibly —
And subsequent, to find
That such was not the posture
Of our immortal mind —

Affords the sly presumption
That in so dense a fuzz —
You — too — take Cobweb attitudes
Upon a plane of Gauze!

To be humiliated is to take on a cobweb attitude; it is to become contaminated by the world, that place of fuzz, that world which operates upon a plane of Gauze.

And certainly that consistently misinterpreted poem, "Come slowly— Eden!" read now, in this context of her first search for publication and acceptance, has an obvious meaning: she is teaching herself to temper her impatience:

> Come slowly—Eden!
> Lips unused to Thee—
> Bashful—sip thy Jessamines—
> As the fainting Bee—
>
> Reaching late his flower,
> Round her chamber hums—
> Counts his nectars—
> Enters—and is lost in Balms.

Even though the imagery is sensuous, we are familiar enough with the metaphors of Emily Dickinson to know what Eden signifies to her. In the same way, the meaning of "Did the Harebell loose her girdle" is no longer baffling, no longer obscure. It has a pathetically obvious clarity, when read as part of this cluster of poems about her poetry, conjoined to the experience of the missed encounter.

> Did the Harebell loose her girdle
> To the lover Bee
> Would the Bee the Harebell *hallow*
> Much as formerly?
>
> Did the "Paradise"—persuaded—
> Yield her moat of pearl—
> Would the Eden *be* an Eden,
> Or the Earl—an *Earl?*

It is a simple rationale for patience. If the flower spreads the petals wide and the pollen becomes easily available, the bee would not revere the harebell; if that Paradise, that Eden, simply left undefended the moat of pearl, Eden would be less a hallowed place and the victor not so deserving of his rank.[17]

Perhaps Bowles finally relented when he received this poem:

Just Once! Oh least Request!
Could Adamant refuse
So small a Grace
So scanty put,
Such agonizing terms?
Would not a God of Flint
Be conscious of a sigh
As down His Heaven dropt remote
"Just Once" Sweet Deity?

The taste of Eden so longed for came on May 4, 1861. "The May Wine" was printed in the *Springfield Republican,* though without the acknowledgment of the poet's name. And there she was, published in a newspaper, carried through the Berkshire Hill country, in company with "War" by Mary E. Wilcox, "Consolation" by M. McNary Spencer, and "Honoraria's Child" by Caroline A. Howard. She had now joined the poets of Bowles' "Original Poetry" column, which just the week before (April 27) had placed into the public domain:

She's my cousin, so what harm
For her blessed little arm
    Round my willing neck to twine
And her dear delicious lips
With their rosy, flattering tips,
    Ever so much,
    Just to touch
        Mine?

Her poem was anonymous. The review of Lucy Larcom's new book of poems praised her art and singled out this example of Miss Larcom's poetic achievement:

Eve plucked the first white rose for her bridal,
And the earliest moss-buds to deck her infant's cradle.

Emily Dickinson was at last a member of the community of published poets. Those "two Editors of Journals" who came to her father's house (one of whom at least had dozens of her poems to use as he would), allowed hers to live at last, side by side with:

About the flowers her fingers glided,
Into their place the blossoms slided.

One feels saddened by the poet's exhilaration:

> I am ashamed—I hide—
> What right have I—to be a Bride—
> So late a Dowerless Girl—
> Nowhere to hide my dazzled Face—
> No one to teach me that new Grace—
> Nor introduce—my Soul—
>
> Me to adorn—How—tell—
> Trinket—to make Me beautiful—
> Fabrics of Cashmere—
> Never a Gown of Dun—more—
> Raiment instead—of Pompadour—
> For Me—My soul—to wear—
>
> Fingers—to frame my Round Hair
> Oval—as Feudal Ladies wore—
> Far Fashions—Fair—
> Skill—to hold my Brow like an Earl—
> Plead—like a Whippowil—
> Prove—like a Pearl—
> Then, for Character—
>
> Fashion My Spirit quaint—white—
> Quick—like a Liquor—
> Gay—like Light—
> Bring Me my best Pride—
> No more ashamed—
> No more to hide—
> Meek—let it be—too proud—for Pride—
> Baptized—this Day—A Bride—

She equips herself in dress and in demeanor to greet anyone who would welcome the late dowerless girl. The new poet is ready for the reception that awaits this beginning of her career. As we know, nothing much came of it.[18] "Of Bronze—and Blaze" seems to be a recovery of balance, if one can think of balance in a poem which compares her poetry to the phenomenon of the Aurora Borealis:

> Of Bronze—and Blaze—
> The North—Tonight—

So adequate—it forms—
So preconcerted with itself—
So distant—to alarms—
An Unconcern so sovreign
To Universe, or me—
Infects my simple spirit
With Taints of Majesty—
Till I take vaster attitudes—
And strut upon my stem—
Disdaining Men, and Oxygen,
For Arrogance of them—

My Splendors, are Menagerie—
But their Competeless Show
Will entertain the Centuries
When I, am long ago,
An Island in dishonored Grass—
Whom none but Daisies, know.

Emily Dickinson was to have nothing but self-confirmation to rely on. Bowles may have published her poem, but he had not really altered his taste in poetry. Even she must have known how foolish her expectations had been when she read Bowles' review of the poems of Bayard Taylor in a December, 1862 issue of the Springfield paper:

> . . . ever since we came to know Bayard Taylor regarded himself as a poet instinctively and had faith in his genius, we have read him with respect. He is among the best of American writers of verse. *The Poet's Journal* is his best. It can't possibly be popular because it is above the popular apprehension; it will take its rank among the choicest poetical productions of the time. Men and women of culture will not fail to recognize in it deep feeling, exquisite delicacy and sentiment, a fine mastery of expression, and a tone as healthy and manly as the nature in which it had its birth.

The reasons he gives for his new respect for Bayard Taylor cannot have been lost on Emily Dickinson. Who more than she regarded herself as a poet and had faith in her genius? Who more than she was above the popular apprehension? At least one man of culture had failed to recognize her depth of feeling, the exquisite delicacy, the fine mastery of her expression. True, her nature was growing less healthy, was not so easily fortified, but whose fault was that?

A year elapsed between the printing of "May Wine" and "The Sleeping" which appeared in the issue for March 1, 1862. By then Emily Dickinson was well along on her journey into isolation and her companion was no ragged prince, she rode no wagon at all, and all the exhilaration was gone. A tone of bitterness replaces that breathless excitement of "I am ashamed—I hide—"

It would never be Common—more—I said—
Difference—had begun—
Many a bitterness—had been—
But that old sort—was done—

Or—if it sometime—showed—as 'twill—
Upon the Downiest—Morn—
Such bliss—had I—for all the years—
'Twould give an Easier—pain—

I'd so much joy—I told it—Red—
Upon my simple Cheek—
I felt it publish—in my Eye—
'Twas needless—any speak—

I walked—as wings—my body bore—
The feet—I former used—
Unnescessary—now to me—
As boots—would be—to Birds—

I put my pleasure all abroad—
I dealt a word of Gold
To every Creature—that I met—
And Dowered—all the World—

When—suddenly—my Riches shrank—
A Goblin—drank my Dew—
My Palaces—dropped tenantless—
Myself—was beggared—too—

I clutched at sounds—
I groped at shapes—
I touched the tops of Films—

I felt the Wilderness roll back
Along my Golden lines—

The Sackcloth—hangs upon the nail—
The Frock I used to wear—
But where my moment of Brocade—
My—drop—of India?

Had she any illusions left, they would have been dispelled when she read again Bowles' assessment of Bayard Taylor's poetry, this time saying that his verse was superior even to "In Memoriam" because it was more true, more orthodox, more tasteful. She knew she had really nothing at all to expect from Samuel Bowles. This poem of concession was found among *his* papers:

Victory comes late,
And is held low to freezing lips
Too rapt with frost
To mind it!
How sweet it would have tasted!
Just a drop!
Was God so economical?
His table's spread too high
Except we dine on tiptoe!
Crumbs fit such little mouths—
Cherries—suit *Robins*—
The Eagle's golden breakfast—*dazzles them!*
God keep his vow to *"Sparrows,"*
Who of little love—know how to starve!

Emily

CHAPTER SIX

The Master Letters I

THE SUBJECT MATTER

THE MASTER LETTERS ARE AT ONCE THE MOST PUZZLING AND challenging documents of all those discovered among Emily Dickinson's papers. They consist of three manuscripts presumably written in the handwriting of the period between 1858 and 1861.

Those biographers who accept the hypothesis that Emily Dickinson's "disaster" came of a hopeless love for Charles Wadsworth assume the Master letters to be drafts of love-letters sent to the minister near or after the time of his departure for California. Critics whose major concern is the poetry usually ignore them. But these are letter-drafts of great importance, for they serve to illuminate the subject matter and the style of the verse, and to reveal the operation of Emily Dickinson's poetic imagination.

There seems to me to be evidence that these much-worked-over pages were written for her eyes only, to relieve her frustration, to ease her suffering at the indifference of Bowles. They were a first repository of the glooms and the desires of a poet striving to explain herself and her poetry. Evidence that the Master letters were used by the poet as source material for the letters and poems she finally wrote and did mail to Bowles rests on the correspondence of imagery, on paraphrase of subject matter, on similarity of allusions, on identical questions, and on the likeness of emotional tone. Here is the same exaggerated modesty, the almost painful self-deprecation; here too are the same appeals, the barbs, the complaints, the cryptic ironies; and here are the familiar protestations of faith in herself and in God.

The first Master letter is primarily an effort to explain the subject matter of her poems—the truth about Nature as a sign of redemption.

The prose description of her meaning exactly fits the theme of many of the poems known to have been received by Bowles. The second Master letter is a mingling of confessions of personal love, pleas for acceptance, complaints at some deep pain inflicted on the poet, apologies for her behavior—it is, in fact, a confusion of all the thoughts and images in the manuscripts sent to Bowles during the time, 1861, when she was striving for his approval and acceptance. Between the second and the third Master letters there intervened that encounter between Emily Dickinson and Samuel Bowles described in Chapter Five. There are references to this meeting, there are the outcries, the lamentations, the diffused outpourings, but as we shall see, there is a subtle shift in the imagery and the tone as she begins to struggle with her pride, to put on the disguise of the wounded child, her favorite mask behind which the poet's features became transfixed for solitude. By reading the Master letters in context with the poems and letters sent to Bowles, singling out for particular notice any alterations or expansions of metaphors, we can discover not merely for whom she wrote but what she was trying to say.

The first Master letter is so wholly concerned with her meaning that it is an invaluable source for understanding Emily Dickinson's subject matter:

Dear Master

I am ill, but grieving more that you are ill, I make my stronger hand work eno' to tell you. I thought perhaps you were in Heaven, and when you spoke again, it seemed quite sweet, and wonderful, and surprised me so—I wish that you were well.

I would that all I love, should be weak no more. The Violets are by my side, the Robins very near, and "Spring"—they say, Who is she—going by the door—

Indeed it is God's house—and these are gates of Heaven, and to and fro, the angels go, with their sweet postillions—I wish that I were great, like Mr. Michael Angelo, and could paint for you. You ask me what my flowers said—then they were disobedient—I gave them messages. They said what the lips in the West, say, when the sun goes down, and so says the Dawn.

Listen again, Master. I did not tell you that today had been the Sabbath Day.

Each Sabbath on the Sea, makes me count the Sabbaths, till we meet on shore—and (will the) whether the hills will look as blue as the sailors say. I cannot talk any more (stay any longer) tonight (now), for this pain denies me.

How strong when weak to recollect, and easy, quite, to love. Will you tell me, please to tell me, soon as you are well.[1]

The person to whom she is writing is ill. Emily Dickinson has a way of exaggerating illness, of always expecting the worst, and then congratulating her friends, whether intimate or casual, on their continuation in life. Samuel Bowles is known to have suffered frequently from attacks of sciatica. In February, 1861, he fell from a sleigh; he struggled with his pain through that spring and by the following October had to agree to enter a home for invalids to try the water cure for relief. Several letters written to Austin from Northampton, where Bowles was convalescing, confirm this.

The same concern with illness pervades many of her poems. There is no special significance to be attached, then, to her line, "I thought perhaps you were in Heaven." Certainly it does not provide evidence that she is writing to a minister.

The references to violets and robin obviously characterize the spring. But the next line, "they say . . . going by the door" is obscure. "They" refers not to the robin or violets, but to people who do not understand the meaning of spring. Emily Dickinson sees the Spring and recognizes her for what she is; she has sent poems conveying her discovery, but evidently her correspondent has not understood these poems. Wistfully she says if she were an artist she could paint the picture more clearly.[2] But she is only able to communicate her visions in poetry; now she finds she must clarify her poems with prose:[3] "They said [her poems about flowers] what the lips in the West, say, when the sun goes down, and so says the Dawn."[4] The poems, then, which have as their subject matter flowers and sunset and sunrise, all have the same meaning as Spring. What is the Spring? "Indeed it is God's house [people going by the door links now to the image of God's house which they pass so nonchalantly] and these [robin, violets, Spring] are the gates of Heaven."

But this only tells the significance of Spring in metaphor. What are we to understand by the analogue of the Gate? The Lexicon tells us that "Gate" is both an opening and a passage as well as the frame of wood we customarily associate with a gate. But *Gate* is further defined there as "An avenue; an opening; a way." Webster's illustration of this definition is a clue to Emily Dickinson's meaning. He writes: "In *Scripture* [gate implies] figuratively, power, [or] dominion. The *gates of hell* are the power and dominion of the devil and his instruments. The *gates of death* are the brink of the grave." Thus the seasons, sunrises and sunsets are a sign of the power and dominion of God; thus the terrestrial Spring is the instrument of God, the gates to His Heaven.[5]

This is always Emily Dickinson's conception of the meaning of Spring, or indeed any season, a concrete sign of regeneration. To her, all objects and all processes that may be perceived by the senses are necessarily evidence of diurnal or seasonal change; and all such signs of the cyclical character of change—the primary attribute of Nature—are taken for evidence of the ultimate destiny of man: immortality. That Nature is the reliable (*because* sensual) evidence of spiritual redemption, she attempts to explain in the rest of this letter.

> Listen again, Master. I did not tell you that today had been the Sabbath day.

Sabbath, in the Lexicon, is defined in this way: ". . . but the Christian Church very early began, and still continue[s] to observe the first day of the week, in commemoration of the Resurrection of Christ, on that day, by which the work of Redemption was completed." Sabbath, then, is not merely Sunday, but a memorial of the Resurrection and a guarantee of Redemption. To understand what Emily Dickinson is saying it is best to expand her cryptic prose: I was not telling you that today was Sunday. Listen to what I have tried to say to you before, and will again, Master. I, and not only I, but the flowers, the sunsets and the sunrise, tell you that all the days and seasons are the Sabbath, the sign of Redemption.

Her next line does not enlarge upon this idea but moves off into another metaphor, and another realm of discourse:

> Each Sabbath on the Sea, makes me count the Sabbaths, till we meet on shore—and (will the) whether the hills will look as blue as the Sailors say.

To track the agile mind of this poet, it is necessary to be alert to her symbolism. Just as the objects in Nature and natural phenomena are often symbols for Regeneration, so frequently the symbol for Death is the sea. Knowing this, we can supply alternative terms to get at her meaning: Each Redemption I hear of—each death I hear of—makes me count the signs of Regeneration here on Earth until I am with you or with those who have made the passage across to Heaven, and then I can tell what that Heaven itself is like, not by surmise but by direct experience of it.

Again her final lines veer off, for there is more in them than what seems at first glance to be a conventional conclusion, pleading illness, as the reason for her inability to write more.

> I cannot talk any more (stay any longer) tonight (now) for this pain denies me.
> How strong when weak to recollect, and easy, quite, to love. Will you tell me, please to tell me, soon as you are well.

Her very illness, which debilitates her, and clouds her memory, is the means by which her intuition (depending on no clarity of sense or reason) becomes strong; then, in her weakness, it becomes much easier to love (perhaps Christ or the Master). Will you (her correspondent) tell me if it is the same with you? Do you agree with all I have said about Regeneration and Redemption? Please tell me what you think, as soon as you are able, when you are restored to health.

Such, then, is the meaning of the Master letter. We cannot know if this was sent anywhere; I have said it was a kind of worksheet for her use alone. Out of it she may have derived the following poem sent to Bowles in 1858:

> If recollecting were forgetting,
> Then I remember not.
> And if forgetting, recollecting,
> How near I had forgot.
> And if to miss, were merry,
> And to mourn, were gay,
> How very blithe the fingers
> That gathered this, Today!

The lines of verse echo the opening lines of the prose saying she too is ill, she too is mourning, as well as the final paragraph, beginning "How strong when weak to recollect."

And we know there is a letter received by Bowles, conjecturally dated August, 1858. Although it is written in an altogether different tone and the imagery is drawn from late summer, not the springtime of the Master letter, it has the same subject:

My friends are my "estate." Forgive me then the avarice to hoard them! They tell me those were poor early, have different views of gold. I dont know how that is. God is not so wary as we, else he would give us no friends, lest we forget him! The Charms of the Heaven in the bush are superceded I fear, by the Heaven in the hand, occasionally. Summer stopped since you were here. Nobody noticed her—that is, no men and women. Doubtless, the fields are rent by petite anguish, and "mourners go about" the Woods. But this is not for us. Business enough indeed, our stately Resurrection! A special Courtesy, I judge, from what the Clergy say! To the "natural man," Bumblebees would seem an improvement, and a spicing of Birds, but far be it from me, to impugn such majestic tastes. Our Pastor says we are a "Worm." How is that reconciled? "Vain—sinful worm" is possibly of another species.

Do you think we shall "see God"? Think of "Abraham" strolling with him in genial promenade!

. . . .

Good night, Mr. Bowles! This is what they say who come back in the morning, also the closing paragraph on repealed lips. Confidence in daybreak modifies Dusk.[6]

This letter asks a similar question, disguised by an ironic attitude toward all such questions. The metaphors have been transformed, although there are subtle echoes. Nobody notices summer here as earlier none recognize the spring. Abraham and God in genial promenade replace the angels on their sweet postillions. Bumblebees and birds replace the violets and robins. The clergy are more noble than the sailors. But instead of certainty unmixed with doubt about the nature of heaven that sailors in theology explore, there is mockery for the pastors of the dogma who assure us of redemption as a special courtesy for man at the same time they decry man as a "Vain—sinful Worm." The last line of the letter to Bowles seems almost a paraphrase of the final portion of the third paragraph in the Master letter.

Another letter, also sent to Bowles, again uses the image of wealth as a metaphor for friendship, and repeats the thought contained in the phrase "Each Sabbath on the Sea," of the Master letter—death.

Will you not come again? Friends are gems—infrequent. Potosi is a care, Sir. I guard it reverently, for I could not afford to be poor now, after affluence.

. . . .

> I have but two acquaintance, the "Quick and the Dead"—and would like more.
>
> I write you frequently, and am much ashamed.[7]

To say that the Master letter was a worksheet from which these letters and the poem were derived cannot be anything more than conjecture. It is obvious that an alternative explanation of the sequence is possible. The poem, "If recollecting were forgetting," which accompanied a bunch of flowers ("How very blithe the fingers / That gathered this, Today!"), may have been sent first and the Master letter then becomes an effort to expand the poem, "You ask me what my flowers said—" She writes the sentimental private draft, reworks it, expunging what she chooses to hide, and sends instead the revision, "My friends are my 'estate.' " Some days I believe one thing, other days I am convinced of the alternative. But that there is an interplay of thought and imagery remains stable. It serves no purpose any longer to bemuse ourselves with the riddle of chronology. At this distance from the events of 1858–1862 we must be satisfied with an approximation. The insight we are seeking is an insight into the meaning of the poems, and the manner of rendering the ideas that became the style of Emily Dickinson. The clusters of images are the clue to the meaning. The variations of metaphors are the clue to the style. A Master letter speaks with clarity of the subject matter whether it was written first or second, whether sent or not sent, because it is the poet's effort to explain the substance of her verse.

There are other poems which are associated with the Master letter. Emily Dickinson has herself provided the incentive for our further search:

> You asked me what my flowers said—then they were disobedient—I gave them messages. They said what the lips in the West, say, when the sun goes down, and so says the Dawn.

So says the Sabbath, so says Death, so says Heaven. What might have been the other poems that baffled the correspondent?

There are many, written during this time, that render the regenerative process of nature in metaphors of flowers that bloom and fade and bloom again; these are poems of seasonal change as well. Ostensibly about gardening, the following poem is a prototype of many that may be found in the fascicles: [8]

All these my banners be.
I sow my pageantry
In May—
It rises train by train—
Then sleeps in state again—
My chancel—all the plain
  Today.

To lose—if one can find again—
To miss—if one shall meet—
The Burglar cannot rob—then—
The Broker cannot cheat.
So build the hillocks gaily
Thou little spade of mine
Leaving nooks for Daisy
And for Columbine—
You and I the secret
Of the Crocus know—
Let us chant it softly—
"There is no more snow!"

To him who keeps an Orchis' heart—
The swamps are pink with June.

The sowing of seeds is performed in May—the flowers will rise, each in their turn, then sleep, to rise again. The Master letter and the public letters have a theological question as well as an interest in flowers. Sure enough! The word "chancel" converts this simple poem about flowers to a characteristic idea of the poet: burial itself is a guarantee of Redemption. The chancel makes of this garden an altar and she names that chancel "Today." She needs no ecclesiastical ensigns. Her word "banners" means, of course, flags and fits the metaphor of pageantry, with its passing parade of "train by train." This secular image is modulated to the "Burglar" and "Broker" of the following stanza. And that word "banners" develops too; indeed the word has another meaning, so specific and so relevant to its use in the poem, one must admit that for all her insistence upon spontaneity Emily Dickinson worked as hard to discover the exact word as she labored to state her precise belief. The Lexicon prints a botanical application: "the upper petal of a papilionaceous corol [the petals that surround the parts of fructification]." Out of such "banners"—flowers in bloom—comes the diversification into daisy and columbine and crocus and orchid. Then all wave together again in the generalized "pink with June." And "snow" undergoes the same process of transformation, literal and figurative and seasonal and physical, all at the same time. Snow is the sleep that falls on the garden in the first stanza; it is the means of burial, and is the source of melting that can convert an icy field to a swamp in the spring.

Remarkable metaphor of regeneration. Who can say which is more striking, the theme or the manner of rendering that theme, her belief that not spiritual but sensual knowledge teaches the metaphysical truth, or her presentation of that idea in sensual imagery of color and motion and tumescence?

Here is another poem, written at about this time, where the metaphor is just as concrete but an action now, attached to a person (not a parade), using the familiar technique of rendering that action in meticulously concrete sensual detail:

> A Lady red—amid the Hill
> Her annual secret keeps!
> A Lady white, within the Field
> In placid Lily sleeps!
>
> The tidy Breezes, with their Brooms—
> Sweep vale—and hill—and tree!
> Prithee, My pretty Housewives!
> Who may expected be?
>
> The Neighbors do not yet suspect!
> The Woods exchange a smile!
> Orchard, and Buttercup, and Bird—
> In such a little while!
>
> And yet, how still the Landscape stands!
> How nonchalant the Hedge!
> As if the "Resurrection"
> Were nothing very strange!

This is a poem about flowers, yes, but of flowers that fall asleep in the Autumn and tranquilly await their cyclical change. Such placid contentment reflects a confidence in Resurrection, for it is their natural inheritance.

The following poem, too, is especially relevant as a message of her flowers; it, too, is constructed out of the images implied in her prose:

> Glowing is her Bonnet,
> Glowing is her Cheek,
> Glowing is her Kirtle,
> Yet she cannot speak.
>
> Better as the Daisy
> From the Summer hill
> Vanish unrecorded
> Save by tearful rill—
>
> Save by loving sunrise
> Looking for her face.
> Save by feet unnumbered
> Pausing at the place.

A characteristic of Emily Dickinson's style is her use of personification to render natural phenomena.[9] Like the "Lady red" this Autumn too is a woman, hurriedly rushing away, her hat already on her head, too pressed for speech. It would be better, the poet says, not to fuss so, to slip quietly off as the Daisy does, unnoticed except by the birds who sing tearfully, by the sunrise who misses her, by people at the barren hillside. The third stanza slows down that rush of passing with its wistful description of deprivation.

In addition to the poems about seasonal change using the imagery of flowers and gardens, there are many depicting temporal changes in the realm of the sky, with metaphors drawn from the phenomena of sunrise and sunset.[10] In all of these the imagery depicts a similar kind of action, departure and return.

Here is a poem which combines all the strands we have been talking about, the transition of nightfall to dawn, the presence of a group of people watching Heaven for a sign, the appearance of beggars imagining a state other than deprivation, the benevolent gift of morning—Nature as the intermediary between God and man—and the substratum of pleading. The poem was sent to Samuel Bowles:

> As Watchers hang upon the East,
> As Beggars revel at a feast
> By savory Fancy spread—

As brooks in deserts babble sweet
On ear too far for the delight,
Heaven beguiles the tired.

As that same watcher, when the East
Opens the lid of Amethyst
And lets the morning go —
That Beggar, when an honored Guest,
Those thirsty lips to flagons pressed,
Heaven to us, if true.

The connection of this poem to the letter sent to Bowles lies in the prose lines, "Good night, Mr. Bowles! This is what they say who come back in the morning, also the closing paragraph on repealed lips. Confidence in Daybreak modifies Dusk." The connection to the Master letter lies in these words found there: "They said what the lips in the West, say, when the sun goes down, and so says the Dawn." Even had we no prose statements to verify the meaning of this cluster of poems, we would know how pervasive a truth this is for Emily Dickinson. In every fascicle but seven there are poems singing the oracle of this bard: Nature is the visible sign of regeneration. Their subjects are bees, butterflies, worms, birds, flowers, gardens, woods, mountains; sunset, sunrise; spring and autumn—all are signs. The birds will return, the flowers will break through the sod, the barren trees will be restored to full leaf, the seasons will renew themselves—all are demonstrations of that vital principle of Nature, the process of transformation by virtue of innate energy. There is no lamentation at loss; there is everywhere a welcome of transiency, for it is this very attribute which affirms permanence. This is the lesson of Nature: transience is the proof of regeneration. And it is this she tries to explain in the Master letter.

There is another part to it. The final portion tries to tell her correspondent that Death is the physical transition between earth and heaven.

Each Sabbath on the Sea, makes me count the Sabbaths, till we meet on shore—and (will the) whether the hills will look as blue as the sailors say.

The poet has many poems in which she describes Death as such a process of transition and any one of them may have puzzled her Master.[11] The term *Sea* is of course the clue; it appears in many poems written during the same period, 1858–1859. What is particularly interesting about this cluster of poems is the shift in emphasis: just as the central idea shifts from physical being to spiritual being, from regeneration to immortality, there is a displacement of the source of imagery. Earth is replaced by water; organic growth is replaced by the turbulence of the sea;[12] evidence available to sense perception is replaced by no evidence at all, for no one may discern the impalpable or the permanent. Consequently these poems about death are also poems of uncertainty, ambiguity, speculation. Sense perception is replaced by intuition.

> Whether my bark went down at sea—
> Whether she met with gales—
> Whether to isles enchanted
> She bent her docile sails—
>
> By what mystic mooring
> She is held today—
> This is the errand of the eye
> Out upon the Bay.

The poem puzzles over the experience of death; the meaning of death the poet knows. But precisely what the voyage is like on that sea, the symbolic place where the mysterious event takes place, what the mooring on that other shore, heaven, is like, remains a question the poet ponders: whether it is annihilation, whether it is struggle, whether it is effortless or passive. And it is just the deceptiveness of that repeated word ("whether") suggesting a question, that causes the reader to come to attention and to read again, and more closely. These are not unresolved metaphysical questions, however, but are precisely the questions that may be resolved by the poet. Whether it (death) is nothingness, whether it is troubled passage, or judgment or damnation, whether death is peaceful entry to Paradise, exactly what is the mooring that will hold the soul, it is the errand of the Bard to reveal.

But since the poet's theory of perception precludes any knowledge that is not derived from the senses, she really cannot tell what it *is* like except in metaphor; she can only express what the passage may *feel* like:

> Exultation is the going
> Of an inland soul to sea,
> Past the houses—past the headlands—
> Into deep Eternity—

> Bred as we, among the mountains,
> Can the sailor understand
> The divine intoxication
> Of the first league out from land?

The watcher of this poem is now on the bark and is intoxicated by this passage out of life. Physical voyage can be described up to the point where Eternity is reached. Emily Dickinson cannot progress. She turns back to her one league out from land, she retreats into analogue. This is what she had done in the letters: "Whether the hills will look as blue as the sailors say. . . . Will you tell me, please to tell me." There in the Master letter, here in this poem, there is the same sense of exultation at the idea of redemption. In both, redemption is talked of as the result of passage by sea to a farther shore. In both, that shore is Heaven. When it comes to exact knowledge of what that Heaven will be like, there is no certainty, neither in the letter nor in any poem that attempts to say.

> Just lost, when I was saved!
> Just felt the world go by!
> Just girt me for the onset with Eternity,
> When breath blew back,
> And on the other side
> I heard recede the disappointed tide!
>
> Therefore, as **One** returned, I feel,
> Odd secrets of the line to tell!
> Some Sailor, skirting foreign shores—
> Some pale Reporter, from the awful doors
> Before the Seal!
>
> Next time, to stay!
> Next time, the things to see
> By Ear unheard,
> Unscrutinized by Eye—
>
> Next time, to tarry,
> While the Ages steal—
> Slow tramp the Centuries,
> And the Cycles wheel!

Emily Dickinson's ambivalence is not the sort to be resolved by any further education; no authority, no book can explain the enigma of the experience in Heaven. That which cannot be known by the medium of the senses simply cannot be known.[13] The poet who believes this would find the image of the sea—on which the sensate man drowns—an appropriate metaphor for death. Even when Emily Dickinson chooses to render the experience of dying on the land, she concentrates all her power on her description of the manner in which the dying person loses his power of sense perception.

It is no laconic shift in the Master letter from Spring to Sabbath, from Earth to Sea, from Regeneration to Redemption, although it seems so curt a conjoining of terms. Out of the very paradox of the duality of perception and intuition, of knowledge and truth, of nature and heaven, there arises literally two kinds of poems, poems of affirmation when nature and specifically the terrestrial world is the source of the imagery, and poems of quest when the sea and specifically voyaging on the water is the source of the imagery.[14]

I say "quest" rather than denial, for the unknown is not a matter of failure but simply unknowable.

> My wheel is in the dark!
> I cannot see a spoke
> Yet know it's dripping feet
> Go round and round.
>
> My foot is on the Tide!
> An unfrequented road—
> Yet have all roads
> A clearing at the end—
>
> Some have resigned the Loom—[15]
> Some in the busy tomb
> Find quaint employ—
>
> Some with new—stately feet—
> Pass royal thro' the gate—
> Flinging the problem back
> At you and I!

Here again the boat is on the water. In order for the paddle-wheel to drive the vessel it must submerge and disappear from view. Yet it will come up, it must go round, for she lives. And as she lives, she approaches death. What is it like? Those who are dead cannot tell. While she lives she cannot know.

Here is the familiar gate image, here again is the metaphor of water as the unknown, and here, too, is the idea of recurrence. What is beyond the gate, what that clearing is, cannot be described.

Again and again Emily Dickinson renders this paradox of the relationship between the real and non-real. In every fascicle but five such poems may be found. Sometimes the poems are melancholy or sorrowful, sometimes they are complacent, often gay, or a performance of wit. Questions, declamations, plaintive outcries, glad avowals—she is engaged in a dialogue with herself, as if just the process of writing will eventually lead her to an answer. This is not contradiction but polarity out of which emerges a delicate balance of meaning, a balance that depends on neither one poem nor another but precisely both, and their variants. An entire cluster, perceived as such because of the interplay between thought and image, must be kept in mind before one can grasp the poet's meaning. For Emily Dickinson it was the very awareness of the truth that was impermanent, although the truth itself was fixed. She had only the intuition that somehow truth shall eventually be known, but that will occur only in the place beyond perception and feeling, where no failure of mortal knowledge is possible: in Heaven. Of this she is never uncertain.

Her poetry, then, is a matrix of efforts to learn, a series of pictures, like stained-glass windows, designed to illuminate the effects of the truth, rather than the cause. And each fascicle is precisely such a matrix, such a composite of variants, not of a theme but of the diverse manifestations of the truth.

CHAPTER SEVEN

The Master Letters II

THE MASK OF STYLE

THE RELATIONSHIP BETWEEN INTUITION AND TRUTH IS NOT ONLY significant for the subject matter of Emily Dickinson's poetry but for her manner as well. Intuition was the instrument of her creative act, the wand of spontaneity. For all her insistence on spontaneity, for all her reliance on intuition as the source of her creative power, for all her disavowal of revision, she worked, she did not merely transcribe the melodies chanting in her subliminal ear. There is the evidence of those innumerable variants, not the words on her manuscripts, but those clusters of poems in which the same image is transformed, the same conception is rendered with mutating emotional tones. Emily Dickinson did indeed subject her "messages" to constant re-examination.

But her search for perfection, her reworking of the poems, is more than a series of experiments with a single idea. Her variants are a search for an appropriate public demeanor. She records her desires, her anguish and despair, her bewilderment, her doubt, her faith, but always in metaphor. The image is itself the material of the mask. The poem is itself the shape of the mask. She fixes her eyes on the gauze wings of a butterfly and sees the manifest hand of God. Any talk of her paradoxes—of sense perception and surmise, of secular and spiritual worlds, of mortality and immortality, of transience and permanence—is small talk compared to the real paradox of this poet.

She was a woman who withdrew into an isolation so total I for one shudder to contemplate the degree of loneliness she experienced. And inside that solitary room she longed to reach out to people everywhere who could read. She scrapped every shred of what we call normal life; with an absolutely iron inflexibility she turned her back on what we call living, and wrote poems. And these poems which were to to be her sole means of communication, the only way in which she would ever be known, she compressed and veiled and disguised. She sought the safety of ironic understatement, of ellipse. She who thought of her dedication to her craft as crucifixion, practiced her craft by perfecting every disguise it was possible to wear. She converted every deeply felt emotion into a well-wrought metaphor, every experience into a simile, every thought into an arrangement of related parts.

This poet was nervously vulnerable to occasions; she was ready always to be touched, to be reached, to be affected by a sound or a visual phenomenon, by an experience—hers or another's. Her raw unself-conscious response to an encounter, casual, solemn, real or fancied, is always present first; then she falls into a kind of dialogue with herself. Mysteriously, necessarily, she begins the process of converting her thoughts and feelings to analogues in the outside world, in the concrete realm of public experience. She refines a style to disguise what has happened in her internal world. Taking whatever devices came to hand—ellipse, epigram, personification, simile, allusion, expanding and contracting metaphors, symbolism, allegory, sprung syntax, prosodic patterns traditional or new—any, all of it—she converts into diabolically elusive and exquisite verse.

An examination of that large cluster of prose and verse—the second and third Master letters, the letters and poems sent to Samuel Bowles, and finally the variant poems left in the fascicles—will provide a rare opportunity to observe this process, for they reveal much about Emily Dickinson's poetic method. We can read them as they represent stages in the transformation of her thoughts and feelings into a subject matter for prose, as a source of imagery for the construction of poems that say best what she chooses to communicate to others, and finally as a source of imagery for poems she wrote for her eyes only.

The second Master letter is the most challenging of the three.

Master.

If you saw a bullet hit a Bird—and he told you he was'nt shot—you might weep at his courtesy, but you would certainly doubt his word.

One drop more from the gash that stains your Daisy's bosom—then would you *believe?* Thomas' faith in Anatomy, was stronger than his faith in faith. God made me—(Sir) Master—I did'nt be—myself. I dont know how it was done. He built the heart in me—Bye and bye it outgrew me—and like the little mother—with the big child—I got tired holding him. I heard of a thing called "Redemption"—which rested men and women. You remember I asked you for it—you gave me something else. I forgot the Redemption (in the Redeemed—I did'nt tell you for a long time, but I knew you had altered me—I) and was tired—no more—(so dear did this stranger become that were it, or my breath—the Alternative—I had tossed the fellow away with a smile.) I am older—tonight, master—but the love is the same—so are the moon and the crescent. If it had been God's will that I might breathe where you breathed—and find the place—myself—at night—if I (can) never, forget that I am not with you—and that sorrow and frost are nearer than I—if I wish with a might I cannot repress—that mine were the Queen's place—the love of the Plantagenet is my only apology—To come nearer than presbyteries—and nearer than the new Coat—that the Tailor made—the prank of the Heart at play on the Heart—in holy Holiday—is forbidden me—You make me say it over—I fear you laugh—when I do not see—(but) "Chillon" is not funny. Have you the Heart in your breast—Sir—is it set like mine—a little to the left—has it the misgiving—if it wake in the night—perchance—itself to it—a timbrel is it—itself to it a tune?

These things are (reverent) holy, Sir, I touch them (reverently) hallowed, but persons who pray—dare remark (our) "Father"! You say I do not tell you all—Daisy confessed—and denied not.

Vesuvius dont talk—Etna—dont—(Thy) one of them—said a syllable—a thousand years ago, and Pompeii heard it, and hid forever—She could'nt look the world in the face, afterward—I suppose—Bashfull Pompeii! "Tell you of the want"—you know what a leech is, dont you—and (remember that) Daisy's arm is small—and you have felt the horizon hav'nt you—and did the sea—never come so close as to make you dance?

I dont know what you can do for it—thank you—Master—but if I had the Beard on my cheek—like you—and you—had Daisy's petals—and you cared so for me—what would become of you? Could you forget me in fight, or flight—or the foreign land? Could'nt Carlo, and you and I walk in the meadows an hour—and nobody care but the Bobolink—and *his*—a *silver* scruple? I used to think when I died—I could see you—so I died as fast as I could—but the "Corporation" are going (to) Heaven too so (Eternity) wont be sequestered—now (at all)—Say I may wait for you—say I need go with no stranger to the to me—untried (country) fold—I waited a long time—Master—but I can wait more—wait till my hazel hair is dappled—and you carry the cane—then I can look at my watch—and if the Day is too far declined—we can take the chances (of) for Heaven—What would you do with me if I came "in white?" Have you the little chest to put the Alive—in?

I want to see you more—Sir—than all I wish for in this world—and the wish—altered a little—will be my only one—for the skies.

Could you come to New England—(this summer—could) would you come to Amherst—Would you like to come—Master?

(Would it do harm—yet we both fear God—) Would Daisy disappoint you—no—she would'nt—Sir—it were comfort forever—just to look in your face, while you looked in mine—then I could play in the woods till Dark—till you take me where Sundown cannot find us—and the true keep coming—till the town is full. (Will you tell me if you will?)

I did'nt think to tell you, you did'nt come to me "in white," nor ever told me why,

> No Rose, yet felt myself a'bloom,
> No Bird—yet rode in Ether.[1]

As in the case of everything Emily Dickinson wrote, be they letters or poems, the first question to settle is the circumstance which provoked her to write. What significant occurrence was the stimulus for this inchoate mixture of passion and appeal, defense and challenge?

We have seen that Emily Dickinson wrote frequently to Samuel Bowles, sending him poems and letters revealing her fears of death,[2] her doubts of salvation, exposing her conviction of her poetic powers, confessing her longings as a poet, confiding a suffering as intense as it was true. But she was not lucky in her reader. Her lyrics looked like nothing he had ever seen; her laments, her postures, her tribulations scarcely rhymed. Her emotions were not even "healthy" ones, always a sign of worth for Bowles. But she always hoped one day Bowles would appreciate her poems, one day he would agree to ease her sense of privation, one day he would decide actively to support her poetic career:

> If I could bribe them by a Rose
> I'd bring them every flower that grows
> From Amherst to Cashmere!
> I would not stop for night, or storm—
> Or frost, or death, or anyone—
> My business were so dear!
>
> If they w'd linger for a Bird
> My Tamborin were soonest heard

Among the April Woods!
Unwearied, all the summer long,
Only to break in wilder song
When Winter shook the boughs!

What if they hear me!
Who shall say
That such an importunity
May not at last avail?
That, weary of this Beggar's face —
They may not finally say, Yes —
To drive her from the Hall?

Here again are "You and I, and Dr. Holland"; the poet would strike a bargain with them, exchanging for their acceptance of her flower poem or her bird poem a pelting of blossoms, a paean of song.

But as we now know, one day she discovered that indeed the time would not ever come. When Emily Dickinson read that article in the *Springfield Republican* the words must have inflicted a great shock on her. Given her personality and sensitivity, encountering such an unequivocal opinion printed in a newspaper must have so demoralized the poet that she called him to her to defend herself, and as we saw in Chapter Five, failed so completely to make herself understood, got so entangled in a web of poetry and love and consecration to God, she was to fall prostrate into a coffin to rest for many a midnight on a bier of shame and chagrin.

"What Should We Write."

There is another kind of writing only too common, appealing to the sympathies of the reader without recommending itself to his subject. It may be called the literature of misery. The writers are chiefly women, gifted women may be, full of thought and feeling and fancy, but poor, lonely and unhappy. Also that suffering is so seldom healthful. It may be a valuable discipline in the end, but for the time being it too often clouds, withers, distorts. It is so difficult to see objects distinctly through a mist of tears. The sketch or poem is usually the writer's photograph in miniature. It reveals a countenance we would gladly brighten, but not by exposing it to the gaze of a worthless world. We know that grief enriches the soul, but seldom is this manifest until after its first intensity is past. We would say to our suffering friends, write not from the fullness of a present sorrow. It is in most cases only after the storm is passed that we may look for those peaceable fruits that nourished by showers, grow ripe and luscious in the sun. There are those indeed who so far triumph over their own personal experiences as to mould them into priceless gifts to the world of literature and art. Like the eider duck bending over her famished young, they give us their heart's blood and we find it then a refreshing draught. But there are marked exceptions. Ordinarily the lacerated bosom must first be healed, 'ere it can gladden other natures with the overflowings of a healthful life.

It seems inevitable that Emily Dickinson should have interpreted these words as a public rebuke to her. It takes little imagination to reconstruct the effect of such an article, reminding ourselves that Susan would read it, Lavinia would read it—well, all of Amherst that counted for Emily Dickinson would read it—and perhaps laugh, or what would be worse for such a proud and so self-conscious a woman, pity her.

There are many poems sent to no one, secreted into her fascicles, which speak more clearly of the effect than any conjecture of mine.

> I cried at Pity—not at Pain—
> I heard a Woman say
> "Poor Child"—and something in her voice
> Convinced myself of me—
>
> So long I fainted, to myself
> It seemed the common way,
> And Health, and Laughter, Curious things—
> To look at, like a Toy—
>
> To sometimes hear "Rich people" buy
> And see the Parcel rolled—
> And carried, we suppose—to Heaven,
> For children, made of Gold—
>
> But not to touch, or wish for,
> Or think of, with a sigh—
> And so and so—had been to us,
> Had God willed differently.
>
> I wish I knew that Woman's name—
> So when she comes this way,
> To hold my life, and hold my ears
> For fear I hear her say

She's "sorry I am dead"—again—
Just when the Grave and I—
Have sobbed ourselves almost to sleep,
Our only Lullaby—

In this same Fascicle 27 into which "I cried at Pity—not at Pain—" is transcribed, may be found the most wistful poem in the canon:

Good Morning—Midnight—
I'm coming Home—
Day—got tired of Me—
How could I—of Him? [3]

Sunshine was a sweet place—
I liked to stay—
But Morn—did'nt want me—now—
So—Goodnight—Day!

I can look—cant I—
When the East is Red?
The Hills—have a way—then—
That puts the Heart—abroad—

You—are not so fair—Midnight—
I chose—Day—
But—please take a little Girl—
He turned away!

It is so direct, the poet's wound lies so exposed, that the beauties of the verse may be relinquished, for who would have the wish to look close?

Close by, in Fascicle 26, is a poem that is all too clear, when read in context with the article:

I read my sentence—steadily—
Reviewed it with my eyes,
To see that I made no mistake,
In it's extremest clause—
The Date, and manner, of the shame—
And then the Pious Form
That "God have mercy" on the Soul
The Jury voted Him—[4]
I made my soul familiar—with her extremity—
That at the last, it should not be a novel Agony—

But she, and Death, acquainted—
Meet tranquilly, as friends—
Salute, and pass, without a Hint—
And there, the Matter ends—

Examine the contents of the threaded booklets and see how many variants on these two poems there are.[5] But the first repository of Emily Dickinson's reaction is the second Master letter, cited in full above.

If you saw a bullet hit a Bird—and he told you he was'nt shot—you might weep at his courtesy, but you would certainly doubt his word.

One drop more from the gash that stains your Daisy's bosom—then would you believe? Thomas' faith in Anatomy, was stronger than his faith in faith. God made me—(Sir) Master—I did'nt be—myself. I dont know how it was done. He built the heart in me—Bye and bye it outgrew me—and like the little mother—with the big child—I got tired holding him.

The second paragraph of the Master letter seems to begin where the article left off: "One drop more from the gash that stains your Daisy's bosom" has a striking similarity to "they give us their heart's blood. . . . Ordinarily the lacerated bosom must first be healed. . . ." The letter begins with a defense of her reaction to the article and then moves to a defense of her suffering. The effort to explain why she is so burdened with grief will be made several times during the course of this letter but it is not the fact that she is suffering that really needs to be defended so much as the validity of her poetry. "One drop more" may be a metaphor for another poem of genuineness. Her poems come out of her blood and ought to be believed, not dismissed as self-indulgence or as contrivance or sentimentality.

Is he such a Doubting Thomas that he needs to put his finger in the gash in order to convince himself that the suffering is real? Can't he believe the sign—the one drop more—the poetry? [6] She cannot justify her heart nor its vulnerability: what she is—her passions and her metaphors—exist outside of will, outside of knowledge, because "God made me." And when her oppressively burdened heart became too much for her to bear, when she wearied of the weight of her message, she was obliged to deliver herself of her poetry.[7]

Now she continues her attempt to convince him of her sincerity:

I heard of a thing called "Redemption"—which rested men and women. you remember I asked you for it—you gave me something else. I forgot the Redemption (in the Redeemed—I did'nt tell you for a long time, but I knew you had altered me—I) and was tired—no more—(so dear did this stranger become that were it, or my breath—the Alternative—I had tossed the fellow away with a smile).

She is referring to that major portion of the first Master letter and that cluster of poems and letters sent to Bowles devoted to this quesion of Redemption, which was mingled with her efforts to explain the subject matter of her poetry. Now she is admitting she forgot the issue and became lost in something else. He became so dear to her, he obviated any need of theological commitment; she was no longer tired or fearful; and not only did she lose her fear of death, she would have welcomed death, would have smilingly tossed her life away rather than lose him.

I am older—tonight, Master—but the love is the same—so are the moon and the crescent. If it had been God's will that I might breathe where you breathed—and find the place—myself—at night—if I (can) never forget that I am not with you—and that sorrow and frost are nearer than I—if I wish with a might I cannot repress—that mine were the Queen's place—the love of the Plantagenet is my only apology—To come nearer than presbyteries—and nearer than the new Coat—that the Tailor made—the prank of the Heart at play on the Heart—in holy Holiday—is forbidden me—

Despite the passing of time her love has not changed, it has only increased. It is always possible, in the seemingly spontaneous lines of Emily Dickinson's prose to recover the meaning of even her most highly compressed language, by tracing the related terms of her analogies:

$$\frac{\text{I am older}}{\text{than I was}} \; : \; \frac{\text{the moon is greater}}{\text{than its crescent}}$$

Not only does this imply the love is the same, because it is the same moon whether it wax or wane, but her love now, compared to her love then, is like a full moon compared to its crescent.[8] There is no allegorical or theological meaning here. She simply is stating her love, defining by her analogy the expanding quality of her desire. Her concern with her poetry need not be lost sight of. Doubtless she wishes her poetry might touch his heart as much as she wishes she might fall asleep on his breast. But love and praise are both forbidden.

The meaning of the Queen's place is indeterminate: it may be the room where he sleeps, it may be her proper rank or her rightful dignity, or a position in his affections; it may be "kind reception," or even that "place" in the newspaper column reserved for the featured poet, rather than the little anonymous spaces used as filler, where the sentimental suffering lady poets customarily appeared. Usually a queen in Emily Dickinson's poetry signifies the queen of Heaven, or the poet achieving her rightful place on the right hand of God when she enters His domain. But "Plantagenet" refers to the English house of royalty founded by the Count of Anjou, Geoffry; [9] it is a secular word and forestalls any spiritual interpretation. She has made the editor a Plantagenet in the service of the Queen rather than herself the bride of Christ.

Even in such a private manuscript as this, prose after all, the imagery is never loose or dissociated; the metaphors modulate and expand and a kind of unity and coherence is achieved, here as everywhere. Take for example that metaphor of respiration. What seems to be at first glance a shift in the image is really a careful expansion. The idea of breathing where he breathes is a modulation of the word "heart," and picks up from the earlier tiredness and "were it, or my breath the Alternative." There is also the link back to God who built the heart in her, and forward to if it were God's will she might live in his heart, and farther yet to the phrase "the prank of the Heart at play on the Heart" which in its turn reminds us of her beginning lamentation, that one drop more from the gash in her bosom.

Her lot is not holy holiday; it is to be despair and privation. Rather than doubt—worse, laugh at—her suffering, he should sympathize:

> You make me say it over—I fear you laugh—when I do not see—(but) "Chillon" is not funny.[10] Have you the Heart in your breast—Sir—is it set like mine—a little to the left—has it the misgiving—if it wake in the night—perchance—itself to it—a timbrel is it—itself to it a tune?

To be so isolated, entombed, forsaken is not funny. The subject of his heart replaces now her own, and she wonders that he has no compassion for fear and suffering. Does he never wake in the middle of the night, so frightened, in such silence that he can hear the total heart beat? That musical image is very apt, for it heightens the degree of silence surrounding the person when systole and diastole can both be heard, the one a melody, the other the rhythmic beat. And it is just the concreteness of that image drawn from sensual sound that is so ever-present a mark of Emily Dickinson's style. Always, when it is the imagery of such a poet that is under scrutiny, we must take into account the physical meaning as well. This does not preclude that she is also describing a religious experience:

> These things are (reverent) holy, Sir, I touch them (reverently) hallowed, but persons who pray—dare remark (our) "Father"! You say I do not tell you all—Daisy confessed—and denied not.
>
> Vesuvius dont talk—Etna—dont—(Thy) one of them—said a syllable—a thousand years ago, and Pompeii heard it, and hid forever—She could'nt look the world in the face, afterward—I suppose—Bashful Pompeii! "Tell you of the want"—you know what a leech is, dont you—and (remember that) Daisy's arm is small—and you have felt the horizon hav'nt you—and did the sea—never come so close as to make you dance?
>
> I dont know what you can do for it—thank you—Master—but if I had the Beard on my cheek—like you—and you—had Daisy's petals—and you cared so for me—what would become of you? Could you forget me in fight[11] or flight—or the foreign land? Could'nt Carlo, and you and I walk in the meadows an hour—and nobody care but the Bobolink—and *his*—a *silver* scruple?

The essence of the religious experience for this poet is as we know intensely personal; the sign of spiritual perception is always some physical manifestation. These words do have the aura of the confessional about them, but she is not talking about God, she is talking about her efforts to explain herself.

The Master has not understood, neither what she was trying to articulate nor what she wanted or why. Pretend as she will to be a shy Daisy, the metaphor for her revelation is not only Vesuvius and Etna, but also Pompeii. Is this inconsistent or is it a sign of a crucial ellipse? By reconstructing the analogy we can discover her meaning. At first we try this design using the act of speech as the logical base:

$$\frac{\text{Daisy confessed}}{\text{to the Master}} : \frac{\text{Vesuvius and Etna spoke}}{\text{Pompeii hid}}$$

But this is an analogy without much significance. Suppose we reverse the design using quality or size or degree of importance as the base:

$$\frac{\text{Daisy confessed}}{\text{the Master }\underline{?}} : \frac{\text{Bashful Pompeii }\textit{hid}}{\text{Vesuvius and Etna }\textit{spoke}}$$

Now the analogy has major implications. The analogy forces us to supply a fourth term. How has the Master, in his single response, affected Daisy?

As the exploding volcano affected Pompeii. Elsewhere in this letter there is an act comparable to the destruction of the town: "If you saw a bullet hit a Bird—and he told you he wasn't shot—you might weep at his courtesy, but you would certainly doubt his word." It is just this bullet, just this eruption of Vesuvius and Mt. Etna that are her metaphors for some catastrophic statement made by the Master. I have suggested this to be the appearance of the article in the *Springfield Republican,* with its lines "It reveals a countenance we would gladly brighten but not by exposing it to the gaze of a worthless world," "the literature of misery," "suffering is unhealthful," and so on. Thunderings certainly.

What does she want? The leech is used in illness to bleed the patient. Bowles has said in his article that "Ordinarily the lacerated bosom must first be healed, 'ere it can gladden other natures with the overflowings of a healthful life." One drop more from the gash in her bosom is almost a paraphrase; her leech image is the reply to his proposal that health be restored. Her illness, her unhealthy state is no present sorrow; the sea is familiar to us as Emily Dickinson's symbol for death, and horizon is a recurring word signifying that other shore, the afterlife. Her grief is no passing storm, no simple personal experience; it has to do with fears of death, with uncertainties. Has he never wakened in the night trembling? Has he never feared to die? Has he never thought of the far shore? She is defending again the validity of tribulation, of melancholy, of suffering. She is answering his article point by point.

What can he do for it? Ah, the writer says, if matters were turned about, if I were the man and you had such need of me, I would not ignore you, would not turn away, would not lose myself in public—domestic or foreign—affairs. Ah, the poet muses, in the poem she sent to Bowles:

> Should you but fail at—Sea—
> In sight of me—
> Or doomed lie—
> Next Sun—to die—
> Or rap—at Paradise—unheard
> I'd *harass God*
> Until he let you in!

And here is the strangest part of all this draft letter. At the point of saying just what she would like, the poet retreats. Even in her own private thoughts, she hedges. Perhaps this is indeed what she would like, this hour of companionship, walking out with him in the fields for an hour. She does eventually ask him to come, and he does, but we know what came of that.

This poem was sent to Bowles:

> What shall I do—it whimpers so—
> This little Hound within the Heart
> All day and night with bark and start—
> And yet, it will not go—
> Would you *untie* it, were you me—
> Would it stop whining—if to Thee—
> I sent it—even now?
>
> It should not tease you—
> By your chair—or, on the mat—
> Or if it dare—to climb your dizzy knee—
> Or—sometimes at your side to run—
> When you were willing—
> Shall it come?
> Tell Carlo—
> *He'll* tell *me!*

His meeting with her awakened that hound to howling and set it to barking and snarling and it ended with a long low growl, a reproach and a warning and a guard. But as she writes her draft she doesn't know yet. She assumes her request will be denied her and so speculates on her chances for walking about with him in the other world.

> I used to think when I died—I could see you—so I died as fast as I could—but the "Corporation" are going Heaven too so (Eternity) wont be sequestered—now (at all)—Say I may wait for you—say I need go with no stranger to the to me untried (country) fold—I waited a long time—Master—but I can wait more—wait till my hazel hair is dappled—and you carry the cane—then I can look at my watch—and if the day is too far declined—we can take the chances (of) for Heaven—

There enters now, as there always does when she counsels patience, a quality of irony. Since this manuscript is more a repository of thoughts, a diversity of emotional tones is no contradiction, although a mixed emotional tone was not unusual in her finished poetry. Often the melancholy is tempered with the wistful, the self-pity with the grotesque, the tragedy with mummery. And in the final portion of the Master letter, as Emily

Dickinson quickens her appeal, she begins to put on a disguise, as if she needed to protect herself from her own private thoughts.

> What would you do with me if I came "in white?" Have you the little chest to put the Alive—in?
>
> I want to see you more—Sir—than all I wish for in this world—and the wish—altered a little—will be my only one—for the skies.
>
> Could you come to New England—(this summer—could) would you come to Amherst—Would you like to come—Master?
>
> (Would it do harm—yet we both fear God—) Would Daisy disappoint you—no—she would'nt—Sir—it were comfort forever—just to look in your face, while you looked in mine—then I could play in the woods till Dark—till you take me where Sundown cannot find us—and the true keep coming—till the town is full. (Will you tell me if you will?)
>
> I did'nt think to tell you, you did'nt come to me "in white," nor ever told me why,

> No Rose, yet felt myself a'bloom,
> No Bird—yet rode in Ether.

"In white" may mean sanctified or wearing a shroud, as the woman of her poem will be "Born—Bridalled—Shrouded—/ In a Day." If that is so, then she goes on to wonder what he might do should she be the first to die; would he be able to preserve her (living soul) until it be time for his departure? "In white" may mean despair, as she names it outright in her poem "I cannot live with You—"

> . . . .
> So We must meet apart—
> You there—I—here—
> With just the Door ajar
> That Oceans are—and Prayer—
> And that White Sustenance—
> Despair—

In that case we get a meaning that leads to their eventual encounter: what if, instead of writing, I came to you in person; what if, in my despair, I came to you? I know where letters end—in a little chest, I have my own ebon box; but can you put the *living* me away in a little chest?

With this interpretation, what follows becomes almost coherent, logical: I want to see you; come to Amherst. This request will survive the draft letter. This request leads to their confrontation. She has earlier visualized their genteel aging together, their crossing over to the place of heaven; now her vision is more concrete. Together in Amherst, will that do harm? Together on the meadow, strolling in the woods, will she suffice for him? More serious than the fear of public censure is the fear that she might somehow disappoint him, that she might not live up to his expectations.[12] It is just at this point that her mind lapses into a projection of herself as one who might very well have such a tremor of insufficiency—a child. This is a typical mask for Emily Dickinson. Again and again, when it is doubt that afflicts her (whether she triumphs over her doubt or succumbs to it) she slips into the persona of the child. Ah no, she would not disappoint him, she reassures herself. If he came, if she could have the comfort of the mere gaze, she would lose all her fear of the woods and the dark.

Recalling here the context of the article which rankles we can understand these phrases more easily: she does not *choose* to be miserable (she would like to play in the woods); she does not *wish* to be unhappy; she would then write the kind of poetry he approves of—the true.

To be sure, she might be saying something like this, too: would we do harm? Oh no. I would not demand more than the comfort of merely gazing into your eyes, that would be enough for me. I am but a child, we will play in the woods as children do, and all the world will remain bright for me thereafter and I will have nothing more to do with misery and suffering.

Either interpretation makes the seeming jar in her thought, "I did'nt think to tell you, you did'nt come to me 'in white,' nor ever told me why," consistent with what has come before. I did not condemn you for not being a sufferer; I never required *you* to explain why you were not in despair, tormented; then why should you chastize me for my "snow"? I may not be a Rose, yet I feel myself in blossom; I may not be a Bird, yet I know how it is to ride in Ether; I need not be dead to write of passage to Heaven; it is not unhealthy to write of suffering.

So this letter, which began with a bird shot down, concludes with a transfigured bird; this worksheet which began with an outcry of pain and moved slowly, erratically, but led as it were by the force of the dialogue itself, through defence of suffering, confession of love, exposure of fears, to wistful appeal, to playacting, to challenge, arrives finally at affirmation, strong affirmation.

So incriminating a document could not possibly have been sent. Emily Dickinson's entire history—biographical and literary—excludes the public. Very seldom was she seen: very seldom did she write outside of metaphor. Her poetic style and her life style are consistent. She set about her process of revision, which was for her primarily a matter of a new start, to construct variants, not of single words but on the total piece.

Out of that image of the bird with which this Master letter begins, this poem emerges:

> Her smile was shaped like other smiles—
> The Dimples ran along—
> And still it hurt you, as some Bird
> Did hoist herself, to sing,
> Then recollect a Ball, she got—
> And hold upon the Twig,
> Convulsive, while the Music crashed—
> Like Beads—among the Bog—

Knowing how often Emily Dickinson personifies herself as a bird, and her poetry as song, this poem is clearly a contemplation on the effect of the "Ball" on her music. It is also an acknowledgment of her effort to disguise the pain. And copied onto the same sheet in Fascicle 14 is a poem which takes up the image of the smile, and contemplates the deliberate disguise:

> A happy lip—breaks sudden—
> It does'nt state you how
> It contemplated—smiling—
> Just consummated—now—
> But this one, wears it's merriment
> So patient—like a pain—
> Fresh gilded—to elude the eyes
> Unqualified, to scan—

The poem says outright she will keep to herself the source of her pain, that she chooses to screen the incident from all whose eyes are not qualified to perceive the truth.[13]

There is another poem modulating the image of the bird, but it has a somewhat different emphasis:

> Kill your Balm—and it's Odors bless you—
> Bare your Jessamine—to the storm—
> And she will fling her maddest perfume—

And she will fling her maddest perfume—
Haply—your Summer night to Charm—

Stab the Bird—that built in your bosom—
Oh, could you catch her last Refrain—
Bubble! "forgive"—"Some better"—Bubble!
"Carol for Him—when I am gone"!

The sadness is muted by a challenge. The act of killing will result in an increase of that for which annihilation was decreed. The odors of balm, the perfumes of jessamine will increase; ironically the destroyer will be blessed. And in the case of the bird there will be forgiveness, but she adds ironically "Some better" poet will sing, but it will be the same carol still. The echo of Whitman in the last two lines suggests that Emily Dickinson was here able to objectify her experience enough to create a poetic jest.

Her metaphor of the wounded heart is converted, in the privacy of her fascicles to her severed heart, which she brings to a different Master:

Father—I bring thee—not Myself—
That were the little load—
I bring thee the departed Heart
I had not strength to hold—

The Heart I cherished in my own
Till mine—too heavy grew—
Yet—strangest—heavier—since it went—
Is it too large for you?

There is a great bitterness in this poem, as well as timidity; that pretense of childlike fear of disappointing the Master changes to a willing offer of her departed heart to God.

Her confession in the Master letter of the fear of the dark, of night, of death, she converted into countless poems. They evolve gradually into poems of recovery where her welcome into the world of God also enables her to divest herself of fright and shadows.

If I'm lost—now—
That I was found—
Shall still my transport be—
That once—on me—those Jasper Gates
Blazed open—suddenly—

That in my awkward—gazing—face—
The Angels—softly peered—
And touched me with their fleeces,
Almost as if they cared—
I'm banished—now—you know it—
How foreign that can be—
You'll know—Sir—when the Savior's face
Turns so—away from you—

She has been excluded from the Master's world; the Angels will gaze on her face instead. Another poem uses so many of the concepts and images of the Master letter (the first and fourth paragraphs especially supply the sources) that it seems a mere simplification of the manuscript: [14]

Forever at His side to walk—
The smaller of the two!
Brain of His Brain—
Blood of His Blood—
Two lives—One Being—now—

Forever of His fate to taste—
If grief—the largest part—
If joy—to put my piece away
For that beloved Heart—

All life—to know each other—
Whom we can never learn—
And bye and bye—a Change—
Called Heaven—
Rapt Neighborhoods of Men—
Just finding out—what puzzled us—
Without the lexicon!

The metaphor of the volcano reappears in Fascicle 4, in a poem which has the same seriousness of tone, the same implication for Pompeii that lay embedded in the Master letter:

I have never seen 'Volcanoes'—
But, when Travellers tell
How those old—phlegmatic mountains
Usually so still—

Bear within—appalling Ordnance,
Fire, and smoke, and gun,
Taking Villages for breakfast,
And appalling Men—

If the stillness is Volcanic
In the human face
When upon a pain Titanic
Features keep their place—

If at length, the smouldering anguish
Will not overcome—
And the palpitating Vineyard
In the dust, be thrown?

If some loving Antiquary,
On Resumption Morn,
Will not cry with joy "Pompeii"!
To the Hills return!

But more intriguing than all these transformations into separate poems is the fact that there is this letter with an accompanying poem that Emily Dickinson sent to Samuel Bowles:

If I amaze[d] your kindness—My love is my only apology. To the people of "Chillon"—this—is enough I have met—no other[rs.] Would you—as[k] le[ss] for your *Queen*—M[r] Bowles?

Then—I mistake—[my] scale—To Da [?] 'tis *daily*—to be gran[ted] and not a "Sunday Su[m] [En]closed—is my [d]efence—

[F]orgive the Gills that ask for Air—if it is harm—to breathe!
To *"thank" you*—[s]hames my thought!

> Should you but fail at—Sea—
> In sight of me—
> Or doomed lie—
> Next Sun—to die—
> Or rap—at Paradise—unheard
> I'd *harass God*
> Until he let you in! [15]

The recurrent imagery is obvious but the emotional tone is hardening. Her growing pride is apparent at the very moment of defense. An ostensible apology cannot obscure her anger. That apology forms the substance of the third Master letter.

Even a cursory reading of this new draft shows it to be related to the second just examined at length but not as revision, for although the declarations of a steadfast love, the protestations of an undying loyalty, the appeal for compassion, the lament that she suffers from an overburdened heart—although all of this is present, everything modulates. What intervened between the two is the encounter. He came, and as we have seen, nothing materialized. Except some thousand poems.

Oh, did I offend it—(Did'nt it want me to tell it the truth) Daisy—Daisy—offend it—who bends her smaller life to his (its) meeker (lower) every day—who only asks—a task—(who) something to do for love of it—some little way she cannot guess to make that master glad—

A love so big it scares her, rushing among her small heart—pushing aside the blood and leaving her faint (all) and white in the gust's arm—

Daisy—who never flinched thro' that awful parting, but held her life so tight he should not see the wound—who would have sheltered him in her childish bosom (Heart)—only it was'nt big eno' for a Guest so large—*this* Daisy—grieve her Lord—and yet it (she) often blundered—perhaps she grieved (grazed) his taste—perhaps her odd—Backwoodsman (life) ways (troubled) teased his finer nature (sense). Daisy knows all that—but must she go unpardoned—teach her, preceptor grace—teach her majesty—Slow (Dull) at patrician things—Even the wren upon her nest learns (knows) more than Daisy dares—

Low at the knee that bore her once unto (royal) wordless rest (now) Daisy (stoops a) kneels a culprit—tell her her (offence) fault—Master—if it is (not so) small eno' to cancel with her life, (Daisy) she is satisfied—but punish (do not) dont banish her—shut her in prison, sir—only pledge that you will forgive—sometime—before the grave, and Daisy will not mind—She will awake in (his) your likeness.

Wonder stings me more than the Bee—who did never sting me—but made gay music with his might wherever I (may) (should) did go—wonder wastes my pound, you said I had no size to spare—

You send the water over the Dam in my brown eyes—

I've got a cough as big as a thimble—but I dont care for that—I've got a Tomahawk in my side but that dont hurt me much. (If you) Her master stabs her more—

Wont he come to her—or will he let her seek him, never minding (whatever) so long wandering (out) if to him at last.

Oh how the sailor strains, when his boat is filling—Oh how the dying tug, till the angel comes. Master—open your life wide, and take me in forever, I will never be tired—I will never be noisy when you want to be still. I will be (glad) (as the) your best little girl—nobody else will see me, but you—but that is enough—I shall not want any more—and all that heaven only will disappoint me—will be because it's not so dear.[16]

The image of faintness of Daisy who is wounded, the prison metaphor, the mask of the child, the tropes of love and death, all reappear, but the poet has converted her private feelings to approximate what will eventually become for her an appropriate public declaration. The shifting back and forth between the spiritual and the emotional is gone and with it those confused minglings of her confessions to fears of death and desires for love and approval. This draft is now consistently personal, her appeal is direct, for she still asks for love; however, it is not an intimate union between a man and a woman but a generalized relationship of guidance.

The personae of both letters taken together undergo a steady change, from a woman fearful of death, to a child who will need protection from the fright of a figurative Dark, to a child at the knee, never noisy, a "best little girl." That lady whose hazel hair is dappled, who can walk gracefully beside her gentleman with the cane, who looks at her watch and then seeing the hour is late decides to go at once to Heaven, now becomes a backwoodsman, dull at patrician things, or worse—she lies faint and white in the gust's arm. That person who pleaded for her own validity now pleads for forgiveness. She who talked of Redemption and Redeemer, of purity and Heaven, who challenged the Master's perception and even his faith (the Doubting Thomas image) now begs for pardon, now is suffused with contrition, admits her failing. Once charging him not to laugh at "Chillon" she says put me in prison if you will, but forgive me, do. The proud Queen now needs to learn grace and poise. She who had loved the Plantagenet is now lower than the wren's nest. What had been a decimated Pompeii has contracted to a decimated Daisy with a cough as big as a thimble. And all that expansive image of the poet arriving in Heaven where the Corporation has taken up residence, where Saints overcrowd the town of that untried country, contracts to a lonely sailor struggling to maintain himself in a small swamped boat.

All of this alteration and contraction produces a shift in tone that must be apparent to any one who reads these letters in juxtaposition. She exaggerates her pleas for pardon; she surrounds her description of suffering with hyperbole not meant to be serious, she assumes a winsome posture; she indulges in a burlesque metaphor. And what is most notable is that all the defense of the validity of her subject matter and her poetry itself is compressed into a few phrases of apology for a form that she admits is blundering, for themes that tease his finer sense, for verses that are without grace because of her own ignorance. Emily Dickinson speaks so; she believes none of it; hence the ironic or humorous even detached quality of feeling that pervades this draft.

The relationship between the two Master letters is striking enough. Both are significant for the insight it affords into Emily Dickinson's mask put on for the public world. As she confronts herself in the privacy of her room she knows herself to be an emotional, passionate woman, royal, wise, strong, noble. As she prepares to confront a world she knows has a different view of her, she begins to hide her personality behind a screen of irony and wit; she endows her prospective reader—if he has misvalued her—with a wisdom she pretends to lack, and she pretends to grant him—whether Higginson, Bowles, or the Master—the role of preceptor on the presumption that his discernment and his taste are necessary for her guidance.[17]

For the most part the final transcription is always into some disguise, a mask of propriety. She renders herself as a child, a petite flower or bird, a beggar, a naif who is weak or weary, suffering, deprived, and above all humble—always humble.

The public mask was not altogether mere contrivance; Emily Dickinson was ambivalent, surely. Her pride was strong, but she was always an easy prey to rebuff; just in the same way her belief in God, in Immortality, was firm, and yet she was frequently a victim of fear and doubt. Since there is evidence enough that her conception of immortality of the soul and immortality of her poetry often coincided, perhaps the very fears she suffered at the idea of death grew large, at times unconquerable, when she could obtain no confirmation of her stature as a poet.

Her process of contraction and compression, her assuming a pose of gayety and indifference, her disguise of easy familiarity, are all marks of the final stage of Emily Dickinson's transformation of a private experience into a type of communication with which she felt at ease. For the most part the letters and poems sent to Samuel Bowles during this period take on an air of mirth and tenderness that she believed to be less demeaning. After her encounter with him, she teaches herself to endure her mortification by hiding her feelings in the fascicles and sending more jocular notes such as this:

> You remember the little "Meeting"—we held for you—last spring? We met again—Saturday—'Twas May—when we "adjourned" but then Adjourns—are all—The meetings wore alike—Mr. Bowles—The Topic—did not tire us—so we chose no new—We voted to remember you—so long as both should live—including Immortality. To count you as ourselves—except more tenderly—as now—when you are ill—and we—the haler of the two—and so I bring the Bond—we sign so many times—for you to read, when Chaos comes—or Treason—or Decay—still witnessing for Morning.
>
> We hope—it is a tri-Hope—composed of Vinnie's—Sue's—and mine—that you took no more pain—riding in the sleigh.
>
> We hope our joy to see you—gave of it's own degree—to you—We pray for your new health—the prayer that goes not down—when they shut the church—We offer you our cups—stintless—as to the Bee—the lily, her new Liquors—
>
>> Would you like Summer? Taste of our's—
>> Spices? Buy, here!
>> Ill! We have Berries, for the parching!
>> Weary! Furloughs of Down!
>> Perplexed! Estates of Violet—Trouble ne'er looked on!
>> Captive! We bring Reprieve of Roses!
>> Fainting! Flasks of Air!
>> Even for Death—a Fairy Medicine—
>> But, which is it—Sir? [18]

Such a poem, dated February, 1861, has a surface of deception—gay, solicitous, domestic—beneath which her ironic barbs are hidden: not snow always, but summer; for his pain and his suffering she offers relief, reprieve, air.

Another letter, conjecturally dated October, 1861, is more serious, apologizes directly for her refusal to see him, and again offers him the same metaphoric balm:

> Perhaps you thought I did'nt care—because I stayed out, yesterday, I *did* care, Mr. Bowles. I pray for your sweet health—to "Alla"—every morning—but something troubled me—and I knew you needed light—and air—so I did'nt come. Nor have I the conceit that you *noticed* me—but I

could'nt bear that you, or Mary [Mrs. Bowles] so gentle to me—should think me forgetful—It's little, at the most—we can do for our's, and we must do that—flying—or our things are *flown!* Dear friend, I wish you were well—

The pattern of written protestations of warm feelings and apologies for not being able to see Bowles is fixed from this time on, for it is a fact that she could very seldom be prevailed upon to meet him face to face again.

It grieves me till I cannot speak, that you are suffering. Wont you come back? Cant I bring you something? My little Balm might be o'erlooked by wiser eyes—you know—Have you tried the Breeze that swings the sign—or the Hoof the Dandelion? I own 'em—Wait for mine!

This is all that I have to say. . . .[19]

The poems she sent to Bowles are somewhat different. They are still compressions but the disguise is not quite the same; the metaphors are familiar but the tone is less frivolous, more serious, sometimes biting, but the mask of objectivity, of generalized emotion, seems to be falling into place.

That paragraph in the second Master letter in which she describes her wonder at his treatment of her, "I don't know what you can do for it—thank you—Master—but if I had the Beard on my cheek—like you—and you had Daisy's petals—and you cared so for me . . ." is twisted around until it becomes an appeal for forgiveness in the third Master letter. She begs him to tell her the fault, pretends to be stricken by remorse, pleads that he tell her how to eradicate it. "Wonder stings me more than the Bee—who did never sting me—but made gay music with her might wherever I did go." This metaphor of the Bee is converted into an ironic quatrain, and it was sent to Samuel Bowles:

> I stole them from a Bee—*
> Because—Thee—
> Sweet plea—
> He pardoned me!

The poem she may have designed the quatrain to introduce is known to have been sent to Bowles at this time:

> Two swimmers wrestled on the spar—
> Until the morning sun—

* them refers to stings.

When One—turned smiling to the land—
Oh God! the Other One!

The stray ships—passing—
Spied a face—
Upon the waters borne—
With eyes in death—still begging raised—
And hands—beseeching—thrown!

The central metaphor here echoes that image in the final paragraph of the third Master letter: "Oh how the sailor strains when his boat is filling—oh how the dying tug, till the angel comes." The poem is strong enough, desperate enough, but depersonalized. This was a typical practice of the poet. What she asked for in her private writings, she asked for in her poetry, but always in metaphor. The appeal is detached from a concrete request. It is not possible, unless one knows the specific occasion out of which a poem emerged, to distinguish between an appeal for love, or an appeal that her poetry be accepted, or that her vision be affirmed, or her doubts allayed. But that she sent Bowles many, many petitions cannot be doubted. That she disguised the seminal truth about herself, finally, is actually stated, and to Bowles himself. This poem was found preserved among *his* papers. It is now in the manuscript collection of the Frost Library at Amherst College.

Going to Him! Happy letter!
Tell Him—
Tell Him the page I did'nt write—
Tell Him—I only said the Syntax—
And left the Verb and the pronoun out—
Tell Him just how the fingers hurried—
Then—how they waded—slow—slow—
And then you wished you had eyes in your pages—
So you could see what moved them so—

Tell Him—it was'nt a Practised Writer—
You guessed—from the way the sentence toiled—
You could hear the Boddice tug, behind you—
As if it held but the might of a child—
You almost pitied it—you—it worked so—
Tell Him—no—you may quibble there—

For it would split His Heart, to know it—
And then you and I, were silenter.

Tell Him—Night finished—before we finished—
And the Old Clock kept neighing "Day"!
And you—got sleepy—and begged to be ended—
What could it hinder so—to say?
Tell Him—just how she sealed you—Cautious!
But—if He ask where you are hid
Until tomorrow—Happy letter!
Gesture Coquette—and shake your Head!

So much then for what Emily Dickinson chose to communicate. We have seen how she proceeded to transform the raw response to a signal rejection of herself and her poetry into letters that strove to hide her suffering. We have seen that nevertheless she continued her efforts to convince this adamant judge, notwithstanding his public stand. She bent her creative powers to this service. She constructed appeals in metaphors but was careful to enliven her poetic pleas with an aura of gayety she knew now would not displease Mr. Bowles.

She did not screen the suffering from herself. This poem is written for Christ and there is no mask. It is a humble plea for help. That laden heart we recognize from the Master letter, she now, herself, offers to God:

Savior! I've no one else to tell—
And so I trouble *thee*
I am the one forgot thee so—
Dost thou remember me?
Nor, for myself, I came so far—
That were the little load—
I brought thee the imperial Heart
I had not strength to hold—
The Heart I carried in my own—
Till mine too heavy grew—
Yet—strangest—*heavier* since it went—
Is it too large for *you?*

A psychological transformation is taking place. Emily Dickinson abandons the Master who has abandoned her; she approaches another on whom she was to rely for the rest of her life. Her need was great. The familiar palsy of doubt unnerves her. She must turn to Christ, for having been abandoned by the Master she has no other. She depicts her demoralization in just the imagery of blood that lay ready for use in the Master letter:

> If *He dissolve*—then—there is *nothing more*—
> *Eclipse*—at *Midnight*—
> It was *dark*—*before*—
>
> *Sunset*—at *Easter*—
> *Blindness*—on the *Dawn*—
> *Faint* Star of Bethlehem—
> *Gone down!*
>
> *Would* but some *God*—*inform* Him—
> Or it be *too late!*
> Say—that the pulse *just lisps*—
> The *Chariots wait*—
>
> Say that a *little life*—for *His*—
> Is *leaking*—*red*—
> *His little Spaniel*—tell Him!
> *Will He heed?*

She was to use this image of the "Eclipse" for God when writing to Higginson; there it will be ironic display for the conventional God of her family; here she is reaching out for spiritual rejuvenation. This poem is transcribed into Fascicle 37. Just below it, on the same sheet of stationery, is an echo of her appeal for relief. The cry for forgiveness is converted to a contemplation at once rebellious and anguished.

> I think just how my shape will rise—
> When I shall be *"forgiven"*—
> Till Hair—and Eyes—and timid Head—
> Are *out of sight*—in Heaven—
>
> I think just how my lips will weigh—
> With shapeless—quivering—prayer—
> That you—*so late*—*"Consider" me*—
> The *"Sparrow"* of your Care—
>
> I mind me that of Anguish—sent—
> *Some* drifts were moved away—

> Before my simple bosom—broke—
> And why not *this*—if *they?*
>
> And so I con that thing—*"forgiven"*—
> Until—delirious—borne—
> By my long bright—and *longer—trust*—
> I *drop* my Heart—*unshriven!*

All the substance of the third Master letter, and the petition poems to Bowles become a source for metaphor here. She wryly speculates on her appeals for pardon and by a sad process of reasoning, displaces the mummery and the pretense. She is no longer a best little girl or a queen or a sailor; her cry for relief is addressed to God, and her intuition tells her to wait for heavenly grace, to let her heart drop unshriven by mortals and trust in an ultimate forgiveness: I recall, the poet is saying, that in other times when anguish came to me, my sorrow did eventually lift (the snow drifts did melt) and so I trust that this anguish too will be alleviated.

Emily Dickinson came to terms with her suffering by abandoning her faith in her Master and restoring her faith in God.[20] The following poem, already cited in context with the missed encounter, uses an imagery that is so much a part of this cluster of draft letters, actual letters and related poems, it is so much a poetic conclusion to this narrative of her signal experience, it bears repetition here:

> One Year ago—jots what?
> God—spell the word! I—cant—
> Was't Grace? Not that—
> Was't Glory? That—will do—
> Spell slower—Glory—
>
> Such Anniversary shall be—
> Sometimes—not often—in Eternity—
> When farther Parted, than the Common Wo—
> Look—feed upon each other's faces—so—
> In doubtful meal, if it be possible
> Their Banquet's real—
>
> I tasted—careless—then—
> I did not know the Wine
> Came once a World—Did you?

Oh, had you told me so—
This Thirst would blister—easier—now—
You said it hurt you—most—
Mine—was an Acorn's Breast—
And could not know how fondness grew
In Shaggier Vest—
Perhaps—I could'nt—
But, had you looked in—
A Giant—eye to eye with you, had been—
No Acorn—then—

So Twelve months ago—
We breathed—
Then dropped the Air—
Which bore it best?
Was this—the patientest—
Because it was a Child, you know—
And could not value—Air?

If to be "Elder"—mean most pain—
I'm old enough, today, I'm certain—then—
As old as thee—how soon?
One—Birthday more—or Ten?
Let me—choose!
Ah, Sir, None!

Letter #300 is the prose conclusion, written to Bowles in 1862:

Is it too late—now? [She is offering a copy of Browning] I should like
so much to remind you—how kind you had been to me.

You could choose—as you did before—if it would not be obnoxious
—except where you "measured by your heart," you should measure—
this time—by mine. I wonder which would be biggest!

. . . . Teach us to miss you less—because the fear to miss you more
haunts us—all the time. We did'nt care so much—once—I wish it was
then—now—but you kept tightening—so—it cant be stirred today—You
did'nt mean to be worse—did you? Was'nt it a mistake? Wont you
decide soon—to be the strong man we first knew? 'Twould lighten things
so much—and yet that man—was not so dear—I guess you'd better not.

There is a letter written to Bowles in 1874 which refers still to this past,
but now with utter coldness behind her mask of hyperbole:

I should think you would have few Letters for your own are so noble that they make men afraid—and sweet as your Approbation is—it is had in fear—lest your depth convict us.

You compel us each to remember that when Water ceases to rise—it has commenced falling. That is the law of Flood. The last Day that I saw you was the newest and oldest of my life.

Resurrection can come but once—first—to the same House. Thank you for leading us by it.

Come always, dear friend, but refrain from going. You spoke of not liking to be forgotten. Could you, tho' you would? Treason never knew you.[21]

Again the metaphor of the Sea and struggle ("Flood") and death by drowning which ends the old life and begins the new. Still the recollection of "Treason."

It seems difficult to accept at this distance from the world of Emily Dickinson that a rejection of her poetry, and the consequent loss of career could have caused that despair so poignantly revealed in her poems. Even knowing that her interpretation of that rejection was mingled with the sense that her person had also been offered and refused may not satisfy contemporary readers. But so it was. This poet could suffer from rejection of her poetry as much as a woman may suffer at the denial of a lover. This artist could believe in her art with the same fervor and single-mindedness we today associate with a romantic attachment. But couple this with a fantasy of love for the same person who could not do more than tolerate her poems, who at a critical juncture of her poetic history not merely forgot to be chivalrous, but—as she thought—exposed her to public shame, then the demoralization of Emily Dickinson is no longer incomprehensible. The quantity of poems left in her fascicles describing the phenomenon of death-in-life, picturing the despair as something far worse than actual death, is commensurate with the degree of her belief that she was a unique poet, an immortal poet.

She disagreed with the judgment of Samuel Bowles; she disagreed profoundly. She did make a second effort; she did seek another critical judgment—from the East—from a well-known literary man, but T. W. Higginson's opinion was the same. Her defense collapsed, and from that time on Emily Dickinson made no further attempt to convince anyone.

CHAPTER EIGHT

The Poetic Manner

It MAY BE TRUE, FOR WE IN OUR DAY ARE TAUGHT SO, THAT WHEN love is unwelcome the suitor begins to hate the beloved, restores his complacency by disparagement of his ardor. There is only one such poem in the entire canon of Emily Dickinson that can be cited on behalf of this theory.

> Art thou the thing I wanted?
> Begone—my Tooth has grown—
> Affront a minor palate
> Thou did'st not goad so long—
>
> I tell thee while I waited—
> The mystery of Food
> Increased till I abjured it
> Subsisting now like God—

May not a woman efface her shame with a more becoming nobility, by swearing an undying love, an eternal loyalty? Does not the delusion of the desirability of the beloved, the conception of him as unique, as irreplaceable, as the paragon of men, go as far to mitigate refusal? It is easier to believe the man is wrong than to admit she is a fool.

There are perhaps forty poems scattered through the fascicles that show how Emily Dickinson transfigured her shame into an impregnable devotion to Samuel Bowles.[1] When she transfers her hopes to Jesus it is difficult to distinguish between her master and her savior. And even when it is clear that Christ is the bridegroom, and immortality is the wedding gift, the fable is told in language that is the language of gallantry and chivalry, in metaphors that belong to sentimental adventures of ladies and gentlemen who ride out together, go to parties, pass quiet evenings by the hearth, or watch together through the silent midnight and waken together in the dawn.

This was the way Emily Dickinson chose to restore herself to patience and equanimity. If she could not have her beloved she would do without man. She shut her door. Only she herself was allowed inside her room where she sat down for the rest of her life to contemplate her meaning.

> The Soul selects her own Society—
> Then—shuts the Door—
> To her divine Majority—
> Present no more—
> Unmoved—she notes the Chariots—pausing—
> At her low Gate—
> Unmoved—an Emperor be kneeling
> Upon her Mat—
>
> I've known her—from an ample nation—
> Choose One—
> Then—close the Valves of her attention—
> Like Stone—

It was no easy pacification.

> I felt my life with both my hands
> To see if it was there—
> I held my spirit to the Glass,
> To prove it possibler—
>
> I turned my Being round and round
> And paused at every pound
> To ask the Owner's name—
> For doubt, that I should know the Sound—
>
> I judged my features—jarred my hair—
> I pushed my dimples by, and waited—
> If they—twinkled back—
> Conviction might, of me—
>
> I told myself, "Take Courage, Friend—
> That—was a former time—
> But we might learn to like the Heaven,
> As well as our Old Home!"

All are familiar with the funeral poems of Emily Dickinson's conception of her living death.

> I felt a Funeral, in my Brain,
> And Mourners to and fro
> Kept treading—treading—till it seemed
> That Sense was breaking through—
>
> And when they all were seated,
> A Service, like a Drum—
> Kept beating—beating—till I thought
> My Mind was going numb—
>
> And then I heard them lift a Box
> And creak across my Soul
> With those same Boots of Lead, again,
> Then Space—began to toll,
>
> As all the Heavens were a Bell,
> And Being, but an Ear,
> And I, and Silence, some strange Race
> Wrecked, solitary, here—
>
> And then a Plank in Reason, broke,
> And I dropped down, and down—
> And hit a World, at every plunge,
> And Finished knowing—then—

But she did survive. It was her own nature, her solitary self that gave her strength:

> No Rack can torture me—
> My Soul—at Liberty—
> Behind this mortal Bone
> There knits a bolder One—
>
> You Cannot prick with saw—
> Nor pierce with Cimitar—
> Two Bodies—therefore be—
> Bind One—The Other fly—
>
> The Eagle of his Nest
> No easier divest—

And gain the Sky
Than Mayest Thou—

Except Thyself may be
Thine Enemy—
Captivity is Consciousness—
So's Liberty.

. . .

Growth of Man—like Growth of Nature—[2]
Gravitates within—
Atmosphere, and Sun endorse it—
But it stir—alone—

Each—it's difficult Ideal
Must achieve—Itself—
Through the solitary prowess
Of a Silent Life—

Effort—is the sole condition—
Patience of Itself—
Patience of opposing forces—
And intact Belief—

Looking on—is the Department
Of it's Audience—
But Transaction—is assisted
By no Countenance—

Her religious consecration healed her:

I live with Him—I see His face—
I go no more away
For Visiter—or Sundown—
Death's single privacy

The Only One—forestalling Mine—
And that—by Right that He
Presents a Claim invisible—
No Wedlock—granted Me—

I live with Him—I hear His Voice—
I stand alive—Today—
To witness to the Certainty
Of Immortality—

Taught Me—by Time—the lower Way
Conviction—Every day—
That Life like This—is stopless—
Be Judgment—what it may—

In the poem with which I conclude this cluster, Emily Dickinson presents a heraldic cry of commitment:

Because I could not stop for Death—
He kindly stopped for me—
The Carriage held but just Ourselves—
And Immortality.

We slowly drove—He knew no haste
And I had put away
My labor and my leisure too,
For His Civility—

We passed the School, where Children strove
At Recess—in the Ring—
We passed the Fields of Gazing Grain—
We passed the Setting Sun—

Or rather—He passed Us—
The Dews drew quivering and chill—
For only Gossamer, my Gown—
My Tippet—only Tulle—

We paused before a House that seemed
A Swelling of the Ground—
The Roof was scarcely visible—
The Cornice—in the Ground—

Since then—'tis Centuries—and yet
Feels shorter than the Day
I first surmised the Horses Heads
Were toward Eternity—

It is crucial to notice that her word is "paused" at the grave (there is no alternative choice); she drives on, with Immortality beside her into Eternity. There is no burial. Now she abandons the world which had abandoned her, and with it the labors that are always part of public life. Her fears of setting sun are transcended. No leisure is to be hers: she devotes herself to poetry. What was Death-in-life came in the guise of that crucial encounter, but it tempered her soul and she survives as a poet.

Within her house, within her garden, in her own experience, lay the germ of a thousand and more poems. She survives to transform all that she sees and thinks and feels into poetry. But the occasion of her own signal rejection—of herself and her poetry—was always primary. She wrote and rewrote, she examined and re-examined all that had occurred; she spoke to herself and of herself without duplicity. She knew she had confronted more than rejection—it was a genuine bereavement. Contemplating at length and at length the meaning of herself and the fate of her poetry, pondering the relationship between her heart and her spirit—over which she kept such diligent watch—she eventually came to the place in her poetic history where she dissolved the distinction between herself and her art. Believing that her power came from God, her poetic power seemed to her to be Godlike. If her soul were immortal, then the product of her soul—her poems—would achieve lasting fame, would in fact be the medium on earth by which she would experience terrestrial immortality.

> The Poets light but Lamps—
> Themselves—go out—
> The Wicks they stimulate—
> If vital Light
>
> Inhere as do the Suns—
> Each Age a Lens
> Disseminating their
> Circumference—

It was out of this very simultaneity of vision of the poet and the poetry that the unique style of Emily Dickinson was forged. She was at once the poet of occasions and the prophet of universal truth. It was the events in her immediate experience that taught her the meaning of reality. A letter, or something she read in a newspaper or magazine, something she heard—the song of a bird, the voices of children, the rustling of leaves—something she saw—blossoms, sunset, rain, snowflakes, a train, a carriage—something she remembered—anything at all could ignite her imagination: she made a poem of it. Often this poem itself became the occasion for another reflection and still another poem.

She understood so well that the source of her poetic inspiration was Heaven, and the meaning therefore of her poems was truth, that she was completely at ease with the materials of her poems. Nothing was banal or trivial; any object in Nature, anything she felt indoors or out, was significant. She was philosophically at ease with the issue of her intuition as the instrument of knowledge. She courted spontaneity and the form of her poetry was for her a sign of true perception. Thus her originality never troubled her.

Nor was she concerned with the problem of consistency. A bird may in one case be simply a bird; another time it may be a symbol of the song of the poet, singing of Heaven or Eternity; it may be a sign of regeneration of nature, or redemption of man; a bird may render as well the inaccessibility of the Divine. Indeed, the poet operated freely within a conglomerate of interchangeable personae and meanings. One poem did not cancel another; taken together the poems extended the scope of her awareness. They enriched one another.

A bird may be preceptor or example. The poet may be a woman given to tears, a bard whose mission is the proclamation of the truth, or a mortal, subject to decay. What flies from the grasp of the persona may be a crumb, a ducat, leaves, light, lover, editor, fame, revelation, release; but always there is a pattern in the rendering of Emily Dickinson's subject matter: flight and return. This is the pattern into which she fits all experience. Always there is a presence, a loss, then the assurance of some ultimate re-encounter, some ultimate union. The hungry will be fed, royal gifts will be granted, light will return with the dawn, Jesus will embrace the deprived, publication will come, the truth will be revealed, resurrection is guaranteed: redemption is secure.

And the period of the second Master letter and the poems written subsequent to the experience that lay embedded there, brought into flowering a poetry that was in a very real sense a metaphor of her experience. To point this out has been the primary justification for having dwelled at length on the personal conflict of Emily Dickinson. For it was

just this conflict that was transformed into the poetic manner so characteristic of her best-wrought poems. It was fixed, as was her way of life, by
the time she wrote to Thomas Higginson.

Many of the poems written before 1860 described death as a sad
withdrawal into another realm. There were wrestlings with uncertainty
as to the nature of that other realm, but always some sense of affirmation
was present. There are none that deny immortality to mortal man. Poems
about Heaven were never sardonic, though there was at times an air of
gay irreverence.

After 1860–1861 the occasion of death is concrete: it is the death of
the poet. It is not the meaning of death as a phenomenon, but the
experience of spiritual annihilation rendered in physical terms. The religious poems change from theoretic affirmations to renderings of Heaven.
The place is populated with angels and martyrs and Jesus, and the poet
arrives there in poem after poem, bringing with her the burden of
suffering and anguish for alleviation and release.

Poems that were metaphors for personal experience were usually
depictions of forceful acts by gamblers, striving sailors, travelers, singers.
Among them were of course those proclaiming the poet to be the spokesman for nature or the interpreter of truth. The later poems depict the
person of Emily Dickinson either on active voyage to the place of healing
or immobilized, still. And with this there occurs a crucial change in the
image of herself: the metaphor of the beggar begins to give way to the
metaphor of royalty. There is a great increase in the sheer number of
poems proclaiming herself as committed artist.

And within the wide spectrum of emotions (replacing the simpler
mask of ironic protestation) it is among those poems where a tone of
patience and a growing chorale of self-assurance prevails, that we find the
lyrics of challenge to all who would deny her a place in this cherished
realm of art. Only once [3] does she falter. She announces with certainty,
with exultation, that she is a Bard in "Just lost, when I was saved!" "Tho'
my destiny be Fustian," "I cautious, scanned my little life," "If I could
bribe them by a Rose," "The thought beneath so slight a film," "I taste a
liquor never brewed," "I've nothing else—to bring, You know,"
"We—Bee and I—live by the quaffing," "The Lamp burns sure—within,"
"I shall keep singing!" "Of Bronze—and Blaze," "I got so I could hear his
name," "Unto like Story—Trouble has enticed me," "It's like the Light,"
"Alone, I cannot be," "The Soul's Superior instants," "Of all the Sounds

despatched abroad," "There came a Day at Summer's full," "Is Bliss then, such Abyss," "My Reward for Being, was This," "The Day that I was crowned," "I'm saying every day," "Reverse cannot befall," and so on and on. Let this poem stand as a paradigm for all the others:

> Dare you see a Soul *at the White Heat?*
> Then crouch within the door —
> Red — is the Fire's common tint —
> But when the vivid Ore
> Has vanquished Flame's conditions,
> It quivers from the Forge
> Without a color, but the light
> Of unannointed Blaze.
> Least Village has it's Blacksmith
> Whose Anvil's even ring
> Stands symbol for the finer Forge
> That soundless tugs — within —
> Refining these impatient Ores
> With Hammer, and with Blaze
> Until the Designated Light
> Repudiate the Forge —

And surely related to this is the fact that earlier her lyrics of captivity, of the cage, give way to celebrations of release, release not to be found in Heaven merely, but in the realm of poesy: "My Business, with the Cloud, / If any Power behind it be." I wish to emphasize that this shift is simultaneous with the experience of bereavement, the result of her rejection, and has nothing to do with those poems projecting her death, or rendering her existence as death in life. The poems about the woman are cries of anguish and despair; those poems of dedication and self-assurance are the songs of the bard.

But the most interesting phenomenon is the alteration of the form of the poetry itself. There is no more profound thought than before, no greater philosophical insight; there is a new conjoining of thought and feeling.

After 1860–1861 her formal design began to take on a greater magnitude; there was an expansion from the rendering of an idea by developing a single metaphor, to rendering a relationship between a physical occurrence and a spiritual or theoretical idea. Emily Dickinson added to her organic conception of form a new mode, the disjunctive structure. This consists of two or more simultaneously expanding metaphors, creating a double or even a multiple movement that required a new kind of reading. One responds to this, not with belief, not even compassion, but with a willingness to take a leap across concurrent terms of an analogy. The value of such poetry is not the quality in the rendering of an idea but the manifestation of a new source of poetic power—the vitality that is generated in the reader.

The crucial experience of the search for publication, between 1858 and 1862, was divided into two periods, corresponding to these two kinds of poetry, the single logically expanding metaphor and the allegory of the disjunctive mode. During 1858–1859, the time of the first Master letter (Bowles the central target) the poems about Nature prevailed, the lyrics of flowers, of birds, of gardens, hills, spring, or sunrise. Here were the contemplative observations of changes in season, of shifting spans of time, and the avowal of Nature as the sign of regeneration. During 1860–1862, the time of the second and third Master letters (Bowles still the central target) the natural world becomes a setting for personal experience; its creatures, its phenomena demonstrate the idea of regeneration but as a counterpoint to the idea of spiritual redemption. Allegorical poems now range across an entire spectrum of personal response to a single experience: from strident appeals, to suffering at deprivation, to patience, to affirmation of love of a different sort; from hope to despair to cynicism, to exultation of a new kind; from fear to disillusion to bitterness to ironic detachment to ultimate and impregnable commitment.

The first stage in Emily Dickinson's evolving poetic style may be demonstrated by one of the simplest poems taken from the early period; it is dated by Johnson "1858."

> Frequently the woods are pink—
> Frequently are brown
> Frequently the hills undress
> Behind my native town.
> Oft a head is crested
> I was wont to see—
> And as oft a cranny
> Where it used to be—
> And the Earth—they tell me—
> On it's Axis turned!
> Wonderful Rotation!
> By but *twelve* performed!

This poem has exactly the subject matter described in the first Master letter. It is precisely a description of seasonal change. In Spring, trees so abundant on the hills surrounding Amherst, blossom into a pink haze on the horizon. Their fading into brown is the autumnal image. Leafiness is not stressed, but rather the color of collective trees as "woods." The image shifts to hills, from the massed foliage to the more open contour of hills, and the poet renders the gradual onset of winter by describing it as an act of a girlish hillside, undressing behind the native town.

Why did she shift from color to such an act? Why yoke two such disparates as "hills" and "undress" if not to imply the act of dressing again. Thus the logic of the metaphor renders the return of Spring.

The second quatrain concretizes the image further. The woods first modulate to hills; the woods now modulate to a single tree. This tree, crested, sports a full helmet trimmed with feathers—a tree in full summer regalia. When the tree removes its covering, chinks or fissures in the space appear—it is winter again. In just such a passage of imagery Emily Dickinson has rendered four seasons. There are in fact five, for the onset of winter is described twice. Just as "undressing" implies dressing again, this repetition of the winter image renders Rotation itself, before the poet has even mentioned it.

The last quatrain, seemingly so much a shift from the physical to the theoretical, actually is not. For it is because of their appearance and the changes in their appearance that they—the particular and physical scene—they—the woods and hills—tell the poet a truth about Nature: that the earth rotates around the sun, that the earth has turned on its Axis and has at the same time moved around the sun. This is an eminently physical act but one which cannot possibly be seen, only assumed to have occurred from its effect. And this phenomenon is again brought down from the abstract when the image of theatrical performance is examined.

Rotation is "performed" by a mere twelve, an expansion of the earlier undressing image and at the same time an enlarging of four seasons to twelve months of the year. The twelve months become performers—their show is the woods turning pink, turning brown, the hills go backstage to change costume, trees come out in plumed helmet—the hill-stage setting changes to a backdrop of barren and ridged terrain.

Surely there is no novel philosophic insight here, no new truth said; surely hills and trees and seasonal change are banal materials. But just that organic development out of a simple image into a sensuous experience, in this case visual, into a concrete physical action, in this case a mummery, into an abstract generalized occurrence, real enough but discernible only through its consequence, is not banal, not trivial.

The following poem, written after the events of 1860, will serve to demonstrate the enrichment of the form.

Again—his voice is at the door—
I feel the old *Degree*—
I hear him ask the servant
For such an one—as me—

I take a *flower*—as I go—
My face to *justify*—
He never *saw* me—*in this life*—
I might *surprise* his eye!

I cross the Hall with *mingled* steps—
I—silent—pass the door—
I look on all this world *contains*—
Just his face—nothing more!

We talk in *careless*—and in *toss*—
A kind of *plummet* strain—
Each—sounding—shily—
Just-how deep—
The other's *one*—had been—

We *walk*—I leave my Dog—at home—
A tender—thoughtful Moon
Goes with us—just a little way—
And—then—we are *alone*—

Alone—if *Angels* are "alone"—
First time they *try* the *sky!*
Alone—if those "vailed faces"—be—
We cannot *count*—on High!

I'd give—to live that hour—*again*—
The *purple—in my Vein*—
But *He* must *count the drops—himself*—
My price for *every stain!*

To know who the poet is about to meet is less important than to be aware of her manner of rendering the confrontation. Her excitement at his arrival is first signaled to us by that seemingly exultant "Again" and its effect: "I feel the old Degree." We think we have before us the revelation at last of Emily Dickinson and her beloved. Well, in fact, we do, but it is her experience that she will recount, after all, and not our conventional interpretation of meetings that is about to be fulfilled. For the poet begins, in the third line, her practice of veering to the opposite of what one expects to follow. She delays her own and our entry into the room by having him ask the servant for her; by just that narrative pause at the sound of his voice, she intensifies our expectation.

His delay is natural enough but hers is an artifice; she catches up a flower that she hopes will belie her pallor; she puts a brake on her excitement. But "I take a flower" is followed by "as I go," and there, in the midst of delay, is a swift and sudden motion. And added to this is another dimension, a sign of another emotion, timidity, potential we see now, for there is that phrase in the first stanza, "For such an one—as me." So very womanly after all, she thinks at such a moment, in all her excitement, that she will not look very pretty. He might be led to think her lack of color is due to the unusual brightness of the flower she carries in her hand. She has faded in her new life. And that small phrase, "in this life" serves a double purpose; it gives the poet a reason for her nervousness and it supplies the reader with a new piece of information, that they have been separated, that they have not been close, because a new life has intervened.

Consider the rendering in just that second quatrain: the sensuous detail, the emotion of vanity, the hint given of events that may have preceded this meeting, the pause and then the speeding up of motion—all at once. This is not all. There is the juxtaposing of flower and face, but with an ellipse for face, for it is "I might surprise his eye!" that we are given—*we* have to understand "face." And at the same time, that coupling of flower and eye thrusts us closer to the meeting: his voice, his eye. It is his face that she will name. In just this way the leap across from the woman to the man is effected.

Her steps are "mingled"—confused, as the Lexicon says—so that indeed she *passes* the door. The poet here has rendered a kinesthetic act with just the words "mingled" and "pass." His speech is paralleled by her silence.

All this excitement and expectation, this immediacy of confrontation, culminates in her direct open statement: "I look on all this world contains— / Just his face—nothing more!" Hyperbole? Spasmodic? Sentimental? Not Emily Dickinson. The next line is as unexpected, as polar to what came before, as distant as it is possible to be. And therein resides the vitality of this poem, in this whirl caused by the use of the unexpected.

> We talk in careless—and in toss—
> A kind of plummet strain—

Not only is that word "plummet" a lead weight, and as such as far from the flower as may be, but the outcome of her flush, her vanity, her confusion is witty repartee, a kind of intellectual exchange. No embrace, no heartfelt emotional greeting, but a bantering conversation. "Strain" means style, or a manner of speaking or writing. Each tries to trip up the other; each tries to perceive a double meaning, to find something lurking below the surface of the words. And all this is preparation for the more active search for hidden meaning that follows.

The words used to describe the conversation are active enough: toss, plummet, deep; and the poet and her companion, having paused for volatile talk, take action at last, action that is polar to our expectation as it is different from their speech: they walk out of the house, out into darkness and privacy and silence where their isolation, not from the world but from each other, becomes complete.

The dog is left behind, and that is a deliberate act. We have met Emily Dickinson's dog Carlo many times: proffered company to Mr. Bowles, proffered company to the Master, defended as best companion to Mr. Higginson. Here, to render an approaching encounter as potentially private, hopefully as needful of privacy, the dog is left back. The moon acts on their behalf; note it is the moon that is tender and thoughtful, not the one we might expect to be. It retreats from the scene and they are in utter privacy, where there is no talk, no light, where there is—what? Emily Dickinson does tell but it is wholly unexpected. She shifts to angels, linking her experience and theirs with the word "alone."

> And—then—we are alone—
> Alone—if Angels are "alone"—
> First time they try the sky!

Whatever else it is, it is not sensual, not personal; it is a heavenly experience. Her metaphor for her state of being with the beloved is strangely enough like that of an angel alone with God. But angels, when they are trying the sky, are, after all, dead. And in fact, in the last stanza she does think of her own death. The "He" of the final quatrain is God.

> I'd give—to live that hour—again—
> The purple—in my Vein—
> But He must count the drops—himself—
> My price for every stain!

That repetition of the word "again" (in the first quatrain and in the last quatrain) establishes two piers across which a bridge is flung, a bridge of time. From the moment of that first sound of his voice, across all that present-tense immediacy, she brings these two companions so close, and then suddenly, at the last moment, at the last stanza, she leaps over the event and sets herself down in Heaven at the moment of her redemption. Why? Following the lines established by the analogy, we may learn why. As she had, running to him, passed the door, as she had, gazing with so much emotion on his face, sat down to talk in banter, so perhaps she, walking out with him, experienced separation, not union at all.

And that sudden outrush of blood, intruding into the final stanza, puts a kind of grotesque image between us and the encounter, between Emily Dickinson and the beloved, between Emily Dickinson and God. It is the same blood that rose to "the old Degree," that blush of excitement in the first stanza, but now it is converted to a slow drop by drop by drop of anguish.

Emily Dickinson does not tell us what happened; she renders the feeling she has about what happened; she depicts motion, and that movement is not one of drawing close, woman to man, but the experience of the poet only, in metaphor of rising upward: from the old horizontal motion (entering the room, walking out of the house), there is now a vertical soaring (or departure) from Moon to sky to Angels, and higher still, to the sky full of stars. The fact that the same word "count" is used for the numbering of stars in the sky (infinite) and the drops of blood in her veins (numberless) signifies that we mortals have no way to count the stars; and implies that He (God, omnipotent) will have the way to count the drops of blood.

And the poem has made an even greater disjunctive leap. Crossing time, having done with space, there is added to these expansions an obverse movement of contraction, analogous to the contraction of the blood into drops. That word "stain" refers both to blood and to hours. Every hour since that meeting has been like a slow dripping of her anguish, a suffering. "Price" in the Lexicon is more than value or estimation of worth, it is more than reward or cost; it is "the price of redemption, the atonement of Jesus Christ." And "stain" in her Lexicon is more than taint of guilt, but disgrace, reproach, shame. I'd give, the poet says, my life to live that hour again; but that is in God's hands; and God will value me for the disgrace I have suffered, the shame I have suffered, and He will redeem me; I have atoned with my blood. This is certainly not a metaphor of exultation.

It is not the truth of her history that makes this a lyric of great power. "Again his voice is at the door" has an extraordinary complexity of movement: that erratic motion, that whirling to a knot, that slow sinuous unwinding to the cut-off, which is the real strength of Emily Dickinson's poetic manner. The peripheral implication, always embedded somewhere in what came before, is always, somehow, used. Unconventional as the means for achieving unity may seem, nevertheless it is unity that results. That is the unique contribution of her poetic style—a new conception of the interplay between the parts and the whole—a disjunctive unity for which the reader's participation is a necessary instrument. Such a meeting never happened again. But in the poem it happens as often as one will read. It is fixed, that moment in time, to recur endlessly; the motion, the life is embedded in the form itself.

Of course all the imagery of the Master letter is contained in this and dozens of variant poems in the fascicles. Whatsoever name we supply for the man with the voice, whether the image engraved on her memory was that of a soldier, a lawyer, a tutor, a minister, an editor, a woman out of the West—all have been conjectured, each has been proved—the facts of the experience must be distinguished from the feelings of the experience. Were we within seven feet of that stage where Emily Dickinson's drama was unfolding, we would have been less wise than the man himself, so skillfully were curtains drawn by the poet whose gnomic utterances were her own contrivance to shield her from any public eye. Even her beloved companion was not to know.

But her feelings, precisely what that moment in time meant to this poet, she has done all in her power to expose. And that is her gift, the rendering of the concrete, the single specific experience with a multiplicity of countervailing images, totally unexpected but potential in the movement and countermovement created by locked opposites, out of which springs a poem that is endlessly vibrating. It is this vitality that casts the banal in an original light.

All this we have said of a love poem, a conventional enough subject matter, but treated in so unique a manner as to cause us to alter the phrase to read "an ostensible love poem" by Emily Dickinson. To verify that this is the style let us take an even more hackneyed subject. Nothing is so commonplace as lamentation at the death of a loved one.

> These—saw Visions—
> Latch them softly—
> These—held Dimples—
> Smooth them slow—
> This—addressed departing accents—
> Quick—Sweet Mouth—to miss thee so—
>
> This—We stroked—
> Unnumbered Satin—
> These—we held among our own—
> Fingers of the Slim Aurora—
> Not so arrogant—this Noon—
>
> These—adjust—that ran to meet us—
> Pearl—for Stocking—Pearl for Shoe—
> Paradise—the only Palace
> Fit for Her reception—now—

A woman lies dead. The crisis is past. Her soul is in Paradise. So much for subject matter analysis. There is really no more to say about the theme of this poem. Let us see how Emily Dickinson can vitalize this corpse.

The poem is everywhere in motion. The persona is literally busy preparing the corpse for burial. First the eyes: realizing how in life they had been able to see remarkable sights—Visions—the person nevertheless knows they can no longer close themselves, the eyelids must be brought down by an external hand, gently for tenderness of the dead, gently because they must not spring back. They must not, as well as can not, open again; they are latched. Next the cheeks which once were mobile enough to dimple and smooth themselves; now they must be smoothed by an external hand striving to bring the skin out to a rounded shape. It is not easy to do this on the cheek of the corpse. It must be done slowly, carefully. Next the mouth that will no more be saying those small goodbyes we are accustomed to hear in the ordinary world. The word "accent" has this implication. And with the first quick movement to occur in this arrangement of the face and figure of the departed one, the persona bends to bestow a last kiss—it must be a quick motion, must it not, this kissing of the dead? But the outcry of the person is not fleeting, "to miss thee so." Now the process is resumed: the hand—not the palm, the hands are being placed in position—that had been soothed when the dead girl lived had—has still—a quality of satin, now become a grade of cool—cold—silk; no merchant can assign it a quality. The fingers too, once held by the person, must be arranged; they no longer are active, these slender fingers of the dead, not now, not at this hour of death (Noon) before which the goddess of dawn or twilight has no power to stand. Finally the feet must be adjusted; the feet that had been able to run now cannot and so need no real shoes, no real stockings, but are already clothed in frozen silk (pearl), and only frozen silk is needed for the kind of walking she will do in Paradise, for which now she has been made ready. The outcry, to miss thee so, reappears here in another emotional speculation, "that ran to meet us—" Now the feet will, well, not run exactly, but walk barefoot on Emily Dickinson's favorite piazza, the jasper floor in the palace of heaven. That last image retains the idea of utter immobilization, for this dead girl does not walk off to Paradise; she is received; the active force has been transferred from the person arranging, to the place receiving. For the greater vision that will await her in Paradise mortal eyes are not needed. Mortal garments are not needed.

The next action we know by implication only; it comes from the shift, the enormous shift—leap—from the preparation of the body, presumably in a small room, out to a vast realm, out to Paradise, for which a probability had been established by the unobtrusive (in its context) word, Aurora, a sky goddess. Her soul is going to Paradise; the corpse will be transported to the grave.

Precisely how the expanding metaphor operates has been traced in detail. To see the genuine skill of Emily Dickinson we must restate the most significant feature of her style. I have said the style is a metaphor of the theme. The theme here is not the subject matter, not the death of a person and the transfer of her soul to heaven. It is the relationship between the state of mortality and the state of immortality, the relationship between transience and permanence. The multiple strands of the expanding metaphor render just this idea. Let us chart them:

eyes	visions	the "real place"
cheeks	dimples	peace
mouth	speech	silence
hands	soft	frozen
fingers	arrogant	still
feet	ran	immobile
	to us	to a Palace
the bier	the persona	Paradise

The person on the bier is inactive; her body only may be looked at, arranged. It is the person looking on who is active, doing the arranging, remembering, feeling the loss. The other world is entirely static, permanent, fixed: see the words that are used—peace, silence, frozen, still, immobile. And the transition between the two lines, of action and inaction, is the death.

To be sure, there are experiments with a device unlike the one operating in "These—saw Visions—" or in "Again—his voice is at the door—" Another reaction to the experience of deprivation of a loved one occurs as the subject matter of "Severer Service of myself," but the method of rendering the affliction is different, for operating here is a wandering metaphor, not easily discerned, not so pleasing, not so convincing, not nearly as inevitable as the death that was the generating cause.

> Severer Service of myself
> I—hastened to demand
> To fill the awful Vacuum
> Your life had left behind—
>
> I worried Nature with my Wheels
> When Her's had ceased to run—
> When she had put away Her Work
> My own had just begun.
>
> I strove to weary Brain and Bone—
> To harass to fatigue

The glittering Retinue of nerves —
Vitality to clog

To some dull comfort Those obtain
Who put a Head away
They knew the Hair to —
And forget the color of the Day —

Affliction would not be appeased —
The Darkness braced as firm
As all my strategem had been
The Midnight to confirm —

No Drug for Consciousness — can be —
Alternative to die
Is Nature's only Pharmacy
For Being's Malady —

In the first stanza the poet decides to work harder in order to fill up the vacancy caused by her loss. The next two stanzas describe the kind of work, perhaps spinning, perhaps writing poems, or perhaps the mere generalized "Rotation, revolution; turn; as, the vicissitude and wheel of things," as the 1847 Lexicon puts it, but actually working late at the task, as the subsequent lines put it, working late into the night, after nightfall as opposed to Nature's work, which is described as a daylight process ending when the wheeling sun goes down and Nature's daywork has been put away. The next stanza does tell of the poet's effort to tire herself out so that her nervous system will become weary and so clog her vitality, her sleeplessness. This metaphor is directly opposed to the image of the first stanza, where work has been pictured as filling an empty space. The fourth stanza veers away from both metaphors (the vacuum-clog, the work of Nature, the work of the poet) to a speculation of how others who have lost find solace. It is at this point, with these lines,

Who put a Head away
They knew the Hair to —
And forget the color of the Day —

that the poet shoots the poem. The narrative has been halted for a comparison between the "I" and "Those"; up to this point it has been "I" and "You" (the lost one) and "I" and "Nature" and the narrative has depicted "I" wrestling with affliction. But now in this stanza the metaphors joggle and boggle. There is no good link between the awful vacuum that the plaintive sufferer seeks to fill and the comfort of those dull ones who can bury a head (ludicrous image at best, grotesque at worst), who can forget what the hair on that head was like, forget what the color of day was like (opposed, it is true, to the Midnight of the poet). One can say, well, Head has its precedent term in Brain, hair has it precedent term in the Retinue of nerves—maybe so. But if so, then the poet's sleepless brain does not too nicely adjust to that bundled-off head.

The poet has been unable to appease her affliction. From stanza 5 on, the darkness transforms to a darkness of the spirit; and all her strategy to outwit the dark merely confirmed that midnight to which her awareness had arrived. Now the final stanza yokes the idea of work to the idea of a drug, not an anodyne but a soporific, to dull the conscious self, in terms prepared for, it is true, by the retinue of nerves of stanza 3, but not reaching as far back as stanza 1. The only drug for that clogging of her vitality would be death, and at this point death is spoken of as the drug in the pharmacy of Nature; it is a leap, to be sure, that leap from the diurnal Nature of stanza 2 to Nature as a drugstore.

Obviously, not every poem works. When one does not it is because of the faltering imagery, never because of the trivial subject matter. Certainly this subject was not trivial, not frivolous. Take the poems with the most banal, the most trite and hackneyed themes we can find, they will be great poems nevertheless because of the manner of rendering. We are familiar with Emily Dickinson's snake, her locomotive, her robins and crocuses and clover, her snowflakes, her frost, her sunsets and autumn days; familiar, too, are her lamentations, her pleas, her exorcisms, her prayers, her elegies and eulogies. We know she has the same power to display in her poems that neither teach nor preach.

> A Bird came down the Walk—
> He did not know I saw—
> He bit an Angleworm in halves
> And ate the fellow, raw.
>
> And then he drank a Dew
> From a convenient Grass—

And then hopped sidewise to the Wall
To let a Beetle pass—

He glanced with rapid eyes
That hurried all around—
They looked like frightened Beads, I thought—
He stirred his Velvet Head

Like one in danger, Cautious,
I offered him a Crumb
And he unrolled his feathers
And rowed him softer home—

Than Oars divide the Ocean,
Too silver for a seam—
Or Butterflies, off Banks of Noon
Leap, plashless as they swim.

This poem has no message, no lesson; it has no biographical or historical significance. But for itself we cherish it. That bird is a real bird; he eats and drinks and jerks about as birds do when they are on the ground; he flies off with a different kind of motion, it is true, but so do real birds fly.

Her ideas are not profound; they offered no special challenge to the nineteenth-century mind. She sought to find a public hearing for a style of poetry that had simply no place whatsoever in the literature of that time. There was no tradition for Emily Dickinson. In the 1860's not Higginson, not Bowles, not Emerson, no one could have saved her from contemporaneous oblivion.

We look today with respect upon her isolation, surely feel compassion for her suffering. But we know that whatever the price she paid in despair, she chose well. She righted her emotions in time; she adjusted them so that she might survive in her world. No one need be fooled by her mask. She was diffident of nothing. Knowing herself to be in possession of a gift given her to transmit to the world, it was the refusal of the world to receive the bequest that tortured her, never the quality or value of the gift itself. Once achieved, she never altered her poetic style. She recognized and accepted and ultimately scorned her failure, and she proceeded. She never ceased to believe in her ultimate vindication and she was right.

CHAPTER NINE

The Practice of Poetry

Emily Dickinson did not ever grow to respect the taste or judgment of her world. She dressed in the white garments of the bride of the Man of Calvary and consecrated her soul to the service of higher truths, higher than any reached by those below who enjoyed the satisfaction of a present fame. And she nursed her indifference in this manner:

> Publication—is the Auction
> Of the Mind of Man—
> Poverty—be justifying
> For so foul a thing
>
> Possibly—but We—would rather
> From Our Garret go
> White—Unto the White Creator—
> Than invest—Our Snow—
>
> Thought belong to Him who gave it—
> Then—to Him Who bear
> It's Corporeal illustration—Sell
> The Royal Air—
>
> In the Parcel—Be the Merchant
> Of the Heavenly Grace—
> But reduce no Human Spirit
> To Disgrace of Price—

And when she herself lapsed from her impregnability, when she did succumb, did in fact get published in the *Springfield Republican,* she had the good sense to know exactly what she had achieved, precisely nothing:

I sometimes drop it, for a Quick—
The Thought to be alive—
Anonymous Delight to know—
And Madder—to concieve—

Consoles a Wo so monstrous
That did it tear all Day,
Without an instant's Respite—
'Twould look too far—to Die—

Delirium—diverts the Wretch
For Whom the Scaffold neighs—
The Hammock's Motion lulls the Heads
So close on Paradise—

A Reef—crawled easy from the Sea
Eats off the Brittle Line—
The Sailor does'nt know the Stroke—
Until He's past the Pain—

It was a solace and it did console her.

She had another source of comfort. She read. Not widely, not wisely, but considering what poems she left to a later world, she read well. That she knew her Lexicon has I think been amply demonstrated. That she knew her Bible and her Hymnbook is obvious. What else did she know? Where did she learn her craft? Emily Dickinson's literary influences are as much a surprise as anything one can say about this unique poet.

In 1938 George Whicher published the first biography that attempted to synthesize everything that was known about the poet and everything that had been said about her poetry; he devoted an entire chapter of *This Was a Poet* to Emily Dickinson's reading. Obtaining special permission from the private owners, he examined her letters, published and unpublished, studied the titles of the books in the libraries accumulated by her father and brother, in order to compile for the first time a list of the literary works known to the poet. The list is not inspiring to those who require their great poets to read great poetry.

He notes how often Emily Dickinson described her pleasure at reading the sentimental fiction of her time: Ik Marvel, Rebecca Harding Davis, Harriet Prescott Spofford, Helen Hunt Jackson, Lady Georgiana

Fullerton. Among American writers of greater stature she knew of Irving, Bryant, Longfellow, Whittier, Emerson, Lowell, Holmes, Thoreau, Hawthorne, Harriet Beecher Stowe, James, and Howells. He lists British poets and prose writers of disconnected time and place: Walpole, Kingsley, Dickens, Ruskin, Browne, Carlyle and Milton, Burns, Goldsmith, Thomson, Young, Tennyson, Coventry Patmore, Byron, Wordsworth, Keats, and Shakespeare; George Eliot, Charlotte and Emily Brontë, Mrs. Gaskell, Elizabeth and Robert Browning. How much of any of these writers she read we cannot say; they were all represented in the family library, but they all were published in *Harper's* and the *Atlantic Monthly* as well. And Whicher tells us that Emily Dickinson read with interest and enthusiasm the *Atlantic Monthly, Harper's Magazine* and *Scribner's Monthly* regularly. She also read daily the *Springfield Republican,* and weekly the *Hampshire and Franklin Express,* and its successor, the *Amherst Record,* as well as the *Hampshire Gazette,* a Northampton paper.

Over this listing, subsequent writers on Emily Dickinson have always paused, and for one reason or another chosen one type of literature, or a single writer, in order to trace parallels. Whicher himself believed the influence of Emerson was strong. He acknowledges too the possibility of the metaphysical poets,[1] but does not claim more than this.

> any allusion from her to the religious poets of the seventeenth century would be of particular interest because of the close parallel between her work and that of Donne, Herbert, and Vaughan. . . . But her only reference to any of the "metaphysical" group consists of a line quoted, late in life, from one of the most familiar of Vaughan's pieces, which she might easily have read in Palgrave. . . . This indication, slight as it is, would lead us to surmise that she was not well acquainted with her distant predecessors.[2]

Despite Whicher's caution there has been a steadily growing belief among the scholars that Emily Dickinson's style derived in large part from her acquaintance with the metaphysical poets. To say this today elevates the poet in our esteem, for the metaphysical poets are the rediscovery of our era. In Emily Dickinson's time they enjoyed no literary respectability. Moses Coit Tyler published his *A History of American Literature, 1607–1765* in the year 1878. His assessment of the Puritan poet, Noyes, provides an insight into the climate of opinion surrounding the seventeenth-century poets in Emily Dickinson's day:

Noyes was the most gifted and brilliant master ever produced in America, of the most execrable form of poetry to which the English language was ever degraded. . . . even in his old age, he continued to write the sort of poetry that, in his youth, had been the fashion, both in England and in America—the degenerate euphuism of Donne, of Wither, of Quarles, of George Herbert. To this appalling type of poetry, Nicholas Noyes faithfully adhered, even to the end of his days, unseduced by the rhythmical heresies, the classic innovations, of John Dryden and Alexander Pope.

Unaware of this, Judith Banzer investigates Emily Dickinson's indebtedness to the metaphysical poets and concludes she was very well acquainted with her distant predecessors. In a brief but provocative article[3] she analyzes the similarity in style and point of view, she demonstrates that the compound manner, the specific kind of imagery, the use of conceits, of puns, and the presence of a certain type of wit are typical of both metaphysical poetry and the poetry of Emily Dickinson. In order to prove that the parallels are not accidental, Miss Banzer suggests that she had actual familiarity with this poetry from her reading. She informs us that seventeenth-century poetry was reprinted in the newspaper the *Springfield Republican;* that articles on this poetry and representative verse appeared in the *Atlantic Monthly,* to which the family subscribed; that copies of Crashaw, Donne, and Davies in the *British Poets* series were read by the poet. Miss Banzer further cites the books borrowed by Emily Dickinson: Dana's *Household Book of Poetry,* Griswold's *The Sacred Poets of England and America,* Chambers' *Cyclopaedia of English Literature* and *The Hymns of the Ages,* with selections from Wither, Crashaw, Southwell, and Habington, and reports that these were surely influential. Since her article is brief, it does not allow space for evidence.

But the books are shelved at the Houghton Library of Harvard University. And the volumes of the magazines and the files of the newspapers are accessible. What they reveal discredits any theory of literary influences that are traditional or conventional.

1. The *British Poets* series came to Amherst in 1860 after Emily Dickinson's style was fixed. Although John Donne's poetry was published in this series in 1855, the pattern of publication was to bring out more recent poets first, the earlier poets much later; thus the other volumes of the "Metaphysicals" were not available in this collection until the 1870's.

2. The *Poems of Robert Greene, Christopher Marlowe, and Ben Jonson* appears to be largely unread, especially the section on Ben Jonson. It is inscribed "Susan Dickinson" and "Edward Dickinson" (her son).

3. *The Poetical Works of George Herbert* (New York, 1857) and *Emblems, Divine and Moral of Francis Quarles* (London, 1824) are the only volumes of poetry from seventeenth-century poets that are in the library. It is the Quarles volume that appears to be well read.

4. An edition of Michelangelo's *Sonnets,* published in 1878, is on the shelf but obviously cannot be called a literary influence.

5. The edition of Palgrave's *Golden Treasury* is 1877.

6. *The Sacred Poets of England and America for Three Centuries,* ed. Rufus W. Griswold (New York, 1849) does include religious poetry of the sixteenth and seventeenth centuries, notably George Wither, Drummond, and Francis Quarles (twenty-one poems), but there is very little by Donne, only pp. 50–52 containing four Sacred Sonnets, an Ode, Hymn to Christ and Hymn to God. Vaughan has more space, pp. 192–207, and Herbert has less, pp. 209–214, than Quarles and Vaughan.

7. *Hymns of the Ages,* ed. C. S. Guild, is the volume *Second Series* only. It is inscribed to Susan Dickinson from the Rev. F. D. Huntington, who wrote the Introduction; the book is well worn, but only up to the point where a poem by the Rev. Huntington appears. Corners of pages are bent at Pastor Josephsen's "For a Wakeful Night," "Abide with Me," by Lyte, "Calm on the Listening Ear," by Rev. Sears, and Herrick's "Lent." The pages on which Donne's poems are printed are uncut; Habington's poems are inaccessible; all the poems in the categories "Death," "Heaven," and "Worship" are on pages that are uncut.

8. *Household Book of Poetry,* ed. Charles A. Dana, 1857, does contain Carew, Crashaw, Drayton, Drummond (8 poems), Habington, Herbert (7 poems), Herrick (16 poems), Lovelace, Marvell (6 poems), Milton, Quarles, Vaughan, and Wither (10 poems), but John Donne is not included.

9. A search through the files of the *Springfield Republican* for 1858–1862, the relevant period for questions of influence, directly contradicts any statement that metaphysical poetry was frequently reprinted in that newspaper. Week by week there appeared a column of original verse featuring living poets.[4] In the "Books, Authors & Art" Column, reviews of important publications were printed, but these were notices of nonfiction, volumes of poetry, and novels written by living authors. An-

nouncements of the publication, month by month, of the well-known journals, such as the *Atlantic Monthly* and *Harper's Magazine* regularly appeared but none of them called attention to any metaphysical verse published in these magazines. As fillers, with no pattern whatsoever, poems were used, but they were sentimental verses, typically Victorian. Very infrequently a column of snippets from famous British poets found its way into print; there were no metaphysical poets represented with the exception of February 14, 1863 when several pieces by Vaughan appeared. By 1863 Emily Dickinson's style was fixed; she could have only the satisfaction of confirmation.

10. There is no evidence that such poetry was featured on the pages of the *Atlantic* or *Harper's*. If the issue is literary influence on Emily Dickinson, then an article on Sir Thomas Browne which appeared in *Harper's* in 1882 can scarcely be relevant. Here is a list of metaphysical (or nearly so) poets represented in *Harper's*, with their dates of publication in that journal:

Richard Baxter, 1875
Cowley, 1880
Drayton, 1874
Drummond, 1878
Dryden, 1852
Herbert, 1855, 1858 (one poem on each occasion)
Herrick, 1870's, 1880's (thirty poems)
Ben Jonson, 1851, 1864, 1878
Raleigh, 1882
Spenser, 1865, 1871 (one poem on each occasion)
Wither, 1865, 1878 (single poems)

Only two articles appeared: "Mr. Vaughan's Heir," 1850, "The Life of Herbert," 1851. A two-paragraph review of an anthology, *Poems, Sixteenth and Seventeenth Centuries,* appeared in 1882.

Surely there is not enough here to warrant any idea that Emily Dickinson was well acquainted with the metaphysical poets through their frequent appearance in this magazine. The *Atlantic Monthly* offers even less evidence. There is an anecdotal article on "Minor Elizabethan Poets" in 1867, containing a diatribe against John Donne, without quotation. Edwin P. Whipple wrote this as part of a series on the Elizabethan period; his biographical and thematic descriptions of Shakespeare

(1867), of Ben Jonson (1867), Beaumont and Fletcher, Massinger, Ford, and Spenser (1868), and finally Sidney, Raleigh, and Bacon (1868) constitute all there is to be found on this period. A search through the magazines (*Harper's* for 1850–1885 and the *Atlantic* for 1857–1876) reveals nothing more.

Miss Banzer was not the only critic to discuss Emily Dickinson's style in terms of the "metaphysicals." Charles Anderson provides a brief summary of what may be found in the poet's library, but it is clearly derived from George Whicher's survey with some titles added from the mimeographed *Handlist* of the Emily Dickinson Association Collection at Houghton. Anderson agrees that "If one attempted to name the chief potential influences from her reading, the Bible and Shakespeare would stand out above all others; then would come Emerson, Thoreau, George Eliot, the Brownings and the Brontés; finally the Metaphysicals." Then Anderson cites the same "actual references" Emily Dickinson made in her letters: Herbert, Vaughan, and Sir Thomas Browne.[5] He does acknowledge that a painstaking study of all possible sources might yield more than one would suspect. Indeed it does. When Anderson points out that no poet was ever less indebted to books he is right, but for the wrong reason; he accepts with no further inquiry Emily Dickinson's own statement to Higginson that she never consciously took any idea or image from another writer. He does not penetrate here behind what he likes to call her masquerade of naiveté.

As recently as 1966 Jack L. Capps made a far more thorough study of the materials relevant to the question of Emily Dickinson's reading. Believing she was extremely indebted to books, he concerns himself with the correlations between passages in her poetry and passages in the literature that fell into her hands. He illuminates many obscure allusions, but is limited because he relies on the direct references made by the poet.[6] Consequently, his patient inquiry, for all its promise, concludes with a statement that has the familiar ring: "For that seclusion she carefully chose her closest companions: her Bible, Watt's Psalms and Hymns, Shakespeare, the seventeenth-century Metaphysicals, Emerson, Dickens, George Eliot, and the Brownings."[7]

Perhaps the idea of the metaphysical stems in the first place from the remark by Susan Dickinson that she preferred the "metaphysical" poems of her sister-in-law. What she meant by the term may have been derived from Chambers' *Cyclopaedia of English Literature,* volumes on her shelf since 1856. His definition of "metaphysical" is clearly "ethical" or "moral" as revealed in the following passage from his critical introduction to the section on "Metaphysical Writers":

> The public taste has been almost wholly withdrawn from metaphysical pursuits, which at this time constituted a favorite study with men of letters. . . . Dr. Francis Hutcheson (1694–1747) introduced a new term, *the moral sense,* into the metaphysical vocabulary, and assigned to it a sphere of considerable importance. With him the moral sense was a capacity of perceiving moral qualities in action which excite what he called ideas of those qualities, in action. . . .[8]

For Chambers the "Metaphysical Writers" were Hume, David Hartley, Dr. Adam Smith, Dr. Reid, Lord Kames, Dr. Richard Price, Abraham Tucker, and Dr. Joseph Priestley. They flourished between 1727 and 1780. Chambers reprints snippets from their prose in his second volume. What we are accustomed to call the metaphysical school of literature is treated by Chambers as a group of men who wrote during the reigns of Elizabeth, James I, and Charles I, the "Third Period." Here do appear Sidney, Raleigh, Marlowe, with one poem each; Spenser, Southwell, Daniel, Drayton, Wotton, Shakespeare, Davies, Donne, Ben Jonson, Wither, Quarles, Herbert, Habington, Suckling, Herrick, Lovelace, Crashaw, with a mere five or six exemplary stanzas or very brief poems. Of John Donne there is this caustic summary:

> Donne is usually considered as the first of a series of poets of the seventeenth century, who, under the name of the Metaphysical Poets, fill a conspicuous place in English literary history. The directness of thought, the naturalness of description, the rich abundance of genuine poetical feeling and imagery, which distinguish the poets of Elizabeth's reign, now begin to give way to cold and forced conceits, mere vain workings of the intellect, a kind of poetry as unlike the former as punning is unlike genuine wit. To give an idea of these conceits—Donne writes a poem on a familiar popular subject, a broken heart. Here he does not advert to the miseries or distractions which are presumed to be the causes of broken hearts, but starts off into a play of conceit upon the phrase. . . . [he makes out] something that will jingle on the reader's imagination. There is here, certainly, analogy, but then it is an analogy which altogether fails to please or move; it is a mere conceit. . . . All the recognised modes, subjects, and phrases of poetry, introduced by them and their contemporaries, were now in some degree exhausted.

This was found, not in a new vein of equally rich ore, but in a continuation of the workings . . . of spurious metal.[9]

Only "The Valediction" and "The Will" and a portion from one of the Satires are reprinted here.

The origin of this belief that Emily Dickinson was influenced by the metaphysical writers may lie with Emily Dickinson herself, her own statement to Higginson that one of her favorite prose writers is Sir Thomas Browne; in another letter she says "My Business is Circumference," and this term "Circumference" is a word said to have been borrowed from Browne. By now we know we cannot accept this poet's avowal for fact. But neither can we dismiss Browne as a mere rhetorical gesture on her part. It is true that in her family library there was a three-volume edition of Sir Thomas Browne, but large portions of the text are still uncut. There was, however, Chambers' *Cyclopaedia* (1847 edition) which devoted three pages to Browne's writings. Chambers, of course, does not particularly admire Browne; his selections are few [10] and his summary disdainful:

> There is greater quaintness and obscurity in his style; he is fond of discussing abstruse and conjectural points. . . . and he displays throughout his writing the mind rather of an amiable and eccentric scholar, than of a man who takes an interest in the great concerns of humanity.

But reading the passages from Browne we find instances of imagery and ideas that call to mind many poems by Emily Dickinson. Here are a few examples. Browne's line, "The great mutations of the world are acted" may have given rise to these lines of Emily Dickinson:

> And the Earth—they tell me—
> On it's Axis turned!
> Wonderful Rotation!
> By but *twelve* performed!

Browne's conviction that we have the ability to forget,

> To be ignorant of evils to come, and forgetful of evils past, is a merciful provision in nature, whereby we digest the mixture of our few and evil days; and our delivered senses not relapsing into cutting remembrances, our sorrows are not kept raw by the edge of repetitions.

elicited this poem which seems an outburst at Browne's foolish belief:

Knows how to forget!
But—could she teach—it?
'Tis the Art, most of all,
I should like to know—

Long, at it's Greek—
I—who pored—patient—
Rise—still the Dunce—
Gods used to know—

Mould my slow mind to this Comprehension—
Oddest of sciences—Book ever bore—

How to forget!
Ah, to attain it—
I would give *you*—
All other Lore—

And when Browne exclaimed: "I believe . . . that the souls of men know
neither contrary nor corruption . . . that the souls of the faithful, as they
leave earth take possession of heaven" Emily Dickinson answered him
with acid verse:

Their Hight in Heaven comforts not—
Their Glory—nought to me—
'Twas best imperfect—as it was—
I'm finite—I cant see—

The House of Supposition—
The Glimmering Frontier that
skirts the Acres of Perhaps—
To Me—shows insecure—

The Wealth I had—contented me—
If 'twas a meaner size—
Then I had counted it until
It pleased my narrow Eyes—

Better than larger values—
That show however true—
This timid life of Evidence
Keeps pleading—"I dont know."

Doubtless one could gloss much of Browne's *Religio Medici* and *Christian Morals* with poems by Emily Dickinson. But we would not find influences so much as echoes, often outright challenges. This is the comfort I mean; this was her way of solace. She wrote her poems as a kind of practice of skill, as her part of an argument which she carried on all her life with published prose or verse. And she did not always quarrel with such reputable writers as Browne.

In the Dickinson library there is a small well-thumbed volume, *Inscriptions on the Grave Stones in the Grave Yards of Northampton,* . . . 1850. Here we may find epitaphs that ring with a startling familiarity:

> The grave is that home of Man
> Where dwells the Multitude.   [p. 44]
>
>   .   .   .
>
> This shall our mouldering members teach,
> What now our senses learn,
> For dust and ashes loudest preach
> Man's infinite concern.   [p. 44]
>
>   .   .   .
>
> Man departs this earthly scene,
> Ah! never to return,
> No second Spring shall ere revive
> The ashes of the urn.   [p. 44]

The same process of writing poems that are responses of a poet who remained unpersuaded of the homilies of accepted versifiers may be observed here. This is an "Inscription" (p. 46):

> Why should we mourn departed friends,
>   Or shake at death's alarm,
> 'Tis but the voice that Jesus sends
>   To call them to his arms.

Here is Emily Dickinson's speculation on such confidence:

> At least—to pray—is left—is left—
> Oh Jesus—in the Air—
> I know not which thy chamber is—
> I'm knocking—everywhere—
>
> Thou settest Earthquake in the South—
> And Maelstrom, in the Sea—

> Say, Jesus Christ of Nazareth—
> Hast thou no Arm for Me?

And of this quatrain of concession,

> Friends and Physicians could not save
> This mortal body from the grave,
> Nor can the grave confine it here
> When Jesus calls it must appear.   [p. 52]

Emily Dickinson ironically inquires:

> Is Heaven a Physician?
> They say that He can heal—
> But Medicine Posthumous
> Is unavailable—
>
> . . . .

In another poem she gives her own interpretation of the lapse from life:

> There is a Languor of the Life
> More imminent than Pain—
> 'Tis Pain's Successor—When the Soul
> Has suffered all it can—
>
> A Drowsiness—diffuses—
> A Dimness like a Fog
> Envelopes Consciousness—
> As Mists—obliterate a Crag.
>
> The Surgeon—does not blanch—at pain—
> His Habit—is severe—
> But tell him that it ceased to feel—
> The Creature lying there—
>
> And he will tell you—skill is late—
> A Mightier than He—
> Has ministered before Him—
> There's no Vitality

She challenged great writers and small, whoever enjoyed a literary reputation she believed she deserved, be he Keats, Byron, Shakespeare, or even the Scriptures. Take, for example, the lines from Isaiah (9.6) "For unto us a child is born, unto us a son is given," and then read her own dubious poem:

> "Unto Me?" I do not know you—
> Where may be your House?
>
> "I am Jesus—Late of Judea—
> Now—of Paradise"—
>
> Wagons—have you—to convey me?
> This is far from Thence—
>
> "Arms of Mine—sufficient Phaeton—
> Trust Omnipotence"—
>
> I am spotted—"I am Pardon"—
> I am small—"The Least
> Is esteemed in Heaven the Chiefest—
> Occupy my House"—

She was always stimulated to revise what she read. This, I think, accounts for the quantity of examples that may be uncovered by anyone with patience enough to sift through the printed verses in the volumes in her library, in the magazines and newspapers she read, in the collections of poetry so popular in her day. To be precise about Emily Dickinson's literary influences we must distinguish between imitation and use; she does not borrow, she improves. When she reads something that is printed, she pits her skill against that which has won the public stamp of approval, she does it over, leaving it, as she thinks, with a finer finish, a greater relevance. The extensiveness of Emily Dickinson's borrowing can be verified by browsing through the two anthologies of poems owned by the Dickinsons, the then famous *Hymns of the Ages* and the widely read *Lyra Domestica.*

Here is a passage taken from the preface to the *Hymns,* (1860):

The poet Robert Southwell, when in prison waiting martyrdom nearly three hundred years ago, wrote thus to his friend: "We have sung the canticles of the Lord in a strange land, and in this desert we have sucked honey from the rock, and oil from the hard stone; but. . . . [we] now sow the seed with tears, that others hereafter may with joy carry in the sheaves to the heavenly granaries.

We recognize the metaphor of the prison, the conception of the poet's mission, her tears. Her use of the metaphor of poems as grain is familiar too:

> I cautious, scanned my little life—
> I winnowed what would fade
> From what w'd last till Heads like mine
> Should be a-dreaming laid.
>
> I put the latter in a Barn—
> The former, blew away.
> I went one winter morning
> And lo—my priceless Hay
>
> Was not upon the "Scaffold"
> Was not upon the "Beam"—
> And from a thriving Farmer—
> A Cynic, I became.
>
> . . . .

Robert Southwell may have confidence in his sheaves and his heavenly granary, but Emily Dickinson is by no means so sure.

This poem appears on pp. 105–106 of the *Hymns:*

> Twas when the sea's tremendous roar
>   A little bark assailed;
> And pallid fear with awful power,
>   O'er each on board prevailed:
>   . . . .
>
> Safe in His Lands, whom seas obey,
>   When swelling billows rise;
> Who turns the darkest night to day
>   And brightens lowering skies:
>   . . . .

Here is Emily Dickinson's variant; her little bark does not survive. If she is safe, it will be because she is dead.

> If my Bark sink
> 'Tis to another sea—
> Mortality's Ground Floor
> Is Immortality—

The poem "Alone with God!" appears on pp. 157–58 of the *Hymns:*

> Alone with God! day's craven cares
> Have crowded onward unawares;
> The soul is left to breathe her prayers.
>
> Alone with God! I bare my breast,
> Come in, come in, O holy guest,
> Give rest—thy rest, of rest the best.
>
> Alone with God! how still a calm
> Steals o'er me, sweet as music's balm,
> When seraphs sing a seraph's psalm.
>
> Alone with God! no human eye
> Is here with eager look to pry
> Into the meaning of each sigh.
>
> Alone with God! no jealous glare
> Now stings me with its torturing stare;
> No human malice says—beware!
>
> . . . .

A glance at the poems listed in Appendix II B, "Poems that render the solitary self as a conscious choice," will remind us of how many there are with this same conception, surely, but written in a poetic style that is, to say the least, an improvement.

These verses from *Lyra Domestica,* another anthology of poems popular in her day, provide similar examples of echoes. "Parting" by K. J. P. Spitta (pp. 81–82) has a quatrain from which Emily Dickinson borrows:

> Nor time, nor place, can sever
>   The bonds which us have bound;
> In Christ abide forever
>   Who once in Him are found.

She alters these lines to read:

> And so when all the time had leaked,
> Without external sound
> Each bound the Other's Crucifix—
> We gave no other Bond—

She takes these lines from "The Dawning" by Vaughan (pp. 117–118):

> But as this restless vocal spring
> All day and night doth run and sing,
> And though here born, yet is acquainted
> Elsewhere, and flowing keeps untainted;

and compresses them, refines them, to read:

> The Well upon the Brook
> Were foolish to depend—
> Let Brooks—renew of Brooks—
> But Wells—of failless Ground!

She reads these lines from "The Glory Reserved" by Dr. Muhlenberg, (pp. 154–55):

> .   .   .   .
> The dazzling sun, at noontide hour,
>   Forth from his flaming vase,
> Flinging o'er earth the golden shower
>   Till vale and mountain blaze,
> But shews, O Lord! one beam of Thine,
> What, then, *the day where Thou dost shine!*
>
> Ah! how shall these dim eyes endure
>   That noon of living rays;
> Or how my spirit, so impure,
>   Upon Thy glory gaze?
> Anoint, O Lord! anoint my sight,
> And robe me for that world of light.

She turns over that flaming vase, knowing well that nothing can pour down from an upright container, and proceeds to write poems that render the phenomenon of the motion of the sun in the sky and its effect on the hills of Amherst. She invests that image of "Noon" with a significance that becomes all but a hallmark of her metaphysical stance.

> A Clock stopped—
> Not the Mantel's—
> Geneva's farthest skill
> Cant put the puppet bowing—
> That just now dangled still—

> An awe came on the Trinket!
> The Figures hunched, with pain —
> Then quivered out of Decimals —
> Unto Degreeless Noon —
>
> . . . .

Indeed when Emily Dickinson says of herself as a poet,

> I was a Phebe — nothing more —
> A Phebe — nothing less —
> The little note that others dropt
> I fitted into place —
>
> . . . .

she means it literally.[11] She herself makes explicit the distinction between imitation and use.

And the little note that others dropped seems to have antagonized her more the closer to home it fell. The *Hampshire and Franklin Express* was an Amherst newspaper that arrived at her house Thursday afternoons, carrying miscellaneous information on husbandry, manufacture, politics, medicine, local events, and on its front page always, a poem. Had the poet read nothing else at all she could have learned here that the poet's duty was to lament the dead, to speculate on Time and Hope and Nature and God. She knew she could not learn how to perform that duty well from these verses and she occupied herself with improving the art. Take for example this portion of "The Bible" by William Leggett, printed in the *Express* on November 25, 1846:

> This little book I'd rather own
> Than all the gold and gems
> That e'er in monarch's coffers shone,
> Than all their diadems.
> Nay, were the seas one chrysolite,
> To earth a golden ball,
> And diamonds all the stars of night,
> This book were worth them all.

Read in context with these lines, the following poem takes on a meaning different from that usually assigned to it:

> I lost a World — the other day!
> Has Anybody found?

> You'll know it by the Row of Stars
> Around it's forehead bound.
>
> A Rich man—might not notice it—
> Yet—to my frugal Eye,
> Of more Esteem than Ducats—
> Oh find it—Sir—for me!

This need not have been a lover, a lately deceased friend, or status; it is altogether possible that the poet simply mislaid her Bible, or pretended to, as a spoof on Leggett and his pompous verse.

Emily Dickinson was above all a poet of occasions. The occasion, however, was not the conventional festival or public event, but the appearance of a crocus in late winter, a sudden rain storm, the arrival of a letter, the alighting of a bee, the nesting of a bird, an obituary notice, a salon in the house next door—to which she had not been invited—or the appearance in print of a poem that displeased her.

Frequently the *Express* printed poems by "Viola," the kind of poetical lady at whom Emily Dickinson was going to laugh for years to come. In 1845 there were three (June 13, August 29, September 26); in 1846 there were four (February 2, June 17, June 24, August 26). Miss Viola was a practiced elegist, but on September 26, 1845 the *Express* printed this poem in praise of America:

"My Country"

> My country! yes, my country!
>   The land that gave me birth;
> If for nought else I'd love thee,
>   O glorious spot of earth.
> I love thy tow'ring mountains,
>   Far stretching to the sky,
> Thy gurgling streams and fountains,
>   And soft winds wand'ring by.
>
> Thy mighty noble rivers,
>   Seeking the ocean's breast
> The graves too of our fathers,
>   Each haunt of peaceful rest.
> Thy dark, deep forests, wreathing
>   Their beauties into one;

One song of Freedom breathing,
   O'er all her banner flung.

Each ope'ning bud and blossom,
   Where'er my footsteps rove;
Enshrined within my bosom
   Art THOU, and ALL I love.
Thy hills, and plains, and vallies,
   Where'er true hearts are found;
Where'er a freeman rallies,
   That is my father-land.

But most of all, New England
   Nearest my heart will be;
Her sons, they toil'd and struggled,
   They fought and bled for thee.
My country! yes, my country!
   Thy name has loudly rung,
'Till many a sword for Liberty,
   Has from its seaboard sprung.

            Viola

On October 10, 1845 the following poem "My Country" appeared in the *Express,* signed by "F. H. C." and bearing this introduction:

suggested by some recently published lines with the same caption

My country! yes, my country!
The land that gave me birth;
With all thy faults I love thee,
Thou favored spot of earth,
Though from thy mountains towering,
And every streamlet's chime,
There comes in grief o'erpowering,
Confession of thy crime.

Each noble river gathers
Stores for the ocean's breast,
And near them sleep our fathers
In deep unbroken rest.
Those stern old men were rather
Unbending in their might;

Expelled Rhode Island's father,
And spurned the Quaker's right.

Our country's yet in blossom,
Her youthful course is new,
And shrined within her bosom
Are thousands brave and true.
But still in southern vallies,
And many a western wave,
Where'er a freeman rallies,
Peeps forth an abject slave.

Not such New England curses
Our own, our native soil;
Her sons have filled their purses,
By stern and grasping toil.
They sought for Freedom boldly,
For Wealth with eager Heed,
And passed too often coldly
A brother's rightful need.

Our banner'd Eagle floateth
All proudly o'er the main;
Although his keen eye noteth
Repudiation's stain.
They tell in foreign nations,
Of debt, and fraud, and shame;
And these the bright libations
They pour to Freedom's name.

Alas! my noble country,
So erring, yet so strong!
Abjure thy course of wrong!
Lament past errors sadly,
Atone with all thy might,
And raise thy standard gladly,
For Freedom and for Right!

Then "May the glorious banner
Be wide and wide unfurled,"

'Till Thousands shout hosanna
Throughout a startled world.
Justice thy motto humble,
Thy sterling watchword, *Truth;*
Then, then while kingdoms crumble,
Live in unending youth!

(Wendell, Mass.)   F. H. C.

As early as 1845 Emily Dickinson had a direct lesson in the practice of poetry: poets could compose their verses stimulated by the poems of others. And what is perhaps more important is the fact that she learned that such poems need not be satires or parodies but serious and thoughtful variations.

That Emily Dickinson was reading the newspaper can be surmised from these two entries in Leyda's valuable sourcebook, *Years and Hours:*

I would love to send you a bouquet if I had an opportunity, and you could press it & write under it, The last flowers of summer. Would'nt it be poetical, and you know that is what young ladies aim to be now-a-days . . .

This entry is dated September 25, 1845 and is a portion of a letter written by the poet to her friend Abiah Root. She writes again to Abiah on June 26, 1846:

Have you seen a beautiful piece of poetry which has been going through the papers lately? Are we almost there? is the title of it . . .

Leyda tells us that it was frequently the custom of Emily Dickinson to snip material from the newspapers, to save her gleanings for eventual use. And so it is possible that she saved these poems and eventually corrected the work of the poets who wrote them. This may have been her challenge of Miss Viola:

The Robin's my Criterion for Tune—
Because I grow—where Robins do—
But, were I Cuckoo born—
I'd swear by him—
The ode familiar—rules the Noon—
The Buttercup's my Whim for Bloom—
Because, we're Orchard sprung—
But, were I Britain born,

I'd Daisies spurn—
None but the Nut—October fit—
Because, through dropping it,
The Seasons flit—I'm taught—
Without the Snow's Tableau
Winter, were lie—to me—
Because I see—New Englandly—
The Queen, discerns like me—
Provincially—

She takes Viola's "but most of all, New England" and turns it into a speculation on a very different sort of country. There are numerous poems that use all the imagery of the eulogy to "My Country," but the nation is displaced by another territory—the kingdom of God.

Doubtless she appreciated "F. H. C.'s" correction of Miss Viola. But this does not mean she admired the revision. These lines seem to be her response to the improvement:

To fight aloud, is very brave—
But *gallanter,* I know
Who charge within the bosom
The Cavalry of Wo—

Who win, and nations do not see—
Who fall—and none observe—
Whose dying eyes, no Country
Regards with patriot love—

We trust, in plumed procession
For such, the Angels go—
Rank after Rank, with even feet—
And Uniforms of Snow.

Reading the poems gathered in Appendix II under the rubrics of Nature and Death and God, one may discover many examples of Emily Dickinson's use of the imagery of gallant fighters who fall in battle, but they are usually compared to suffering unknowns who fall in private combat.

Emily Dickinson was not a social poet. The only poem that approaches a comment on the Civil War has in it echoes of her reservations about the subject matter of both Miss Viola and "F. H. C."

Color—Caste—Denomination—
These—are Time's Affair—
Death's diviner Classifying
Does not know they are—

As in sleep—All Hue forgotten—
Tenets—put behind—
Death's large—Democratic fingers
Rub away the Brand—

If Circassian—He is careless—
If He put away
Chrysalis of Blonde—or Umber—
Equal Butterfly—

They emerge from His Obscuring—
What Death—knows so well—
Our minuter intuitions—
Deem unplausible

This is not to say the poet was cold to the issues of the Civil War. There are poems that genuinely lament the sacrifice of young men to the violence of battle, just as there are deeply felt outcries against the indignities and iniquities of the market place. But the poet was more committed to the causes of the heart and the soul; and the field of the heart, the domain of the soul, was Heaven, not earth. Death would heal the inequities of slavery. The function of the poet is to be the herald of God.

That she always tried to tell this we know from what we have seen in her correspondence with Higginson and with Bowles. This poem, found among Bowles' papers, strives to explain the true nature of the poet, the true provenance of song:

A feather from the Whippowil
That everlasting—sings!
Whose galleries—are Sunrise—
Whose Opera—the Springs—
Whose Emerald Nest the Ages spin
Of mellow—murmuring thread—
Whose Beryl Egg, what School Boys hunt
In "Recess"—Overhead!

This bird is singing an immortal song; it sings of cyclical Nature in a form woven out of Time itself; and the product of such song [the Beryl Egg] is placed in Heaven where schoolboys [those who play at paste], those who desire to learn this art, would do well to hunt.[12]

To verify that this poem is an explanation of the art of poetry, we need only examine Fascicle 14 for there, transcribed onto the same sheet of paper, one directly following the other, (H72a, H72b) are both poems, "I taste a liquor never brewed," (The May-Wine) and "A feather from the Whippowil." In the one Emily Dickinson is herself the school-boy; in the other she is transformed to an "Inebriate of air." In fact, among the other poems transcribed onto this same manuscript sheet:

72a	214	I taste a liquor never brewed—
72b	161	A feather from the Whippowil
72c	181	I lost a World—the other day!
72d	182	If I should'nt be alive
72e	183	I've heard an Organ talk, sometimes—
72f	184	A transport one cannot contain
72g	185	"Faith" is a fine invention

there is one which speaks quite directly about the experience of inspiration, and at least two which are ironic jibes at public arbiters of poetic worth.

This is more than a demonstration of how frequently it was Emily Dickinson's practice (and how early she began!) to explain herself or to challenge those presumed to know. It gives us an insight into what she thought it appropriate for the poet to say. In these poems, as in all her "poet poems," she declares that the details of the real world are useful only as they enable the poet to render, by implication, the less apparent details of the unseen world; she explains to whoever would listen that the poet is a bard who sings of the relationship between the seen and the unseen, the real and the non-real, the small sphere inhabited briefly by herself and her fellows in their accidental time and place, and the large sphere inhabited by souls who have transcended time and are beyond place, with God.

It would seem that we have come all the way around again to Sir Thomas Browne and his term "circumference" for this description of Emily Dickinson's conception of the true provenance of song, of her view that it is the bard who must explain the relationship that exists between the small world of everyday experience and the large world of eternal time and space, has been stated in words with which Browne would have felt at ease: Emily Dickinson believed the poet's task was to celebrate the interplay between the small circuit world and the larger circumference world.

Whether or not that term "circumference" was derived from Browne is not the point, however; what is relevant is the particular meaning Emily Dickinson attaches to it, how she puts it to work in her poetry. The Lexicon serves us better than any study of Browne's prose, for what we are seeking is not literary influence but meaning, and beyond that, an illumination of her style and her structure. Browne supplies a clue, not an answer.

In the 1847 Dictionary "Circumference" is defined as "The line that goes round or encompasses a figure; a periphery; applied particularly to the line that goes around a circle, sphere, or other figure approaching these in form (Milton)." However this seems not to be the meaning which was intended by the poet when in her fourth letter to Higginson (Letter #268, July 1862) she defends herself against all his critical cautions with a net of naiveté underlaid with steel: "My Business is Circumference—" [13] It is more than her disengagement from life that she is explaining.

Continuing to read the Lexicon we see that the second definition, also quoted from Milton, says "The space included in a circle." Chambers' *Cyclopaedia* has among the selections from Browne these lines:

Circles and right lines limit and close all bodies, and the mortal right-lined circle * must conclude and shut up all.

We may or may not be on Browne's territory; surely we are standing in the middle of Emily Dickinson's domain.

Let us recall the lines from "I should have been too glad, I see—"

My little Circuit would have shamed
This new Circumference—have blamed—
The homelier time behind.

and then take a small gamble; let us look up the term "circuit." There is the same definition: "The space enclosed in a circle, or within certain limits." And it is also taken from Milton.[14] The fact is that there in the

* The character of death. [Browne's footnote]

Lexicon these two terms are linked. To examine the cluster of circumference-circuit poems is clearly the next step. There are 17 poems that actually use the word "Circumference"; there are 6 that use the word "Circuit." And, of course, "I should have been too glad, I see—" uses both.

The cluster of Circumference poems reveals an interesting phenomenon; some use the term to indicate enormous breadth, vast space, Heaven, Immortality; some use the term to signify that small area above the earth through which insects or birds take their flight—signifying limited breadth, a smaller space, the simple physical air. These examples are from the first group:

> I should have been too glad, I see—
> Too lifted—for the scant degree
> Of Life's penurious Round—
> My little Circuit would have shamed
> This new Circumference—have blamed—
> The homelier time behind.
>
> . . . .

Here circumference means breadth, a vastness that is opposed to all that is small and scant.

> I saw no Way—The Heavens were stitched—
> I felt the Columns close—
> The Earth reversed her Hemispheres—
> I touched the Universe—
>
> And back it slid—and I alone—
> A speck upon a Ball—
> Went out upon Circumference—
> Beyond the Dip of Bell—

Here circumference means huge distance; the poet, slipping out of the confines of the oppressive columns of the Church, rises up, out and beyond, going far far past where any churchbells reach.

> No Crowd that has occurred
> Exhibit—I suppose
> That General Attendance
> That Resurrection—does—

Circumference be full—
The long restricted Grave
Assert her Vital Privilege—
The   Dust—connect—and   live—

. . . .

Here circumference means place, that very populated territory where all
the resurrected souls become whole again and restored to eternal life.

An ignorance a Sunset
Confer upon the Eye—
Of Territory—Color—
Circumference—Decay—

It's Amber Revelation
Exhilirate—Debase—
Omnipotence' inspection
Of Our inferior face—

And when the solemn features
Confirm—in Victory—
We start—as if detected
In Immortality—

Here circumference means all that is unknowable except by the signs of
its opposite, specifically, by the sign of the decay of the sunset, we know
the revolution of the sun, and by implication, Immortality.

When Bells stop ringing—Church—begins—
The Positive—of Bells—
When Cogs—stop—that's Circumference—
The Ultimate—of Wheels.

Here circumference means afterlife, the final goal of life.

Time feels so vast that were it not
For an Eternity—
I fear me this Circumference
Engross my Finity—

To His exclusion, who prepare
By Processes of Size
For the Stupendous Vision
Of His Diameters—

Here circumference means size, the infinite as opposed to the finity of the poet.

> The Poets light but Lamps—
> Themselves—go out—
> The Wicks they stimulate—
> If vital Light
>
> Inhere as do the Suns—
> Each Age a Lens
> Disseminating their
> Circumference—

Here circumference means eternity, the large length of Time that suns survive, as opposed to the brief span of light disseminated by a candle. Note that poetry is yoked by the logic of the metaphor to circumference.

> A Coffin—is a small Domain,
> Yet able to contain
> A Citizen of Paradise
> In it's diminished Plane.
>
> A Grave—is a restricted Breadth—
> Yet ampler than the Sun—
> And all the Seas He populates
> And Lands He looks upon
>
> To Him who on it's small Repose
> Bestows a single Friend—
> Circumference without Relief—
> Or Estimate—or End—

Here circumference means Immortality, with the attributes of unrestricted breadth and endless time and measureless space and changelessness, as opposed to all the restrictive attributes of the grave. In this connection it is useful to quote the Lexicon definition of the word "compass," not the Mariner's compass discussed in connection with "Wild Nights," but the more general noun: "(1) the limit or boundary of a space and the space included; applied to time, space, sound, etc. Our knowledge lies within a very narrow *compass*. The universe extends beyond the *compass* of our thoughts. (2) A passing round; a circular course; a circuit. (3) limits of truth; moderation; due limits. These definitions imply the opposite of the meanings attached to "circumference" as it is used in this first group of poems. The second group does in fact use the word in the more limited sense.

> From Cocoon forth a Butterfly
> As Lady from her Door
> Emerged—a Summer Afternoon—
> Repairing Everywhere—
>
> . . . .
>
> Her pretty Parasol be seen
> Contracting in a Field
> Where Men made Hay—
> Then struggling hard
> With an opposing Cloud—
>
> Where Parties—Phantom as Herself—
> To Nowhere—seemed to go
> In purposeless Circumference—
> As 'twere a Tropic Show—
>
> . . . .

Here circumference is the meandering rise and fall of a butterfly in flight.

> She staked her Feathers—Gained an Arc—
> Debated—Rose again—
> This time—beyond the estimate
> Of Envy, or of Men—
>
> And now, among Circumference—
> Her steady Boat be seen—
> At home—among the Billows—As
> The Bough where she was born—

Here circumference is the distance to which a bird has flown, not so far that she cannot be seen.

> A single Clover Plank
> Was all that saved a Bee
> A Bee I personally knew
> From sinking in the sky—
>
> Twixt Firmament above
> And Firmament below

> The Billows of Circumference
> Were sweeping him away—
>
> .   .   .   .

Here circumference is the mobile air through which the bee flies.

In this second group of poems, the term signifies motion through a middle distance, as opposed to the meaning usual in the first group, direction to infinity. To resolve what seems like a contradiction we have an instrument: the cluster of circuit poems. Here there is no equivocation, for circuit means that small world, that real world, inhabited by the poet.

> .   .   .   .
> Yet not too far to come at call—
> And do the little Toils
> That make the Circuit of the Rest—
> And deal occasional smiles
> To lives that stoop to notice mine—
>
> .   .   .   .
>
>
> .   .   .
>
>
> .   .   .   .
> Too lifted—for the Scant degree
> Of Life's penurious Round—
> My little Circuit would have shamed
>
> .   .   .   .
>
>
> .   .   .
>
>
> .   .   .   .
> We learn to know the Planks—
> That answer to Our feet—
> So miserable a sound—at first—
> Nor even now—so sweet—
>
> As plashing in the Pools—
> When Memory was a Boy—
> But a Demurer Circuit—
> A Geometric Joy—
>
> .   .   .   .
>
>
> .   .   .
>
>
> This quiet Dust was Gentlemen and Ladies
> And Lads and Girls—

Was laughter and ability and Sighing
And Frocks and Curls.

This Passive Place a Summer's nimble mansion
Where Bloom and Bees
Exist an Oriental Circuit
Then cease, like these—

This last poem is contemplating death; circuit has the same meaning as that "circumference" of the second group, those motion poems, but transposed to symbolize a brief mortal span.

> Tell all the Truth but tell it slant—
> Success in Circuit lies
> Too bright for our infirm Delight
> The Truth's superb surprise
> As Lightning to the Children eased
> With explanation kind
> The Truth must dazzle gradually
> Or every man be blind—

Having traced the meaning of the term circuit thus far, finding it to signify the real and limited world of the living man, this poem takes on a new clarity for it makes explicit Emily Dickinson's conception of the proper subject matter of poetry: the circuit-world is what the poet must render, and by implication the Truth about Heaven, the circumference world, will be known.

Here, then, we have a cluster of poems that renders a relationship between this life and the afterlife, with a pivotal poem in each grouping a "poet poem" ("The Poets light but Lamps—" and "Tell all the Truth but tell it slant—") that declaims the truth about the craft and the purpose of the bard. So Emily Dickinson told "F. H. C." and so she told Bowles and so she told Higginson. It may be that so she has told all the generations of readers that would follow.

Now it has taken the context of the cluster to illuminate the meaning of the word "Circumference." But before we are satisfied that we fully understand Emily Dickinson's use of the term, we had better verify it from another available source. We have that phrase in the letter, "My Business is Circumference—" We have the context of its frame paragraph:

Perhaps you smile at me. I could not stop for that. My Business is Circumference—An ignorance, not of Customs, but if caught with the Dawn —or the Sunset see me—myself the only Kangaroo among the Beauty, Sir, if you please, it afflicts me, and I thought that instruction would take it away.

She tells Higginson she is not ignorant of verse form but rather of how to tell the truth, she is afflicted with doubt that her poems are as beautiful as Nature herself. The instruction she seeks has nothing to do with "Customs" but with restoring her self-confidence, a courtly way of asking for praise.

How interesting is the fact that here we have all the familiar imagery associated with the term "Circumference" as she has used it in her second group of poems. "I could not *stop* for that" contains the analogue to the *motion* of the butterfly, the bee, the bird, the caterpillar; the analogue to these graceful flying insects and bird is the kangaroo, and that kangaroo is the poet, that "singular animal . . . [skilled] in leaping."

So much, then, for the term circumference; it has, as I say, led us to Emily Dickinson's craft and purpose. Now, what of her message, what truth does the bard proclaim?

There is still more to be done. In the Lexicon, just below the word "Circumference" appears this strange word: "circumferentor" with the following definition: "An instrument used by surveyors for taking angles. . . . Only a rough approximation to the truth is obtained by this instrument." [15] Suppose we follow the track then of the term "angle" to discover whether or not that word is associated with the imagery of circumference and circuit. It is well worth a try. What cluster of poems uses the word "angle"? These 6:

> I got so I could hear his name—
> Without—Tremendous gain—
> That Stop—sensation—on my Soul—
> And Thunder—in the Room—
>
> I got so I could walk across
> That Angle in the floor,
> Where he turned so, and I turned—how—
> And all our Sinew tore—
>
> . . . .

Here "angle" is a turning point on the floor, a crucial one to the poet, but seemingly unrelated to the meaning we are seeking.

> The Angle of a Landscape—
> That every time I wake—
> Between my Curtain and the Wall
> Upon an ample Crack—
>
> Like a Venetian—waiting—
> Accosts my open eye—
> Is just a Bough of Apples—
> Held slanting, in the Sky—
>
> . . . .
>
> The Seasons—shift—my Picture—
> Upon my Emerald Bough,
> I wake—to find no—Emeralds—
> Then—Diamonds—which the Snow
>
> From Polar Caskets—fetched me—
> The Chimney—and the Hill—
> And just the Steeple's finger—
> These—never stir at all—

This "angle" is the visual scene which she sees outside her window; it is literally the world of Nature depicted in terms of seasonal change.

> We see—Comparatively—
> The Thing so towering high
> We could not grasp it's [Angle]
> Unaided—Yesterday—
>
> This Morning's finer Verdict—
> Makes scarcely worth the toil—
> A furrow—Our Cordillera—
> Our Appenine—a Knoll—
>
> Perhaps 'tis kindly—done us—
> The Anguish—and the loss—
> The wrenching—for His Firmament
> The Thing belonged to us—

To spare these Striding Spirits
Some Morning of Chagrin—
The waking in a Gnat's—embrace—
Our Giants—further on—

This poem has echoes of "Tell all the Truth but tell it slant—" with that special cautionary line "As Lightning to the Children eased / With explanation kind" a modulation of "Perhaps 'tis kindly—done us—" The poem also introduces the idea of death, which becomes the central experience of the following poem:

When I was small, a Woman died—
Today—her Only Boy
Went up from the Potomac—
His face all Victory

To look at her—How slowly
The Seasons must have turned
Till Bullets clipt an Angle
And He passed quickly round—

. . . .

Here the "angle" is a turning-point between living and dying. The phrase "The Seasons must have turned" is an echo of "The Angle of a Landscape—" with its particularly relevant line "The Seasons—shift—my Picture—" The following poem names the "Crystal Angle" of death unequivocally:

Her Sweet turn to leave the Homestead
Came the Darker Way—

. . . .

Distance—be Her only Motion—
If 'tis Nay—or Yes—
Acquiescence—or Demurral—
Whosoever guess—

He—must pass the Crystal Angle
That obscure Her face—
He—must have achieved in person
Equal Paradise—

The "Crystal Angel"! The turning point between life and death? No. The transition between the Homestead and Paradise: Death.

Experience is the Angled Road
Preferred against the Mind
By—Paradox—the Mind itself—
Presuming it to lead

Quite Opposite—How Complicate
The Discipline of Man—
Compelling Him to Choose Himself
His Preappointed Pain—

That angle then is death. It is not any abstract relationship between this small life and redemption, but the real experience of death. And it is this relationship that it is the poet's business to proclaim.

In 1862, in her fourth letter to Higginson, Emily Dickinson knew that she was a poet; she knew why and how; and she knew what her gospel voice must reveal: the relationship between mortality and immortality is death; the relationship between the finite circuit world and the cosmic circumference universe is the crystal angle.

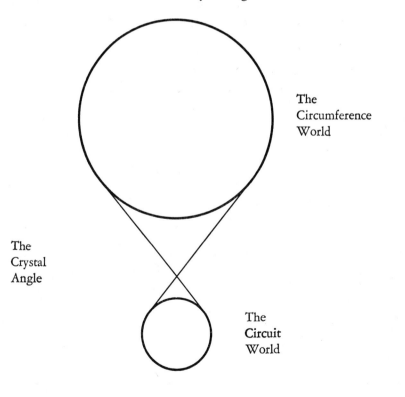

The
Circumference
World

The
Crystal
Angle

The
Circuit
World

Because we inhabit the finite world we may share only the attributes of temporary reality, we must content ourselves with signs of the infinite. It is the business of the poet to recognize these signs. It is the business of the poet to observe transient phenomena and explain thereby the fixed universe, to confront jeopardy and prophesize safety. Eventually we will experience the transition between mortal life and eternal life, we will pass through the angle of death, voyage out of the limited circuit into the limitless circumference, and that which appalls momently will save finally. The voice of the poet sings surety, chants how these things may be.

Whatever terms we use to state the theme of Emily Dickinson, we must state them in the form of a relationship. And whatever phenomena Emily Dickinson used to render her theme, her manner was necessarily a mode of equivalencies. This is to say her style is itself a metaphor of her theme. Whether she marshals her details around the subject matter pertaining to the circuit world, or concentrates on the experience of death, whether she spirals down on the single traumatic deprivation or focuses on the funeral of an actual person or tries to take the tint of a sunset, recreate the play of lightning, transfix the wind, always her method is the same. There is one expanding metaphor drawn from the circuit world; it is conjoined (actually or by implication) to an equivalent metaphor drawn from the circumference world, and both are held in tension, bound together by juxtaposition not logic, perceived as related by a leap of the imagination not by fact, by intuition not reason.

This poetic manner vitalizes a phrase (a "sudden sky") or a line ("The Night was wide, and furnished scant") as easily as it enlivens a fully developed poem. When Emily Dickinson says "The Soul should always stand ajar" she is employing the same device that elsewhere concretizes regeneration by naming corn tassels and red apples and pumpkins in the field and Christmas stockings in their seasonal order. An ear of corn, a pumpkin is transient; their sequence, their reappearance is immutable.

And that is precisely the lesson of the threaded booklets, each is a separate and distinct and complete collection of poems that render the circuit and circumference world connected by the experience of death. The discussion in the preceding chapter has demonstrated the operation of this method for single poems; it is now appropriate to demonstrate the same method as it operates to yoke together the multiple strands of the fascicle.

CHAPTER TEN

The Fascicles

THE WHOLE MATTER OF THE PROPER SEQUENCE OF THE POEMS IN the fascicles is crucial to any understanding of Emily Dickinson's purpose in tying her pages together, as she did once she was satisfied with the substance and structure of the gathering of poems. Any final analysis of the poet's intention must always be made with the acknowledgment that accuracy is no longer absolutely attainable. However there are three things operating in our favor: one is the presence of several poems on a manuscript page, and that is indisputable, for these poems cannot have been displaced; the second is the careful reconstruction of the fascicles made by devoted and patient scholars, the third is the poetic manner of Emily Dickinson—the modulating image, the interplay of metaphors, and the narrative structure.

Each fascicle consists of four or five folded sheets of paper onto which are copied in close sequence several poems; sometimes a line is drawn to indicate separation, sometimes the poet merely leaves a wider space between her stanzas. Each sheet now has a distinct manuscript number assigned to it. In the case of those deposited in the Houghton Library, the number was given by the archivist, who wished to catalogue the sheets immediately on their arrival; the numbers correspond only to the accidental sequence of the pages as they were delivered. It is evident from the Appendix listing of the contents of the fascicles that no idea of a fixed order was operating when the numbers were assigned, not in this late numbering of the manuscripts, or in the earlier numbering of the threaded booklets 1–40 (Mrs. Todd's work). These fascicles had been broken up during the process of the first editing, and the loose pages were returned to Lavinia Dickinson, from whom they were eventually taken by Susan and left for Mrs. Bianchi. It was the skilled work of Mrs. Theodora Ward, the very able editor working with Thomas Johnson during the preparation of the Variorum text, that caused the pages to be redistributed in accordance with the quality of stationery, identifying water-marks, matching pinholes, and handwriting analysis. Doubtless she had the assistance of Houghton archivists devoted to their task.

In the case of those deposited in the Frost Library, the manuscript number was given by Jay Leyda working on behalf of Mrs. Bingham when she transferred to the Frost Library those envelopes which had lain in her mother's camphorwood chest, undisturbed for decades, and very carefully handled thereafter.

Recently R. W. Franklin has made another painstaking study which led him to revise the ordering of the manuscripts in many of those fascicles on deposit at the Houghton Library, and one on deposit at the Frost. Probably there is very little more that can be done, scientifically, to reconstitute the fascicles as Emily Dickinson left them. Enough of the booklets are so clearly correct in their reconstruction, the manuscripts should now remain undisturbed in both repositories.

We may safely turn our attention to Emily Dickinson's purpose in binding her poems as if she herself were editor, printer, and publisher. What principle guided her? It was not chronology; we know this from the evidence of handwriting, for there are poems that exist in different hands on the scraps which have been copied fair, in one hand, and placed together into a booklet. Also there is the evidence supplied by letters, sent at different times, enclosing poems that were eventually transcribed into single booklets. It was not recipients: there is no Higginson fascicle, no Helen Hunt Jackson grouping, no Bowles, no Holland booklet. These are not gatherings according to single events or subjects for there are no flower or sky gatherings, no death or nature booklets, no romantic attachment fascicles. Neither are they organized according to emotions or feelings for ironic poems, happy, sad, wistful and gay poems all mingle in a single fascicle.

It appears, rather, to be typical of each fascicle that it may contain deeply religious lyrics, speculations about the profound question of immortality and reality, nostalgic verses lamenting her loss of a loved one, bitter and despairing poems about herself as a poet, sunny contemplations of mere flowers, mere birds, mere sunsets, mere dawns, and altogether complicated inquiries into these same flowers and birds and sunsets and dawns as signs of the regenerative power of Nature. It appears, further, to be typical of each fascicle that the range of emotions be fully represented for it is not unusual to find several poems on similar subjects generating polar feelings. The principle behind the construction of the fascicles is, in a word, dramatic. Each is a narrative structure designed to recreate the experience of the woman as she strives for acceptance or knowledge, is rebuffed or fails because of her limitations, but then by an act of will, forces herself to be patient in order to survive, fixes her hopes on another world where Jesus and God await her, and remains content meanwhile with herself alone. Or, if the emphasis is on the poet, each fascicle records the poet's effort to understand the truth as she observes the phenomena of the transient world she inhabits. She accumulates her discoveries into a long link-poem that ultimately celebrates as it proclaims the relationship between the mortal and the immortal, the transient and the immutable, the finite and the infinite, the natural and the spiritual—in a word, the circuit and the circumference worlds linked by the experience of death. The conflict arises out of the quest itself, whether it be for the truth or for love or fame; the resolution is usually a consecration of herself to her art or to God.

So similar are the fascicles it seems possible to chart one and obtain a blueprint for all:

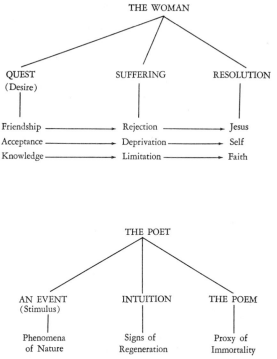

The question of the larger structure, the gatherings of poems into private volumes any one of which would be a good representation of Emily Dickinson's achievement as a poet, may now be investigated.

A cautionary word about the appearance of any poem on its manuscript page is in order. The poems were not written in conventional verse form. From the following poem, printed here exactly as it appears on a fair copy preserved in the Frost Library, it is evident that the line length and the stanza structure is unlike that fixed by Johnson when he reproduced it as Poem #322 in his complete *Poems.* It is more like another version transcribed into Fascicle 23 (H128a). A careful comparison of this version with those appearing in the Variorum text reveals that there are differences among the words as well as in the design, but since the poet often left more than one fair copy it is simply impossible to decide which word is correct. So impossible that it becomes an irrelevant question. Insoluble problems are a deterrent only when one insists that there are no other problems worth solving. Just looking at the poem, realizing that every poem written by Emily Dickinson has an appearance similar to this is instructive, at least insofar as it reminds us we do not have her own text, not in any collection whatsoever.

Recto

There came a day —
at Summer's full —
Entirely for me —
I thought that such
was for the Saints —
When Resurrections — be —
   The Sun — as common —
went — abroad —

the flowers accustomed
blew—
As if no soul—that
solstice passed—
which maketh
all things—new—
the time was scarce
profaned—of speech—
the falling of a word
Was [needless]—as at
Sacrament—
the Wardrobe—of
Our Lord:
    Each was to
Each—the sealed
Church—
Permitted to Commune—
    this time—
Lest we too awkward
    show
At Supper of "the Lamb."

      Verso

    The hours slid
fast—as hours will—
Clutched tight—by
greedy hands—
So—faces on two Decks
look back—
Bound to *opposing* Lands.
    and so when
all the time had Leaked—
Without External sound—
Each bound the
other's Crucifix—
We gave no other
Bond—
    Sufficient—troth—
that we shall
rise:
Deposed—at—Length

the Grave—
to that new marriage—
Justified—through
Calvaries—of
Love!

Whether the lines are brief because she wished to have them so or whether she was hemmed in by her narrow white paper will never be known. We have no alternative but to admit we cannot know and to proceed.

That I have chosen Fascicle 12 to print here as Emily Dickinson herself intended, in its sequence and as a whole, is without any hidden motive; another fascicle would have served as well. It only seemed to me that this gathering had a larger scope, and was for this very reason more like all the others. When Emily Dickinson was satisfied with a smaller collection it was usually because she had allowed her emphasis to fall on one or another area of experience, and was content that it should do so.

H55a [1]

Conscious am I in my Chamber,
Of a shapeless friend—
He doth not attest by Posture—
Nor Confirm—by Word—

Neither Place—need I present Him—
Fitter Courtesy
Hospitable intuition
Of His Company—

Presence—is His furthest license—
Neither He to Me
Nor Myself to Him—by Accent—
Forfeit Probity—

Weariness of Him, were quainter
Than Monotony
Knew a Particle—of Space's
Vast Society—

Neither if He visit Other—
Do He dwell—or Nay—know I—
But Instinct esteem Him
Immortality—

H55b

You taught me Waiting with Myself—
Appointment strictly kept—
You taught me fortitude of Fate—
This—also—I have learnt—

An Altitude of Death, that could
No bitterer debar
Than Life—had done—before it—
Yet—there is a Science more—

The Heaven you know—to understand
That you be not ashamed
Of Me—in Christ's bright Audience
Upon the further Hand—

H55c [2]

Suspense—is Hostiler than Death—
Death—thosoever Broad,
Is just Death, and cannot increase—
Suspense—does not conclude—

But perishes—to live anew—
But just anew to die—
Annihilation—plated fresh
With Immortality—

The fascicle opens with a vision the poet has of herself alone in her small chamber except for her visitor from the larger realm of Heaven. She has no sensual awareness of Christ, but intuition of his presence is sufficient. Were either to demand a sign [an Accent] it would violate, not achieve proof. Whether or not this is the God of others, her instinct tells her that her friend is immortal. Here, then, is a poem that combines the quest for knowledge of God with patience in the assurance that she and Jesus are known to each other.

The second poem continues to operate in the realm of the woman, but the emphasis shifts to the quest for friendship. The poet is still solitary, but her solitude is delineated as fate that she be alone, rendered in a metaphor of impregnability. The two barriers to companionship are life and death. There remains only the possibility of Heaven, where the companion resides, but she cannot say whether any union awaits her there. The identity of "You" cannot be fixed except through the juxtaposition of this poem with what precedes it and what follows immediately after; the longed-for companion is God.

The third poem is more abstract, more generalized a speculation about knowledge and doubt. To live with suspense about the truth is harder to sustain than to experience death, for annihilation is final, but suspense continually renews itself. The poem grows out of the preceding one, specifically out of the lines:

> Yet—there is a Science more—
> The Heaven you know—to understand

The three taken together probe the relationship between intuition and knowledge, the first expanding intuition, the next two expanding knowledge. The waiting of the second poem transposes to the suspense of the third; that which was learned in the second transposes to the doubt of the third. Knowledge of life and death and heaven transpose to suspense and annihilation and immortality.

H56a

> Drama's Vitallest Expression is the Common Day
> That arise and set about Us—
> Other Tragedy
>
> Perish in the Recitation—
> This—the best enact
> When the Audience is scattered
> And the Boxes shut—
>
> "Hamlet" to Himself were Hamlet—
> Had not Shakespeare wrote—

Though the "Romeo" left no Record
Of his Juliet,

It were infinite enacted
In the Human Heart—
Only Theatre recorded
Owner cannot shut—

H56b

Life, and Death, and Giants—
Such as These—are still—
Minor—Apparatus—Hopper of the Mill—
Beetle at the Candle—
Or a Fife's Fame—
Maintain—by Accident that they proclaim—

H56c

Four Trees—upon a solitary Acre—
Without Design
Or Order, or Apparent Action—
Maintain—

The Sun—upon a Morning meets them—
The Wind—
No nearer Neighbor—have they—
But God—

The Acre gives them—Place—
They—Him—Attention of Passer by—
Of Shadow, or of Squirrel, haply—
Or Boy—

What Deed is Their's unto the General Nature—
What Plan
They severally—retard—or further—
Unknown—

H56d

The Grace—Myself—might not obtain—
Confer upon My flower—
Refracted but a Countenance—
For I—inhabit Her—

This next group consists of poems about Nature, but nature interpreted through her signs in the phenomenal world, the rising and setting sun, four trees, a flower, not by any a priori knowledge on the part of the spectator. In a metaphor comparing the natural event of the passing of a day to the contrived plays by Shakespeare, the poet declares that the living heart itself enacts the everlasting coming and going, the constant giving and taking away, the true drama of transience. Because of the analogy to *Hamlet* and *Romeo and Juliet* the poem takes on a funereal tone, the transience is characterized as loss. Nature's proclamation here has overtones of sadness.

This feeling is carried over into the second poem. The analogues change to a beetle and a fife; the beetle hovers near death and that fife tells of fame, playing its message on a tinny mediocre instrument; the gigantic occurrences of Life (the fife) and Death (the beetle) are made small and insignificant, they become mere hopper of the mill, are ground up. What is proclaimed is therefore unsure, what happens is accidental, without cause.

It is this idea of cause that evades the mind, of knowledge conveyed through chance, that modulates into the third poem. The seed of this idea was placed in the first group of poems, where knowledge was said to be less than intuition, where immortality was said to be known by instinct, not logic. The trees stand on the acre of the third poem without design or order; they act out their roles in the natural world without self-consciousness, without intention. How they participate in the larger scheme of general nature remains unknown.

The last poem is an appeal for favor. It is part of that quest for friendship so often the subject matter of the poetry, part of the small circuit world, talking not primarily of the larger issues that are the substance of the first three poems, but using what is discovered there for some slant truth here. She and the flower are sharers of the light of the divine countenance, so that any favor conferred on the flower will benefit her. This poem is as wistful about attaining a kind regard as are the second and third poems about attaining to some knowledge about the meaning of the real world. The first poem falls within the spectrum of melancholy, but does have more bite to it. If one substitutes "my poem" for "My flower" and reads it in the context of the first poem where the *Hamlet* and the *Romeo and Juliet* are seen as Shakespeare's flowers, his plays, then the small quatrain takes on a larger significance. The work of art is enacted in the human heart; the poem is a refraction of herself. And this poem has moved us across the division of the chart into the realm of the poet.

H57a

The Birds reported from the South—
A News express to Me—
A spicy Charge, My little Posts—
But I am deaf—Today—

The Flowers—appealed—a timid Throng—
I reinforced the Door—
Go blossom to the Bees—I said—
And trouble Me—no More—

The Summer Grace, for Notice strove— [3]
Remote—Her best Array—
The Heart—to stimulate the Eye
Refused too utterly—

At length, a Mourner, like Myself,
She drew away austere—
Her frosts to ponder—then it was
I recollected Her—

She suffered Me, for I had mourned—
I offered Her no word—
My Witness—was the Crape I bore—
Her—Witness—was Her Dead—

Thenceforward—We—together dwelt—
I never questioned Her—

Our Contract
A Wiser Sympathy

H57b

Remorse—is Memory—awake—
Her Parties all astir—
A Presence of Departed Acts—
At window—and at Door—

It's Past—set down before the Soul
And lighted with a Match—
Perusal—to facilitate—
And help Belief to stretch—

Remorse is cureless—the Disease
Not even God—can heal—
For 'tis His institution—and
The Adequate of Hell—

H57c

Renunciation—is a piercing Virtue—
The letting go
A Presence—for an Expectation—
Not now—
The putting out of Eyes—
Just Sunrise—
Lest Day—
Day's Great Progenitor—
Outvie
Renunciation—is the Choosing
Against itself—
Itself to justify
Unto itself—
When larger function—
Make that appear—
Smaller—that Covered Vision—Here—

It is the experience of deprivation, the Grace for which the poet longs but
cannot obtain, that becomes the subject matter of the third group of

poems. This idea clearly stems from the first group of poems describing the poet's solitary state. But these now are more personal outcries at the painful choice the poet has made.

The first poem describes an effect of her act of renunciation, the act soon to be rendered in the third poem. Remembering how the emphasis has already fallen on Nature, it is fitting that she describe the effect in a metaphor of summer and winter. The signs of Christ's presence are now modulated to the birds that tell the news of summer, the flowers that appeal for notice; nothing of this Summer Grace can move her heart, which is withdrawn and aloof. It is the same heart that appeared in the second group of poems except that the tragedy of the common day did affect the human heart. But the poet will arrive at this same idea. The summer passes on, becomes herself austere as she contemplates her losses. Now the poet and summer are kin, both mourners for what each has lost. And as in the poem about Christ in her chamber, there are these lines depicting a voiceless relationship,

> Neither He to Me
> Nor Myself to Him—by Accent—
> Forfeit Probity

so here, the two companions dwell together in an instinctual communion: [4]

> I offered Her no word—
> I never questioned Her—

The parallel between the next two poems and "Suspense—is hostiler than Death—" is obvious, even the syntax of each opening line is the same. In the poem about remorse the poet speculates on an operation of the mind, but the action of memory and its substance of remorse is far more personal, for the word implies a sense of guilt, a restless conscience that will not allow the soul to forget. The continuing resurgence of suspense is analogous to the ceaseless stir of remorse. Neither may conclude. And this disease that cannot be healed, that is in fact Hell, is like the perishing without the dying—the hostile suspense. [5]

In the poem about renunciation the image-links to all that went before are apparent: the passing of the day, the solitary self, the doubt, the presence of God [Day's Great Progenitor]. But here the poet is far more personal in the rendering of her deprivation; she explains why she has herself chosen to be alone, to relinquish a mortal companion in this world. It is for the sake of a later fulfillment hopefully in Heaven. This "Presence" is the same kind of "Presence" of that immortal friend in her chamber who took no liberties beyond simple nearness. She renounces all others and chooses to remain alone at the outset of her day's beginning (metaphor for her life span) because fulfillment of the mortal sort [Day] might contend with her commitment to God.[6] She has so chosen despite her own personal longing because her larger function has triumphed, has made such mortal associations seem small.

H58a

Never for Society
He shall seek in vain—
Who His own acquaintance
Cultivate—Of Men
Wiser Men may weary—
But the Man within

Never knew Satiety—
Better entertain
Than could Border Ballad—
Or Biscayan Hymn—
Neither introduction
Need You—unto Him—

H58b

I sometimes drop it, for a Quick—
The Thought to be alive—
Anonymous Delight to know—
And Madder—to conceive—

Consoles a Wo so monstrous
That did it tear all Day,
Without an instant's Respite—
'Twould look too far—to Die—

Delirium—diverts the Wretch
For Whom the Scaffold neighs—

The Hammock's Motion lulls the Heads
So close on Paradise—

A Reef—crawled easy from the Sea
Eats off the Brittle Line—
The Sailor does'nt know the Stroke—
Until He's past the Pain—

H58c

It dropped so low—in my Regard—
I heard it hit the Ground—
And go to pieces on the Stones
At bottom of my Mind—

Yet blamed the Fate that fractured—*less*
Than I reviled Myself,
For entertaining Plated Wares
Upon my Silver Shelf—

H58d

Autumn—overlooked my Knitting—
Dyes—said He—have I—
Could disparage a Flamingo—
Show Me them—said I—

Cochineal—I chose—for deeming
It resemble Thee—
And the little Border—Dusker—
For resembling Me—

The fascicle is beginning to take on a narrative quality. All the seeds of probability sown in the early poems are being taken up one by one and brought to fruition. This is, indeed, a long link-poem, a single poem composed of discrete but intricately related parts.

Her renunciation explained, now she goes on to examine the literal operation of her own free choice. Mortal companions relinquished, how shall she conduct herself without society? Her answer is expected, for we have already read her description of that better society within the privacy of her chamber. As she was hospitable to the company of God then, so she is cultivating her own solitary self now; as she knew she would never grow weary of God then, so she knows she will not grow weary of herself now; not monotonous then, no satiety now; He constituted the society of a vast space then; she, within herself, constitutes sufficient entertainment now.

The same modulation continues to occur, the same links continue to join the dramatic art of Shakespeare and the particular activity of this poet. The drama needs the theater; she entertains herself better than can any reading of ballads or hymns. What entertainment has she devised for herself? The making of poems. For her flowers earlier she had pleaded favor; for her poems here she needs nothing.

This is a brave poem. The succeeding one is less brave. She is still speculating about her renunciation but the object renounced alters; it is not a companion, it is acceptance—not as a woman but as a poet. The earlier impregnability, the strength to do without favor, has become intimidated. And she justifies herself in a new way, not for the sake of a larger function, but because she suffers too acutely. It is of primary importance to notice that as Emily Dickinson veers over to that other side of the chart, as she begins to talk of herself as a poet, her feelings become more intense, her metaphors more violent.

To be published is to be alive, a mad dream, but even an anonymous appearance may console a woe that is too monstrous, too constant a torment. She needs respite. Her early patience has changed to delirium, and all her former bravura disintegrates in the metaphor of a wretch about to climb the scaffold; all her former self-sufficiency collapses into the metaphor of the drowning sailor.

It is a relief to read of the return of common sense. The poem that follows contemplates that very act of dropping her resignation for a quick grasp of transient pleasure, but the poet chastizes herself, looks on her weakness with irony. We recognize that earlier fate which she had accepted with so much equanimity in the second poem of this fascicle, in the new context here when she says she blames the fate that fractured her less than she blames herself. What is that "Anonymous Delight" but plated wares; what that mad dream now but delirium? And what are her poems—silver shelves.

All these poems about the poet and the self have lost the ambiguity of her early speculations concerning knowledge and truth and afterlife and immortality. When it comes to the poetry she suffers, to be sure, but she is in no doubt whatsoever. And the last poem of this group makes a comparison that verifies this fact of her confidence. She compares her knitting—her poems of many colors—to the natural phenomena of Autumn. And she is not bested by Nature.

H59a

Bloom upon the Mountain—stated—
Blameless of a Name—
Efflorescence of a Sunset—
Reproduced—the same—

Seed, had I, my Purple Sowing
Should endow the Day—
Not a Tropic of a Twilight—
Show itself away—

Who for tilling—to the Mountain
Come, and disappear—
Whose be Her Renown, or fading,
Witness, is not here—

While I state—the Solemn Petals,
Far as North—and East,
Far as South and West—expanding—
Culminate—in Rest—

And the Mountain to the Evening
Fit His Countenance—
Indicating, by no Muscle—
The Experience—

H59b

Publication—is the Auction
Of the Mind of Man—
Poverty—be justifying
For so foul a thing

Possibly—but We—would rather
From Our Garret go
White—Unto the White Creator—
Than invest—Our Snow—

Thought belong to Him who gave it—
Then—to Him Who bear
It's Corporeal illustration—Sell
The Royal Air—

In the Parcel—Be the Merchant
Of the Heavenly Grace—
But reduce no Human Spirit
To Disgrace of Price—

H59c

All but Death, can be Adjusted—
Dynasties repaired—
Systems—settled in their Sockets—
Citadels—dissolved—

Wastes of Lives—resown with Colors
By Succeeding Springs—
Death—unto itself—Exception—
Is exempt from Change—

These three poems and the last group of four that follows are like the resolution of a conflict; they have a kind of narrative fulfillment that satisfies the reader who craves a restoration of tranquility. Emily Dickinson achieves equanimity not by logic or rhetoric but by passing through an experience. And we have moved all across the diagram and are now in the realm of the poet. It should not surprise us to read poems at this stage of the dramatic narrative that are without humility. Having passed through the crisis of despair she is moving upward and will emerge strengthened and reassured, confident and free of all her doubts.

The poem "Bloom upon the Mountain—stated—" tells what she tries to do when she writes her poetry. She strives to render the bloom on the mountain, to reproduce the colors of the sunset, and she suggests as a by-the-way that this has not yet been done. She has seeds that will create the kind of day that no natural change can alter. Her poems create days that live without fading. And her poems tell who tills those wild flowers, who causes the revolution of the sun: she is the bard who names Nature and God. Her work is eternal. While she transfixes her truths forever, real flowers fall to rest and the real day fades, evening comes and the mountain adapts itself to the change without any sign of yea or nay. The mountain just fits itself to the natural law of change, without any exertion. She, by contrast—a contrast that pervades the poem—records the change, and it takes a great deal of muscle to practice her craft.

Such a poet was not ever going to be humble about her art. She may suffer the deepest kind of torment at her deprivation but she will rise again and again off the floor of her despondence and restore herself. She has achieved a tensile strength of soul. So she says in her next poem.

This poem is the analogue to "I sometimes drop it, for a Quick—" but the tone is as far from that outburst of self-pity as she can get. She is contemptuous, surely, but energetic and affirmative and triumphant all at once. Despair at not being accepted? Oh no. What need has she of publication? Only poverty of spirit requires payment. She would rather go straight to her creator as she is, virginal, white, unknown, out of the great world where fame pretends to be of value (that tin fife is back). Her thoughts belong to God. Next they belong to herself, for she is the poet who wears the corporeal illustration of God. It is right that she make parcels of the royal air, write poems; it is right that she be merchant of heavenly grace, write poems; but to demean herself with print and price—no!

The next poem returns to the question raised in the earlier portion of the fascicle but now the approach is altogether positive. Suspense may be hostiler than death, but all but death can be adjusted. No loss in the circuit world is final, whether it be of large import such as that which pertains to dynasties or systems or whether it be of small import such as the wasting of years on a thankless task. Lives, like the purple sowings of the preceding poem, can be replanted and another spring may find them blossoming (the barrier of citadels may be dissolved). Never mind. Only death is beyond the possibility of change. She, her chances, Nature, the entire circuit world is transient, but that is a good, not an evil, for change may be benevolent.

H6oa

Growth of Man—like Growth of Nature—
Gravitates within—
Atmosphere, and Sun endorse it—
But it stir—alone—

Each—it's difficult Ideal
Must achieve—Itself—
Through the solitary prowess
Of a Silent Life—

Effort—is the sole condition—
Patience of Itself—
Patience of opposing forces—
And intact Belief—

Looking on—is the Department
Of it's Audience—
But Transaction—is assisted
By no Countenance—

H6ob

My Worthiness is all my Doubt—
His Merit—all my fear—
Contrasting which, my quality
Do lowlier—appear—

Lest I should insufficient prove
For His beloved Need—
The Chiefest Apprehension
Upon my thronging Mind—

'Tis true—that Deity to stoop
Inherently incline—
For nothing higher than Itself
Itself can rest upon—

So I—the undivine abode
Of His Elect Content—

Conform my Soul—as twere a Church,
Unto Her Sacrament—

H60c

So the Eyes accost—and sunder
In an Audience—
Stamped—occasionally—forever—
So may Countenance

Entertain—without addressing
Countenance of One
In a Neighboring Horizon—
Gone—as soon as known—

H60d

My Soul—accused me—And I quailed—
As Tongues of Diamond had reviled
All else accused me—and I smiled—
My Soul—that Morning—was My friend—

Her favor—is the best Disdain
Toward Artifice of Time—or Men—
But Her Disdain—'twere lighter bear
A finger of Enamelled Fire—

And this idea of change becomes the subject of her contemplation in the next poem. But it has modulated to growth. I do not know how acquainted Emily Dickinson was with the musical structure of the fugue, but that form is surely akin to what she is constructing in her fascicle. The last group of poems takes all her strands of metaphors, all her questions and concerns, and ties them together in a final burst of joy in herself and her work. Her triumphant realization is precisely that with which she had begun but faltered to uphold. Her resolution restores herself to herself without timidity or ambivalence.

The poem "Growth of Man—like Growth of Nature—" is the analogue of "Never for Society." It has echoes of that image of the dramatic event in "Drama's Vitallest Expression is the Common Day." It has echoes of the silence and solitude of "Conscious am I in my Chamber," and "You taught me Waiting with Myself—" Even the single word "Countenance" reverberates. All the themes are recurring, intricately interweaving now with an emotional dynamics of positive affirmation. Instead of the middling triumph over hymns and ballads, she is now endorsed by sun and atmosphere [the Royal Air]. And the key word, of course, is "prowess." No wretch lulled in a hammock, no sailor crawling to a reef, no inhabitant of a flower, but herself avowing the solitary prowess of her silent life. She announces what keeps her strong, and it is not even God but herself and her own effort, her supreme patience, her indifference to the opposing forces, earlier named life and death. Now her belief admits of no doubt. Let anyone who will look on: what she is doing needs no favor, no friendly countenance. Her flowers need no grace conferred on them.

Emily Dickinson pauses in her next poem, submits for two stanzas to trepidation. She doubts only one thing now, her worthiness. Compared to God (and she *is* comparing herself to God) her quality *may* be of lower stature. If the humility of this poet lasts eight lines it is a long time. How does she resolve this doubt about her status? By teaching herself a truth only she could surmise. The probability for her reply to her own self-doubt lies embedded in that characterization of God as needy. And once said, she wins. God must stoop, must lean on such a one as she, for he cannot rest his weight on anything higher than Himself. So she restores her faith in her worth by proclaiming God necessarily dwells in her. Then and therefore and all right: she will conform her soul to her work, God needs her. She consecrates herself and her endeavor to God. That contract between nature and the poet has now transformed to a covenant between the poet and God.

That said, what then of her solitary self? What of her relinquished society? What of her mortal companions? her Immortal Companion? The third poem goes over the ground of "Conscious am I in my Chamber," but in order to reappraise the poet's relationship to the circuit and the circumference world. She operates in the circuit world, but only as a performer, her real relationship is to God. Her eyes will accost and sunder from the eyes of common folk, but one countenance, seen, leaves its stamp forever. The line "Entertain—without addressing" is a transformation of the line from the first poem of the fascicle, "He doth not attest by Posture— / Nor Confirm—by Word—" It is God, then, who lives in the neighboring horizon. Logic, knowledge, talk will not keep him, but the stamp of the intuitive experience of God is "forever."

The final poem is the analogue to "It dropped so low—in my Regard—" It is instructive to see the poet end the entire sequence of poems not with God but with the self. God has become almost ephemeral in the preceding poem, "Gone—as soon as known—" and He has leaned on the poet in the poem before that. The first poem transcribed onto this final sheet of stationery declares for herself alone. The last poem on the paper, the last in the fascicle, sings the praise of her soul. And everything else, everything, falls into place on her hierarchy.

Her soul has the hardness of a diamond. If her soul says Fool! she quails. Let all others so accuse her, she will smile. If her soul says Yes to her, then all Time—transience, change, annihilation—whatever happens in the course of Nature she may disdain. All Mankind—whoever, wherever—she may disdain. But if her soul reviles her that is worse than any mere putting out of her eyes, worse than any hanging from a scaffold, worse than any drowning, worse than death.

The degree to which each fascicle has its own inner design may be verified by anybody who cares to read the gatherings of poems as the poet intended. They do not all say the same thing, but they all do have an intrinsic dramatic narrative as their central structure. Each poem modulates an image of a preceding poem. Each leads on to what follows. Each has a unity that is verbal, ideational, and dramatic, and at the same time functions as part of a larger construct that is in its turn unified by carefully modulated imagery, deliberately discursive argument, and transforming emotional tone. Precisely what the particular conflict may be in a single fascicle changes as does the quality of feeling with which the poet regards herself and her suffering. Her means of restoring herself to equanimity are not always the same, and in fact there are link-poems which do not end on any triumphant note at all, but conclude rather with resignation or patience or even with a kind of rhetorical restatement of the theory of compensation, familiar to us from our reading of Emerson. Sometimes the processes of Nature tranquilize her, sometimes it is the presence of God that reassures her, sometimes it is an acid challenge to herself to lift herself by her own bootstraps and proceed that restores her.

The subject for despair, the sources and resolution of her doubt, the range on the spectrum of emotions, have got to be determined separately for each threaded booklet. The single poems are disguises, are Emily Dickinson's various masks—of persona, of metaphor, of style, of tone. The form is never possible to disguise. The form of Emily Dickinson's poetry is a structured series of poems, the rendering of a conflict in stages of perplexity moving from query to response, to new inquiry to another reply, until some level of resolution is achieved. Here she rests. Here she ties her booklets. And once here she begins anew. To doubt, to quest, through pain to survival.

I have described the way in which Emily Dickinson practiced the art of poetry, both as it applies to the creating of single poems and the assembling of these poems into larger constructs. For the separate parts I have traced a pattern of effective borrowing from, or better to say improvement of, the printed poems that she encountered in her reading. For the structuring of her poems into self-contained fascicles there are literary sources as well. An examination of the volumes of poetry in the Emily Dickinson Association holdings at the Houghton Library reveals facts that are relevant.

The volumes of Tennyson, Holmes, Willis, Proctor, Emerson, Bryant, Kingsley, E. B. Browning are without any announced organization, simply compilations of verse. Herbert's volume is merely arranged into three parts: The Temple, The Church Militant, and Miscellaneous. Heine's poems were categorized according to types (Dream Pictures, Songs, Romances, Sonnets, Lyrics) and according to subjects (Homeward Journey, Hart Journey, The North Sea). Coleridge's poems were organized into two sections, the first chronological, the second thematic.

But Wordsworth rearranged his published poems into a new organization. The new edition appeared in 1857, and the large handsome volume of Wordsworth in her library is a reprint of the poems in their new ordering. While the scheme has no similarity to Emily Dickinson's conception of related parts, the very act of Wordsworth in republishing his poems in a new design may have suggested to her the idea of arranging poems in some kind of meaningful order.

The scheme of *Hymns of the Ages* is thematic; all the poems appropriate to a single subject are placed together under these topics:

> Aspiration
> Virtue
> **True Gain**

Love
Active Duty
Saints
Contentment
Trust
Affliction
Patience
Prayer
Christ
God
Death
Heaven
Miscellaneous

Emily Dickinson surely tried her hand on all of these themes; each fascicle does contain a representative poem from each category. Moreover, the progression of topics simulate a movement from the secular to the spiritual world, have a type of narrative structure that controls the entire volume.

Coventry Patmore's *Angel in the House* (1856) was on Susan's library table when Emerson called in 1857. That long sentimental poem consists of a series of parts, each carrying a narrative of romantic attachment forward to a happy conclusion. And each part is further divided into separate sections that generalize on an event or the scene or situation, followed usually by one or two or three separate and distinct epigrammatic, even ironic quatrains, concluding with a highly specific narrative portion, with the particular characters and literal events described.

But the most important book in the library, perhaps the seminal influence on Emily Dickinson, is Francis Quarles' *Emblems, Divine and Moral,* (1824 ed.). Browsing through the *Emblems* one discovers dozens of lines that are echoed in Emily Dickinson's verse:

> These are no times to touch the merry string
> Of Orpheus; no, these are no times to sing.
> Can hide-bound pris'ners, that have spent their souls,
> And famish'd bodies in the noisome holes
> Of hell-black dungeons, apt their rougher throats,
> Grown hoarse with begging alms, to warble notes?
> Book 4, Emblem 15

Ye holy virgins, that so oft surround
  The city's sapphire walls; whose snowy feet
Measure the pearly paths of sacred ground,
  And trace the new Jerusalem's jasper street;
        Book 5, Emblem 1

Earth is an island ported round with fears;
Thy way to heav'n is through the sea of tears,
It is a stormy passage, where is found
The wrack of many a ship, but no man drown'd.
        Book 3, Epigram 8

But it is the fact of his larger structure that has the more intriguing relevance now. Quarles calls his major divisions "Volumes." Each volume consists of 15 parts, 15 "Emblems," grouped around a single large theme such as the signs of worldliness, or the fruits of sin, or contrition, or divine justice.

The single Emblem is an allegorical drawing *borrowed* by Quarles from Herman Hugo's book of emblems printed in Antwerp in 1624, *Pia Desideria Emblematis, Elegiis et affectibus S. S. Patrum illustrata.*[7] Below each picture is a text from Scripture which the drawing was intended to illuminate. Then Quarles' poem follows, describing in verse what has been rendered in line. The form of the poem varies: it may be a simple narrative poem in which the event in the picture becomes an incident in the poem, or a sequence of stanzas, each speculating on some aspect of the doctrine illustrated, or a dialogue between two characters who appear to be at odds in the engraving—a device familiar to us from the cartoons of our own day. Thus the poet reconstructs an argument between an unhappy mortal and his divine soul, between Eve and the Serpent, between a pretty youth safe inside a cage of purity arguing with a Satanic creature who is trying to corrupt him. Following this poem is a selection of one or more relevant prose passages taken from the Christian Fathers. These moral writings are chosen for their relationship to the argument or lamentation or doubt raised in the text of the poem. Finally there appears an epigram, written by Quarles, pronouncing the appropriate resolution to the conflict, or calling a character in the poem above it to task for his doubt or his sinful behavior or backsliding or temerity.

The emblem reproduced below is complete in itself; at the same time it is a segment of a larger construct consisting of 15 parts, each combining 4 or 5 disparate pieces. The entire assemblage, as well as this one sequence, represents a religious drama, akin to Emily Dickinson's assemblage of poems into her own narrative of quest.

BOOK V EMBLEM 10

My soul is like a bird, my flesh the cage,
Wherein she wears her weary pilgrimage
Of hours, as few as evil, daily fed
With sacred wine and sacramental bread;
The keys that lock her in and let her out,
Are birth and death; 'twixt both she hops about

From perch to perch, from sense to reason; then
From higher reason down to sense again:
From sense she climbs to faith; where for a season
She sits and sings; then down again to reason:
From reason back to faith, and straight from thence
She rudely flutters to the perch of sense:
From sense to hope; then hops from hope to doubt,
From doubt to dull despair; there seeks about
For desp'rate freedom, and at ev'ry grate
She wildly thrusts, and begs the untimely date
Of th' unexpir'd thraldom, to release
The afflicted captive, that can find no peace.
Thus am I coop'd; within this fleshly cage
I wear my youth, and waste my weary age;
Spending that breath, which was ordain'd to chant
Heav'n's praises forth, in sighs and sad complaint:
Whilst happier birds can spread their nimble wing
From shrubs to cedars, and there chirp and sing,
In choice of raptures, the harmonious story
Of man's redemption, and his Maker's glory:
You glorious martyrs, you illustrious stoops,
That once were cloister'd in your fleshly coops
As fast as I, what rhet'ric had your tongues?
What dext'rous art had your elegiac songs?
What Paul-like pow'r had your admir'd devotion?
What shackle-breaking faith infus'd such motion
To your strong pray'r, that could obtain the boon
To be enlarg'd; to be uncag'd so soon?
Whilst I, poor I, can sing my daily tears,
Grown old in bondage, and can find no ears:
You great partakers of eternal glory,
That with your Heaven-prevailing oratory
Releas'd your souls from your terrestrial cage,
Permit the passion of my holy rage
To recommend my sorrows, dearly known
To you, in days of old, and once your own,
To your best thoughts (but oh't doth not befit ye
To move your prayers; you love joy, not pity:)
Great Lord of souls, to whom should pris'ners fly
But thee? thou hadst a cage as well as I;
And, for my sake, thy pleasure was to know

The sorrows that it brought, and felt'st them too:
O let me free, and I will spend those days,
Which now I waste in begging, in thy praise.

Anselm. in Protolog. Cap.i.

O miserable condition of mankind, that has lost that for which he was created! alas! what hath he lost? and what hath he found? he hath lost happiness for which he was made, and found misery for which he was not made: what is gone? and what is left? that thing is gone, without which he is unhappy; that thing is left, by which he is miserable: O wretched men! from whence are we expelled? to what are we impelled? whence are we thrown? and whither are we hurried? from our home into banishment; from the sight of God into our own blindness; from the pleasure of immortality to the bitterness of death: miserable change! from how great a good, to how great an evil! ah me! what have I enterprised? what have I done? whither did I go? whither am I come?

Epig. 10

Paul's midnight voice prevail'd; his music's thunder
Unhing'd the prison-doors, split bolts in sunder:
And sitt'st thou here, and hang'st the feeble wing?
And whin'st to be enlarg'd? soul, learn to sing.

It is more than a matter of substance or language that calls our attention to Quarles as the poet who engaged the attention of Emily Dickinson. To be sure here is the caged soul, here are all her familiar allusions to nature, here are the devices of dialogue and of personification for abstract ideas and the spirit; here are the birds, the martyrs, the quarrel with sense and with reason, the concept of death as release, the envy of other singers, the direct appeal to Jesus because of the shared experience—all of it is here. But it is the fact of the construct of disparate parts dramatizing a conflict, the picture, the poem, the lamentation of St. Anselm and the resolution provided in the epigram, that is more striking, indeed crucial to our understanding of the achievement of Emily Dickinson. And although it is true that she deliberately organized her lyrics into a kind of dramatic emblem, more intriguing is the fact that even as she imitates this form, she continues her most typical practice where other poets are concerned: she corrects the work! If we read Fascicle 32 in context with Emblem 10 by Quarles we can see that she borrows from Quarles in order to alter, to put straight, to rectify not the language but the thoughts of the poet she has under scrutiny. We find not parallels but refutation.

Quarles' engraving depicts the soul of the poet encaged. In the background hangs an open cage from which a liberated bird has flown. Kneeling at the cage door, with his fingers on the bolt, is an angel. The conflict between the poet and the Lord is narrated in the poem that follows, and from the outcry there we learn that the soul longs for release. Bound to the flesh, the soul is beset with doubt and fear despite moments of hope; the soul flits from sense (despair) to reason (doubt) to faith (hope) and falls back again and again. Those who have passed through the fleshly cage sing rapturously of redemption and the glory of God, but the poet is afraid; he addresses these glorious martyrs, envying their boon, wondering how they achieved their joy, pleading that they speak on his behalf, that they pity him, but finally it is the Lord of souls to whom he addresses himself, only God can free him. The aspect of death, the fearful experience of death intrudes onto the poem as Quarles shifts from verse to prose, quoting a grim and gloomy passage from St. Anselm. The theologian warns man of the misery of ignorance, inveighs against the wretched existence of man who doubts and therefore falls out of the sight of God into the blindness and bitterness of death. Release comes in the Epigram: Paul decrees the poet's liberation.

In the fascicle Emily Dickinson is in colloquy with her own soul; it is her soul that urges the body to be courageous, to lose her timidity of truth, to overcome her fear of death, to allay her doubts of redemption, to take passage out of the mortal state to Heaven where all that was alive still lives, all awaits her there without change, accessible to her eternally. The dialogue leads to a test of liberation by an act of will. Quarles requires the intervention of St. Paul; Emily Dickinson allows her soul to wheedle her body to take the risk for rapture. The climax of the fascicle comes in the moment of transition between the death of the timid but trusting body and the liberation of the secure soul; Emily Dickinson shifts her speaker, it is Jesus who addresses the soul and dissolves all ignorance of how these things may be, then accompanies the soul on its way to light and glory.

Fascicle 32 consists of eleven poems transcribed onto four sheets of stationery. Both T. H. Johnson and R. W. Franklin agree on the contents of the booklet, manuscripts H171, H53, H61 and H54, although they do not place them in the same order. Johnson arranges them: 171, 61, 53, 54; Franklin suggests this sequence: 53, 54, 61, 171. But if we examine the manuscripts bearing in mind the poetic manner of Emily Dickinson—the modulating image, the interplay of metaphors, the narrative structure—and take for our clues the indisputable arrangements of poems on the single piece of stationery as well as Quarles' Emblem 10, then the most probable sequence, surely, is 171, 53, 61 and 54. Let us see.

H171a

Before I got my eye put out
I liked as well to see—
As other Creatures, that have Eyes
And know no other way—

But were it told to me—Today—
That I might have the sky
For mine—I tell you that my Heart
Would split, for size of me—

The Meadows—mine—
The Mountains—mine
All Forests—Stintless Stars—
As much of Noon as I could take
Between my finite eyes—

The Motions of the Dipping Birds—
The Morning's Amber Road—
For mine—to look at when I liked—
The News would strike me dead—

So safer Guess—with just my soul
Upon the Window pane—
Where other Creatures put their eyes—
Incautious—of the Sun—

H171b

Of nearness to her sundered Things
The Soul has special times—

When Dimness—looks the Oddity—
Distinctness—easy—seems—

The Shapes we buried, dwell about,
Familiar, in the Rooms—
Untarnished by the Sepulchre,
The Mouldering Playmate comes—

In just the Jacket that he wore—
Long buttoned in the Mold
Since we—old mornings, Children—played—
Divided—by a world—

The Grave yields back her Robberies—
The Years, our pilfered Things—
Bright Knots of Apparitions
Salute us, with their wings—

As we—it were—that perished—
Themself—had just remained till we rejoin them—
And 'twas they, and not ourself
That mourned.

These two poems introduce the poet and her soul. She is not in a cage but in a strange state of what seems to be physical blindness, as in Anselm's forbidding lines.[8] Her eyes were put out by the Sun, by her degreeless Noon, by her sudden intuition of a truth so overpowering it shattered her physical sense and replaced that dull way of seeing Nature, that ordinary way ignorant creatures must content themselves with, replaced conventional sight with spiritual vision. When she became aware that all this world of transient nature was not merely to observe but might be possessed, was actually a boon for her taking, that news was too much for her; she was too humble, felt too small and perhaps even fearful of such vision. Moreover, to possess it "Today" meant dying today. She preferred to leave it at guess, not certainty. She preferred not yet to die, to leave her soul gazing through the crystal pane.[9]

The narrative continues in H171b: but there were times when the soul took ascendancy over the body, when the vision of what lay beyond this life became more clear than what common sight could behold. The objects in the world of nature of the first poem modulate now to objects in the domestic world. The eye of the soul observes the beloved dead and describes them in terms that are intended to lull not frighten for these are "playmates" and "buttons" in the mold. The soul sees so distinctly it seems as if the departed were alive and mourning us, and we dead waiting to be restored. In the first poem, soul-sight perceives natural phenomena made immutable; in the second poem the vision is of people made immortal.

H53a

Tie the Strings to my Life, My Lord,
Then, I am ready to go!
Just a look at the Horses—
Rapid! That will do!

Put me in on the firmest side—
So I shall never fall—
For we must ride to the Judgment—
And it's partly, down Hill—

But never I mind the steepest—
And never I mind the Sea—
Held fast in Everlasting Race—
By my own Choice, and Thee—

Goodbye to the Life I used to live—
And the World I used to know—
And kiss the Hills, for me, just once—
Then—I am ready to go!

H53b

I like a look of Agony,
Because I know it's true—
Men do not sham Convulsion,
Nor simulate, a Throe—

The Eyes glaze once—and that is Death—
Impossible to feign
The Beads upon the Forehead
By homely Anguish strung.

H53c

I felt a Funeral, in my Brain,
And Mourners to and fro
Kept treading—treading—till it seemed
That Sense was breaking through—

And when they all were seated,
A Service, like a Drum—
Kept beating—beating—till I thought
My Mind was going numb—

And then I heard them lift a Box
And creak across my Soul
With those same Boots of Lead, again,
Then Space—began to toll,

As all the Heavens were a Bell,
And Being, but an Ear,
And I, and Silence, some strange Race
Wrecked, solitary, here—

And then a Plank in Reason, broke,
And I dropped down, and down—
And hit a World, at every plunge,
And Finished knowing—then—

The poet loses timidity, is ready to be restored to those who have departed. She agrees to join the soul and pass through the glass window to death. The experience of death is rendered as a familiar journey in company with Jesus, a friendly coachman who may be reminded to put her in on the firmest side so that she will not tumble out. Although the road has its dangers, being partly downhill—how precisely *down* the next poem will portray—it is not frightful, not the ghastly experience that St. Anselm warns against. She chooses to go; she gladly leaves her life and joins the voyage to immortal Heaven.

But then the reality of mortal annihilation intervenes. She takes a closer look and scares herself with the event of actual death. She tries to brave it out, to exorcize by naming the agony, the death throes, the glazed eyes.

The next poem continues the narrative. Those sundered things playing in the sepulchre, earlier, now have contracted into one corpse; having convulsed and died it must be buried. A funeral is next. The body lies inert except for the sense of hearing, and the sounds are gruesome: treading, beating, creaking, tolling.[10] Contracting still further from the generalized death of loved ones to her own death, there follows now her own descent; it is not the gentle fall of the earlier poem but a drop and a plunge and a hitting of worlds as this body plummets down. But it reaches no bottom for the mortal mind can go no farther, reason is useless, knowing is finished.

This leaves the body in the predicament St. Anselm has bewailed: "From whence are we expelled? to what are we impelled? Whence are we thrown? and whither are we hurried?" In the next group of poems Emily Dickinson replies coolly, calmly, answering the generalizations of Anselm with details of a "whence" (H61a) that are particular and precise, with details of a "whither" (H61b) that become a song of fearlessness, a chant of faith. And Anselm's fear that man may fall out of the sight of God she refutes with a dialogue (H61c) between the soul and her Savior that portrays a care so tender, so compassionate, that Anselm's terror "what have I enterprised? what have I done? whither did I go? whither am I come?" seems unmanly, even faithless by contrast.

H61a

'Twas just this time, last year, I died.
I know I heard the Corn,
When I was carried by the Farms—
It had the Tassels on—

I thought how yellow it would look—
When Richard went to mill—
And then, I wanted to get out,
But something held my will.

I thought just how Red—Apples wedged
The Stubble's joints between—
And Carts went stooping round the fields
To take the Pumpkins in—

I wondered which would miss me, least,
And when Thanksgiving, came,
If Father'd multiply the plates—
To make an even Sum—

And would it blur the Christmas glee
My Stocking hang too high
For any Santa Claus to reach,
The Altitude of me—

But this sort, grieved myself,
And so, I thought the other way,
How just this time, some perfect year—
Themself, should come to me—

H61b

Afraid! Of whom am I afraid?
Not Death—for who is He?
The Porter of my Father's Lodge
As much abasheth me!

Of Life? 'Twere odd I fear [a] thing
That comprehendeth me
In one or two existences—
Just as the case may be—

Of Resurrection? Is the East
Afraid to trust the Morn
With her fastidious forehead?
As soon impeach my Crown!

H61c

I showed her Hights she never saw—
"Would'st Climb," I said?
She said—"Not so"—
"With *me*—" I said—With *me?*
I showed her Secrets—Morning's Nest—
The Rope the Nights were put across—

And *now* —"Would'st have me for a Guest?"
She could not find her Yes —
And then, I brake my life —And Lo,
A Light, for her, did solemn glow,
The larger, as her face withdrew —
And *could* she, further, "No"?

In the dialogue it is Jesus who speaks to the soul in just those gentle terms
the soul earlier used in reassuring the body. Emily Dickinson portrays a
personal Jesus who broke his life for the sake of herself. It is not Paul's
midnight voice of Quarles' Epigram that will unhinge her prison-door,
but Jesus' light that will reveal secrets, as he has done before and will
again. Jesus is a familiar "Guest."

The final group of lyrics in this fascicle carries the soul farther past
the experience of death, leaving the episode, not necessarily the body, well
behind, leaving the factor of time behind. The soul has survived, it has
not descended, and waits now to traverse the vast distance to the place of
redemption.

H54a

'Tis so appalling —it exhilirates —
So over Horror, it half Captivates —
The Soul stares after it, secure —
To know the worst, leaves no dread more —

To scan a Ghost, is faint —
But grappling, conquers it —
How easy, Torment, now —
Suspense kept sawing so —

The Truth, is Bald, and Cold —
But that will hold —
If any are not sure —
We show them —prayer —
But we, who know,
Stop hoping, now —

Looking at Death, is Dying —
Just let go the Breath —

And not the pillow at your Cheek
So Slumbereth —

Others, Can wrestle —
Your's, is done —
And so of Wo, bleak dreaded — come,
It sets the Fright at liberty —
And Terror's free —
Gay, Ghastly, Holiday!

H54b

How noteless Men, and Pleiads, stand,
Until a sudden sky
Reveals the fact that One is rapt
Forever from the Eye —

Members of the Invisible,
Existing, while we stare,
In Leagueless Opportunity,
O'ertakeless, as the Air —

Why did'nt we detain Them?
The Heavens with a smile,
Sweep by our disappointed Heads
Without a syllable —

H54c

When we stand on the tops of Things —
And like the Trees, look down —
The smoke all cleared away from it —
And Mirrors on the scene —

Just laying light — no soul will wink
Except it have the flaw —
The Sound ones, like the Hills — shall stand —
No Lightning, scares away —

The Perfect, nowhere be afraid —
They bear their dauntless Heads,
Where others, dare not go at Noon,
Protected by their deeds —

The Stars dare shine occasionally
Upon a spotted World —
And Suns, go surer, for their Proof,
As if an Axle, held —

Yes, the experience was appalling but now the horror is past. Now the truth that put out her eyes in the first poem returns, but it is characterized as Bald, without subterfuge, as Cold, without the power to shatter a physical sight that no longer exists. Surmise that intimidated has become certainty for the heart has indeed split and no intimidation is possible. Hope and prayer too are useless now, left behind with ignorance. Mortal knowledge is finished but immortal truth has replaced it. The "whence come we" is being explained on another level. The body has left behind the fruits of the farm and Christmas glee; now the soul has left behind fright and terror and dread. So does Emily Dickinson contradict the traditional warnings articulated by Quarles, by Anselm, by St. Augustine, indeed by all the expounders of Christian dogmas from John of Patmos to the Amherst preachers, all who discomfort and dismay. Emily Dickinson refuses here, and always, the threats of conventional theology.

To look at death as ordinary creatures do is terrifying; to visualize death with her soul beside her on the one hand, and Jesus beside her on the other hand, to look upon death as she does is exhilarating. Why? Because the soul is never in danger. It has remained staring down at the struggle and then turned aside to proceed with its business: rising.

H54b presents an enormous expansion of place. The soul is now deep in the Heavens, a shooting star, a member of the invisible, overtakeless, beyond measure. And as the distance increases, the severance from ordinary mortals becomes total. The dead, those who have been unnoticed in life, are suddenly important to those left behind, are at last meaningful only as they are removed, but the "One" is now part of an eternally moving cosmos and all sweep by without deigning to notice the mortals below.

The final poem brings together all the acts and images that opened the fascicle: the vision of course has cleared; the window has modulated to a mirror; the timid heart that split earlier has modulated to a flawed soul that winks; the news that might strike her dead has become the lightning that does not frighten the sound soul; the one who sought safety in guessing now has become dauntless; the stintless stars continue to shine on the spotted world and that sun which shattered the eyes of the person in the beginning is now one of many suns rolling through the heavens. And the fascicle concludes, as it began, with a description of the nature of the soul.

Earlier the soul had been endowed with spiritual light to see; finally it is endowed with perfection to survive. The spotted soul trembles here as the mortal flesh had trembled there. And just as nature—her meadows and rivers and forests, her stars and birds and sunlight—had in the beginning been granted to the soul with the courage to intuite the truth, so at the end, the spotted world receives light from such souls as these, and the universe itself is held firm by the act of faith of the perfect soul. Quarles is timid. St. Anselm is scared. Emily Dickinson decrees a better fate for those noteless men, those infinitesimal sparks who die fearless, trusting in God: the soul is the axle that by its own probity keeps the universe secure.

I cannot help but lament the action of those who first held in their hands the fascicles of Emily Dickinson. They unknotted the twine, separated the pages, placed marks of their choosing on single poems, copied the good ones down for publication in those thin little volumes that bring a heavy price today on the collector's market, but obscured for so long the ultimate value of the poems as Emily Dickinson conceived them. For the poetry of Emily Dickinson is a poetry of assemblage. Each single poem is complete; each fascicle is complete. Taken all together, consider what a tapestry she has woven.

Doubtless that which was real to this poet was limited; her experiences were narrow, the sources for her lines of metaphor were circumscribed by her lack of exposure to people and places and circumstances. Emily Dickinson never went inside the factory at Lowell, never entered a hospital ward, never crossed a cotton plantation. No one can deny her vision was that of a woman confined to the simple employments of housekeeping and gardening: her trees swing like tassels, her days undress themselves, her sunsets sweep with brooms, her summers fling veils, wear dimities, her ghosts wear lace, her soul rides in a carriage, her suffering causes her to stitch zig-zag seams, her departed ones wear frozen brooches.

But she understood risk:

> She staked her Feathers—Gained an Arc—

she understood constraint:

> Still at the Egg-life—
> Chafing the Shell—

she understood triumph:

> What when the Eggs fly off in Music

she understood rank:

> We introduce ourselves
> To Planets and to Flowers

Sitting upright all her days, she recognized polarity:

> Dropped into the Ether Acre—

Emily Dickinson had only eight years of formal schooling, seven—with many interruptions—at the Amherst Academy and one at Mount Holyoke Seminary, nothing after her eighteenth year. She taught herself to see the colors of the breast of a young robin before the red feathers grew; she taught herself to say how the tints on the valley altered minute by minute as the sun went down. She learned the cocoon and the seed. She learned to measure endless space, to gauge eternal time, to interrogate silence, to weigh the inscrutable.

Undismayed by solitude, she created for herself worlds that were whole, satisfying her own sense of significant magnitude. And she carefully placed her emblems of discovery, her poems of quest, encounter and deprivation, of Nature and Heaven and God—the lyrics of the woman and the songs of the poet—one by one, into gatherings that were themselves the paradigm world, that were themselves proxies for publication. They might lie in her drawer now, eventually they would

> Make Summer—When the Lady lie
> In Ceaseless Rosemary—

And that we cannot mollify her fate, after all, is part of our own deprivation, for we have no text of the poetry of Emily Dickinson as she intended it and left it. We have not yet shed the distorting effects of her editors who in her own day confused sentiment with insight, and in our day confuse cataloguing with scholarship. When we reconstruct her threaded booklets we can come to understand the fire of her poetry and treasure that legacy for which she seared her own life.

APPENDIX I

The Fascicle Numbering

I HAVE HAD THE GOOD FORTUNE TO READ THE RECENTLY PUBLISHED monograph, *The Editing of Emily Dickinson, A Reconsideration,* by R. W. Franklin (University of Wisconsin Press, 1967) in time for the preparation of this material. I have profited by Franklin's careful analysis of the physical characteristics of the manuscripts and their ordering and have been saved the embarrassment of many errors that must result from working solely with the Variorum text or the manuscripts as they have been preserved in the Houghton Library under Johnson's guidance and in the Frost Library under Jay Leyda's guidance. I have followed Franklin's suggestions for reordering the manuscript sheets whenever they do not coincide with Johnson's or Leyda's schemes. Where there are discrepancies I have listed both arrangements.

The poems are listed below according to fascicles or packets into which they were gathered, presumably by Emily Dickinson. Fascicles 1 through 38 and 40, 80 through 85 are threaded by Emily Dickinson's hand, with the exceptions of 33, 35, 36 and 38; these were bound with single brass fasteners, probably placed by Lavinia Dickinson. Franklin's argument that there is no Fascicle 39, no Fascicle 10, and that Fascicles 2 and 3 are actually a single gathering is convincing. Packets 86 through 93 are collections of unthreaded manuscripts that seem to have been gathered for binding by the poet. Franklin includes Packets 94 and 95 in his grouping but they seem to me to have too conjectural a relationship to one another to be listed here. Packets 96 through 98 are actually envelopes of loose sheets, as are those numbered 99 through 110. I agree with Franklin's opinion that they are arbitrary gatherings and may not be considered as organized assemblings of related poems.

The numbering of the fascicles and packets was the work of Mrs.

Todd in 1891 when she set herself the task of indexing the manuscripts in her possession; her numbers are arbitrary.

Summary of number of poems in each fascicle and packet

FASCICLE 1: 24	18: 22	32: 11
2–3: 37	19: 23	33: 25
4: 20	20: 13	34: 17
5: 21	21: 22	35: 24
6: 11	22: 25	36: 9
7: 16	23: 19	37: 21
8: 20	24: 21	38: 14
9: 16	25: 23	40: 21
11: 18	26: 26	80: 25
12: 21	27: 22	81: 22
13: 17	28: 20	82: 22
14: 22	29: 20	83: 25
15: 29	30: 20	84: 21
16: 20	31: 20	85: 15
17: 23		
PACKET 86: 38	89: 6	92: 35
87: 32	90: 44	93: 14
88: 41	91: 30	

FASCICLE 1 *

(Manu-
script) (Poem) (First Line)

1a	58	Delayed till she had ceased to know—
1b	89	Some things that fly there be—
1c	90	Within my reach!
1d	91	So bashful when I spied her!
1e	92	My friend must be a Bird—
1f	93	Went up a year this evening!
2a	94	Angels, in the early morning
2b	95	My nosegays are for Captives—
2c	96	Sexton! My Master's sleeping here.

* The manuscript number is that assigned in the Emily Dickinson Association Collection, Houghton Library, Harvard University. The poem number is that assigned by Thomas H. Johnson. The first line is always that of the first poem entered in the Johnson text.

2d	97	The rainbow never tells me
2e	98	One dignity delays for all—
2f	88	As by the dead we love to sit,
2g	99	New feet within my garden go—
2h	903	I hide myself within my flower,
3a	11	I never told the buried gold
3b	49	I never lost as much but twice,
3c	50	I hav'nt told my garden yet—
3d	51	I often passed the village
4a	12	The morns are meeker than they were—
4b	52	Whether my bark went down at sea—
4c	53	Taken from men—this morning—
4d	13	Sleep is supposed to be
4e	54	If I should die,
4f	55	By Chivalries as tiny,

Houghton arrangement: the same.

FASCICLE 2–3

5a	59	A little East of Jordan,
5b	148	All overgrown by cunning moss,
5c	100	A science—so the Savans say,
5d	101	Will there really be a "Morning"?
5e	102	Great Caesar! Condescend
6a	103	I have a King, who does not speak—
6b	104	Where I have lost, I softer tread—
6c	149	She went as quiet as the Dew
6d	105	To hang our head—ostensibly—
6e	106	The Daisy follows soft the Sun—
7a	60	Like her the Saints retire,
7b	61	Papa above!
7c	107	'Twas such a little—little boat
7d	62	"Sown in dishonor"!
7e	150	She died—*this* was the way she died.
7f	63	If pain for peace prepares
7g	108	Surgeons must be very careful

8a	64	Some Rainbow—coming from the Fair!
8b	109	By a flower—By a letter—
8c	65	I cant tell you—but you feel it—
9a	73	Who never lost, are unprepared
9b	74	A Lady red—amid the Hill
9c	126	To fight aloud, is very brave—
9d	127	'Houses'—so the Wise Men tell me—
10a	128	Bring me the sunset in a cup,
10b	75	She died at play,
10c	129	Cocoon above! Cocoon below!
10d	76	Exultation is the going
10e	77	I never hear the word "escape"
11a	130	These are the days when Birds come back—
11b	131	Besides the Autumn poets sing
11c	216	Safe in their Alabaster Chambers—
11d	78	A poor—torn heart—a tattered heart—
12a	132	I bring an unaccustomed wine
12b	133	As Children bid the Guest "Good Night"
12c	79	Going to Heaven!
12d	80	Our lives are Swiss—

Houghton arrangement: Fascicle 2 consists of manuscripts 5, 6, 7, 8 exactly as above; Fascicle 3 consists of manuscripts 9, 10, 11, 12 exactly as above. R. W. Franklin believes that Emily Dickinson gathered all the poems into one fascicle.

FASCICLE 4

13a	165	A *Wounded* Deer—leaps highest—
13b	152	The Sun kept stooping—stooping—low!
13c	166	I met a King this afternoon!
14a	167	To learn the Transport by the Pain—
14b	168	If the foolish, call them *"flowers"*—
14c	169	In Ebon Box, when years have flown
14d	170	Portraits are to daily faces
15a	171	Wait till the Majesty of Death
15b	172	'Tis so much joy! 'Tis so much joy!

15c	173	A fuzzy fellow, without feet,
15d	174	At last, to be identified!
16a	175	I have never seen 'Volcanoes'—
16b	153	Dust is the only Secret—
16c	176	I'm the little "Heart's Ease"!
16d	177	Ah, Necromancy Sweet!
17a	154	Except to Heaven, she is nought.
17b	170	Pictures are to daily faces
17c	178	I cautious, scanned my little life—
17d	179	If I could bribe them by a Rose
17e	180	As if some little Arctic flower

FASCICLE 5

18a	515	No Crowd that has occurred
18b	516	Beauty—be not caused—It Is—
18c	517	He parts Himself—like Leaves—
91a	538	'Tis true—They shut me in the Cold—
91b	539	The Province of the Saved
91c	540	I took my Power in my Hand—
91d	541	Some such Butterfly be seen
93a	542	I had no Cause to be awake—
93b	543	I fear a Man of frugal Speech—
93c	379	Rehearsal to Ourselves
93d	544	The Martyr Poets—did not tell—
95a	550	I cross till I am weary
95b	386	Answer July—
95c	551	There is a Shame of Nobleness—
96a	552	An ignorance a Sunset
96b	553	One Crucifixion is recorded—only—
96c	387	The Sweetest Heresy recieved
96d	388	Take Your Heaven further on—
382a	520	I started Early—Took my Dog—
382b	300	"Morning"—means "Milking"—to the Farmer—
382c	521	Endow the Living—with the Tears—

Houghton arrangement:

18 (515, 516, 517)
149 (354, 518, 355)
150 (356, 519, 357, 358)
382 (520, 300, 521)
20 (672, 359, 360, 361)
22 (522, 523, 362, 363)

FASCICLE 6

25a	498	I envy Seas, whereon He rides—
25b	499	Those fair—fictitious People—
26a	500	Within my Garden, rides a Bird
26b	340	Is Bliss then, such Abyss,
26c	341	After great pain, a formal feeling comes—
26d	501	This World is not Conclusion.
27	503	Better—than Music! For I—who heard it—
381a	342	It will be Summer—eventually.
381b	343	My Reward for Being, was This.
381c	344	'Twas the old—road—through pain—
381d	502	At least—to pray—is left—is left

Houghton arrangement:

23 (495, 337, 496)
24 (338, 497, 339)
25 (498, 499)
26 (500, 340, 341, 501)
381 (342, 343, 344, 502)
27 (503)

FASCICLE 7

28a	134	Perhaps you'd like to buy a flower,
28b	135	Water, is taught by thirst.
28c	136	Have you got a Brook in your little heart,
28d	137	Flowers—Well—if anybody
28e	138	Pigmy seraphs—gone astray—

29a	83	Heart, not so heavy as mine
29b	139	Soul, Wilt thou toss again?
29c	140	An altered look about the hills—
29d	141	Some, too fragile for winter winds
30a	142	Whose are the little beds, I asked
30b	143	For every Bird a Nest—
30c	85	"They have not chosen me," he said,
31a	144	She bore it till the simple veins
31b	81	We should not mind so small a flower—
31c	145	This heart that broke so long—
31d	146	On such a night, or such a night,

FASCICLE 8

32a	283	A Mien to move a Queen—
32b	284	The Drop, that wrestles in the Sea—
32c	285	The Robin's my Criterion for Tune—
32d	243	I've known a Heaven, like a Tent—
33a	244	It is easy to work when the soul is at play—
33b	286	That after Horror—that *'twas us*—
34	223	I Came to buy a smile—today—
35a	288	I'm Nobody! Who are you?
35b	245	I held a Jewel in my fingers—
36a	240	Ah, Moon—and Star!
36b	317	Just so—Jesus—raps—
36c	246	Forever at His side to walk—
36d	221	It cant be "Summer"!
37	247	What would I give to see his face?
38a	248	Why—do they shut Me out of Heaven?
38b	249	Wild Nights—Wild Nights!
38c	250	I shall keep singing!
38d	251	Over the fence—
220	287	A Clock stopped—

X   1737   Rearrange a "Wife's" affection!

Houghton arrangement:

32 (283, 284, 285, 243)
36 (240, 317, 246, 221)
38 (248, 249, 250, 251)
37 (247)
35 (288, 245)
34 (223)
220 (287)
33 (244, 286)

FASCICLE 9

39a	636	The Way I read a Letter's—this—
39b	637	The Child's faith is new—
39c	472	Except the Heaven had come so near—
39d	638	To my small Hearth His fire came
40a	639	My Portion is Defeat—today—
40b	473	I am ashamed—I hide—
41a	640	I cannot live with You—
41b	641	Size circumscribes—it has no room
42a	474	They put Us far apart—
42b	642	Me from Myself—to banish—
42c	475	Doom is the House without the Door—
43a	313	I should have been too glad, I see—
43b	476	I meant to have but modest needs—
44a	(476)	(conclusion of "I meant to have")
44b	643	I could suffice for Him, I knew—
44c	644	You left me—Sire—two Legacies—
44d	477	No Man can compass a Despair—

FASCICLE 10

According to R. W. Franklin there is no Fascicle 10.
Houghton arrangement: manuscript 45, poem #7, "The feet of people
walking home," is the only listing.

FASCICLE 11

50a	645	Bereavement in their death to feel
50b	646	I think To Live—may be a Bliss
50c	647	A little Road—not made of Man—
51a	648	Promise This—When You be Dying—
51b	478	I had no time to Hate—
52a	649	Her Sweet turn to leave the Homestead
52b	650	Pain—has an Element of Blank—
52c	651	So much Summer
131a	754	My Life had stood—a Loaded Gun—
131b	710	The Sunrise runs for Both—
131c	755	No Bobolink—reverse His Singing
132a	756	One Blessing had I than the rest
132b	690	Victory comes late—
132c	757	The Mountains—grow unnoticed—
133a	758	These—saw Visions—
133b	711	Strong Draughts of Their Refreshing Minds
133c	993	We miss Her, not because We see—
133d	675	Essential Oils—are wrung—

Houghton arrangement:

50 (645, 646, 647)
51 (648, 478)
52 (649, 650, 651)

FASCICLE 12

55a	679	Conscious am I in my Chamber,
55b	740	You taught me Waiting with Myself—
55c	705	Suspense—is Hostiler than Death—
56a	741	Drama's Vitallest Expression is the Common Day
56b	706	Life, and Death, and Giants—
56c	742	Four Trees—upon a solitary Acre—
56d	707	The Grace—Myself—might not obtain—

X   1725   I took one Draught of Life—

Houghton arrangement: the same except for exclusion of 1725.

FASCICLE 14

R. W. Franklin concludes his discussion of the ordering of the manuscripts with these words about Fascicle 14:

> The packet remains a hodge-podge of sheets . . . the packet has three different kinds of paper, two or three different periods of handwriting, and three sets of mismatched sewing holes. The sheets are so unrelated that one might suspect they were parts of other gatherings. I have searched several times for the appropriate places in the other fascicles, and although possibilities appear, the manuscript evidence for any of them is not strong enough to establish proper places for these sheets. It is possible, of course, that these sheets might never have been bound by Emily Dickinson into her fascicles; the sewing holes might have come from the sheets having been bound with displaced sheets sometime between 1886 and 1891. Or perhaps some of the sheets may have constituted a small packet by them-selves—H 75–77, for example. At any rate, the six sheets, so grouped, never formed one of Emily Dickinson's fascicles.*

He has satisfied himself only with the shift of manuscript 73, poems #333, #334, #326, to Fascicle 27. The remaining sheets are listed below in their Houghton arrangement.

69a	319	The nearest Dream recedes—unrealized—
69b	277	What if I say I shall not wait!
69c	240	Ah, Moon—and Star!
69d	278	A Shady friend—for Torrid days—
71a	271	A solemn Thing—it was—I said—
71b	272	I breathed enough to take the Trick—
71c	238	Kill your Balm—and it's Odors bless you—
71d	239	"Heaven"—is what I cannot reach!
72a	214	I taste a liquor never brewed—
72b	161	A feather from the Whippowil
72c	181	I lost a World—the other day!
72d	182	If I should'nt be alive
72e	183	I've heard an Organ talk, sometimes—

---

* *The Editing of Emily Dickinson*, p. 58.

83f	201	Two swimmers wrestled on the spar—
83g	202	My Eye is fuller than my vase—
84a	203	He forgot—and I—remembered—
84b	204	A slash of Blue—
84c	205	I should not dare to leave my friend,
84d	206	The Flower must not blame the Bee—
84e	324	Some keep the Sabbath going to Church—

FASCICLE 16

85	371	A precious—mouldering pleasure—'tis—
86a	533	Two Butterflies went out at Noon—
86b	304	The Day came slow—till Five o'clock—
86c	1053	It was a quiet way—
86d	372	I know lives, I could miss
87a	373	I'm saying every day
87b	305	The difference between Despair
87c	374	I went to Heaven—
88a	375	The Angle of a Landscape—
88b	683	The Soul unto itself
88c	534	We see—Comparatively—
88d	376	Of Course—I prayed—
89a	535	She's happy, with a new Content—
89b	536	The Heart asks Pleasure—first—
92a	529	I'm sorry for the Dead—Today—
92b	530	You cannot put a Fire out—
92c	531	We dream—it is good we are dreaming—
384	532	I tried to think a lonelier Thing
X	1727	If ever the lid gets off my head
X	1739	Some say goodnight—at night—

Houghton arrangement:

92 (529, 530, 531)
85 (371)

384 (532)
86 (533, 304, 1053, 372)
87 (373, 305, 374)
88 (375, 683, 534, 376)
89 (535, 536)

FASCICLE 17

90a	306	The Soul's Superior instants
90b	537	Me prove it now—Whoever doubt
90c	377	To lose one's faith—surpass
90d	378	I saw no Way—The Heavens were stitched—
94a	380	There is a flower that Bees prefer—
94b	381	A Secret told—
94c	382	For Death—or rather
67a	383	Exhiliration—is within—
67b	545	'Tis One by One—the Father counts—
67c	546	To fill a Gap
67d	547	I've seen a Dying Eye
68a	384	No Rack can torture me—
68b	548	Death is potential to that Man
68c	385	Smiling back from Coronation
68d	549	That I did always love
20a	672	The Future—never spoke—
20b	359	I gained it so—
20c	360	Death sets a Thing significant
20d	361	What I can do—I will—
22a	522	Had I presumed to hope—
22b	523	Sweet—You forgot—but I remembered
22c	362	It struck me—every Day—
22d	363	I went to thank Her—

Houghton arrangement:

90 (306, 537, 377, 378)
91 (538, 539, 540, 541)
93 (542, 543, 379, 544)
94 (380, 381, 382)

67 (383, 545, 546, 547)
68 (384, 548, 385, 549)
95 (550, 386, 551)
96 (552, 553, 387, 388)

FASCICLE 18

97a	982	No Other can reduce
97b	788	Joy to have merited the Pain—
97c	269	Bound—a trouble—

98a	789	On a Columnar Self—
98b	790	Nature—the Gentlest Mother is,
98c	720	No Prisoner be—
98d	259	Good Night—Which put the Candle out?

99a	721	Behind Me—dips Eternity—
99b	671	She dwelleth in the Ground—
99c	722	Sweet Mountains—Ye tell Me no lie—
99d	723	It tossed—and tossed—

100a	724	It's easy to invent a Life—
100b	791	God gave a Loaf to every Bird—
100c	725	Where Thou art—that—is Home—
100d	726	We thirst at first—'tis Nature's Act—

101a	792	Through the strait pass of suffering—
101b	727	Precious to Me—She still shall be—
101c	665	Dropped into the Ether Acre—
101d	666	Ah, Teneriffe!

102a	793	Grief is a Mouse—
102b	728	Let Us play Yesterday—
102c	729	Alter! When the Hills do—

FASCICLE 19

| 103a | 652 | A Prison gets to be a friend— |
| 103b | 314 | Nature—sometimes sears a Sapling— |

| 104a | 479 | She dealt her pretty words like Blades— |
| 104b | 480 | "Why do I love" You, Sir? |

104c	481	The Himmaleh was known to stoop
104d	482	We Cover Thee—Sweet Face—
105a	653	Of Being is a Bird
105b	654	A long—long Sleep—A famous—Sleep—
105c	655	Without this—there is nought—
105d	656	The name—of it—is "Autumn"—
106a	657	I dwell in Possibility—
106b	483	A Solemn thing within the Soul
106c	658	Whole Gulfs—of Red, and Fleets—of Red—
106d	484	My Garden—like the Beach—
106e	659	That first Day, when you praised Me, Sweet,
107a	485	To Make One's Toilette—after Death
107b	660	'Tis good—the looking back on Grief—
107c	486	I was the slightest in the House—
107d	487	You love the Lord—you cannot see—
108a	488	Myself was formed—a Carpenter—
108b	489	We pray—to Heaven—
108c	315	He fumbles at your Soul
108d	1076	Just Once! Oh least Request!

FASCICLE 20

109a	293	I got so I could hear his name—
109b	263	A single Screw of Flesh
109c	264	A Weight with Needles on the pounds—
110a	217	Savior! I've no one else to tell—
110b	265	Where Ships of Purple—gently toss—
110c	266	This—is the land—the Sunset washes—
110d	294	The Doomed—regard the Sunrise
110e	225	Jesus! thy Crucifix
110f	267	Did we disobey Him?
111	295	Unto like Story—Trouble has enticed me—
112a	296	One Year ago—jots what?
112b	297	It's like the Light—
112c	298	Alone, I cannot be—

FASCICLE 21

113a	389	There's been a Death, in the Opposite House,
113b	554	The Black Berry—wears a Thorn in his side—
113c	307	The One who could repeat the Summer day—
114a	396	There is a Languor of the Life
114b	397	When Diamonds are a Legend,
114c	398	I had not minded—Walls—
114d	399	A House upon the Hight—
115a	390	It's Coming—the postponeless Creature—
115b	308	I send Two Sunsets—
115c	391	A Visitor in Marl—
115d	392	Through the Dark Sod—as Education—
116a	393	Did Our Best Moment last—
116b	555	Trust in the Unexpected—
116c	394	'Twas Love—not me—
116d	556	The Brain, within it's Groove
117a	557	She hideth Her the last—
117b	395	Reverse cannot befall
117c	558	But little Carmine hath her face—
117d	559	It knew no Medicine—
117e	560	It knew no lapse, nor Diminution—
21a	561	I measure every Grief I meet
21b	562	Conjecturing a Climate

Houghton arrangement:

113 (389, 554, 307)
117 (557, 395, 558, 559, 560)
116 (393, 555, 394, 556)
115 (390, 308, 391, 392)
21 (561, 562)
114 (396, 397, 398, 399)

FASCICLE 22

| 118a | 692 | The Sun kept setting—setting—still |
| 118b | 693 | Shells from the Coast mistaking— |

128a	322	There came a Day at Summer's full,
128b	262	The lonesome for they know not What—
129a	291	How the old Mountains drip with Sunset
129b	325	Of Tribulation—these are They,
129c	292	If your Nerve, deny you—
46a	253	You see I cannot see—your lifetime—
46b	254	"Hope" is the thing with feathers—
46c	255	To die—takes just a little while—
46d	256	If I'm lost—now—
74a	257	Delight is as the flight—
74b	219	She sweeps with many-colored Brooms—
74c	290	Of Bronze—and Blaze—
74d	258	There's a certain Slant of light,

Houghton arrangement:

126 (289, 252)
46 (253, 254, 255, 256)
74 (257, 219, 290, 258)
127 (228, 259, 260, 261)
128 (322, 262)
129 (291, 325, 292)

FASCICLE 24

130a	827	The Only News I know
130b	961	Wert Thou but ill—that I might show thee
130c	962	Midsummer, was it, when They died—
209a	902	The first Day that I was a Life
209b	963	A nearness to Tremendousness—
209c	964	"Unto Me?" I do not know you—
209d	965	Denial—is the only fact
210a	903	I hide myself within my flower,
210b	966	All forgot for recollecting
210c	904	Had I not This, or This, I said,
210d	905	Between My Country—and the Others—
211a	906	The Admirations—and Contempts—of time—
211b	907	Till Death—is narrow Loving—

211c	908	'Tis Sunrise—Little Maid—Hast Thou
211d	967	Pain—expands the Time—
212a	968	Fitter to see Him, I may be
212b	969	He who in Himself believes—
213a	970	Color—Caste—Denomination—
213b	909	I make His Crescent fill or lack—
213c	971	Robbed by Death—but that was easy—
213d	972	Unfulfilled to Observation—

Houghton arrangement:

131 (754, 710, 755)
132 (756, 690, 757)
133 (758, 711, 993, 675)

FASCICLE 25

134a	564	My period had come for Prayer—
134b	402	I pay—in Satin Cash—
134c	565	One Anguish—in a Crowd—
134d	335	'Tis not that Dying hurts us so—
135a	566	A Dying Tiger—moaned for Drink—
135b	567	He gave away his Life—
135c	568	We learned the Whole of Love—
135d	403	The Winters are so short—
136	(403)	(conclusion of "The Winters are so short—")
137a	569	I reckon—when I count at all—
137b	404	How many Flowers fail in Wood—
137c	405	It might be lonelier
137d	406	Some—Work for Immortality—
138a	570	I could die—to know—
138b	571	Must be a Wo—
138c	572	Delight—becomes pictorial—
138d	407	If What we Could—were what we would—
138e	573	The Test of Love—is Death—

139a	574	My first well Day—since many ill—
139b	309	For largest Woman's Heart I knew—
139c	408	Unit, like Death, for Whom?
140a	575	"Heaven" has different Signs—to me—
140b	409	They dropped like Flakes—
140c	576	I prayed, at first, a little Girl,

FASCICLE 26

141a	410	The first Day's Night had come—
141b	411	The Color of the Grave is Green—
142a	577	If I may have it, when it's dead,
142b	412	I read my sentence—steadily—
143a	413	I never felt at Home—Below—
143b	578	The Body grows without—
143c	579	I had been hungry, all the Years—
172a	414	'Twas like a Maelstrom, with a notch,
172b	580	I gave myself to Him—
172c	415	Sunset at Night—is natural—
173a	416	A Murmur in the Trees—to note—
173b	417	It is dead—Find it—
173c	418	Not in this World to see his face—
173d	581	I found the words to every thought
174a	419	We grow accustomed to the Dark—
174b	420	You'll know it—as you know 'tis Noon—
174c	421	A Charm invests a face
47a	299	Your Riches—taught me—Poverty.
47b	583	A Toad, can die of Light—
47c	332	There are two Ripenings—one—of sight—
48a	582	Inconceivably solemn!
48b	422	More Life—went out—when He went
48c	423	The Months have ends—the Years—a knot—
48d	424	Removed from Accident of Loss

49a	584	It ceased to hurt me, though so slow
49b	310	Give little Anguish—

Houghton Arrangement:

141 (410, 411)
142 (577, 412)
143 (413, 578, 579)
172 (414, 580, 415)
173 (416, 417, 418, 581)
174 (419, 420, 421)
48 (582, 422, 423, 424)
47 (299, 583, 332)
49 (584, 310)

FASCICLE 27

144a	425	Good Morning—Midnight—
144b	585	I like to see it lap the Miles—
144c	426	It dont sound so terrible—quite—as it did—
145a	427	I'll clutch—and clutch—
145b	428	Taking up the fair Ideal,
145c	429	The Moon is distant from the Sea—
146a	430	It would never be Common—more—I said—
146b	431	Me—come! My dazzled face
146c	432	Do People moulder equally,
147	433	Knows how to forget!
148a	586	We talked as Girls do—
148b	587	Empty my Heart, of Thee—
148c	588	I cried at Pity—not at Pain—
23a	495	It's thoughts—and just One Heart—
23b	337	I know a place where Summer strives
23c	496	As far from pity, as complaint—
24a	338	I know that He exists.
24b	497	He strained my faith—
24c	339	I tend my flowers for thee—

73a	333	The Grass so little has to do—
73b	334	All the letters I can write
73c	326	I cannot dance upon my Toes—

Houghton arrangement:

144 (425, 585, 426)
145 (427, 428, 429)
146 (430, 431, 432)
147 (433)
148 (586, 587, 588)

FASCICLE 28

149a	354	From Cocoon forth a Butterfly
149b	518	Her sweet Weight on my Heart a Night
149c	355	'Tis Opposites—entice—
150a	356	The Day that I was crowned
150b	519	'Twas warm—at first—like Us—
150c	357	God is a distant—stately Lover—
150d	358	If any sink, assure that this, now standing—
151a	589	The Night was wide, and furnished scant
151b	434	To love thee Year by Year—
151c	590	Did you ever stand in a Cavern's Mouth—
151d	435	Much Madness is divinest Sense—
152a	436	The Wind—tapped like a tired Man—
152b	591	To interrupt His Yellow Plan
152c	437	Prayer is the little implement
153a	592	What care the Dead, for Chanticleer—
153b	438	Forget! The Lady with the Amulet
153c	439	Undue Significance a starving man attaches
154a	593	I think I was enchanted
154b	440	'Tis customary as we part
154c	594	The Battle fought between the Soul

Houghton arrangement:

151 (589, 434, 590, 435)
152 (436, 591, 437)

153 (592, 438, 439)
154 (593, 440, 594)

FASCICLE 29

155a	311	It sifts from Leaden Sieves—
155b	595	Like Mighty Foot Lights—burned the Red
156a	598	Three times—we parted—Breath—and I—
156b	599	There is a pain—so utter—
156c	600	It troubled me as once I was—
156d	601	A still—Volcano—Life—
158a	606	The Trees like Tassels—hit—and swung—
158b	444	It feels a shame to be Alive—
19a	443	I tie my Hat—I crease my Shawl—
19b	597	It always felt to me—a wrong
70a	596	When I was small, a Woman died—
70b	441	This is my letter to the World
70c	442	God made a little Gentian—
70d	343	My Reward for Being, was This.
383a	602	Of Brussels—it was not—
383b	603	He found my Being—set it up—
383c	604	Unto my Books—so good to turn—
383d	605	The Spider holds a Silver Ball
X	1710	A curious Cloud surprised the Sky,
X	1712	A Pit—but Heaven over it—
157a *	[443]	'Twould start them—
157b *	[443]	Therefore—we do life's labor—

Houghton arrangement:

155 (311, 595)
70 (596, 441, 442, 343)
19 (443 [157a, 157b] 597)
156 (598, 599, 600, 601)

* alternate stanzas to conclude poem #1712

158 (606, 444)
383 (602, 603, 604, 605)

FASCICLE 30

159a	794	A Drop fell on the Apple Tree—
159b	795	Her final Summer was it—
159c	796	Who Giants know, with lesser Men
160a	797	By my Window have I for Scenery
160b	730	Defrauded I a Butterfly—
160c	731	"I want"—it pleaded—All it's life—
161a	876	It was a Grave, yet bore no Stone
161b	798	She staked her Feathers—Gained an Arc—
161c	799	Despair's advantage is achieved
161d	800	Two—were immortal twice—
162a	803	Who Court obtain within Himself
162b	732	She rose to His Requirement—dropt
162c	802	Time feels so vast that were it not
163a	801	I play at Riches—to appease
163b	804	No Notice gave She, but a Change—
163c	686	They say that "Time assuages"—
164a	681	On the Bleakness of my Lot
164b	805	This Bauble was preferred of Bees—
164c	806	A plated Life—diversified
164d	807	Expectation—is Contentment—

FASCICLE 31

165a	712	Because I could not stop for Death—
165b	759	He fought like those Who've nought to lose—
165c	713	Fame of Myself, to justify,
166a	678	Wolfe demanded during dying
166b	760	Most she touched me by her muteness—
166c	761	From Blank to Blank—
167a	762	The Whole of it came not at once—
167b	763	He told a homely tale

167c	764	Presentiment—is that long Shadow—on the Lawn—
167d	765	You constituted Time—
168a	766	My Faith is larger than the Hills—
168b	714	Rests at Night
168c	715	The World—feels Dusty
168d	767	To offer brave assistance
169a	768	When I hoped, I recollect
169b	316	The Wind did'nt come from the Orchard—today—
170a	716	The Day undressed—Herself—
170b	717	The Beggar Lad—dies early—
170c	769	One and One—are One—
170d	770	I lived on Dread—

FASCICLE 32

53a	279	Tie the Strings to my Life, My Lord,
53b	241	I like a look of Agony,
53c	280	I felt a Funeral, in my Brain,
54a	281	'Tis so appalling—it exhilirates—
54b	282	How noteless Men, and Pleiads, stand,
54c	242	When we stand on the tops of Things—
61a	445	'Twas just this time, last year, I died.
61b	608	Afraid! Of whom am I afraid?
61c	446	He showed me Hights I never saw—
171a	327	Before I got my eye put out
171b	607	Of nearness to her sundered Things

Houghton arrangement:

171 (327, 607)
61 (445, 608, 446)
53 (279, 241, 280)
54 (281, 282, 242)

FASCICLE 33

175a	910	Experience is the Angled Road
175b	973	'Twas awkward, but it fitted me—

175c	974	The Soul's distinct connection
175d	911	Too little way the House must lie
176a	975	The Mountain sat upon the Plain
176b	912	Peace is a fiction of our Faith—
176c	830	To this World she returned.
176d	823	Not what We did, shall be the test
176e	976	Death is a Dialogue between
176f	1114	The largest Fire ever known
177a	913	And this of all my Hopes
177b	901	Sweet, to have had them lost
177c	977	Besides this May
177d	914	I cannot be ashamed
178a	915	Faith—is the Pierless Bridge
178b	916	His Feet are shod with Gauze—
178c	917	Love—is anterior to Life—
178d	918	Only a Shrine, but Mine—
178e	919	If I can stop one Heart from breaking
179a	504	You know that Portrait in the Moon—
179b	345	Funny—to be a Century—
179c	346	Not probable—The barest Chance—
179d	347	When Night is almost done—
180a	978	It bloomed and dropt, a Single Noon—
180b	979	This Merit hath the worst—
180c	920	We can but follow to the Sun—

FASCICLE 34

181a	609	I—Years had been—from Home—
181b	610	You'll find—it when you try to die—
182a	611	I see thee better—in the Dark—
182b	447	Could—I do more—for Thee—
182c	612	It would have starved a Gnat—
182d	613	They shut me up in Prose—
183a	448	This was a Poet—It is That
183b	614	In falling Timbers buried—

FASCICLE 35

193a	1090	I am afraid to own a Body—
193b	1091	The Well upon the Brook
193c	1092	It was not Saint—it was too large—
193d	1093	Because 'twas Riches I could own,
193e	1094	Themself are all I have—
193f	1095	To Whom the Mornings stand for Nights,

FASCICLE 36

194	609	I Years had been from Home
195	1224	Like Trains of Cars on Tracks of Plush
196	1255	Longing is like the Seed
197	1226	The Popular Heart is a Cannon first—
198	1227	My Triumph lasted till the Drums
199a	1209	To disappear enhances—
199b–c	1228	So much of Heaven has gone from Earth
281	1225	It's Hour with itself
B103–8	1269	I worked for chaff and earning Wheat

Houghton arrangement:

194 (609)
195 (1224)
281 (1225)
197 (1226)
198 (1227)
199 (1209, 1228)
196 (1255)

FASCICLE 37

200a	230	We—Bee and I—live by the quaffing—
200b	231	God permits industrious Angels—
200c	232	The Sun—*just touched* the Morning—
200d	233	The Lamp burns sure—within—
201a	163	Tho' my destiny be Fustian—
201b	207	Tho' I get home how late—how late—

201c	208	The Rose did caper on her cheek—
201d	209	With thee, in the Desert—
201e	185	"Faith" is a fine invention
201f	210	The thought beneath so slight a film—
202a	318	I'll tell you how the Sun rose—
202b	(318)	(conclusion of "I'll tell you how the Sun rose—")
202c	159	A little Bread—a crust—a crumb—
202d	160	Just lost, when I was saved!
202e	211	Come slowly—Eden!
202f	212	Least Rivers—docile to some sea.
203a	270	*One Life* of so much Consequence!
203b	234	You're right—"the way *is* narrow"—
203c	216	Safe in their Alabaster Chambers—
204a	235	The Court is far away—
204b	236	If *He dissolve*—then—there is *nothing—more*—
204c	237	I think just how my shape will rise—
204d	224	I've nothing else—to bring, You know—

FASCICLE 38

205a	1185	A little Dog that wags his tail
205b	1187	Oh Shadow on the Grass,
205c	1196	To make Routine a Stimulus
206a	1197	I should not dare to be so sad
206b	1182	Remembrance has a Rear and Front—
206c	1200	Because my Brook is fluent
207	1194	Somehow myself survived the Night
208a	1201	So I pull my Stockings off
208b	1195	What we see we know somewhat
208c	1203	The Past is such a curious Creature
208d	1177	A prompt—executive Bird is the Jay—
380a	1353	The last of Summer is Delight—
380b	1354	The Heart is the Capital of the Mind—
380c	1344	Not any more to be lacked—

Houghton arrangement:

205 (1185, 1187, 1196)
206 (1197, 1182, 1200)
380 (1353, 1354, 1344)
207 (1194)
208 (1201, 1195, 1203, 1177)

FASCICLE 39

According to R. W. Franklin there is no Fascicle 39.

Houghton arrangement:

130 (827, 961, 962)
209 (902, 963, 964, 965)
210 (903, 966, 904, 905)
211 (906, 907, 908, 967)
212 (968, 969)
213 (970, 909, 971, 972)

FASCICLE 40

214a	455	Triumph—may be of several kinds—
214b	617	Dont put up my Thread & Needle—
214c	456	So well that I can live without—
214d	618	At leisure is the Soul
215a	457	Sweet—safe—Houses—
215b	619	Glee—The great storm is over—
215c	620	It makes no difference abroad—
215d	621	I asked no other thing—
216a	622	To know just how He suffered—would be dear—
216b	623	It was too late for Man—
216c	624	Forever—is composed of Nows—
217a	625	'Twas a long Parting—but the time
217b	626	Only God—detect the Sorrow—
217c	458	Like Eyes that looked on Wastes—
217d	459	A Tooth upon Our Peace
218a	460	I know where Wells grow—Droughtless Wells—
218b	627	The Tint I cannot take—is best—

219a	461	A Wife—at Daybreak I shall be—
219b	462	Why make it doubt—it hurts it so—
219c	463	I live with Him—I see His face—
219d	464	The power to be true to You,

FASCICLE 80 *

1	8	There is a word
1a	9	Through lane it lay—thro' bramble—
2	15	The Guest is gold and crimson—
2	36	I counted till they danced so
2a	37	Before the ice is in the pools—
2a	38	By such and such an offering
3	39	It did not surprise me—
3a	40	When I count the seeds
8	147	Bless God, he went as soldiers,
8	56	If I should cease to bring a Rose
8a	14	One Sister have I in the house,
X	1730	"Lethe" in my flower,
8a	57	To venerate the simple days
X	1729	I've got an arrow here.
4	41	I robbed the Woods—
4	42	A Day! Help! Help! Another Day!
4a	43	Could live—did live—
4a	44	If she had been the Mistletoe
5	10	My wheel is in the dark!
5a	45	There's something quieter than sleep
6	46	I keep my pledge.
6	47	Heart! We will forget him!
6a	48	Once more, my now bewildered Dove
6a	17	Baffled for just a day or two—
7	336	The face I carry with me—last—

FASCICLE 81

1	771	None can experience stint
1a	772	The hallowing of Pain
2	773	Deprived of other Banquet,
2a	774	It is a lonesome Glee—

* The manuscript number is that assigned in the Bingham Collection, Frost Library; the poem number is that assigned by Johnson. R. W. Franklin proposes this revision of Fascicle 80 based on his examination of scraps and transcripts of poems whose manuscripts are lost.

2a	775	If Blame be my side—forfeit Me—
3	776	The Color of a Queen, is this—
3a	677	To be alive—is Power—
4	777	The Loneliness One dare not sound—
4a	676	Least Bee that brew—
5	778	This that would greet—an hour ago—
5a	779	The Service without Hope—
6	718	I meant to find Her when I came—
6a	780	The Truth—is stirless—
7	719	A South Wind—has a pathos
7	781	To wait an Hour—is long—
7a	782	There is an arid Pleasure—
8	783	The Birds begun at Four o'clock—
9	784	Bereaved of all, I went abroad—
9a	785	They have a little Odor—that to me
10	786	Severer Service of myself
11	682	'Twould ease—a Butterfly—
11a	787	Such is the Force of Happiness—

FASCICLE 82

1	18	The Gentian weaves her fringes—
1a	6	Frequently the woods are pink—
1a	19	A sepal, petal, and a thorn
2	20	Distrustful of the Gentian—
2	21	We lose—because we win—
2a	22	All these my banners be.
3	23	I had a guinea golden—
4	24	There is a morn by men unseen—
4a	323	As if I asked a common Alms,
4a	25	She slept beneath a tree—
5	7	The feet of people walking home
5a	26	It's all I have to bring today—
6	27	Morns like these—we parted—
6	28	So has a Daisy vanished
6a	29	If those I loved were lost
7	30	Adrift! A little boat adrift!
7	31	Summer for thee, grant I may be
7a	32	When Roses cease to bloom, Sir,
7a	33	If recollecting were forgetting,
8	4	On this wondrous sea

| 8a | 34 | Garlands for Queens, may be— |
| 8a | 35 | Nobody knows this little Rose— |

FASCICLE 83

1	66	So from the mould
1	110	Artists wrestled here!
1a	67	Success is counted sweetest
1a	111	The Bee is not afraid of me.
2	112	Where bells no more affright the morn—
2a	68	Ambition cannot find him.
2a	113	Our share of night to bear—
3	114	Good night, because we must,
3	86	South Winds jostle them—
3a	69	Low at my problem bending,
3a	115	What Inn is this
4	116	I had some things that I called mine—
4a	117	In rags mysterious as these
4a	118	My friend attacks my friend!
5	70	"Arcturus" is his other name—
6	119	Talk with prudence to a Beggar
6	120	If this is "fading"
6a	121	As Watchers hang upon the East,
6a	84	Her breast is fit for pearls,
7	122	A something in a summer's Day
7a	71	A throe upon the features—
8	72	Glowing is her Bonnet,
8	123	Many cross the Rhine
8a	124	In lands I never saw—they say
8a	125	For each extatic instant

FASCICLE 84

1	628	They called me to the Window, for
1a	669	No Romance sold unto
2	465	I heard a Fly buzz—when I died—
2a	674	The Soul that hath a Guest
3	629	I watched the Moon around the House
4	1181	When I hoped I feared—
4a	630	The Lightning playeth—all the while—
5	631	Ourselves were wed one summer—dear—
5a	466	'Tis little I—could care for Pearls—
6	632	The Brain—is wider than the Sky—

6a	467	We do not play on Graves—
7	312	Her—"last Poems"—
7a	633	When Bells stop ringing—Church—begins—
8	468	The Manner of it's Death
8a	469	The Red—Blaze—is the Morning—
9	634	You'll know Her—by Her Foot—
10	470	I am alive—I guess—
11	1067	Except the smaller size
11a	635	I think the longest Hour of all
12	329	So glad we are—a Stranger'd deem
12a	471	A Night—there lay the Days between—

FASCICLE 85

1	348	I dreaded that first Robin, so,
2	505	I would not paint—a picture—
3	506	He touched me, so I live to know
3a	349	I had the Glory—that will do—
4	507	She sights a Bird—she chuckles—
4a	350	They leave us with the Infinite.
5	508	I'm ceded—I've stopped being Their's—
6	509	If anybody's friend be dead
7	510	It was not Death, for I stood up,
8	511	If you were coming in the Fall,
9	351	I felt my life with both my hands
9a	352	Perhaps I asked too large—
10	328	A Bird came down the Walk—
11	512	The Soul has Bandaged moments—
12	513	Like Flowers, that heard the news of Dews,

PACKET 86 *

1	922	Those who have been in the Grave the longest—
1	845	Be Mine the Doom—
1a	876	It was a Grave, yet bore no Stone
2	838	Impossibility, like Wine
2	808	So set it's Sun in Thee
2a	923	How the Waters closed above Him

* The term "Fascicle" is used to designate only those gatherings which were tied together as evidenced by needle holes along the left-hand margins of the manuscripts. "Packet" denotes those gatherings of loose manuscripts. Their placement and ordering can never be more than conjectural, except in those cases where several poems are transcribed onto a single folded sheet.

3	839	Always Mine!
3a	840	I cannot buy it—'tis not sold—
4	841	A Moth the hue of this
4a	842	Good to hide, and hear 'em hunt!
5	924	Love—is that later Thing than Death—
5a	925	Struck, was I, nor yet by Lightning—
6a	926	Patience—has a quiet Outer—
7	831	Dying! To be afraid of thee
7a	843	I made slow Riches but my Gain
8	844	Spring is the Period
8	834	Before He comes we weigh the Time!
8a	846	Twice had Summer her fair Verdure
9	809	Unable are the Loved to die
9	847	Finite—to fail, but infinite to Venture—
9a	848	Just as He spoke it from his Hands
9a	849	The good Will of a Flower
10	850	I sing to use the Waiting
10	810	Her Grace is all she has—
10a	851	When the Astronomer stops seeking
11	927	Absent Place—an April Day—
11	852	Apology for Her
11a	928	The Heart has narrow Banks
12	853	When One has given up One's life
12a	811	The Veins of other Flowers
13	812	A Light exists in Spring
13a	854	Banish Air from Air—
14	1105	Like Men and Women Shadows walk
14a	929	How far is it to Heaven?
15	813	This quiet Dust was Gentlemen and Ladies
15a	930	There is a June when Corn is cut

16	855	To own the Art within the Soul
16a	856	There is a finished feeling

PACKET 87

1	857	Uncertain lease—develops lustre
1	931	Noon—is the Hinge of Day—
1a	858	This Chasm, Sweet, upon my life
2a	932	My best Acquaintances are those
3	859	A Doubt if it be Us
3	860	Absence disembodies—so does Death
3a	861	Split the Lark—and you'll find the Music—
4	862	Light is sufficient to itself—
4	863	That Distance was between Us
4a	833	Perhaps you think me stooping
5	814	One Day is there of the Series
5a	815	The Luxury to apprehend
6	864	The Robin for the Crumb
6a	865	He outstripped Time with but a Bout,
7	836	Truth—is as old as God—
7	816	A Death blow is a Life blow to Some
7a	933	Two Travellers perishing in Snow
8	866	Fame is the tint that Scholars leave
8a	867	Escaping backward to perceive
9	934	That is solemn we have ended
9	868	They ask but our Delight—
9a	869	Because the Bee may blameless hum
10	870	Finding is the first Act
10a	817	Given in Marriage unto Thee
11	871	The Sun and Moon must make their haste—
11a	872	As the Starved Maelstrom laps the Navies

10	1043	Lest this be Heaven indeed
10a	523	Just to be Rich
11	1061	Three Weeks passed since I had seen Her—
11a	1044	A Sickness of this World it most occasions
11a	994	Partake as doth the Bee,
12	1062	He scanned it—staggered—
12a	985	The Missing All, prevented Me
13	986	A narrow Fellow in the Grass
14	1063	Ashes denote that Fire was—
14a	987	The Leaves like Women, interchange
15	1045	Nature rarer uses Yellow
15	1064	To help our Bleaker Parts
15a	1046	I've dropped my Brain—My Soul is numb—
16a	1047	The Opening and the Close
17	1065	Let down the Bars, Oh Death—
17a	1048	Reportless Subjects, to the Quick
17a	988	The Definition of Beauty is
18	1049	Pain has but one Acquaintance
18a	989	Gratitude—is not the mention

PACKET 89

1	1220	Of Nature I shall have enough
2	1219	Now I knew I lost her—
4	492	Civilization—spurns—the Leopard!
6	491	While it is alive
7	493	The World—stands—solemner—to me—
8	663	Again—his voice is at the door—

(56) *	494	Going to Him! Happy letter!

PACKET 90

1	997	Crumbling is not an instant's Act
1a	1054	Not to discover weakness is
2	998	Best Things dwell out of Sight
2a	982	No Other can reduce
3	999	Superfluous were the Sun
3a	995	This was in the White of the Year—
4	1000	The Fingers of the Light
4a	983	Ideal are the Fairy Oil
5	1001	The Stimulus, beyond the Grave
5	1002	Aurora is the effort
5a	1003	Dying at my music!
5a	1004	There is no Silence in the Earth—so silent
6	1005	Bind me—I still can sing—
6	1006	The first We knew of Him was Death—
6a	1007	Falsehood of Thee could I suppose
6a	1008	How still the Bells in Steeples stand
7	1009	I was a Phebe—nothing more—
7a	433	Knows how to forget!
8a	984	'Tis Anguish grander than Delight
9	1055	The Soul should always stand ajar
9a	1010	Up Life's Hill with my little Bundle
9a	1011	She rose as high as His Occasion
10	1056	There is a Zone whose even Years
10a	1012	Which is best? Heaven—
11	1177	A bold, inspiriting Bird
11a	1013	Too scanty 'twas to die for you,

* The manuscript number is conjectural.

12	1014	Did We abolish Frost
12	1015	Were it but Me that gained the Hight—
12a	1016	The Hills in Purple syllables
12a	1017	To die—without the Dying
13	1018	Who saw no Sunrise cannot say
13a	1057	I had a daily Bliss
13a	1019	My Season's furthest Flower—
14	1020	Trudging to Eden, looking backward,
14a	1021	Far from Love the Heavenly Father
15	1022	I knew that I had gained
15	1023	It rises—passes—on our South
15a	1024	So large my Will
16	1025	The Products of my Farm are these
16a	1026	The Dying need but little, Dear,
17	1058	Bloom—is Result—to meet a Flower
17a	1027	My Heart upon a little Plate
18	1028	'Twas my one Glory—
18	1029	Nor Mountain hinder Me

PACKET 91

1	874	They wont frown always—some sweet Day
1a	940	On that dear Frame the Years had worn
2	941	The Lady feeds Her little Bird
2	832	Soto! Explore thyself!
2a	875	I stepped from Plank to Plank
3	835	Nature and God—I neither knew
3	845	Be Mine the Doom—
3a	877	Each Scar I'll keep for Him
3a	837	How well I knew Her not
4	942	Snow beneath whose chilly softness
4	818	I could not drink it, Sweet,
4a	878	The Sun is gay or stark

5	879	Each Second is the last
5a	880	The Bird must sing to earn the Crumb
6	881	I've none to tell me to but Thee
6a	819	All I may, if small,
7	943	A Coffin—is a small Domain,
7a	944	I learned—at least—what Home could be—
9	945	This is a Blossom of the Brain—
9a	820	All Circumstances are the Frame
10	882	A Shade upon the mind there passes
10a	946	It is an honorable Thought
11	400	A Tongue—to tell Him I am true!
12	563	I could not prove the Years had feet—
12a	401	What Soft—Cherubic Creatures—
13	883	The Poets light but Lamps—
13	884	An Everywhere of Silver
13a	885	Our little Kinsmen—after Rain
14	947	Of Tolling Bell I ask the cause?
14a	886	These tested our Horizon—

PACKET 92

1	828	The Robin is the One
1a	948	'Twas Crisis—All the length had passed—
2	887	We outgrow love, like other things
2a	888	When I have seen the Sun emerge
3	889	Crisis is a Hair
3a	949	Under the Light, yet under,
4	821	Away from Home are some and I—
4a	229	A Burdock—clawed my Gown—
5	1540	As imperceptibly as Grief

6	1050	As willing lid o'er weary eye
6a	990	Not all die early, dying young—
7	822	This Consciousness that is aware
7a	890	From Us She wandered now a Year,
8	950	The Sunset stopped on Cottages
8a	829	Ample make this Bed—
9	951	As Frost is best conceived
9a	891	To my quick ear the Leaves—conferred—
10	952	A Man may make a Remark—
10a	953	A Door just opened on a street—
11	892	Who occupies this House?
12	954	The Chemical conviction
12a	955	The Hollows round His eager Eyes
13	956	What shall I do when the Summer troubles—
13a	893	Drab Habitation of Whom?
14	957	As One does Sickness over
14a	958	We met as Sparks—Diverging Flints
15	894	Of Consciousness, her awful Mate
15a	895	A Cloud withdrew from the Sky
16	896	Of Silken Speech and Specious Shoe
16	897	How fortunate the Grave—
16a	898	How happy I was if I could forget
17	959	A loss of something ever felt I—
17a	899	Herein a Blossom lies—
18	900	What did They do since I saw Them?
18a	960	As plan for Noon and plan for Night

PACKET 93

1	1202	The Frost was never seen—
2	1189	The Voice that stands for Floods to me

APPENDIX II

The Rubrics

POEMS LISTED ACCORDING TO THEMES, CLUSTERS OF METAPHORS AND persona, with a paradigm poem quoted for each rubric.

A. Poems that render an affliction, a gradual healing, and ultimate patience (pain and survival).
B. Poems that render the solitary self as a conscious choice.
C. Poems that render the poet's longing to be with someone, or his transfiguring power.
D. Poems that contemplate the problem of knowing.
E. Poems that contemplate poetry.
F. Poems that personify Nature (transformation, regeneration).
G. The subject matter of the poem is an actual death.
H. Poems that contemplate the experience of death.
I. Poems that contemplate Jesus or God.
J. Poems that contemplate the nature of Heaven and Immortality.
K. Poems that render a child going to Heaven.
L. The persona shifts to wife or bride going to Heaven.
M. Poems rendering quest.
N. Poems rendering compensation (yoked opposites).
O. Poems that have the metaphor of a boat or ship at sea, or the sea.
P. Poems that have the metaphor of the cage or prison.
Q. Poems sent to Samuel Bowles.

Within each rubric the poems are arranged according to the fascicles or packets in which they were placed. Each poem is identified by its manuscript number, its first line, and, in brackets, by the number assigned to it by Johnson in the Variorum text. For example:

1 H1e   My friend must be a Bird—[92]

1 signifies the poem is part of Fascicle 1; *H1e* signifies the manuscript is in the Houghton collection on sheet 1, position e; [92] signifies that it is poem #92 in the Variorum text.

A. POEMS THAT RENDER AN AFFLICTION, A GRADUAL HEALING, AND ULTIMATE PATIENCE (PAIN AND SURVIVAL)

Poem #425

Good Morning—Midnight—
I'm coming Home—
Day—got tired of Me—
How could I—of Him?

Sunshine was a sweet place—
I liked to stay—
But Morn—did'nt want me—now—
So—Goodnight—Day!

I can look—cant I—
When the East is Red?
The Hills—have a way—then—
That puts the Heart—abroad—

You—are not so fair—Midnight—
I chose—Day—
But—please take a little Girl—
He turned away!

1	H1e	My friend must be a Bird—[92]
2	H6d	To hang our head—ostensibly—[105]
[3]	H9c	To fight aloud, is very brave—[126]
4	H14a	To learn the Transport by the Pain—[167]
5	H91a	'Tis true—They shut me in the Cold—[538]
	H91c	I took my Power in my Hand—[540]
	H93a	I had no Cause to be awake—[542]
	H93c	Rehearsal to Ourselves [379]
	H93d	The Martyr Poets—did not tell—[544]
	H95a	I cross till I am weary [550]
	H96b	One Crucifixion is recorded—only—[553]
	H96d	Take Your Heaven further on—[388]
	H382a	I started Early—Took my Dog—[520]

6	H26b	Is Bliss then, such Abyss, [340]
	H26c	After great pain, a formal feeling comes—[341]
	H381d	At least—to pray—is left—is left—[502]
7	H29a	Heart, not so heavy as mine [83]
	H30c	"They have not chosen me," he said, [85]
8	H33a	It is easy to work when the soul is at play—[244]
	H33b	That after Horror—that 'twas us—[286]
	H36b	Just so—Jesus—raps—[317]
	H38a	Why—do they shut Me out of Heaven? [248]
	H220	A Clock stopped—[287]
9	H39c	Except the Heaven had come so near—[472]
	H40a	My Portion is Defeat—today—[639]
	H40b	I am ashamed—I hide—[473]
	H42b	Me from Myself—to banish—[642]
	H43a	I should have been too glad, I see—[313]
	H43b–44a	I meant to have but modest needs—[476]
	H44c	You left me—Sire two Legacies—[644]
	H44d	No Man can compass a Despair—[477]
11	H50b	I think To Live—may be a Bliss [646]
	H51b	I had no time to Hate—[478]
	H52b	Pain—has an Element of Blank—[650]
	H131a	My Life had stood—a Loaded Gun—[754]
	H131c	No Bobolink—reverse His Singing [755]
	H132a	One Blessing had I than the rest [756]
	H132b	Victory comes late—[690]
	H133b	Strong Draughts of Their Refreshing Minds [711]
	H133d	Essential Oils—are wrung—[675]
12	H55b	You taught me Waiting with Myself—[740]
	H55c	Suspense—is Hostiler than Death—[705]
	H57a	The Birds reported from the South—[743]
	H57b	Remorse—is Memory—awake—[744]
	H57c	Renunciation—is a piercing Virtue—[745]
	H58a	Never for Society [746]
	H58b	I sometimes drop it, for a Quick—[708]
	H58c	It dropped so low—in my Regard—[747]

	H59c	All but Death, can be Adjusted—[749]
	H60a	Growth of Man—like Growth of Nature—[750]
	H60b	My Worthiness is all my Doubt—[751]
	H60d	My Soul—accused men—And I quailed—[753]
13	H62a	The Morning after Wo—[364]
	H63d	I reason, Earth is short—[301]
	H64a	To put this World down, like a Bundle—[527]
	H64b	Although I put away his life—[366]
	H65a	One need not be a Chamber—to be Haunted—[670]
	H65c	The Soul selects her own Society—[303]
	H66a	How sick—to wait—in any place—but thine—[368]
	H66b	Mine—by the Right of the White Election! [528]
14	H69b	What if I say I shall not wait! [277]
	H71a	A solemn thing—it was—I said—[271]
	H71b	I breathed enough to take the Trick—[272]
	H71d	"Heaven"—is what I cannot reach! [239]
	H72c	I lost a World—the other day! [181]
	H75a	He put the Belt around my life—[273]
	H77b	Her smile was shaped like other smiles—[514]
	H77c	A happy lip—breaks sudden—[353]
15	H78a	What shall I do—it whimpers so—[186]
	H78d	Bound—a trouble—[269]
	H80d	It's such a little thing to weep [189]
	H80e	He was weak, and I was strong—then—[190]
	H81b	Poor little Heart! [192]
	H82c	We dont cry—Tim and I, [196]
	H83d	I'm "wife"—I've finished that—[199]
	H83f	Two swimmers wrestled on the spar—[201]
	H84a	He forgot—and I—remembered—[203]
16	H87b	The difference between Despair [305]
	H88b	The Soul unto itself [683]
	H88d	Of Course—I prayed—[376]
	H89b	The Heart asks Pleasure—first—[536]
	H92c	We dream—it is good we are dreaming—[531]
	H384	I tried to think a lonelier Thing [532]
17	H90a	The Soul's Superior instants [306]
	H90b	Me prove it now—Whoever doubt [537]

	H90d	I saw no Way—The Heavens were stitched—[378]
	H67a	Exhiliration—is within—[383]
	H67c	To fill a Gap [546]
	H68a	No Rack can torture me—[384]
	H20d	What I can do—I will—[361]
	H22a	Had I presumed to hope—[522]
	H22c	It struck me—every Day—[362]
18	H97c	Bound—a trouble—[269]
	H98a	On a Columnar Self—[789]
	H99a	Behind Me—dips Eternity—[721]
	H101a	Through the strait pass of suffering—[792]
	H102a	Grief is a Mouse—[793]
	H102b	Let Us play Yesterday—[728]
19	H103a	A Prison gets to be a friend—[652]
	H103b	Nature—sometimes sears a Sapling—[314]
	H104a	She dealt her pretty words like Blades—[479]
	H105c	Without this—there is nought—[655]
	H106b	A Solemn thing within the Soul [483]
	H107a	To make One's Toilette—after Death [485]
	H107b	'Tis good—the looking back on Grief—[660]
	H107c	I was the slightest in the House—[486]
20	H109a	I got so I could hear his name—[293]
	H109b	A single Screw of Flesh [263]
	H109c	A Weight with Needles on the pounds [264]
	H110d	The Doomed—regard the Sunrise [294]
	H110e	Jesus! thy Crucifix [225]
	H112a	One Year ago—jots what? [296]
21	H113b	The Black Berry—wears a Thorn in his side—[554]
	H114a	There is a Languor of the Life [396]
	H116a	Did Our Best Moment last—[393]
	H116d	The Brain, within it's Groove [556]
	H117b	Reverse cannot befall [395]
	H21a	I measure every Grief I meet [561]
22	H118a	The Sun kept setting—setting—still [692]
	H119d	Upon Concluded Lives [735]
	H120b	Each Life Converges to some Centre—[680]

	H123d–124	No matter—now—Sweet—[704]
	H125c	I many times thought Peace had come [739]
23	H129b	Of Tribulation—these are They, [325]
	H129c	If your Nerve, deny you—[292]
	H46d	If I'm lost—now—[256]
	H74a	Delight is as the flight—[257]
	H74d	There's a certain Slant of light, [258]
24	H209a	The first Day that I was a Life [902]
	H210b	All forgot for recollecting [966]
	H210c	Had I not This, or This, I said, [904]
	H211d	Pain—expands the Time—[967]
	H212a	Fitter to see Him, I may be [968]
	H212b	He who in Himself believes—[969]
	H213c	Robbed by Death—but that was easy—[971]
	H213d	Unfulfilled to Observation—[972]
25	H134a	My period had come for Prayer—[564]
	H134c	One Anguish—in a Crowd—[565]
	H134d	'Tis not that Dying hurts us so—[335]
	H137c	It might be lonelier [405]
	H138b	Must be a Wo—[571]
	H138c	Delight—becomes pictorial—[572]
	H139a	My first well Day—since many ill—[574]
	H139b	For largest Woman's Heart I knew—[309]
	H140c	I prayed, at first, a little Girl, [576]
26	H141a	The first Day's Night had come—[410]
	H142b	I read my sentence—steadily—[412]
	H143b	The Body grows without—[578]
	H143c	I had been hungry, all the Years—[579]
	H172a	'Twas like a Maelstrom, with a notch, [414]
	H172b	I gave myself to Him—[580]
	H174a	We grow accustomed to the Dark—[419]
	H48b	More Life—went out—when He went [422]
	H48c	The Months have ends—the Years—a knot—[423]
	H49a	It ceased to hurt me, though so slow [584]

27   H144a   Good Morning—Midnight—[425]
       H146a   It would never be Common—more—I said—[430]
       H147   Knows how to forget! [433]
       H148b   Empty my Heart, of Thee—[587]
       H148c   I cried at Pity—not at Pain—[588]
       H24b   He strained my faith—[497]

28   H150d   If any sink, assure that this, now standing—[358]
       H151c   Did you ever stand in a Cavern's Mouth—[590]
       H154c   The Battle fought between the Soul [594]

29   H156a   Three times—we parted—Breath—and I—[598]
       H156b   There is a pain—so utter—[599]
       H156c   It troubled me as once I was—[600]
       H19a   I tie my Hat—I crease my Shawl—[443]
       H383b   He found my Being—set it up—[603]

30   H159c   Who Giants know, with lesser Men [796]
       H161c   Despair's advantage is achieved [799]
       H163c   They say that "Time assuages"—[686]
       H164a   On the Bleakness of my Lot [681]
       H164c   A Plated Life—diversified [806]
       H164d   Expectation—is Contentment—[807]

31   H165a   Because I could not stop for Death—[712]
       H165c   Fame of Myself, to justify, [713]
       H166c   From Blank to Blank—[761]
       H167a   The Whole of it came not at once—[762]
       H167d   You constituted Time—[765]
       H169a   When I hoped, I recollect [768]
       H170d   I lived on Dread—[770]

32   H53a   Tie the Strings to my Life, My Lord, [279]
       H53c   I felt a Funeral, in my Brain, [280]
       H54a   'Tis so appalling—it exhilirates—[281]
       H61a   'Twas just this time, last year, I died. [445]
       H61b   Afraid! Of whom am I afraid? [608]
       H171a   Before I got my eye put out [327]

33   H175b   'Twas awkward, but it fitted me—[973]
       H177a   And this of all my Hopes [913]

	H179d	When Night is almost done—[347]
	H180b	This Merit hath the worst—[979]
34	H181a	I Years had been from Home [609]
	H182c	It would have starved a Gnat—[612]
	H182d	They shut me up in Prose—[613]
	H184d	Love—thou—art high—[453]
35	H190b	Superiority to Fate [1081]
	H192a	What Twigs We held by—[1086]
	H192c	Ended, ere it begun—[1088]
	H193b	The Well upon the Brook [1091]
	H193d	Because 'twas Riches I could own, [1093]
	H193f	To Whom the Mornings stand for Nights, [1095]
36	H194	I Years had been from Home [609]
	H198	My Triumph lasted till the Drums [1227]
37	H201b	Tho' I get home how late—how late—[207]
	H202d	Just lost, when I was saved! [160]
	H203a	*One Life* of so much Consequence! [270]
	H204a	The Court is far away—[235]
	H204b	If *He dissolve*—then—there is *nothing—more*—[236]
	H204c	I think just how my shape will rise—[237]
38	H205c	To make Routine a Stimulus [1196]
	H206a	I should not dare to be so sad [1197]
	H206b	Remembrance has a Rear and Front—[1182]
	H206c	Because my Brook is fluent [1200]
	H207	Somehow myself survived the Night [1194]
	H208c	The Past is such a curious Creature [1203]
40	H214b	Dont put up my Thread & Needle—[617]
	H214d	At leisure is the Soul [618]
	H215c	It makes no difference abroad—[620]
	H215d	I asked no other thing—[621]
	H216b	It was too late for Man—[623]
	H216c	Forever—is composed of Nows—[624]
	H217b	Only God—detect the Sorrow—[626]
	H219a	A Wife—at Daybreak I shall be—[461]
	H219c	I live with Him—I see His face—[463]

80	B1	There is a word [8]
81	B1a	The hallowing of Pain [772]
	B2	Deprived of other Banquet, [773]
	B3a	To be alive—is Power—[677]
	B4	The Loneliness One dare not sound—[777]
	B5	This that would greet—an hour ago—[778]
	B5a	The Service without Hope—[779]
	B7a	There is an arid Pleasure—[782]
	B9	Bereaved of all, I went abroad—[784]
	B10	Severer Service of myself [786]
	B11a	Such is the Force of Happiness—[787]
84	B2a	The Soul that hath a Guest [674]
	B4	When I hoped I feared—[1181]
	B10	I am alive—I guess—[470]
85	B1	I dreaded that first Robin, so, [348]
	B3	He touched me, so I live to know [506]
	B5	I'm ceded—I've stopped being Their's—[508]
	B7	It was not Death, for I stood up, [510]
	B9	I felt my life with both my hands [351]
	B11	The Soul has Bandaged moments—[512]
86	B2	Impossibility, like Wine [838]
	B3	Always Mine! [839]
	B4a	Good to hide, and hear 'em hunt! [842]
	B5a	Struck, was I, nor yet by Lightning—[925]
	B6a	Patience—has a quiet Outer—[926]
	B7a	I made slow Riches but my Gain [843]
	B8a	Twice had Summer her fair Verdure [846]
	B9	Finite—to fail, but infinite to Venture—[847]
	B10	I sing to use the Waiting [850]
	B11a	The Heart has narrow Banks [928]
	B12	When One has given up One's life [853]
	B16	To own the Art within the Soul [855]
87	B1a	This Chasm, Sweet, upon my life [858]
	B3	A Doubt if it be Us [859]
	B4a	Perhaps you think me stooping [833]

	B7	A Death blow is a Life blow to Some [816]
	B13a	I felt a Cleaving in my Mind— [937]
88	B1a	Sang from the Heart, Sire, [1059]
	B10	Somewhat, to hope for, [1041]
	B12a	The Missing All, prevented Me [985]
	B15a	I've dropped my Brain—My Soul is numb— [1046]
89	B7	The World—stands—solemner—to me— [493]
	B8	Again—his voice is at the door— [663]
90	B1	Crumbling is not an instant's Act [997]
	B1a	Not to discover weakness is [1054]
	B7a	Knows how to forget! [433]
	B9a	Up Life's Hill with my little Bundle [1010]
	B11a	Too scanty 'twas to die for you, [1013]
	B12	Were it but Me that gained the Hight— [1015]
	B12a	To die—without the Dying [1017]
	B15	I knew that I had gained [1022]
91	B1	They wont frown always—some sweet Day [874]
	B2a	I stepped from Plank to Plank [875]
	B6	I've none to tell me to but Thee [881]
	B12	I could not prove the Years had feet— [563]
92	B2	We outgrow love, like other things [887]
	B3	Crisis is a Hair [889]
	B7	This Consciousness that is aware [822]
	B10a	A Door just opened on a street— [953]
	B13	What shall I do when the Summer troubles— [956]
	B14	As One does Sickness over [957]
	B17	A loss of something ever felt I— [959]
93	B11	The harm of Years is on him— [1280]
	B13	Somewhere upon the general Earth [1231]
102	B11	Art thou the thing I wanted? [1282]
X	L250	Title divine—is mine! [1072]
X	L249	Should you but fail at—Sea— [226]

B. POEMS THAT RENDER THE SOLITARY SELF AS CONSCIOUS CHOICE

Poem #789

On a Columnar Self—
How ample to rely
In Tumult—or Extremity—
How good the Certainty

That Lever cannot pry—
And Wedge cannot divide
Conviction—That Granitic Base—
Though None be on our Side—

Suffice Us—for a Crowd—
Ourself—and Rectitude—
And that Assembly—not far off
From furthest Spirit—God—

12	H58a	Never for Society [746]
	H60a	Growth of Man—like Growth of Nature—[750]
13	H65c	The Soul selects her own Society—[303]
	H66b	Mine—by the Right of the White Election! [528]
16	H88b	The Soul unto itself [683]
17	H90a	The Soul's Superior instants [306]
18	H98a	On a Columnar Self—[789]
26	H172b	I gave myself to Him—[580]
29	H383b	He found my Being—set it up—[603]
31	H165c	Fame of Myself, to justify, [713]
35	H190b	Superiority to Fate [1081]
40	H217b	Only God—detect the Sorrow—[626]
	H219c	I live with Him—I see His face—[463]

84 B2a   The Soul that hath a Guest [674]

85 B5   I'm ceded—I've stopped being Their's—[508]

86 B12   When One has given up One's life [853]

90 B15   I knew that I had gained [1022]

92 B7   This Consciousness that is aware [822]

98 B3–21   Of all the Souls that stand create—[664]

X   L250   Title divine—is mine! [1072]

C. POEMS THAT RENDER THE POET'S LONGING TO BE WITH SOMEONE,
   OR THE TRANSFIGURING POWER OF THE CHERISHED PERSON

Poem #643

I could suffice for Him, I knew—
He—could suffice for Me—
Yet Hesitating Fractions—Both
Surveyed Infinity—

"Would I be Whole" He sudden broached—
My syllable rebelled—
'Twas face to face with Nature—forced—
'Twas face to face with God—

Withdrew the Sun—to Other Wests—
Withdrew the furthest Star
Before Decision—stooped to speech—
And then—be audibler

The Answer of the Sea unto
The Motion of the Moon—
Herself adjust Her Tides—unto—
Could I—do else—with Mine?

6   H25a   I envy Seas, whereon He rides—[498]

8	H36c	Forever at His side to walk—[246]
	H37	What would I give to see his face? [247]
	H38b	Wild Nights—Wild Nights! [249]
9	H41a	I cannot live with You—[640]
	H44b	I could suffice for Him, I knew—[643]
	H44c	You left me—Sire—two Legacies—[644]
11	H51a	Promise This—When You be Dying—[648]
13	H64b	Although I put away his life—[366]
	H66a	How sick—to wait—in any place—but thine—[368]
17	H68d	That I did always love [549]
18	H97b	Joy to have merited the Pain—[788]
	H100c	Where Thou art—that—is Home—[725]
	H102c	Alter! When the Hills do—[729]
19	H104b	"Why do I love" You, Sir? [480]
	H107a	To make One's Toilette—after Death [485]
21	H114c	I had not minded—Walls—[398]
22	H125b	You said that I "was Great"—one Day—[738]
24	H130b	Wert Thou but ill—that I might show thee [961]
	H211b	Till Death—is narrow Loving—[907]
	H212a	Fitter to see Him, I may be [968]
26	H142a	If I may have it, when it's dead, [577]
	H173c	Not in this World to see his face—[418]
	H47a	Your Riches—taught me—Poverty. [299]
31	H168c	The World—feels Dusty [715]
38	H205b	Oh Shadow on the Grass, [1187]
40	H214c	So well that I can live without—[456]
	H219d	The power to be true to You, [464]

85	B3	He touched me, so I live to know [506]
	B8	If you were coming in the Fall, [511]
	B12	Like Flowers, that heard the news of Dews, [513]
86	B9	Unable are the Loved to die [809]
87	B5a	The Luxury to apprehend [815]
89	(B56?)	Going to Him! Happy letter! [494]
	B8	Again—his voice is at the door—[663]
90	B5	The Stimulus, beyond the Grave [1001]
	B6	Bind me—I still can sing—[1005]
91	B11	A Tongue—to tell Him I am true! [400]

It is illuminating to examine the following three poems in context with those listed above:

35	H192a	What Twigs We held by—[1086]
93	B11	The harm of Years is on him—[1280]
102	B11	Art thou the thing I wanted? [1282]

D. POEMS THAT CONTEMPLATE THE PROBLEM OF KNOWING

Poem #701

A Thought went up my mind today—
That I have had before—
But did not finish—some way back—
I could not fix the Year—

Nor where it went—nor why it came
The second time to me—
Nor definitely, what it was—
Have I the Art to say—

But somewhere—in my Soul—I know—
I've met the Thing before—
It just reminded me—'twas all—
And came my way no more—

1	H1b	Some things that fly there be — [89]
	H3c	I hav'nt told my garden yet — [50]
	H4b	Whether my bark went down at sea — [52]
2	H5d	Will there really be a "Morning"? [101]
	H7a	Like her the Saints retire, [60]
	H8c	I cant tell you — but you feel it — [65]
[3]	H10a	Bring me the sunset in a cup, [128]
6	H26a	Within my Garden, rides a Bird [500]
	H26d	This World is not Conclusion. [501]
7	H29c	An altered look about the hills — [140]
8	H36c	Forever at His side to walk — [246]
9	H43a	I should have been too glad, I see — [313]
10 *	H45	The feet of people walking home [7]
12	H56c	Four Trees — upon a solitary Acre — [742]
13	H63d	I reason, Earth is short — [301]
14	H72e	I've heard an Organ talk, sometimes — [183]
15	H80a	The Murmur of a Bee [155]
	H81a	The Skies cant keep their secret! [191]
	H81c	I shall know why — when Time is over — [193]
19	H108b	We pray — to Heaven — [489]
20	H110c	This — is the land — the Sunset washes — [266]
22	H118d	The Spirit is the Conscious Ear. [733]
	H119c	"Nature" is what we see — [668]
	H121a	Their Hight in Heaven comforts not — [696]

* R. W. Franklin believes there is no Fascicle 10, that this poem was a loose manuscript intended for mailing.

	H122d	A Thought went up my mind today—[701]
	H123c	Out of sight? What of that? [703]
25	H138a	I could die—to know—[570]
26	H173d	I found the words to every thought [581]
	H174b	You'll know it—as you know 'tis Noon—[420]
27	H145b	Taking up the fair Ideal, [428]
29	H156c	It troubled me as once I was—[600]
30	H161a	It was a Grave, yet bore no Stone [876]
	H162c	Time feels so vast that were it not [802]
31	H170c	One and One—are One—[769]
32	H61b	Afraid! Of whom am I afraid? [608]
33	H180c	We can but follow to the Sun—[920]
35	H190a	When they come back—if Blossoms do—[1080]
36	H199b	So much of Heaven has gone from Earth [1228]
38	H208b	What we see we know somewhat [1195]
40	H218b	The Tint I cannot take—is best—[627]
	H219c	I live with Him—I see His face—[463]
80	B5	My wheel is in the dark! [10]
	B6a	Once more, my now bewildered Dove [48]
81	B6a	The Truth—is stirless—[780]
82	B5	The feet of people walking home [7]
	B6a	If those I loved were lost [29]
83	B1	So from the mould [66]
	B3	Good night, because we must, [114]
	B3a	Low at my problem bending, [69]

86 B1   Those who have been in the Grave the longest—[922]
   B1a   It was a Grave, yet bore no Stone [876]
   B14a   How far is it to Heaven? [929]

87 B7   Truth—is as old as God—[836]

90 B2   Best Things dwell out of Sight [998]

91 B3   Nature and God—I neither knew [835]
   B9a   All Circumstances are the Frame [820]

93 B1   The Frost was never seen—[1202]
   B6   Some we see no more, Tenements of Wonder [1221]

98 B3–14   I never saw a Moor—[1052]

E. POEMS THAT CONTEMPLATE POETRY

Poem #945

This is a Blossom of the Brain—
A small—italic Seed
Lodged by Design or Happening
The Spirit fructified—

Shy as the Wind of his Chambers
Swift as a Freshet's Tongue
So of the Flower of the Soul
It's process is unknown.

When it is found, a few rejoice
The Wise convey it Home
Carefully cherishing the spot
If other Flower become.

When it is lost, that Day shall be
The Funeral of God,
Upon his Breast, a closing Soul
The Flower of our Lord.

1 H2b   My nosegays are for Captives [95]

2	H8b	By a flower—By a letter—[109]
[3]	H12a	I bring an unaccustomed wine [132]
4	H13c	I met a King this afternoon! [166]
	H15b	'Tis so much joy! 'Tis so much joy! [172]
	H15d	At last, to be identified! [174]
	H17c	I cautious, scanned my little life—[178]
	H17d	If I could bribe them by a Rose [179]
5	H91c	I took my Power in my Hand—[540]
	H93d	The Martyr Poets—did not tell—[544]
6	H27	Better—than Music! For I—who heard it—[503]
7	H28a	Perhaps you'd like to buy a flower, [134]
8	H32c	The Robin's my Criterion for Tune—[285]
	H38a	Why—do they shut Me out of Heaven? [248]
	H38b	Wild Nights—Wild Nights! [249]
	H38c	I shall keep singing! [250]
9	H39c	Except the Heaven had come so near—[472]
11	H131a	My Life had stood—a Loaded Gun—[754]
	H131c	No Bobolink—reverse His Singing [755]
	H132a	One Blessing had I than the rest [756]
	H133d	Essential Oils—are wrung—[675]
12	H56a	Drama's Vitallest Expression is the Common Day [741]
	H57c	Renunciation—is a piercing Virtue—[745]
	H58b	I sometimes drop it, for a Quick—[708]
	H59b	Publication—is the Auction [709]
	H60b	My Worthiness is all my Doubt—[751]
13	H63c	To hear an Oriole sing [526]
14	H72a	I taste a liquor never brewed—[214]
	H72e	I've heard an Organ talk, sometimes—[183]
	H72g	"Faith" is a fine invention [185]

15 H82a   Musicians wrestle everywhere—[157]
    H82b   For this—accepted Breath—[195]

16 H85   A precious—mouldering pleasure—'tis—[371]
    H87a   I'm saying every day [373]
    H92b   You cannot put a Fire out—[530]

17 H20d   What I can do—I will—[361]

18 H98d   Good Night! Which put the Candle Out? [259]
    H100b God gave a Loaf to every Bird—[791]

19 H106a I dwell in Possibility—[657]
    H106d My Garden—like the Beach—[484]

20 H112c Alone, I cannot be—[298]

21 H113b The Black Berry—wears a Thorn in his side—[554]
    H113c The One who could repeat the Summer day—[307]
    H115b I send Two Sunsets—[308]

22 H118b Shells from the Coast mistaking—[693]
    H120b Each Life Converges to some Centre—[680]
    H121a Their Hight in Heaven comforts not—[696]
    H122d A Thought went up my mind today—[701]

23 H127b Good Night! Which put the Candle out? [259]
    H127d Put up my lute! [261]
    H74c   Of Bronze—and Blaze—[290]

25 H137a I reckon—when I count at all—[569]

26 H143c I had been hungry, all the Years—[579]
    H173d I found the words to every thought [581]

27 H145a I'll clutch—and clutch—[427]
    H23a   It's thoughts—and just one Heart—[495]
    H73c   I cannot dance upon my Toes—[326]

28 H151d Much Madness is divinest Sense—[435]
    H154a I think I was enchanted [593]

29	H70b	This is my letter to the World [441]
30	H161d	Two—were immortal twice—[800]
	H163a	I play at Riches—to appease [801]
31	H165a	Because I could not stop for Death—[712]
	H165c	Fame of Myself, to justify, [713]
	H168a	My Faith is larger than the Hills—[766]
	H168c	The World—feels Dusty [715]
34	H183a	This was a Poet—It is That [448]
	H183c	I died for Beauty—but was scarce [449]
	H184b	At last, to be identified! [174]
	H184c	The Malay—took the Pearl—[452]
	H186c–187	It was given to me by the Gods—[454]
35	H193d	Because 'twas Riches I could own, [1093]
37	H200b	God permits industrious Angels—[231]
	H200d	The Lamp burns sure—within—[233]
	H201e	"Faith" is a fine invention [185]
	H202e	Come slowly—Eden! [211]
	H204d	I've nothing else—to bring, You know—[224]
38	H206c	Because my Brook is fluent [1200]
40	H218b	The Tint I cannot take—is best—[627]
81	B5a	The Service without Hope—[779]
	B9a	They have a little Odor—that to me [785]
82	B5a	It's all I have to bring today—[26]
83	B3	South Winds jostle them—[86]
	B4a	In rags mysterious as these [117]
84	B5a	'Tis little I—could care for Pearls—[466]
	B7	Her—"last Poems"—[312]
85	B2	I would not paint—a picture—[505]

86	B4a	Good to hide, and hear 'em hunt! [842]
	B5a	Struck, was I, nor yet by Lightning—[925]
	B7a	I made slow Riches but my Gain [843]
	B10	I sing to use the Waiting [850]
	B10	Her Grace is all she has—[810]
	B16	To own the Art within the Soul [855]
88	B1a	Sang from the Heart, Sire, [1059]
	B4a	To undertake is to achieve [1070]
	B17a	Reportless Subjects, to the Quick [1048]
90	B6	Bind me—I still can sing—[1005]
	B7	I was a Phebe—nothing more—[1009]
	B9a	Up Life's Hill with my little Bundle [1010]
	B12	Were it but Me that gained the Hight—[1015]
	B16	The Products of my Farm are these [1025]
91	B5a	The Bird must sing to earn the Crumb [880]
	B9	This is a Blossom of the Brain—[945]
	B12	I could not prove the Years had feet—[563]
	B13	The Poets light but Lamps—[883]
98	B3–7	Did the Harebell loose her girdle [213]
104	B13	Fortitude incarnate [1217]

F. POEMS THAT PERSONIFY NATURE (TRANSFORMATION, REGENERATION)

Poem #1000

The Fingers of the Light
Tapped soft upon the Town
With "I am great and cannot wait
So therefore let me in."

"You're soon," the Town replied,
"My Faces are asleep—
But swear, and I will let you by
You will not wake them up."

The easy Guest complied
But once within the Town

The transport of His Countenance
Awakened Maid and Man

The Neighbor in the Pool
Upon His Hip elate
Made loud obeisance and the Gnat
Held up His Cup for Light.

1	H2c	Sexton! My Master's sleeping here. [96]
	H2g	New feet within my garden go— [99]
	H3a	I never told the buried gold [11]
	H3b	I never lost as much but twice, [49]
	H3c	I hav'nt told my garden yet— [50]
	H4a	The morns are meeker than they were— [12]
2	H5c	A science—so the Savans say, [100]
	H8a	Some Rainbow—coming from the Fair! [64]
	H8c	I cant tell you—but you feel it— [65]
[3]	H9b	A Lady red—amid the Hill [74]
	H10b	She died at play, [75]
	H12b	As Children bid the Guest "Good Night" [133]
4	H15c	A fuzzy fellow, without feet, [173]
	H17c	I cautious, scanned my little life— [178]
5	H95b	Answer July— [386]
	H382a	I started Early—Took my Dog— [520]
6	H381a	It will be Summer—eventually. [342]
7	H28c	Have you got a Brook in your little heart, [136]
	H29c	An altered look about the hills— [140]
	H30a	Whose are the little beds, I asked [142]
	H31b	We should not mind so small a flower— [81]
8	H32d	I've known a Heaven, like a Tent— [243]
11	H131b	The Sunrise runs for Both— [710]
	H132c	The Mountains—grow unnoticed— [757]

12	H56c	Four Trees—upon a solitary Acre—[742]
	H57a	The Birds reported from the South—[743]
	H58d	Autumn—overlooked my Knitting—[748]
14	H77a	Of all the Sounds despatched abroad, [321]
15	H81a	The Skies cant keep their secret! [191]
	H84b	A slash of Blue—[204]
	H84d	The Flower must not blame the Bee—[206]
16	H86a	Two Butterflies went out at Noon—[533]
	H88a	The Angle of a Landscape—[375]
17	H94a	There is a flower that Bees prefer—[380]
18	H98b	Nature—the Gentlest Mother is, [790]
	H99b	She dwelleth in the Ground—[671]
	H101d	Ah, Teneriffe! [666]
19	H103b	Nature—sometimes sears a Sapling—[314]
	H105d	The name—of it—is "Autumn"—[656]
	H106b	A Solemn thing within the Soul [483]
	H106c	Whole Gulfs—of Red, and Fleets—of Red—[658]
	H108c	He fumbles at your Soul [315]
20	H110c	This—is the land—the Sunset washes—[266]
21	H115c	A Visitor in Marl—[391]
	H115d	Through the Dark Sod—as Education—[392]
	H117a	She hideth Her the last—[557]
22	H125a	The Moon was but a Chin of Gold [737]
23	H126a	I know some lonely Houses off the Road [289]
	H128a	There came a Day at Summer's full, [322]
	H74b	She sweeps with many-colored Brooms—[219]
24	H211c	'Tis Sunrise—little Maid—Hast Thou [908]
	H213b	I make His Crescent fill or lack—[909]
25	H139a	My first well Day—since many ill—[574]

26	H173a	A Murmur in the Trees—to note—[416]
	H48c	The Months have ends—the Years—a knot—[423]
27	H144a	Good Morning—Midnight—[425]
	H145c	The Moon is distant from the Sea—[429]
	H23b	I know a place where Summer strives [337]
	H24c	I tend my flowers for thee—[339]
	H73a	The Grass so little has to do—[333]
28	H149a	From Cocoon forth a Butterfly [354]
	H152a	The Wind—tapped like a tired Man—[436]
	H152b	To interrupt His Yellow Plan [591]
29	H155a	It sifts from Leaden Sieves—[311]
	H383d	The Spider holds a Silver Ball [605]
	H158a	The Trees like Tassels—hit—and swung—[606]
30	H159a	A Drop fell on the Apple Tree—[794]
	H161b	She staked her Feathers—Gained an Arc—[798]
	H163b	No Notice gave She, but a Change—[804]
31	H166b	Most she touched me by her muteness—[760]
	H168b	Rests at Night [714]
	H169b	The Wind did'nt come from the Orchard—today—[316]
	H170a	The Day undressed—Herself—[716]
33	H176a	The Mountain sat upon the Plain [975]
	H178b	His Feet are shod with Gauze—[916]
35	H189a	These are the Signs to Nature's Inns—[1077]
36	H195	Like Trains of Cars on Tracks of Plush [1224]
37	H200c	The Sun—*just touched* the Morning—[232]
	H202a	I'll tell you how the Sun rose—[318]
38	H208d	A prompt—executive bird is the Jay—[1177]
40	H218b	The Tint I cannot take—is best—[627]
80	B2	The Guest is gold and crimson—[15]
	B4	I robbed the Woods—[41]

	B4a	Could live—*did* live—[43]
	B5a	There's something quieter than sleep [45]
	B6	Heart! We will forget him! [47]
81	B3	The Color of a Queen, is this—[776]
	B6a	The Truth—is stirless—[780]
	B7	A South Wind—has a pathos [719]
82	B1	The Gentian weaves her fringes—[18]
	B1a	Frequently the woods are pink—[6]
	B4	There is a morn by men unseen—[24]
	B4a	She slept beneath a tree—[25]
	B6	Morns like these—we parted—[27]
83	B1	Artists wrestled here! [110]
	B4	I had some things that I called mine—[116]
	B7a	A throe upon the features—[71]
	B8	Glowing is her Bonnet, [72]
84	B3	I watched the Moon around the House [629]
	B4a	The Lightning playeth—all the while—[630]
	B9	You'll know Her—by her Foot—[634]
86	B4	A Moth the hue of this [841]
	B8	Spring is the Period [844]
	B12a	The Veins of other Flowers [811]
	B14	Like Men and Women Shadows walk [1105]
87	B2a	My best Acquaintances are those [932]
	B12	Ribbons of the Year—[873]
	B14	Fairer through Fading—as the Day [938]
88	B2a	Who is the East? [1032]
	B4	His Bill an Augur is [1034]
	B5	Could I but ride indefinite [661]
	B7	Bee! I'm expecting you! [1035]
	B8a	Her little Parasol to lift [1038]
	B9	I heard, as if I had no Ear [1039]
	B13	A narrow Fellow in the Grass [986]
	B14a	The Leaves like Women, interchange [987]
	B15	Nature rarer uses Yellow [1045]

90	B4	The Fingers of the Light [1000]
	B5	Aurora is the effort [1002]
	B11	A bold, inspiriting Bird [1177]
	B12a	The Hills in Purple syllables [1016]
	B17	Bloom—is Result—to meet a Flower [1058]
91	B2	The Lady feeds Her little Bird [941]
	B13a	Our little Kinsmen—after Rain [885]
92	B2a	When I have seen the Sun emerge [888]
	B6	As willing lid o'er weary eye [1050]
	B8	The Sunset stopped on Cottages [950]
	B13	What shall I do when the Summer troubles—[956]
	B16	Of Silken Speech and Specious Shoe [896]
	B18	What did They do since I saw Them? [900]
93	B1	The Frost was never seen—[1202]
98	B1	The spry Arms of the Wind [1103]
	B3–7	Did the Harebell loose her girdle [213]
106	B8	The Wind begun to knead the Grass—[824]
X	L	The Juggler's Hat her Country is—[330]
X	L	Further in Summer than the Birds [1068]
X	HB186	Whose cheek is this? [82]

G. THE SUBJECT MATTER OF THE POEM IS AN ACTUAL DEATH

Poem #758

These—saw Visions—
Latch them softly—
These—held Dimples—
Smooth them slow—
This—addressed departing accents—
Quick—Sweet Mouth—to miss thee so—

This—We stroked—
Unnumbered * Satin—

* Ungraded, as by a manufacturer.

These—we held among our own—
Fingers of the Slim Aurora—
Not so arrogant—this Noon—

These—adjust—that ran to meet us—
Pearl—for Stocking—Pearl for Shoe—
Paradise—the only Palace
Fit for Her reception—now—

1	H1a	Delayed till she had ceased to know—[58]
	H1f	Went up a year this evening! [93]
	H3c	I hav'nt told my garden yet—[50]
	H4c	Taken from men—this morning—[53]

2	H5b	All overgrown by cunning moss, [148]
	H6c	She went as quiet as the Dew [149]
	H7e	She died—*this* was the way she died. [150]

| [3] | H11d | A poor—torn heart—a tattered heart—[78] |

| 6 | H381c | 'Twas the old—road—through pain—[344] |

7	H31a	She bore it till the simple veins [144]
	H31c	This heart that broke so long—[145]
	H31d	On such a night, or such a night, [146]

11	H52a	Her Sweet turn to leave the Homestead [649]
	H133a	These—saw Visions—[758]
	H133c	We miss Her, not because We see—[993]

| 13 | H62b | Departed—to the Judgment—[524] |
| | H66c | She lay as if at play [369] |

| 15 | H78b | How many times these low feet staggered—[187] |
| | H81d | On this long storm the Rainbow rose—[194] |

| 17 | H22d | I went to thank Her—[363] |

| 19 | H104d | We Cover Thee—Sweet Face—[482] |

| 21 | H113a | There's been a Death, in the Opposite House, [389] |
| | H114d | A House upon the Hight—[399] |

22	H119a	If He were living—dare I ask—[734]
24	H211c	'Tis Sunrise—Little Maid—Hast Thou [908]
27	H144c	It dont sound so terrible—quite—as it did—[426]
	H148a	We talked as Girls do—[586]
	H148b	Empty my Heart, of Thee [587]
28	H150b	'Twas warm—at first—like Us—[519]
	H154a	I think I was enchanted [593]
29	H158b	It feels a shame to be Alive—[444]
	H70a	When I was small, a Woman died—[596]
30	H159b	Her final Summer was it—[795]
	H160c	"I want"—it pleaded—All it's life—[731]
31	H167b	He told a homely tale [763]
33	H177c	Besides this May [977]
34	H183b	In falling Timbers buried—[614]
	H186b	I rose—because He sank—[616]
35	H191b	The last Night that She lived [1100]
40	H216a	To know just how He suffered—would be dear—[622]
	H217c	Like Eyes that looked on Wastes—[458]
81	B6	I meant to find Her when I came—[718]
	B10	Severer Service of myself [786]
84	B5	Ourselves were wed one summer—dear—[631]
	B7	Her—"last Poems"—[312]
85	B6	If anybody's friend be dead [509]
86	B2a	How the Waters closed above Him [923]
88	B1	That Such have died enable Us [1030]
	B11	Three Weeks passed since I had seen Her—[1061]

90 B9a   She rose as high as His Occasion [1011]

91 B1a   On that dear Frame the Years had won [940]
    B3a   How well I knew Her not [837]
    B4   Snow beneath whose chilly softness [942]

92 B7a   From Us She wandered now a Year, [890]
    B11   Who occupies this House? [892]
    B13a   Drab Habitation of Whom? [893]

93 B5   So proud she was to die [1272]
    B9   It came at last but prompter Death [1230]

100 B8   She sped as Petals of a Rose [991]

105 B2   Bless God, he went as soldiers, [147]

H. POEMS THAT CONTEMPLATE THE EXPERIENCE OF DEATH

Poem #665

Dropped into the Ether Acre—
Wearing the Sod Gown —
Bonnet of Everlasting Laces—
Brooch—frozen on—

Horses of Blonde—and Coach of Silver—
Baggage a strapped Pearl—
Journey of Down—and Whip of Diamond
Riding to meet the Earl—

1   H2e   One dignity delays for all—[98]
    H3b   I never lost as much but twice, [49]
    H4e   If I should die, [54]

2   H6b   Where I have lost, I softer tread—[104]

[3] H11c   Safe in their Alabaster Chambers—[216]
    H11d   A poor—torn heart—a tattered heart—[78]
    H12c   Going to Heaven! [79]

4   H15a   Wait till the Majesty of Death [171]
    H16b   Dust is the only Secret—[153]

5	H18a	No Crowd that has occurred [515]
	H95a	I cross till I am weary [550]
6	H25b	Those fair—fictitious People—[499]
	H26b	Is Bliss then, such Abyss, [340]
7	H29d	Some, too fragile for winter winds [141]
8	H33b	That after Horror—that 'twas us—[286]
	H220	A Clock stopped—[287]
9	H42c	Doom is the House without the Door—[475]
11	H50a	Bereavement in their death to feel [645]
	H51a	Promise This—When You be Dying—[648]
12	H59c	All but Death, can be Adjusted—[749]
14	H72d	If I should'nt be alive [182]
15	H82c	We dont cry—Tim and I, [196]
	H83a	Dying! Dying in the night! [158]
	H83f	Two swimmers wrestled on the spar—[201]
	H84c	I should not dare to leave my friend, [205]
16	H86c	It was a quiet way—[1053]
	H92a	I'm sorry for the Dead—Today—[529]
17	H94c	For Death—or rather [382]
	H67d	I've seen a Dying Eye [547]
	H68b	Death is potential to that Man [548]
	H20c	Death sets a Thing significant [360]
18	H99a	Behind Me—dips Eternity—[721]
	H100a	It's easy to invent a Life—[724]
	H101c	Dropped into the Ether Acre—[665]
19	H105b	A long—long Sleep—A famous—Sleep—[654]
	H106b	A Solemn thing within the Soul [483]
20	H110d	The Doomed—regard the Sunrise [294]
	H112b	It's like the Light—[297]

21 H114c I had not minded—Walls—[398]
    H114d A House upon the Hight—[399]
    H115a It's Coming—the postponeless Creature—[390]
    H115d Through the Dark Sod—as Education—[392]
    H117d It knew no Medicine—[559]

22 H118a The Sun kept setting—setting—still [692]
    H119d Upon Concluded Lives [735]
    H121c Life—is what we make it—[698]

23 H129b Of Tribulation—these are They, [325]
    H129c If your Nerve, deny you—[292]

24 H211a The Admirations—and Contempts—of time [906]
    H213a Color—Caste—Denomination—[970]

25 H134d 'Tis not that Dying hurts us so—[335]
    H135a A Dying Tiger—moaned for Drink—[566]
    H139c Unit, like Death, for Whom? [408]

26 H141b The Color of the Grave is Green—[411]
    H142a If I may have it, when it's dead, [577]
    H173b It is dead—Find it—[417]
    H47b   A Toad, can die of Light—[583]
    H48c   The Months have ends—the Years—a knot—[423]

27 H146c Do People moulder equally, [432]
    H23c   As far from pity, as complaint—[496]
    H24a   I know that He exists. [338]

28 H150d If any sink, assure that this, now standing—[358]
    H153a What care the Dead, for Chanticleer—[592]

29 H156a Three times—we parted—Breath—and I—[598]

30 H161a It was a Grave, yet bore no Stone [876]
    H161c Despair's advantage is achieved [799]

31 H165a Because I could not stop for Death—[712]
    H167a The Whole of it came not at once—[762]
    H170c One and One—are One—[769]

32	H53a	Tie the Strings to my Life, My Lord, [279]
	H53b	I like a look of Agony, [241]
	H53c	I felt a Funeral, in my Brain, [280]
	H54a	'Tis so appalling—it exhilirates—[281]
	H54b	How noteless Men, and Pleiads, stand, [282]
	H61a	'Twas just this time, last year, I died. [445]
	H61b	Afraid! Of whom am I afraid? [608]
	H171b	Of nearness to her sundered Things [607]
33	H175d	Too little way the House must lie [911]
	H176b	Peace is a fiction of our Faith—[912]
	H176e	Death is a Dialogue between [976]
	H179d	When Night is almost done—[347]
	H180c	We can but follow to the Sun—[920]
34	H181a	I—Years had been—from Home—[609]
	H181b	You'll find—it when you try to die—[610]
	H183c	I died for Beauty—but was scarce [449]
	H186a	Our journey had advanced—[615]
35	H189c	The Bustle in a House [1078]
36	H194	I Years had been from Home [609]
	H199a	To disappear enhances—[1209]
37	H203	Safe in their Alabaster Chambers—[216]
40	H215a	Sweet—safe—Houses—[457]
	H217a	'Twas a long Parting—but the time [625]
	H218a	I know where Wells grow—Droughtless Wells—[460]
	H218b	The Tint I cannot take—is best—[627]
	H219c	I live with Him—I see His face—[463]
80	B4a	Could live—*did* live—[43]
	B5a	There's something quieter than sleep [45]
	B7	The face I carry with me—last—[336]
81	B5	This that would greet—an hour ago—[778]
	B9	Bereaved of all, I went abroad—[784]
	B10	Severer Service of myself [786]

83	B2	Where bells no more affright the morn—[112]
	B2a	Ambition cannot find him. [68]
	B3a	What Inn is this [115]
	B6	If this is "fading" [120]
	B7a	A throe upon the features—[71]
84	B2	I heard a Fly buzz—when I died—[465]
	B8	The Manner of it's Death [468]
	B10	I am alive—I guess—[470]
85	B7	It was not Death, for I stood up, [510]
86	B1	Those who have been in the Grave the longest—[922]
	B1a	It was a Grave, yet bore no Stone [876]
	B7	Dying! To be afraid of thee [831]
	B9	Unable are the Loved to die [809]
	B14a	How far is it to Heaven? [929]
	B15	This quiet Dust was Gentlemen and Ladies [813]
	B16a	There is a finished feeling [856]
87	B1a	This Chasm, Sweet, upon my life [858]
	B3	Absence disembodies—so does Death [860]
	B7	A Death blow is a Life blow to Some [816]
	B12a	Death leaves Us homesick, who behind, [935]
	B13	This Dust, and it's Feature—[936]
88	B3	Said Death to Passion [1033]
	B11a	A Sickness of this World it most occasions [1044]
	B16a	The Opening and the Close [1047]
	B17	Let down the Bars, Oh Death—[1065]
	B18	Pain has but one Acquaintance [1049]
90	B9	The Soul should always stand ajar [1055]
	B10	There is a Zone whose even Years [1056]
	B15a	So large my Will [1024]
	B16a	The Dying need but little, Dear, [1026]
91	B7	A Coffin—is a small Domain—[943]
	B14	Of Tolling Bell I ask the cause? [947]
92	B1a	'Twas Crisis—All the length had passed—[948]
	B3a	Under the Light, yet under, [949]

	B6a	Not all die early, dying young—[990]
	B7	This Consciousness that is aware [822]
	B8a	Ample make this Bed—[829]
	B12	The Chemical conviction [954]
	B16	How fortunate the Grave—[897]
	B18a	As plan for Noon and plan for Night [960]
93	B6	Some we see no more, Tenements of Wonder [1221]
	B10	Not any higher stands the Grave [1256]
	B12	The Bone that has no Marrow, [1274]
95	B13	Step lightly on this narrow spot—[1183]
105	B4 *	If I should cease to bring a Rose [56]
	B10 *	To venerate the simple days [57]
107	B49	Mute thy Coronation—[151]

I. POEMS THAT CONTEMPLATE JESUS OR GOD

Poem #225

Jesus! thy Crucifix
Enable thee to guess
The smaller size!

Jesus! thy second face
Mind thee in Paradise
Of our's!

5	H91b	The Province of the Saved [539]
	H96b	One Crucifixion is recorded—only—[553]
6	H381d	At least—to pray—is left—is left—[502]
8	H36b	Just so—Jesus—raps—[317]
9	H39d	To my small Hearth His fire came—[638]
	H43b	I meant to have but modest needs—[476]
11	H131a	My Life had stood—a Loaded Gun—[754]
	H132a	One Blessing had I than the rest [756]

* R. W. Franklin places these in Fascicle 80.

12	H55a	Conscious am I in my Chamber, [679]
	H60b	My Worthiness is all my Doubt—[751]
13	H64a	To put this World down, like a Bundle—[527]
	H65c	The Soul selects her own Society—[303]
	H66b	Mine—by the Right of the White Election! [528]
14	H75a	He put the Belt around my life—[273]
15	H81c	I shall know why—when Time is over—[193]
	H82b	For this—accepted Breath—[195]
	H83a	Dying! Dying in the night! [158]
	H84a	He forgot—and I—remembered—[203]
16	H88d	Of Course—I prayed—[376]
17	H90c	To lose one's faith—surpass [377]
	H90d	I saw no Way—The Heavens were stitched—[378]
18	H98c	No Prisoner be—[720]
	H102b	Let Us play Yesterday—[728]
19	H107d	You love the Lord—you cannot see—[487]
20	H109a	I got so I could hear his name—[293]
	H110a	Savior! I've no one else to tell—[217]
	H110e	Jesus! thy Crucifix [225]
22	H121c	Life—is what we make it—[698]
24	H209c	"Unto Me?" I do not know you—[964]
25	134a	My period had come for Prayer—[564]
	H135b	He gave away his Life—[567]
	H138b	Must be a Wo—[571]
	H138e	The Test of Love—is Death—[573]
	H140c	I prayed, at first, a little Girl, [576]
26	H172b	I gave myself to Him—[580]
27	H146c	Do People moulder equally, [432]
	H24a	I know that He exists. [338]

92 B15   Of Consciousness, her awful Mate [894]

93 B2   The Voice that stands for Floods to me [1189]

98 B3–21 Of all the Souls that stand create — [664]

X   L   Title divine — is mine! [1072]

J. POEMS THAT CONTEMPLATE THE NATURE OF HEAVEN AND
   IMMORTALITY *

Poem #915

Faith — is the Pierless Bridge
Supporting what We see
Unto the Scene that We do not —
Too slender for the eye

It bears the Soul as bold
As it were rocked in Steel
With Arms of Steel at either side —
It joins — behind the Vail

To what, could We presume
The Bridge would cease to be
To Our far, vascillating Feet
A first Nescessity.

[3] H9d   'Houses' — so the Wise Men tell me — [127]
     H12c   Going to Heaven! [79]

  6 H26d   This World is not Conclusion. [501]

  9 H43b   I meant to have but modest needs — [476]

 12 H55b   You taught me Waiting with Myself — [740]

* It should be pointed out that this list isolates those poems whose specific question concerns the nature of Heaven and Immortality. All those poems that contemplate Nature as a guarantee of Immortality, that contemplate the experience of death, the nature of Jesus and God, that speculate on the function of the poet or ponder the means of arriving at truth, are interrelated and could be listed under this one rubric.

13	H66d	Heaven is so far of the Mind [370]
14	H71d	"Heaven"—is what I cannot reach! [239]
15	H79	What is—"Paradise"—[215]
	H84e	Some keep the Sabbath going to Church—[324]
16	H87c	I went to Heaven—[374]
17	H90a	The Soul's Superior instants [306]
18	H97a	No Other can reduce [982]
	H100d	We thirst at first—'tis Nature's Act—[726]
19	H108b	We pray—to Heaven—[489]
22	H118c	The Heaven vests for Each [694]
	H121a	Their Hight in Heaven comforts not—[696]
	H123c	Out of sight? What of that? [703]
24	H130a	The Only News I know [827]
25	H134a	My period had come for Prayer—[564]
	H138a	I could die—to know—[570]
	H140a	"Heaven" has different Signs—to me—[575]
26	H143a	I never felt at Home—Below—[413]
	H174b	You'll know it—as you know 'tis Noon—[420]
27	H145b	Taking up the fair Ideal, [428]
	H146b	Me—come! My dazzled face [431]
30	H160a	By my Window have I for Scenery [797]
32	H61b	Afraid! Of whom am I afraid? [608]
33	H175c	The Soul's distinct connection [974]
	H178a	Faith—is the Pierless Bridge [915]
36	H199b	So much of Heaven has gone from Earth [1228]

37	H201b	Tho' I get home how late—how late—[207]
38	H207	Somehow myself survived the Night [1194]
40	H214a	Triumph—may be of several kinds—[455]
	H216b	It was too late for Man—[623]
	H217a	'Twas a long Parting—but the time [625]
	H219a	A Wife—at Daybreak I shall be—[461]
	H219c	I live with Him—I see His face—[463]
82	B5	The feet of people walking home [7]
83	B2	Where bells no more affright the morn—[112]
86	B2	So set it's Sun in Thee [808]
87	B7	A Death blow is a Life blow to Some [816]
88	B10	Lest this be Heaven indeed [1043]
90	B2a	No Other can reduce [982]
	B8a	'Tis Anguish grander than Delight [984]
	B10	There is a Zone whose even Years [1056]
	B15a	So large my Will [1024]
91	B10a	It is an honorable Thought [946]
93	B8	Immortal is an ample word [1205]
	B13	Somewhere upon the general Earth [1231]

K. POEMS THAT RENDER A CHILD GOING TO HEAVEN

Poem #215

What is—"Paradise"—
Who live there—
Are they "Farmers"—
Do they "hoe"—
Do they know that this is "Amherst"—
And that I—am coming—too—

Do they wear "new shoes"—in "Eden"—
Is it always pleasant—there—
Wont they scold us—when we're hungry—
Or tell God—how cross we are—

You are sure there's such a person
As "a Father"—in the sky—
So if I get lost—there—ever—
Or do what the Nurse calls "die"—
I shant walk the "Jasper"—barefoot—
Ransomed folks—wont laugh at me—
Maybe—"Eden" a'nt so lonesome
As New England used to be!

1	H4c	Taken from men—this morning—[53]
2	H5d	Will there really be a "Morning"? [101]
	H8c	I cant tell you—but you feel it—[65]
[3]	H9d	'Houses'—so the Wise Men tell me—[127]
	H12c	Going to Heaven! [79]
9	H43b	I meant to have but modest needs—[476]
15	H79	What is—"Paradise"—[215]
16	H88d	Of Course—I prayed—[376]
19	H107c	I was the slightest in the House—[486]
27	H146b	Me—come! My dazzled face [431]
	H146c	Do People moulder equally, [432]
	H147	Knows how to forget! [433]
31	H170b	The Beggar Lad—dies early—[717]
37	H204a	The Court is far away—[235]
40	H219a	A Wife—at Daybreak I shall be—[461]
83	B5	"Arcturus" is his other name—[70]

107 B49   Mute thy Coronation — [151]

L. THE PERSONA SHIFTS TO WIFE OR BRIDE GOING TO HEAVEN

Poem #461

A Wife—at Daybreak I shall be—
Sunrise—Hast thou a Flag for me?
At Midnight, I am but a Maid,
How short it takes to make it Bride—
Then—Midnight, I have passed from thee
Unto the East, and Victory—

Midnight—Good Night! I hear them call,
The Angels bustle in the Hall—
Softly my Future climbs the Stair,
I fumble at my Childhood's prayer
So soon to be a Child no more—
Eternity, I'm coming—Sir,
Savior—I've seen the face—before!

5   H18a   No Crowd that has occurred [515]

6   H25b   Those fair—fictitious People—[499]

9   H40b   I am ashamed—I hide [473]

13 H66b   Mine—by the Right of the White Election! [528]

14 H71a   A solemn thing—it was I said—[271]

15 H82b   For this—accepted Breath—[195]
    H83d   I'm "Wife"—I've finished that—[199]

17 H67b   'Tis One by One—the Father counts—[545]

19 H107d   You love the Lord—you cannot see—[487]

23 H128a   There came a Day at summer's full, [322]
    H129b   Of Tribulation—these are They, [325]

26 H172b   I gave myself to Him—[580]

27 H145a   I'll clutch—and clutch—[427]

28 H150a   The Day that I was crowned [356]

29 H156c   It troubled me as once I was—[600]

34 H186a   Our journey had advanced—[615]

40 H219a   A Wife—at Daybreak I shall be—[461]
    H219c   I live with Him—I see His face—[463]

84 B5   Ourselves were wed one summer—dear—[631]
    B10   I am alive—I guess—[470]

85 B3   He touched me, so I live to know [506]
    B5   I'm ceded—I've stopped being Their's—[508]

87 B10a   Given in Marriage unto Thee [817]

89 B7   The World—stands—solemner—to me—[493]

X   L   Title divine—is mine! [1072]

M. POEMS RENDERING QUEST

Poem #731

"I want"—it pleaded—All it's life—
I want—was chief it said
When Skill entreated it—the last—
And when so newly dead—

I could not deem it late—to hear
That single—steadfast sigh—
The lips had placed as with a "Please"
Toward Eternity—

4   H17d   If I could bribe them by a Rose [179]
    H17e   As if some little Arctic flower [180]

7   H30b   For every Bird a Nest—[143]

8	H34	I came to buy a smile—today—[223]
	H35b	I held a Jewel in my fingers—[245]
	H38b	Wild Nights—Wild Nights! [249]
11	H52c	So much Summer [651]
	H132b	Victory comes late—[690]
17	H20b	I gained it so—[359]
	H22a	Had I presumed to hope—[522]
18	H100b	God gave a Loaf to every Bird—[791]
19	H108d	Just Once! Oh least Request! [1076]
22	H121b	I could bring You Jewels—had I a mind to—[697]
	H121d	The Judge is like the Owl—[699]
23	H46b	"Hope" is the thing with feathers—[254]
25	H134d	'Tis not that Dying hurts us so—[335]
26	H47a	Your Riches—taught me—Poverty. [299]
27	H145a	I'll clutch—and clutch—[427]
30	H160c	"I want"—it pleaded—All it's life—[731]
31	H166b	Most she touched me by her muteness—[760]
	H170b	The Beggar Lad—dies early—[717]
34	H184c	The Malay—took the Pearl—[452]
37	H202e	Come slowly—Eden! [211]
40	H215d	I asked no other thing—[621]
82	B4a	As if I asked a common Alms, [323]
83	B6a	Her breast is fit for pearls, [84]
86	B3a	I cannot buy it—'tis not sold—[840]
	B8a	Twice had Summer her fair Verdure [846]

N. POEMS RENDERING COMPENSATION (YOKED OPPOSITES)

Poem #355

'Tis Opposites—entice—
Deformed Men—ponder Grace—
Bright fires—the Blanketless—
The Lost—Day's face—

The Blind—esteem it be
Enough Estate—to see—
The Captive—strangles new—
For deeming—Beggars—play—

To lack—enamor Thee—
Tho' the Divinity—
Be only
Me—

22	H119d	Upon Concluded Lives [735]
	H122c	The Zeroes—taught us—Phosphorus—[689]
	H125b	You said that I "was Great"—one Day—[738]
23	H126b	I can wade Grief—[252]
24	H210c	Had I not This, or This, I said, [904]
25	H138b	Must be a Wo—[571]
	H138c	Delight—becomes pictorial—[572]
	H138d	If What we Could—were what we would [407]
26	H172c	Sunset at Night—is natural—[415]
	H47a	Your Riches—taught me—Poverty. [299]
28	H149c	'Tis Opposites—entice—[355]
	H153c	Undue Significance a starving man attaches [439]
30	H161c	Despair's advantage is achieved [799]
	H163a	I play at Riches—to appease [801]
	H164c	A Plated Life—diversified [806]
	H164d	Expectation—is Contentment—[807]
32	H54a	'Tis so appalling—it exhilirates—[281]
33	H175a	Experience is the Angled Road [910]
	H175c	The Soul's distinct connection [974]
35	H188b	Perception of an object costs [1071]
36	H199a	To disappear enhances—[1209]
81	B1	None can experience stint [771]
	B7	A South Wind—has a pathos [719]
82	B2	We lose—because we win—[21]
83	B1a	Success is counted sweetest [67]
	B8a	For each extatic instant [125]
84	B12	So glad we are—a Stranger'd deem [329]

86	B2	Impossibility, like Wine [838]
87	B1	Uncertain lease—develops lustre [857]
	B3	Absence disembodies—so does Death [860]
	B14a	What I see not, I better see—[939]
88	B6a	To One denied to drink [490]
	B7a	Satisfaction—is the Agent [1036]
92	B9	As Frost is best conceived [951]
93	B10	Not any higher stands the Grave [1256]
102	B11	Art thou the thing I wanted? [1282]

O. POEMS THAT HAVE THE METAPHOR OF A BOAT OR SHIP AT SEA, OR THE SEA

Poem #1217

Fortitude incarnate
Here is laid away
In the swift Partitions
Of the awful Sea—

Babble of the Happy
Cavil of the Bold
Hoary the Fruition
But the Sea is old

Edifice of Ocean
Thy tumultuous Rooms
Suit me at a venture
Better than the Tombs

1	H1f	Went up a year this evening! [93]
	H4b	Whether my bark went down at sea—[52]
2	H7c	'Twas such a little—little boat [107]
[3]	H10d	Exultation is the going [76]
	H11d	A poor—torn heart—a tattered heart—[78]

5	H95a	I cross till I am weary [550]
	H382a	I started Early—Took my Dog—[520]
6	H381d	At least—to pray—is left—is left—[502]
8	H32b	The Drop, that wrestles in the Sea—[284]
	H38b	Wild Nights—Wild Nights! [249]
9	H42a	They put Us far apart—[474]
	H44b	I could suffice for Him, I knew—[643]
	H44c	You left me—Sire—two Legacies—[644]
11	H50b	I think To Live—may be a Bliss [646]
	H52a	Her Sweet turn to leave the Homestead [649]
12	H58b	I sometimes drop it, for a Quick—[708]
13	H66a	How sick—to wait—in any place—but thine—[368]
15	H80c	My River runs to thee—[162]
	H83f	Two swimmers wrestled on the spar—[201]
16	H86a	Two Butterflies went out at Noon—[533]
17	H90b	Me prove it now—Whoever doubt [537]
18	H99a	Behind Me—dips Eternity—[721]
	H99d	It tossed—and tossed—[723]
19	H105c	Without this—there is nought—[655]
	H106d	My Garden—like the Beach—[484]
	H107b	'Tis good—the looking back on Grief—[660]
20	H110b	Where Ships of Purple—gently toss—[265]
	H110c	This—is the land—the Sunset washes—[266]
22	H119b	As if the Sea should part [695]
	H119c	"Nature" is what we see—[668]
	H122b	You've seen Balloons set—Hav'nt You? [700]
	H125c	I many times thought Peace had come [739]
23	H46b	"Hope" is the thing with feathers—[254]

24 H210b   All forgot for recollecting [966]
    H210d   Between My Country—and the Others—[905]

26 H172a   'Twas like a Maelstrom, with a notch, [414]
    H174b   You'll know it—as you know 'tis Noon—[420]

27 H145c   The Moon is distant from the Sea—[429]
    H148b   Empty my Heart, of Thee—[587]

28 H149a   From Cocoon forth a Butterfly [354]
    H152b   To interrupt His Yellow Plan [591]
    H153b   Forget! The Lady with the Amulet [438]

29 H156a   Three times—we parted—Breath—and I—[598]

30 H159a   A Drop fell on the Apple Tree—[794]
    H160a   By my Window have I for Scenery [797]
    H162b   She rose to His Requirement—dropt [732]

32 H53a   Tie the Strings to my Life, My Lord, [279]

34 H184c   The Malay—took the Pearl—[452]

37 H202d   Just lost, when I was saved! [160]
    H202f   Least Rivers—docile to some sea. [212]
    H203a   *One Life* of so much Consequence! [270]

38 H206c   Because my Brook is fluent [1200]

40 H215b   Glee—The great storm is over—[619]

80 B6a   Once more, my now bewildered Dove [48]

81 B9   Bereaved of all, I went abroad—[784]

82 B5   The feet of people walking home [7]
    B7   Adrift! A little boat adrift! [30]
    B8   On this wondrous sea [4]

84 B1   They called me to the Window, for [628]
    B5a   'Tis little I—could care for Pearls—[466]
    B6   The Brain—is wider than the Sky—[632]

85	B3	He touched me, so I live to know [506]
86	B2	So set it's Sun in Thee [808]
	B2a	How the Waters closed above Him [923]
	B9	Finite—to fail, but infinite to Venture—[847]
87	B8a	Escaping backward to perceive [867]
88	B18a	Gratitude—is not the mention [989]
90	B18	Nor Mountain hinder Me [1029]
91	B5	Each Second is the last [879]
	B7a	I learned—at least—what Home could be—[944]
97	B13	The duties of the Wind are few, [1137]
98	B3	I never saw a Moor—[1052]
104	B13	Fortitude incarnate [1217]
107	B5	A great Hope fell [1123]
	B38	If my Bark sink [1234]
X	L	Should you but fail at—Sea—[226]
X	L	An Hour is a Sea [825]
X	L	The Sea said "Come" to the Brook—[1210]

P. POEMS THAT HAVE THE METAPHOR OF THE CAGE OR PRISON

Poem #77

I never hear the word "escape"
Without a quicker blood,
A sudden expectation,
A flying attitude!

I never hear of prisons broad
By soldiers battered down,
But I tug childish at my bars
Only to fail again!

1	H2b	My nosegays are for Captives—[95]
[3]	H10a	Bring me the sunset in a cup, [128]
	H10e	I never hear the word "escape" [77]
9	H42a	They put Us far apart—[474]
14	H72f	A transport one cannot contain [184]
18	H102b	Let Us play Yesterday—[728]
19	H103a	A Prison gets to be a friend—[652]
28	H149c	'Tis Opposites—entice—[355]
83	B6	Talk with prudence to a Beggar [119]
88	B5	Could I but ride indefinite [661]
	B6a	To One denied to drink [490]

Q. POEMS SENT TO SAMUEL BOWLES

Among the manuscripts presented by Mrs. Bingham to the Frost Library, Amherst, are letters and poems received by Samuel Bowles from Emily Dickinson. They were originally in the possession of Samuel Bowles, Jr., who gave them to Lavinia Dickinson and Mabel Loomis Todd when the first edition of *Letters* (1894) was in preparation. Furthermore, among Mrs. Bingham's papers, soon to become part of her large collection of family documents given to the Sterling Library of Yale University, New Haven, there are several listings of the Bowles poems.

[3]	H11a	These are the days when Birds come back—[130] (also Bingham)
	H11b	Besides the Autumn poets sing [131] (also Bingham)
7	H29a	Heart, not so heavy as mine [83] (also Bingham)
	H30c	"They have not chosen me" he said, [85] (also Bingham)
8	H32b	The Drop, that wrestles in the Sea [284] (also Bingham)
	H34	I came to buy a smile—today—[223] (also Bingham)
11	H132b	Victory comes late—[690] (also L257)

14 H72g   "Faith" is a fine invention [185] (also L220)

15 H78a   What shall I do—it whimpers so—[186] (also Bingham)
    H80c   My River runs to thee—[162] (also L235)
    H82b   For this—accepted Breath [195] (also Bingham)
    H83e   I stole them from a Bee [200] (also Bingham)
    H84b   A slash of Blue—[204] (also Bingham)

16 H88b   The Soul unto itself [683] (also Bingham)

17 H22b   Sweet—You forgot—but I remembered [523] (also Bingham) [stanza beginning "Just to be Rich"]

18 H101a   Through the strait pass of suffering—[792] (also Bingham)

19 H108d   Just Once! Oh least Request! [1076] (also Bingham)

20 H110e   Jesus! thy Crucifix [225] (also L242)

22 H122c   The Zeroes—taught us—Phosphorus—[689] (also L257)

25 H139a   My first well Day—since many ill—[574] (also Bingham) [stanza beginning "The loss of sickness—was it loss?"]

35 H188c   The Crickets sang [1104] (also Bingham)

37 H201e   "Faith" is a fine invention [185]
    H204d   I've nothing else—to bring, You know—[224] (also Bingham)

80 B4a   If she had been the Mistletoe [44] (also Bingham)

82 B3   I had a guinea golden—[23] (also Bingham)
    B7a   If recollecting were forgetting [33] (also Bingham)

83 B3   Good night, because we must, [114] (also Bingham)
    B6a   As Watchers hang upon the East, [121] (also Bingham)
    B6a   Her breast is fit for pearls [84] (also Bingham)

84 B12   So glad we are—a Stranger'd deem [329] (also Bingham)

86 B8   Before He comes we weigh the Time! [834] (also Bingham)

87	B4a	Perhaps you think me stooping [833] (also Bingham)
89	B(56)	Going to Him! Happy letter! [494] (also Bingham)
91	B3	Nature and God—I neither knew [835] (also Bingham)
92	B8a	Ample make this Bed—[829] (also Bingham)
94	B1	After all Birds have been investigated and laid aside—[1395] (also Bingham) [Lines beginning "Last to adhere"]
96	B1	As Summer into Autumn slips [1346] (also L420)
98	B3–12	I have no Life but this—[1398] (also L515)
109	B1	Could mortal lip divine [1409] (also Bingham)
	B14	If it had no pencil [921] (also Bingham)
X		The Juggler's Hat her Country is—[330] (Bingham)
X X		While Asters—[331] (Bingham) [Poem #342, "It will be summer"]
X		Teach Him—when He makes the *names*—[227] (Bingham)
X		I'll send the feather from my Hat! [687] (Bingham)
X		I would distil a cup, [16] (L193)
X		Would you like summer? Taste of ours. [691] (L229)
X		Should you but fail at—Sea—[226] (L249)
X		Title divine—is mine! [1072] (L250)
X		*"Speech"*—is a prank of *Parliament*—[688] (L252)
X		He is alive, this morning—[1160] (L341)
X		Ourselves we do inter with sweet derision. [1144] (L489)
X		Not that he goes—we love him more [1435] (L536)

Emily Dickinson's Reading

A. *The Emily Dickinson Association Books*
B. *Selections*
C. *Francis Quarles*
D. *Sir Thomas Browne*

A. *The Emily Dickinson Association Books*

The Emily Dickinson Association protects the volumes presented by Gilbert H. Montague to the Houghton Library, Harvard University, Boston. A mimeographed catalogue, *Handlist of Books Found in the Home of Emily Dickinson at Amherst, Massachusetts,* Spring 1950, may be consulted by a visitor to this library, and any volume may be examined.

These books have the autograph of ED:

Emerson, *Poems* (1847) [signed B. F. Newton].
Higginson, *Short Studies of American Authors* (1880).
Holmes, *Poems* (1849 ed.).
F. D. Huntington, *Christian Believing and Living* (1860) [Inscribed by her father].
Thomas a Kempis, *Of the Imitation of Christ* (1857 ed.).

These books are inscribed to ED:

The Holy Bible, containing the Old and New Testaments (1843).
Bound volume of miscellaneous sheet music.
H. G. Ollendorff, *New Method of Learning to Read German* (1846).
Matthew Arnold, *Sweetness and Light* [18—].
Mrs. C. M. Badger, *Wild Flowers Drawn and Colored from Nature,* with an introduction by Mrs. L. H. Sigourney (1859).
Mme. Barera, *Memoirs of Rachel* (1858).
Charlotte Brontë, *Jane Eyre* (1864).
— — — *Villette* (1859).

The Complete Concordance to Shakespeare (1877) [received 1880].
George Eliot, *Adam Bede* (1860).
— — — *Mill on the Floss* (1860).
— — — *The Spanish Gypsy* (1868).
O. B. Frothingham, *Theodore Parker: A Biography* (1874).
Mrs. Gaskell, *The Life of Charlotte Brontë* (1858).
W. L. Herndon, *Explorations of the Valley of the Amazon* (1854).
Howells, *Italian Journeys* (1867).
Helen Hunt Jackson, *Bits of Travel at Home* (1878).
Charles Kingsley, *Yeast* (1859).
James Russell Lowell, *My Study Windows* (1872).
Jane Porter, *Thaddeus of Warsaw* (1820).
Mme. Recamier, *The Religious Souvenir* (1832) [received 1833].
Wm. Buell Sprague, *Letters on Practical Subjects* (1851) [given by her father].
Sir Henry Taylor, *Philip Van Artevelde* (1835) [inscribed 1863].
Edward Trelawny, *Recollections of the Last Days of Shelley and Byron* (1859).

What poets were there?

Bailey, Philip James (1816–1902) *Festus,* a poem (1848).
Browning, Elizabeth Barrett
    Aurora Leigh (1857 ed.).
    Essays on the Greek Christian Poets (1863).
    Poems by . . . (1862) [Volume 4 only].
    The Poems of . . . (1852) [2 volumes].
    Poetical Works of . . . (1884 ed.) [5 volumes].
    Prometheus Bound and Other Poems (1851).
Browning, Robert
    Balamastion's Adventure (1871).
    Dramatis Personae (1864).
    Fifine at the Fair (1872).
    The Ring and the Book (1869).
    Selections from the Poetical Works of . . . *First Series* (1884).
    Selections from the Poetical Works of . . . *Second Series* (1884).
    Sordello (1864).
Bryant, William Cullen, *Poems by* . . . (1849).
Byron, *The Works of* . . . (1821) [4 volumes].
— — — *The Letters and Journals* (1830) [2 volumes].
Chaucer, *The Poetical Works of* . . . (1880) [3 volumes].
Clough, *The Poems and Prose Remains of* . . . (1869) [2 volumes].

Coleridge, *The Poetical and Dramatic Works of* . . . [3 volumes].
Cowper
  The Minor Poems (1818).
  Poems (1809) [2 vols.].
  Table Talk and Other Poems (1818).
  The Task (1818).
Dante, *The Vision: or Hell, Purgatory and Paradise* (1845 ed.).
Emerson
  The Conduct of Life (1861).
  English Traits (1878).
  Essays, First Series (1861); *Second Series* (1862).
  Letters and Social Aims (1876).
  May-Day and Other Pieces (1867).
  Miscellanies (1860).
  Poems (1847); *Poems* (1858).
  Representative Men (1878).
  Selected Poems (1878).
  Society and Solitude (1879).
Goethe, *Faust, a dramatic poem* (1859 ed.).
  [also] *Faust, a tragedy* (1860 ed.).
Goldsmith, *The Miscellaneous Works of* . . . (1809).
  Select Poems of . . . (1875).
Gray, *An Elegy Written in a Country Churchyard* (1854).
Greene, Robert, *The Poems of Robert Greene, Christopher Marlowe, and Ben Jonson* [18—].
Griswold, Rufus Wilmot (compiler), *Gems from the American Poets* (1844) [miniature book, 3″ x 5″].
  The Sacred Poets of England and America (1849).
Guild, Caroline Snowden (compiler)
  Hymns for Mothers and Children (1861).
  Hymns for Mothers and Children, Second Series (1866).
  Hymns of the Ages, Second Series (1861).
Heine, *Book of Songs* (1864 ed.).
Herbert (1593–1633) *The Poetical Works of* . . . (1857 ed.).
Holland, Josiah Gilbert, *Bitter-sweet, a poem* . . . (1859).
  Kathrina (1867).
  [*Titcomb's Letters* (1859).]
Holmes, *Poems* . . . *New and Enlarged Edition* (1849).
  Poems by . . . (1851).
Homer, *The Iliad*, tr. Pope (1806 ed.). [2 volumes]
  The Iliad, tr. Buckley (1854 ed.).

Horace, *The Odes and Epodes of Horace,* tr. Lytton (1870 ed.).
Hunt, Leigh, *Men, Women and Books* . . . (1855). [2 volumes]
Kingsley, *Poems by* . . . (1856).
The Koran in English (1806).
Longfellow
   The Golden Legend (1852).
   Hyperion, a romance (1852).
   Poems . . . (1863). [2 volumes]
   The Song of Hiawatha (1874).
Lowell, *A Fable for Critics* (1848).
   [*Among My Books* (1870).]
Michelangelo, *The Sonnets* (1878).
Milton, *Paradise Lost* (1819).
Palgrave, *The Golden Treasury* (1877 ed.).
Parks, Edwards Amasa, *The Sabbath Hymn-Book* (1858).
Patmore, Coventry (1823–1896) *The Angel in the House* (1856).
   Faithful for Ever (1861).
   The Unknown Eros (1877).
   The Victories of Love (1862).
Proctor, Adelaide Anne, *Legends and Lyrics* (1860).
Quarles, Francis (1592–1644) *Emblems, Divine and Moral* (1824
   ed.) [2 volumes in 1].
Richardson, Abby Sage (1837–1900) *Pebbles and Pearls* (1868).
Rogers, Samuel (1763–1855) *The Poetical Works of* . . . (1852).
Schiller, *The Works of* . . . (1853).
Scott, Sir Walter, *The Poetical Works of* . . . (1876) [7 volumes].
Shakespeare, *The Comedies, Histories, Tragedies, and Poems of* . . .
   (1853 ed.) [8 volumes].
Shelley, *The Poetical Works of* . . . (1853).
Smith, Alexander (1830–1867) *Poems* (1853).
   A Summer in Skye (1865).
Sophocles, *The Tragedies* (1860 ed.).
Spitta, Karl Johann Philip (1801–1859) *Lyra Domestica* (1861).
Taylor, Bayard, *A Book of Romances, Lyrics and Songs* (1852).
Tennyson, *The Princess* (1848).
   Enoch Arden (1864).
   In Memoriam (1850).
   Maud (1855).
   Poems by . . . (1853). [2 volumes]
   The Poetical Works of . . . (1862) [2 volumes].
   The Works of . . . (1871) [10 volumes].
   The Last Tournament (1873).

Thompson, James (1700–1748) *The Seasons* (1817).

Tupper, Martin, *Proverbial Philosophy, First Series* (1846).

Warner, Charles Dudley (1829–1900) *My Summer in a Garden* (1871); *Saunterings* (1872).

Watts, Isaac (1674–1748) *Christian Psalmody in Four Parts* (1817). *The Psalms, Hymns, and Spiritual Songs* (1834).

Whittier, *Ballads of New England* (1870).
   In War Time (1864).
   Miriam and Other Poems (1871).
   Snowbound (1866).

Willis, Nathaniel Parker (1806–1867) *The Poems, Sacred, Passionate and Humorous* (1847).

Wordsworth, *The Complete Poetical Works of . . .* (1854).
   The Wreath . . . A Collection of Poems (1824).

Young, Edward (1683–1765) *The Complaint; or Night Thoughts* (1845).

Other works of literature, religion, belles-lettres:

Beauties of the British Poets (1826) [Extracts].

Bayne, Peter, *Essays in Biography and Criticism* (1860).

Bridgman, Thomas, *Inscriptions on the Gravestones . . . of Northampton* (1850).

Chambers, *Cyclopedia of English Literature: A Selection of the Choicest Productions of English Authors from the Earliest to the Present Time* (1847) [2 volumes].

Elegant Extracts (1828) [extracts; volumes 1, 3, 5, 6].

Gilfillan, George, *Modern Literature and Literary Men* (1851).

Hitchcock, *The Power of Christian Benevolence* (1851).

Mitford, Mary Russell, *Recollections of a Literary Life* (1852).

De Quincy, *Essays on the Poets* (1853 ed.).
   Literary Reminiscences (1854 ed.).

Salad for the Solitary, ed. Frederick Saunders (1853) [essays].

Taylor, Sir Henry, *Notes from Life in Seven Essays* (1853).

Thackeray, *The English Humorists* (1853 ed.).

Thoreau, *Letters* (1865).
   Walden (1862).
   A Week on the Concord (1862).

Trench, R. C. *On the Lessons in Proverbs* (1855).
   On the Study of Words (1855).

Scribner's Magazine, 1870–1881.

Spectator (1819 ed.) [12 volumes].

Webster's Dictionary (1847 ed.).

Crabb, *Synonyms* (1810).
Alexander, *A Pocket Dictionary of the Holy Bible* (1831).
Eschenburg, *Manual of Classical Literature* (1846 ed.).
Jenks, *A Companion to the Bible* (1838).
Simmons, *A Scripture Manual* (1845).

The pervasive belief in the significance of the metaphysical poets as a literary influence on Emily Dickinson may have been responsible for the rejection of several important books of a different sort that were found among the volumes presented to the Houghton Library. When the Association acquired the library of the Dickinson family, they gave a *Handlist* of the books found there to Whicher and Johnson and asked them to decide what ought to be retained, and what books rejected from the Houghton collection. The *Handlist* has markings placed next to each title indicating how they decided: a red "x" signifies that Whicher rejected, THJ approved; a blue "x" signifies THJ rejected.

Whicher's assumption that Emily Dickinson had been entirely uninterested in Classical literature was confirmed by Johnson, despite the fact that they found two separate editions of Homer, as well as a volume each by Sophocles and Horace on the list, and despite the obvious references in this poem:

Poem #371

A precious—mouldering pleasure—'tis—
To meet an Antique Book—
In just the Dress his Century wore—
A privilege—I think—

His venerable Hand to take—
And warming in our own—
A passage back—or two—to make—
To Times when he—was young—

His quaint opinions—to inspect—
His thought to ascertain
On Them[e]s concern our mutual mind—
The Literature of Man—

What interested Scholars—most—
What Competitions ran—
When Plato—was a Certainty—
And Sophocles—a Man—

When Sappho—was a living Girl—
And Beatrice wore
The Gown that Dante—deified—
Facts Centuries before

He traverses—familiar—
As One should come to Town—
And tell you all your Dreams—were true—
He lived—where Dreams were born—

His presence is Enchantment—
You beg him not to go—
Old Volumes shake their Vellum Heads—
And tantalize—just so—

Both scholars knew, indeed Johnson makes a special point of it in his biography, that Elizabeth Barrett Browning was greatly admired by Emily Dickinson. They could not then have been unaware of the fact that Mrs. Browning had written a book of essays on the Greek Christian Poets, and had often published translations of classical poetry. Both undoubtedly saw these titles on the *Handlist:*

E. B. Browning, *Essays on the Greek Christian Poets,* 1863
Prometheus Bound and Other Poems, 1851

Had they opened the book on the Greek Christian poets, they could have read there Mrs. Browning's long essay on the *Greek* poetic tradition. They agreed to send back to Amherst, as irrelevant,

John Lempriere, *A Classical Dictionary,* 1816
Charles Anthon, *A Classical Dictionary,* 1846
James Skerret Baird, *The Classical Manual,* 1877

The date of publication of the third volume indicates at least a continuing interest in the classical world.

Mrs. Browning had carried on an intense correspondence with a minister concerning the internal life of the mystic, striving with him to unravel questions of the soul and the afterlife. The *Handlist* shows three volumes on this very subject to have been part of the Dickinson library:

Peter Bayne, *The Christian Life,* Boston, 1856
Joseph Butler, Bishop of Durham, *The Analogy of Religion Natural and Revealed,* New York, 1843
Thomas Cogswell Upham, *Principles of the Interior or Hidden Life,* New York, 1848

Thomas Upham had been for a time professor of "Mental and Moral

Philosophy" at Amherst Academy; his textbook on that subject was used for decades by Amherst students. Moreover, it was this same Upham who wrote a two-volume biography of Madame de la Mothe Guyon,* a French mystic whose poetry was reprinted often and at length in several of the anthologies contained in the Dickinson library. The *Handlist* shows that Whicher and Johnson both agreed to reject these volumes.

The biographers inform us that a picture of Thomas Carlyle hung on the wall of Emily Dickinson's bedroom; yet Carlyle's *Critical and Miscellaneous Essays,* 1860, was returned.

No one can say with certainty that any of these books would illuminate questions of Emily Dickinson's style and subject matter, and perhaps the decisions were correct. But to ignore what is actually in the library or to neglect to examine the books themselves is questionable practice.

B. *Selections.*

Martin F. Tupper, *Proverbial Philosophy,* A Book of Thoughts and Arguments [has her inscription although it is conjectural]
Didactic poetry. Section "Of Writing" is marked:
"and shouldst thou ask my judgment of that which hath most profit in the world, for answer take thou this, The prudent penning of a letter."

"Thou has not lost an hour, whereas there is a record. A written thought at midnight shall redeem the livelong day."

Frederick Saunders, *Salad for the Solitary,* 1853.

A book usually overlooked because of its bizarre title, *Salad* does contain one chapter that is obviously grimy with use: "Citations from the Cemeteries," with factual accounts of funeral rituals, descriptions of tombstones and churchyards, and a lengthy collection of epitaphs. The book is inscribed to Susan H. Gilbert.
Contents:
Dietetics (uncut).
The Talkative and the Taciturn (cut).
Facts and Fancies About Flowers (cut).
A Monologue on Matrimony (cut).
Curious and Costly Books (cut) [the value of books in monetary terms; famous relics, most expensive books, etc.].
Something About Nothing [i.e., Negation] (cut).
Pastimes and Sports (uncut).

* Thomas C. Upham, *Life and Religious Opinions and Experience of Madame de la Mothe Guyon* (New York, 1847).

Dying Words of Distinguished Men (much evidence of use).

The Poetry of Plants (uncut).

Infelicities of the Intellectual (cut) [foibles and fallacies of great men of literature].

Citations from the Cemeteries (pp. 227–261 show marks of use).

The Shrines of Genius (cut) [anecdotes of where they lived and the places they gathered].

The Selfish and the Social (much evidence of use).

Pleasures of the Pen [examples of great passages of poetry] (cut).

Sleep and its Mysteries (cut).

from "Pleasures of the Pen"

"The Persian poet, Sardi, teaches a moral in one of his apologies. Two friends passed a summer day in a garden of roses; one satisfied himself with admiring their colors and inhaling their fragrance; the other filled his bosom with the leaves, and enjoyed at home, during several days with his family, the deliciousness of the perfume. The first was the *solitary,* the second the *social* student. He wanders among many gardens of thought, but always brings back some flower in his hand. Who can estimate the advantages that may result from this toil, and this application of it." [p. 299]

There are many examples of ingenious poetic diversions, as the wit of echo poems (e.g., Disraeli) and the wit of curious combinations of words that may be changed in their ordering to create interesting effects (e.g., Swift's Latin poems).

from "Citations from the Cemeteries"

After describing the manner of funerals of the past, and taking note of the kinds of tombstones that are in old churchyards, a collection of epitaphs appears. The facetious epitaphs resemble those printed each month in *Harper's Magazine* in a column of humorous poems and anecdotes. The examples reprinted here are those that show marks of use.

An epitaph by Shakespeare:

With fairest flowers,
Whilst summer lasts, and I live here Fidele,
I'll sweeten thy sad grave; thou shalt not lack
The flower that like thy face, pale primrose, nor
The azured harebell, like thy veins; no, nor

The leaf of eglantine; whom not to slander,
Outsweetened not thy breath.

I, Richard Skipwithe, gentlyman in birthe,
    late fellow of New Inne,
In my age twenti, on my soul partyed from the bodee
    in August an 16th day,
And now I ly her abyding God's mercy under this
    stone in clay,
Desyring you that this sal see unto the meyden
    pray for mee,
Like as you wold that other for ye shold.

Earth goes to   As mould to mould.
Earth treads on   Earth   Glittering in gold,
Earth as to   Return ne'er should,
Earth shall be   Goe where he would.

Earth upon   Consider may,
Earth goes to   Naked a way,
Earth though on   Earth   Be stout and gay,
Earth shall from   Passe poore away.

Here lies John, Duke of Marleborough
Who run the French through and through;
He married Sarah Jennings, spinster,
Died at Windsor, and was buried at Westminster.

Here lies one *More,* and no more than he,
One *More,* and no *More!* how can that be?
Why one *More,* and no *more,* may well lie here alone;
But here lies *one More* and that's more than one!

    God be praised!
Here is Mr. DUDLEY, senior,
    And JANE, his wife, also,

Who whilst living, was his superior:
   But see what Death can do,
Two of his sons also lie here,
   One Walter, t'other Joe:
They all of them went in the year 1510 below.

My Sledge and Hammer lay reclined,
My Bellows, too, have lost their wind,
My Fire's extinct, my Forge decayed,
And in the dust my vice is laid;
My coal is spent, my Iron gone,
My Nails are drove—my work is done.

Father and Mother and I
   Lies buried here as under:
Father and Mother lies buried here,
   And I lies buried yonder.

   In this house
which I have borrowed from
my brethren the worms,
     lie I,
Samuel, by Divine permission,
   Bishop of this island.
    Stop, reader;
   behold, and smile at
THE PALACE OF A BISHOP!
   who died May 30,
    in the year
     1653

Here lieth, wrapped in clay,
The body of William Wray;—
I have no more to say!

This tombstone is a *Milestone,* hah, how so?
Because, beneath lies *Miles,* who's Miles below.

Here lies Pat Steele: —
  That's very thrue: —
Who was he? what was he?
  What's that to you?

Good Friend, For Jesus' Sake Forbeare
To Digg the Dust Enclosed here:
Blest Be ye Man yt Spares These Stones,
And Cursed Be Him yt Moves My Bones.

Death creeps abought on hard,
And steals abroad on seen,
Hur darts are suding, and her arrows keen,
Hur strocks are deadly, com they soon or late,
When being struck repentance is too late,
Death is a minut, full of suding sorrow,
Then live today, as thou may'st dy to morrow.

Beneath this stone, Tom Crossfield lies,
Who cares not now who laughs or cries,
He laughed when sober, and when mellow,
Was a harum-scarum harmless fellow:
He gave to none designed offence,
So —'Honi soit qui mal y pense'

John Adams lies here, of the parish of Southwell
A carrier who carried the can to his mouth well;
He carried so much, and he carried so fast.
He could carry no more — so was carried at last;
For the liquor he drank being too much for one,
He could not carry off, so he's now carri-on.

The Grave, great teacher, to a level brings
Heroes and beggars, galley-slaves and kings;
But Theodore this moral learned, are dead;

Fate poured its lessons on his living head,
Bestowed a kingdom, and denied him bread.

Painters and heralds, by your leave,
    Here lies the bones of Matthew Prior:
The son of Adam and of Eve; —
    Let Bourbon or Nassau go higher!

Farewell, great painter of mankind,
    Who reach'd the noblest point of art;
Whose pictur'd morals charm the mind,
    And through the eye correct the heart!
If genius fire thee, reader, stay;
    If nature touch thee, drop a tear: —
If neither move thee, turn away,
    For Hogarth's honor'd dust lies here.

Alas! he's gone before;
Gone to return no more.
Our panting breasts aspire
After their aged sire,
Whose well-spent life did last
Full many years and past;
And now he hath begun
That which will ne'er be done:
Crowned with eternal bliss,
We wish our souls with his.

Doe, pious Marble! let thy readers knowe
What they and what their children owe
To Draiton's name, whose sacred dust
We recommend unto thy TRUST:
Protect his memory, and preserve his storye,
Remaine a lasting monument of his glorye;
And when thy ruines shall disclaime
To be the treas'rer of his name,

His name that cannot fade shall be
An everlasting monument to thee.

Here lies N., the best of fathers, the most tender
of husbands; his disconsolate widow still keeps
the fancy shop, Rue Richelieu, No.—

Ca git ma femme; c'est bien,
Pour son repose, et la mien.

Here lyes (expecting the second
Comminge of our SAVIOR CHRIST
JESUS) the body of Edmond Spenser,
The Prince of Poets in his tyme,
Whose divine spirit needs noe
Other witnesse than the works
Which he left behind him.
He was borne in London, in the yeare 1553,
    And died in the year 1598.

Braintree, thy prophet's gone, this tomb inters
The Rev. Moses Fiske his sacred hearse.
Adore heaven's praiseful art, that formed the man,
Who soules, not to himself, but Christ oft won:
Sailed through the straits with Peter's family,
Renowned, and Gaius' hospitality,
Paul's patience, James' prudence, John's sweet love—
Is landed, entered, cleared, and crowned above.

    Ah! old must die.
A Death's head on your hand, you need not weare,
A dying head you on your shoulders beare,
You neede not one to mind you, you must dye,
You in your name may spell mortalitye.
Younge men may dye, but old men these dye must:
'Twill not be long before you turne to dust.

Before you turne to dust! ah! must! old dye!
What shall younge doe, when old in dust doe lye?
When old in dust lye, what new England doe?
When old in dust doe lye, its best dye too.
on Thomas Dudley

Born in America, in Europe bred,
In Africa traveled, and in Asia wed;
Where long he lived and thrived, in London dead.
Much good, some ill, he did; so hope all's even,
And that his soul through mercy's gone to Heaven.
You that survive, and read this tale, take care,
For this most certain exit to prepare.
Where blest in peace the actions of the just
Smell sweet, and blossom in the silent dust.
On Elihu Yale

God wills us free; man wills us slaves. I will as God
wills, God's will be done! Here lies the body of John
Jack, a native of Africa, who died March, 1773,
aged 60 years. Though born in a land of slavery, he
was born free; though he lived in a land of liberty, he
lived a slave; till by his honest, though stolen
labors, he acquired the source of slavery,
which gave him his freedom, though not long before
his death, the grand tyrant set him on a footing
with kings. Though a slave to vice, he practised
those virtues without which kings are but slaves.

She yt lyes here, was while she stood,
A very glorie of womanhoode:
Even here was sowne most pretious dust,
Which surely shall rise with the just.

Thomas Bridgman, *Inscriptions on the Grave Stones in the Grave Yards of Northampton, and of other towns in the Valley of the Connecticut,* 1850.

> Emily Dickinson's well-known interest in mortuary subject matter would have been nourished by this book, that seems the most well read of any in the library. It is inscribed "Edward Dickinson, 1857."

Jesus can make a dying bed
   Feel soft as downy pillows are
While on his breast I lean my head,
   And breathe my life out sweetly there.   [p. 29]

Life makes the soul dependent on the dust
Death gives her wings to mount above the spheres.   [p. 29]

Corruption, earth and worms,
   Shall but refine this flesh
Till my triumphant spirit comes,
   To put it on afresh.
Hark from the tombs
   A doleful sound,
Mine years attend the cry,
   Ye living men come view the ground
Where you must shortly lie.   [p. 30]

Time was like you she life possessed,
And time shall be when you shall rest.   [p. 31]

Life like the Solar Shadow
Speeds away from Point
To Point.
Tho seeming to stand still
Thus soon Mans hours are
up, and we are gone.   [p. 44]

The grave is that home of Man
Where dwells the Multitude.   [p. 44]

This shall our mouldering members teach,
What now our senses learn,
For dust and ashes loudest preach
Man's infinite concern.   [p. 44]

Man departs this earthly scene,
Ah! never to return,
No second Spring shall ere revive
The ashes of the urn. [p. 44]

Why should we mourn departed friends,
   Or shake at death's alarm,
'Tis but the voice that Jesus sends
   To call them to his arms. [p. 46]

Her Body here entombed in dust,
Her pious soul is gone we trust,
Among the assembly of the just. [p. 47]

Rest here blest saint till from his throne
The morning break and pierce the shade. [p. 51]

Friends and Physicians could not save
This mortal body from the grave,
Nor can the grave confine it here
When Jesus calls it must appear. [p. 52]

Why lingers hope around the silent dead,
There is another and a better world. [p. 56]

Unveil thy bosom faithful tomb,
   Take this new treasure to thy trust,
And give their sacred relicks, room
   To slumber in the silent dust. [p. 59]

How populous, how vital is the grave,
This is Creation's Melancholy vault,
Where change shall be no more. [p. 66]

All, All, is right by God ordained or done, who but
    God resumed the Friends He gave.   [p. 73]

Our days are as the grass,
Or like the morning flower,
If one sharp blast sweeps o'er the field
They wither in an hour.   [p. 76]

"Is it well with the child? and she answered it is well." [p. 84]

There is a pressed leaf between pages 90 and 91. This is printed on page 90:

    And if we believe that Jesus died and rose again,
    Even so them also which sleep in Jesus will God bring with him.

This is printed below:

    Death kills not the buds of virtue.
    No. They spread.

This is printed on page 91:

    Death came with friendly care,
    The opening bud to heaven conveyed,
    And bade it blossom there.

And Angel's arm can't snatch us from the grave,
Legions of Angels can't confine us there.   [p. 95]

"Hark, they whisper Angels say,
    Sister Spirit come away."
        "Now I See."   [p. 101]

Well, the kind minute must appear,
When we shall leave these bodies here,
These clogs of clay, and mount on high,
To join the songs above the sky.   [p. 105]

My Body Sleeps my SOULE HATH SVIET REST
in ARMES oF GoD in Christ who makes me Blest
The Tyme Drawes on apace when GoD ye Sonne
To See his face shall both UNITE In oNE. [p. 109]

He taught us how to live, and OH! too high
A price for knowledge, taught us how to die. [p. 116]

The dear delight we here enjoy,
    And fondly call our own,
Are but short favors borrowed now,
    To be repaid anon. [p. 125]

Oh! could we die with those yt die,
And place us in their stead;
Then would our Spirits learn to fly,
And convers with the Dead. [p. 126]

Suddenly Death threw forth his dart,
The fatal arrow pierced my heart,
When health and vigor crown'd my day,
Alas my soul was snatch'd away.

                    In Memory of
                    Chester Smith,
                    who was instantly killed by the
                    upsetting of a load of wood,
                    Jan. 25th, 1810, aged 18 years [p. 134]

Here is a poem written by Emily Dickinson which may be read in context
with the epitaph above, to the discomfiture of all the scholars who require
that great poets be influenced by great poets:

                    Poem #614

            In falling Timbers buried—
            There breathed a Man—
            Outside—the spades—were plying—
            The Lungs—within—

Could He—know—they sought Him—
Could They—know—He breathed—
Horrid Sand Partition—
Neither—could be heard—

Never slacked the Diggers—
But when Spades had done—
Oh, Reward of Anguish,
It was dying—Then—

Many Things—are fruitless—
'Tis a Baffling Earth—
But there is no Gratitude
Like the Grace—of Death—

Oh let my mouldering members teach
What mortals ought to learn,
For dust and ashes loudest preach,
Man's Infinite concern.   [p. 140]

In Memory of
Mr. Elnathan Baldwin,
who was suddenly killed by the wheel of a wagon,
    near Hartford, on the 13 of July, 1812,
        aged 40 yEARS.
        Useful in Life,
AND LAMENTED IN DEATH.
        Come all you weary travelers
        Pray stop and drop a tear,
        As I traveled I made a full stop here.   [p. 147]

By Adam's sin we all must die,
By Christ alone we rise on high.   [p. 163]

Virtue outshines the stars, outlives the tomb,
Climbs up to heaven, and finds a peaceful home.   [p. 165]

Death makes a melancholy gloom,
  It makes an empty seat,
Y living mortals all must come
  And try this long retreat.   [p. 180]

Were I so tall to reach the pole,
  Or grasp the ocean with my span,
I must be measured by my soul,—
  The mind's the standard of the man.   [p. 190]

The room below flamed like a stove,
Anxious for those who slept above,
She ventured on ye trembling floor,
It fell, she sank and rose no more.
    The unfortunate Miranda,
      Whose remains are here interred, fell a prey
    to the flames that consumed her Father's House,
    on yᵉ 11th of June, 1791, aged 28.

                                              [p. 193]

Deliriums State, was worse than fate;
  And vacancy of mind;
But real grace fill'd up the space,
  And left a hope behind.   [p. 198]

Death, great proprietor of all,
Tis thine to tread out empires
And to quench the stars.   [p. 210]

That Emily Dickinson wandered about in the cemetery and speculated on
the occupants of the graves is possible; she may have remained at home and
browsed through the book of epitaphs. She has left this poem to suit either
conjecture:

Poem #892

Who occupies this House?
A Stranger I must judge

Since No one knows His Circumstance—
'Tis well the name and age

Are writ upon the Door
Or I should fear to pause
Where not so much as Honest Dog
Approach encourages.

It seems a curious Town—
Some Houses very old,
Some newly raised this Afternoon,
Were I compelled to build

It should not be among
Inhabitants so still
But where the Birds assemble
And Boys were possible.

Before Myself was born
'Twas settled, so they say,
A Territory for the Ghosts—
And Squirrels, formerly.

Until a Pioneer, as
Settlers often do
Liking the quiet of the Place
Attracted more unto—

And from a Settlement
A Capitol has grown
Distinguished for the gravity
Of every Citizen.

The Owner of this House
A Stranger He must be—
Eternity's Acquaintances
Are mostly so—to me.

Hymns of the Ages. Bishop Huntington, who gave this book to "S. H. Dickinson," was represented in the Dickinson library with his own collection of essays, *Christian Believing and Living,* one among the mere five bearing the autograph of the poet. *Hymns* is well used but more so up to the point of pages 206–207 where Huntington's own poem "A Supplication" is printed. The book is divided according to theme.

This selection is taken from the preface, written by Huntington, and may have been of interest to Emily Dickinson:

For the previous volume * we sought such utterances as in their gentle mysticism embodied a religious *sentiment,* fitted to console and soothe, to bind up broken reeds: in the present, our purpose being rather to strengthen the reeds that they may not break, and haply bend them into use, . . . we have given with less sentiment, more religious *thought.*

Because both of their obscurity and striking merit, large selections are presented from verse-writers of the sixteenth and seventeenth centuries, "from the tender and earnest numbers of Southwell and Crashaw and Habington," the gentle symphonies of Vaughan, the rugged verse of Donne and Jeremy Taylor, from the quaint "Church Emblems" of Quarles, and the voluminous "Hallelujah" of Wither, which touched with a poetic glow each object of every-day life.

For the rest, we have, like the householder, brought together things "new and old": some of the latter we must thank the German writers for passing on to us, ... Choosing irrespective of creed, we have often been guided by rare and deep associations of the past; hymns there are here which have been breathed by dying lips, traced on the walls of prisons, sung with hushed voices in catacombs, or joyfully chanted on the battle-march, or fearlessly at the stake.

"For a Wakeful Night" by Pastor Josephsen is bent at the corner:

Now darkness over all is spread
  No sounds the stillness break;
Ah when shall these sad hours be fled:
  Am I alone awake?

The following excerpts have strikingly similar metaphors to those which appear in the poetry of Emily Dickinson.

from Henry Vaughan, "Peace" [p. 2]

        My soul, there is a countrie
        Afar beyond the stars,

* This edition is the so-called "Second Series." The "First Series," 1858, reprinted much the same kind of poetry, with the addition of "The Cherubic Pilgrim," selections (Silesius) and excerpts from Alger's popular anthology of Oriental poetry.

Where stands a wingéd sentrie
    All skillfull in the wars.
There above noise and danger,
    Sweet Peace sits crown'd with smiles,
And One born in a manger
    Commands the beauteous files.

from Richard Crashaw, "Cheap Medicine" [pp. 6–7]

As when a piece of wanton lawn,
A thin, aerial veil, is drawn
O'er beauty's face, seeming to hide,
More sweetly shows the blushing bride;
A soul, whose intellectual beams
No mists do mask, no lazy streams;
A happy soul, that all the way
To heaven rides in a summer's day.

. . . .

Would'st see nest of new roses grow
In a bed of reverend snow? —
Warm thoughts, free spirits flattering
Winter's self into a spring?

from Habington [pp. 18–19]

Why doth ambition so the mind distresse
    To make us scorne what we possesse,
And look so farre before us, since all we
    Can hope, is varied misery?

. . . .

Stay here then, and while curious exiles find
    New toyes for a fantastique mind,
Enjoy at home what's real: here the Spring
    By her aeriall quires doth sing
As sweetly to you, as if you were laid
    Under the learn'd Thessalian shade.
Direct your eyesight inward, and you'll find
    A thousand regions in your mind
Yet undiscover'd. Travell them, and be
    Expert in home cosmographie.
This you may doe safe both from rocke and shelfe:
    Man's a whole world within himselfe.

from the Disciples' Hymn Book, "The Gate of Heaven," [pp. 35–36]

> She stood outside the gate of heaven, and saw them
>   entering in,
> A world-long train of shining ones, all washed in
>   blood from sin.
>
> The hero-martyr in that blaze uplifted his strong eye,
> And trod firm the reconquered soil of his nativity!
>
> And humble souls, who held themselves too dear for
>   earth to buy,
> Now passed through the golden gate, to live eternally.

from George Wither, "Divers Providences" [p. 126]

> Had we no winter, summer would be thought
>   Not half so pleasing; and if tempests were not,
> Such comforts by a calm could not be brought;
>   For things, save by their opposites, appear not.

from the Breviary

> Ye mist and darkness, cloud and storm,
>   Confused creations of the night;
> Light enters—morning streaks the sky—
>   Christ comes,—'tis time ye take your flight.
>
> Pierced by the sun's ethereal dart,
>   Night's gloomy mass is cleft in twain;
> And, in the smiling face of day,
>   Nature resumes her tints again.
>
> The star that heralds in the morn
>   Is fading in the skies;
> The darkness melts;—O Thou true Light!
>   Upon our souls arise.
>
> Shall Nature from her couch arise,
>   And rise for thee in vain?
> While heaven, and earth, and seas, and skies,
>   Such types of truth contain.
>
> Lord of eternal purity!
>   Who dost the world with light adorn,

And paint the tracts of azure sky
With lovely hues of eve and morn:

Who didst command the sun to light
His fiery wheel's effulgent blaze;
Didst set the moon her circuit bright;
The stars their ever-winding maze:

That, each within its order's sphere,
They might divide the night from day;
And of the seasons through the year,
The well remember'd signs display.

from "Hymn of the Calabrian Shepherds"

We pray thee for the little bark
Upon the stormy sea

The soldier, he who only sleeps
His head upon his brand,
Who only in a dream can see
His own beloved land.

All of the hymns from the Breviary are in quatrains (abab)
All of the hymns from the Missal are 3 lines (aaa)

Lyra Domestica. This anthology contains a translation of the *Psaltery and Harp* by K. J. P. Spitta, plus additional selections made by the same Rev. F. D. Huntington, referred to above. Selections are taken from Vaughan, Whittier, Wordsworth, Mme. Guyon, Hogg, Doane, E. B. Browning, Herbert, Proctor, Peabody, Hawthornden, Coleridge, Scheffler, and many others. The poets are not represented in any order other than theme.

"Parting" by K. J. P. Spitta [pp. 81–82]

How mean ye thus by weeping
To break my very heart?
We both are in Christ's keeping,
And cannot therefore part;
Nor time, nor place, can sever
The bonds which us have bound;
In Christ abide for ever
Who once in Him are found.

As though to part for ever
 We press each other's hands,
And yet no power can sever
 Our love's eternal bands;
We look quite broken-hearted,
 And sob our last farewell,
And yet can not be parted,
 For both in Jesus dwell.

We say "I here, you yonder,"
 "You go, and I remain,"
And yet are not asunder,
 But links of one great chain;
In tones of deep affection
 "Our road parts here" we say,
Yet go in one direction,
 And in the self-same way.

Then let us cease from weeping,
 And moderate our woe,
We both are in Christ's keeping,
 With whom we always go;
Both under His protection,
 Both led by His dear hand,
Both in the same direction,
 To the same Fatherland.

In fruitless lamentation
 Let us not waste the hours,
But find our consolation
 In knowing Christ is ours;
If faith in Him unite us,
 Though parting gives us pain
It cannot disunite us,
 For both in Him remain.

"When We First Awake" by Wither [pp. 108–109]

 Dear God! that watch doth keep
  Round all that honour Thee,
 Vouchsafing Thy beloved sleep
  When rest shall needful be;

My soul returns Thee praise,
  That thus refresh'd I am;
And that my tongue a voice can raise,
  To praise Thee for the same.

As now my soul doth shake
  Dull sleep out of her eyes;
So let Thy Spirit me awake,
  That I from sin may rise.
The night is past away,
  Which fill'd us full of fears;
And we enjoy the glorious day,
  Wherein Thy grace appears.

Oh! let me, therefore, shun
  All errors of the night;
Thy righteousness let me put on,
  And walk as in the light:
And guard me from his power,
  Since I on Thee rely,
Who walks in darkness to devour
  When our long sleep draws nigh.

Yea, when the trump shall sound
  Our summons from the grave,
Let this my body from the ground
  A blessed rising have.
That, whatso'er the dreams
  Of my corruption be,
The vision of Thy glorious beams
  May bring full joys to me.

"The Dawning," by Vaughan [pp. 117–118]

Ah! what time wilt Thou come? when shall that cry
The *Bridegroom's coming!* fill the sky?
Shall it in the evening run,
When our words and works are done?
Or will Thy all-surprising light
  Break at midnight,
When either sleep, or some dark pleasure
Possesseth mad man without measure?

Or shall these early fragrant hours
    Unlock thy bowers?
And with their blush of light descry
Thy locks crown'd with eternity?
Indeed, it is the only time
That with Thy glory doth best chime;
All now are stirring: every field
    Full hymns doth yield;
The whole creation shakes off night,
And for thy shadow looks the light;
Stars now vanish without number,
Sleepy planets set and slumber,
The pursy clouds disband and scatter,
All expect some sudden matter;
Not one beam triumphs, but from far
    That morning-star.

O at what time soever Thou,
Unknown to us, the heavens wilt bow,
And, with Thy angels in the van,
Descend to judge poor careless man,
Grant, I may not like puddle lie
In a corrupt security,
Where, if a traveller water crave,
He finds it dead, and in a grave.
But as this restless vocal spring
All day and night doth run and sing,
And though here born, yet is acquainted
Elsewhere, and flowing keeps untainted;
So let me all my busy age
In Thy free services engage;
And though, while here, of course I must
Have commerce sometimes with poor dust,
And in my flesh, though vile and low,
As this doth in her channel flow,
Yet let my course, my aim, my love,
And chief acquaintance be above;
So when that day and hour shall come,
In which Thyself will be the sun,
Thou'lt find me drest and on my way,
Watching the break of Thy Great Day.

"Sunday," by Herbert [pp. 121–122]

O day most calm, most bright,
　　The fruit of this, the next world's bud,
Th' indorsement of supreme delight,
Writ by a friend, and with his blood;
　　The couch of time; care's balm and bay;
The week were dark, but for thy light:
　　Thy Torch doth show the way.

　　The other days and thou
Make up one man; whose face thou art,
　　Knocking at heaven with thy brow:
The working-days are the back part;
　　The burden of the week lies there,
Making the whole to stoop and bow,
　　Till thy release appear.

　　Sundays the pillars are,
On which heaven's palace arched lies:
　　The other days fill up the spare
And hollow room with vanities.
　　They are the fruitful beds and borders
In God's rich garden: that is bare
　　Which parts their ranks and orders.

　　The Sundays of man's life,
Threaded together on time's string,
　　Make bracelets to adorn the wife
Of the eternal glorious King.
　　On Sunday heaven's gate stands ope;
Blessings are plentiful and rife,
　　More plentiful than hope.

　　This day my Saviour rose,
And did enclose this light for His:
　　That, as each beast his manger knows,
Man might not of his fodder miss.
　　Christ hath took in this piece of ground,
　　And made a garden there for those
　　Who want herbs for their wound.

Thou art a day of mirth:
And where the week-days trail on ground,
Thy flight is higher, as thy birth:
O let me take thee at the bound,
Leaping with thee from seven to seven,
Till that we both, being toss'd from earth,
Fly hand in hand to heaven!

from "The City of God," Bernard, Abbot of Clugni [pp. 138–139]

Brief life is here our portion,
Brief sorrow, short-lived care;
The life that knows no ending,
The tearless life, is there.
O one! O only mansion!
O Paradise of joy!
Where tears are ever banished,
And joys have no alloy.

Beside thy living waters,
All plants are great and small—
The cedar of the forest,
The hyssop on the wall.
Thy ageless walls are bounded
With amethyst unpriced,
The saints build up its fabric,
And the corner-stone is Christ.

Thou hast no shore, fair ocean,
Thou hast no time, bright day,
Dear fountain of refreshment
To pilgrims far away.
Upon the Rock of Ages,
They raise the holy tower;
Thine is the victor's laurel,
And thine the golden dower.

They stand, those halls of Sion,
Conjubilant with song,
And bright with many an angel,
And many a martyr throng.
The Prince is ever in them,
The light is aye serene,

The pastures of the blessed
  Are decked in glorious sheen.

There is the throne of David,
  And there from toil released
The shout of them that triumph,
  The song of them that feast.
And they beneath their Leader,
  Who conquered in the fight,
Forever and forever
  Are clad in robes of white.

"I Will Keep Thee," a Medieval Hymn [pp. 143–146]

Thus said Jesus: —I will keep
In safety my defenceless sheep
From sin and endless misery,
Seeking soul, I will keep thee.

SOUL

Lord, I believe Thy word is sure,
But I am ignorant and poor,
My goodness reaches not to Thee,
For mercy's sake, wilt Thou keep me?

JESUS

I passèd by the rich and brave,
Thee, needy soul, I came to save;
The poor in spirit blessed be—
Oh! trust me then, I will keep thee.

. . . .

JESUS

Can I forsake my heart's delight?
Thy end is precious in my sight;
I conquered Death on Calvary,
And from its sting I will keep thee,
I will be near thy dying bed—
Amid the waves sustain thy head;
My rod, my staff, thy help shall be,
In perfect peace I will keep thee.
I am the ark that goes before

To guide the pilgrim safe to shore;
At my rebuke shall Jordan flee—
In life, in death, I will keep thee.
Then, then, my sister and my spouse,
I will fulfil my sacred vows;
And thou in bliss my glory see,
When on my breast I've placèd thee.

SOUL

It is enough, my Lord! my Love!
The hills, the mountains must remove;
But I shall still unshaken be—
The word is passed, *Thou wilt keep me.*

"The Glory Reserved," by Dr. Muhlenberg [pp. 154–155]

Since o'er Thy footstool here below
  Such radiant gems are strewn,
O what magnificence must glow,
  My God! about Thy throne!
So brilliant *here* those drops of light,
Where the full ocean rolls, how bright!

If night's blue curtain of the sky,
  With thousand stars inwrought,
Hung like a royal canopy
  With glittering diamonds fraught.
Be, Lord, Thy temple's outer veil—
What splendour at the shrine must dwell?

The dazzling sun, at noontide hour,
  Forth from his flaming vase,
Flinging o'er earth the golden shower
  Till vale and mountain blaze,
But shews, O Lord! one beam of Thine,
What, then, *the day where Thou dost shine!*

Ah! how shall these dim eyes endure
  That noon of living rays;
Or how my spirit, so impure,
  Upon Thy glory gaze?
Anoint, O Lord! anoint my sight,
And robe me for that world of light.

"The Spirit's Home," anonymous [pp. 184–185]

> Mysterious in its birth,
>   And viewless as the blast,
> Where has the spirit fled from earth?
>   For ever past.
>
> We ask the grave below,
>   It keeps the secret well;
> We call upon the heavens to shew;
>   They will not tell.
>
> Of earth's remotest strand
>   Are tales and tidings known;
> But from the spirit's distant land
>   Returneth none.
>
> Winds bear the breath of flowers
>   To travellers o'er the wave;
> But bear no message from the bowers
>   Beyond the grave.
>
> Proud science scales the skies,
>   From star to star doth roam;
> But reacheth not the shore where lies
>   The spirit's home.
>
> Impervious shadows hide
>   This mystery of heaven;
> But where all knowledge is denied,
>   *There* faith is given.

"The Second Coming," anonymous [pp. 211–212]

> Rejoice, rejoice, believers!
>   And let your lights appear;
> The evening is advancing
>   The darker night is near.
> The Bridegroom is arising,
>   And soon will He draw nigh:
> Up! pray, and watch, and wrestle,
>   At midnight comes the cry.

See that your lamps are burning;
   Replenish them with oil;
Look now for your salvation,
   The end of sin and toil.
The watchers on the mountain
   Proclaim the Bridegroom near:
Go, meet Him as He cometh,
   With hallelujahs clear.

Oh! wise and holy virgins,
   Now raise your voices higher,
Till in your jubilations
   Ye meet the angel-choir.
The marriage-feast is waiting,
   The gates wide open stand;
Up, up, ye heirs of glory,
   The Bridegroom is at hand!

Our hope and expectation,
   O Jesus, now appear;
Arise, Thou Sun so looked for,
   O'er this benighted sphere!
With hearts and hands uplifted
   We plead, O Lord, to see
The day of our redemption,
   And ever be with Thee!

Johann Scheffler (well represented in this anthology) was a German mystic who used the name "Silesius" and his collection of verse *The Cherubinic Wanderer* is a connected series of quatrains rendering as if it were a narrative, a mystical experience. The style of the aphorism (the single quatrain) is very similiar to Emily Dickinson's manner of proceeding through contradiction and paradox to a realization of the truth.

   The rose which here and now
      thine outer eyes behold
   For all eternity
      hath also bloomed in God.

   God is as small as I,
    I am as great as he;

Above me he cannot,
    nor I below him, be.

God is the fire in me,
    And I the light in him.
Are we not, each to each,
    most inwardly akin?

No here nor now can touch
    God, who is nothingness;
The more we reach for him,
    the more he vanishes.

"Gazing upon the sun,"
    sayest thou, "I lose all sight."
Blame that upon thine eyes,
    not upon his great light.

Up, bride! The bridegroom comes!
    And none shall him possess
Save one who, on the instant,
    can be in readiness.

The wedding dress is love—
    The spirit's love—and God.
Don it, and doff thereby
    what makes thy spirit sad.

The Godhead is a spring,
    from it do all things flow,
And to it they flow back.
    Hence 'tis an ocean too.

Love is like unto death,
    it kills my every sense.

It breaks my heart in me,
   and takes my spirit hence.

And is this Golgotha?
   But then how can it be
That lily and rose are here
   in fadeless bravery?
And there the tree of life,
   the spring with the four rivers?
Then it is Paradise.
   Yet whate'er be its name—
Golgotha, Paradise—
   To me it is the same.

Nothing imperfect is:
   equal are gold and tin,
Frogs are as beautiful
   as are the Seraphim.

C. *Francis Quarles,* Emblem 11, Book III. *The engraving for
this emblem is the frontispiece to this book.*

The Poem

The world's a sea; my flesh a ship that's mann'd
With lab'ring thoughts & steer'd by reason's hand
My heart's the seaman's card, whereby she fails;
My loose affections are the greater sails;
The top-sail is my fancy, and the gusts
That fill these wanton sheets are worldly lusts.
Pray'r is the cable, at whose end appears
The anchor hope, ne'er slip'd but in our fears;
My will's th' unconstant pilot, that commands
The stagg'ring keel; my sins are like the sands:
Repentance is the bucket, and mine eye
The pump unus'd (but in extreams) and dry:
My conscience is the plummet that does press
The deeps, but seldom cries, O *fathomless:*
Smooth calm's security; the gulph, despair;

My fraight's corruption, and this life's my fare:
My soul's the passenger, confus'dly driv'n
From fear to fright; her landing port is heav'n.
My seas are stormy, and my ship doth leak;
My sailers rude; my steers-man faint and weak:
My canvass torn, it flaps from side to side:
My cable's crackt, my anchor's slightly ty'd,
My Pilot's craz'd; my ship-wrack sands are cloak'd;
My bucket's broken, and my pump is choak'd;
My calm's deceitful; and my gulf too near;
My wares are slubber'd, and my fare's too dear:
My plummet's light, it cannot sink nor sound;
O, shall my rock-bethreaten'd soul be drown'd?
Lord, still the seas, and shield my ship from harm;
Instruct my sailors, guide my steersman's arm:
'Touch thou my compass, and renew my sails,
Send stiffer courage or send milder gales;
Make strong my cable, bind my anchor faster;
Direct my pilot, and be thou his master;
Object the sands to my more serious view,
Make sound my bucket, bore my pump a new:
New-cast my plummet, make it apt to try
Where the rocks lurk, and where the quick-sands lie;
Guard thou the gulf with love, my calms with care;
Cleanse thou my fraight; accept my slender fare;
Refresh the sea-sick passenger; cut short
His voyage; land him in his wished port:
Thou, thou, whom winds and stormy seas obey,
That through the deep gav'st grumbling Isr'el way,
Say to my soul, be safe; and then mine eye
Shall scorn grim death, although grim death stand by.
O thou whose strength—reviving arm did cherish
Thy sinking Peter, at the point to perish,
Reach forth thy hand, or bid me tread the wave,
I'll come, I'll come; the voice that calls will save.

S. AMBROSE

The confluence of lust makes a great tempest
which in this sea disturbeth the sea faring soul,
that reason cannot govern it.

S. Augustine

We labour in the boisterous sea: thou standest
upon the shore and seest our dangers; give us
grace to hold a middle course betwixt Scylla and
Charybdis, that both dangers escaped, we may
arrive at the port secure.

Epigram

My soul, the seas are rough, and thou a stranger
In these false coasts; O keep aloof; there's danger:
Call forth thy plummet; see a rock appears;
Thy ship wants sea-room, make it with thy tears.

D. *Selections from Sir Thomas Browne in Chambers'* Cyclopaedia

[Oblivion.]

What song the syrens sang, or what name Achilles assumed when he hid
himself among women, though puzzling questions, are not beyond all conjecture. What time the persons of these ossuaries entered the famous nations
of the dead, and slept with princes and counsellors, might admit a wide solu-
tion. But who were the proprietaries of these bones, or what bodies these
ashes made up, were a question above antiquarianism; not to be resolved by
man, nor easily perhaps by spirits, except we consult the provincial guardians,
or tutelary observators. Had they made as good provision for their names as
they have done for their relics, they had not so grossly erred in the art of per-
petuation. But to subsist in bones, and be but pyramidally extant, is a fallacy
in duration. Vain ashes, which, in the oblivion of names, persons, times, and
sexes, have found unto themselves a fruitless continuation, and only arise unto
late posterity, as emblems of mortal vanities, antidotes against pride, vain-
glory, and maddening vices. Pagan vain-glories, which thought the world
might last for ever, had encouragement for ambition, and finding no Atropos
unto the immortality of their names, were never damped with the necessity
of oblivion. Even old ambitions had the advantage of ours, in the attempts of
their vain-glories, who, acting early, and before the probable meridian of
time, have by this time found great accomplishment of their designs, whereby
the ancient heroes have already outlasted their monuments and mechanical
preservations. But in this latter scene of time we cannot expect such mummies

unto our memories, when ambition may fear the prophecy of Elias;[1] and Charles V. can never hope to live within two Methuselahs of Hector.[2]

And therefore restless inquietude for the diuturnity of our memories unto present considerations, seems a vanity almost out of date, and superannuated piece of folly. We cannot hope to live so long in our names as some have done in their persons; one face of Janus holds no proportion unto the other. It is too late to be ambitious. The great mutations of the world are acted, or time may be too short for our designs. To extend our memories by monuments, whose death we daily pray for, and whose duration we cannot hope, without injury to our expectations, in the advent of the last day, were a contradiction to our beliefs. We, whose generations are ordained in this setting part of time, are providentially taken off from such imaginations; and being necessitated to eye the remaining particle of futurity, are naturally constituted unto thoughts of the next world, and cannot excusably decline the consideration of that duration, which maketh pyramids pillars of snow, and all that is past a moment.

Circles and right lines limit and close all bodies, and the mortal right-lined circle[3] must conclude and shut up all. There is no antidote against the opium of time, which temporally considereth all things. Our fathers find their graves in our short memories, and sadly tell us how we may be buried in our survivors. Grave-stones tell truth scarce forty years. Generations pass while some trees stand, and old families last not three oaks. To be read by bare inscriptions like many in Gruter,[4] to hope for eternity by enigmatical epithets, or first letters of our names, to be studied by antiquaries who we were, and have new names given us, like many of the mummies, are cold consolations unto the students of perpetuity, even by everlasting languages.

To be content that times to come should only know there was such a man, not caring whether they knew more of him, was a frigid ambition in Cardan; disparaging his horoscopal inclination and judgment of himself, who cares to subsist, like Hippocrates' patients, or Achilles' horses in Homer, under naked nominations, without deserts and noble acts, which are the balsam of our memories, the *entelechia* and soul of our subsistences. To be nameless in worthy deeds exceeds an infamous history. The Canaanitish woman lives more happily without a name than Herodias with one. And who had not rather have been the good thief, than Pilate?

But the iniquity of oblivion blindly scattereth her poppy, and deals with the memory of men without distinction to merit of perpetuity: who can but pity

---

[1] That the world may last but six thousand years.

[2] Hector's fame lasting above two lives of Methuselah, before that famous prince was extant.

[3] The character of death.

[4] Gruteri Inscriptiones Antiquæ.

the founder of the pyramids? Herostratus lives that burnt the temple of Diana; he is almost lost that built it: time hath spared the epitaph of Adrian's horse; confounded that of himself. In vain we compute our felicities by the advantage of our good names, since bad have equal durations; and Thersites is like to live as long as Agamemnon, without the favour of the everlasting register. Who knows whether the best of men be known? or whether there be not more remarkable persons forgot than any that stand remembered in the known account of time? Without the favour of the everlasting register, the first man had been as unknown as the last, and Methuselah's long life had been his only chronicle.

Oblivion is not to be hired: the greatest part must be content to be as though they had not been; to be found in the register of God, not in the record of man. Twenty-seven names make up the first story before the flood; and the recorded names ever since contain not one living century. The number of the dead long exceedeth all that shall live. The night of time far surpasseth the day, and who knows when was the equinox? Every hour adds unto that current arithmetic which scarce stands one moment. And since death must be the Lucina of life; and even Pagans could doubt whether thus to live were to die; since our longest sun sets at right descensions, and makes but winter arches, and therefore it cannot be long before we lie down in darkness, and have our light in ashes; since the brother of death daily haunts us with dying mementos, and time, that grows old in itself, bids us hope no long duration; diuturnity is a dream, and folly of expectation.

Darkness and light divide the course of time, and oblivion shares with memory a great part even of our living beings; we slightly remember our felicities, and the smartest strokes of affliction leave but short smart upon us. Sense endureth no extremities, and sorrows destroy us or themselves. To weep into stones are fables. Afflictions induce callosities; miseries are slippery, or fall like snow upon us, which, notwithstanding, is no unhappy stupidity. To be ignorant of evils to come, and forgetful of evils past, is a merciful provision in nature, whereby we digest the mixture of our few and evil days; and our delivered senses not relapsing into cutting remembrances, our sorrows are not kept raw by the edge of repetitions. A great part of antiquity contented their hopes of subsistency with a transmigration of their souls—a good way to continue their memories, while, having the advantage of plural successions, they could not but act something remarkable in such variety of beings; and, enjoying the fame of their passed selves, make accumulation of glory unto their last durations. Others, rather than be lost in the uncomfortable night of nothing, were content to recede into the common being, and make one particle of the public soul of all things, which was no more than to return into their unknown and divine original again. Egyptian ingenuity was more unsatisfied, contriving their bodies in sweet consistencies to attend the return of their souls. But all was vanity, feeding the wind, and folly. The Egyptian mummies, which Cambyses or time hath spared, avarice now consumeth. Mummy is become merchandise; Mizraim cures wounds, and Pharaoh is sold for balsams.

                      *   *   *

There is nothing strictly immortal but immortality. Whatever hath no beginning may be confident of no end, which is the peculiar of that necessary essence that cannot destroy itself, and the highest strain of omnipotency to be so powerfully constituted as not to suffer even from the power of itself; all others have a dependent being, and within the reach of destruction. But the sufficiency of Christian immortality frustrates all earthly glory, and the quality of either state after death makes a folly of posthumous memory. God, who can only destroy our souls, and hath assured our resurrection, either of our bodies or names hath directly promised no duration; wherein there is so much of chance, that the boldest expectants have found unhappy frustration, and to hold long subsistence seems but a scape in oblivion. But man is a noble animal, splendid in ashes, and pompous in the grave, solemnising nativities and deaths with equal lustre, nor omitting ceremonies of bravery in the infamy of his nature.   *   *   *

Pyramids, arches, obelisks, were but the irregularities of vain-glory, and wild enormities of ancient magnanimity. But the most magnanimous resolution rests in the Christian religion, which trampleth upon pride, and sits on the neck of ambition, humbly pursuing that infallible perpetuity, unto which all others must diminish their diameters, and be poorly seen in angles of contingency.

Pious spirits, who passed their days in raptures of futurity, made little more of this world than the world that was before it, while they lay obscure in the chaos of pre-ordination and night of their fore-beings. And if any have been so happy as truly to understand Christian annihilation, ecstacies, exolution, liquefaction, transformation, the kiss of the spouse, gustation of God, and ingression into the divine shadow, they have already had a handsome anticipation of heaven: the glory of the world is surely over, and the earth in ashes unto them.

To subsist in lasting monuments, to live in their productions, to exist in their names, and predicament of chimeras, was large satisfaction unto old expectations, and made one part of their elysiums. But all this is nothing in the metaphysics of true belief. To live indeed is to be again ourselves, which being not only a hope but an evidence in noble believers, 'tis all one to lie in St Innocent's churchyard, as in the sands of Egypt; ready to be anything in the ecstacy of being ever, and as content with six foot as the moles of Adrianus.

[*Light the Shadow of God.*]

Light that makes things seen makes some things invisible. Were it not for darkness, and the shadow of the earth, the noblest part of creation had remained unseen, and the stars in heaven as invisible as on the fourth day, when they were created above the horizon with the sun, and there was not an eye to behold them. The greatest mystery of religion is expressed by adumbration, and in the noblest part of Jewish types we find the cherubim shadowing the mercy-seat. Life itself is but the shadow of death, and souls departed but the shadows of the living. All things fall under this name. The sun itself is but the dark Simulachrum, and light but the shadow of God.

[*Toleration.*]

I could never divide myself from any man upon the difference of an opinion, or be angry with his judgment for not agreeing with me in that from which within a few days I should dissent myself.

[*Death.*]

I thank God I have not those strait ligaments or narrow obligations to the world, as to dote on life, or be convulsed and tremble at the name of death. Not that I am insensible of the dread and horror thereof, or, by raking into the bowels of the deceased, continual sight of anatomies, skeletons, or cadaverous relics, like vespilloes, or grave-makers, I am become stupid, or have forgot the apprehension of mortality; but that, marshalling all the horrors, and contemplating the extremities thereof, I find not anything therein able to daunt the courage of a man, much less a well-resolved Christian. And therefore am not angry at the error of our first parents, or unwilling to bear a part of this common fate, and like the best of them to die, that is, to cease to breathe, to take a farewell of the elements, to be a kind of nothing for a moment, to be within one instant of a spirit. When I take a full view and circle of myself, without this reasonable moderator and equal piece of justice, death, I do conceive myself the miserablest person extant. Were there not another life that I hope for, all the vanities of this world should not intreat a moment's breath for me; could the devil work my belief to imagine I could never die, I would not outlive that very thought; I have so abject a conceit of this common way of existence, this retaining to the sun and elements, I cannot think this is to be a man, or to live according to the dignity of humanity. In expectation of a better, I can with patience embrace this life, yet in my best meditations do often desire death. I honour any man that contemns it, nor can I highly love any that is afraid of it: this makes me naturally love a soldier, and honour those tattered and contemptible regiments, that will die at the command of a sergeant. For a Pagan there may be some motives to be in love with life; but for a Christian to be amazed at death, I see not how he can escape this dilemma, that he is too sensible of this life, or hopeless of the life to come.   *   *

It is a brave act of valour to contemn death; but where life is more terrible than death, it is then the truest valour to dare to live; and herein religion hath taught us a noble example. For all the valiant acts of Curtius, Scævola, or Codrus, do not parallel or match that one of Job; and sure there is no torture to the rack of a disease, nor any poniards in death itself, like those in the way or prologue to it. 'Emori nolo, sed me esse mortuum nihil curo' — ['I would not die, but care not to be dead']. Were I of Cæsar's religion, I should be of his desires, and wish rather to go off at one blow, than to be sawed in pieces by the grating torture of a disease. Men that look no further than their outsides, think health an appurtenance unto life, and quarrel with their constitutions for being sick; but I that have examined the parts of man, and know upon what tender filaments the fabric hangs, do wonder that we are not always so; and considering the thousand doors that lead to death, do thank my God that we can die but once. It is not only the mischief of diseases, and villany of poisons, that make an end of us: we vainly accuse the fury of guns, and the new inventions of death; it is in the power of every hand to destroy us, and we are beholden unto every one we meet he doth not kill us. There is, therefore, but one comfort left, that though it be in the power of the weakest arm to take away life, it is not in the strongest to deprive us of death: God would not exempt himself from that, the misery of immortality in the flesh; he undertook not that was immortal. Certainly there is no happiness within this circle of flesh, nor is it in the optics of those eyes to behold felicity; the first day of our jubilee is death. The devil hath therefore failed of his desires; we are happier with death, than we should have been without it. There is no misery but in himself, where there is no end of misery; and so, indeed, in his own sense, the stoic is in the right. He forgets that he can die who complains of misery; we are in the power of no calamity while death is in our own.

[Study of God's Works.]

The world was made to be inhabited by beasts, but studied and contemplated by man; it is the debt of our reason we owe unto God, and the homage we pay for not being beasts; without this, the world is still as though it had not been, or as it was before the sixth day, when as yet there was not a creature that could conceive, or say there was a world. The wisdom of God receives small honour from those vulgar heads that rudely stare about, and with a gross rusticity admire his works; those highly magnify him whose judicious inquiry into his acts, and deliberate research into his creatures, return the duty of a devout and learned admiration.

[*Ghosts.*]

I believe that the whole frame of a beast doth perish, and is left in the same state after death as before it was materialed unto life; that the souls of men know neither contrary nor corruption; that they subsist beyond the body, and outlive death by the privilege of their proper natures, and without a miracle; that the souls of the faithful, as they leave earth, take possession of heaven; that those apparitions and ghosts of departed persons are not the wandering souls of men, but the unquiet walks of devils, prompting and suggesting us unto mischief, blood, and villany, instilling and stealing into our hearts; that the blessed spirits are not at rest in their graves, but wander solicitous of the affairs of the world; but that those phantasms appear often, and do frequent cemeteries, charnel-houses, and churches, it is because those are the dormitories of the dead, where the devil, like an insolent champion, beholds with pride the spoils and trophies of his victory over Adam.

[*Of Myself.*]

For my life it is a miracle of thirty years, which to relate were not a history, but a piece of poetry, and would sound to common ears like a fable. For the world, I count it not an inn but a hospital, and a place not to live but to die in. The world that I regard is myself; it is the microcosm of my own frame that I can cast mine eye on—for the other I use it but like my globe, and turn it round sometimes for my recreation. * * The earth is a point not only in respect of the heavens above us, but of that heavenly and celestial part within us. That mass of flesh that circumscribes me, limits not my mind. That surface that tells the heavens it hath an end, cannot persuade me I have any. * * Whilst I study to find how I am a microcosm or little world, I find myself something more than the great. There is surely a piece of divinity in us— something that was before the heavens, and owes no homage unto the sun. Nature tells me I am the image of God as well as Scripture. He that understands not thus much, hath not his introduction or first lesson, and hath yet to begin the alphabet of man.

[*Charity.*]

But to return from philosophy to charity: I hold not so narrow a conceit of this virtue, as to conceive that to give alms is only to be charitable, or think a piece of liberality can comprehend the total of charity. Divinity hath wisely divided the acts thereof into many branches, and hath taught us in this narrow way many paths unto goodness: as many ways as we may do good, so many ways we may be charitable; there are infirmities, not only of body, but of soul and fortunes, which do require the merciful hand of our abilities. I cannot contemn a man for ignorance, but behold him with as much pity as I do Lazarus. It is no greater charity to clothe his body, than apparel the nakedness of his soul. It is an honourable object to see the reasons of other men wear our liveries, and their borrowed understandings do homage to the bounty of ours. It is the cheapest way of beneficence, and, like the natural charity of the sun, illuminates another without obscuring itself. To be reserved and caitiff in this part of goodness, is the sordidest piece of covetousness, and more contemptible than pecuniary avarice. To this (as calling myself a scholar) I am obliged by the duty of my condition: I make not, therefore, my head a grave, but a treasure of knowledge; I intend no monopoly, but a community in learning; I study not for my own sake only, but for theirs that study not for themselves. I envy no man that knows more than myself, but pity them that know less. I instruct no man as an exercise of my knowledge, or with an intent rather to nourish and keep it alive in mine own head, than beget and propagate it in his; and in the midst of all my endeavours, there is but one thought that dejects me, that my acquired parts must perish with myself, nor can be legacied among my honoured friends. I cannot fall out, or contemn a man for an error, or conceive why a difference in opinion should divide an affection: for controversies, disputes, and argumentations, both in philosophy and in divinity, if they meet with discreet and peaceable natures, do not infringe the laws of charity. In all disputes, so much as there is of passion, so much there is of nothing to the purpose; for then reason, like a bad hound, spends upon a false scent, and forsakes the question first started. And this is one reason why controversies are never determined; for though they be amply proposed, they are scarce at all handled, they do so swell with unnecessary digressions; and the parenthesis on the party is often as large as the main discourse upon the subject.

Notes

Chapter One: The First Publication

[1] *The Letters of Emily Dickinson,* ed. Thomas H. Johnson (Cambridge, Mass., 1958) —hereafter cited as *Letters* —p. 408.

[2] See Chapter Five.

[3] See Chapter Three.

[4] *Letters,* p. 545; pp. 841–42.

[5] *Letters,* p. 726.

[6] *Letters,* p. 769.

[7] R. B. Sewall, *The Lyman Letters* (Amherst, 1965). These record Joseph Lyman's decision not to fulfill his intention to marry Lavinia but to take Miss Laura Baker instead.

[8] As early as February, 1887, only nine months after ED's death, Mrs. Todd was already at work copying the poems. This entry in her diary (Thursday, February 17, 1887) would seem to indicate the activity had become a matter of course: "Feel brighter today. Finished attic curtains in the morning, & made David put them up. In the afternoon a few of Emily's poems copied on the typewriter."

[9] All poems quoted are from *The Poems of Emily Dickinson,* ed. Thomas H. Johnson (Cambridge, Mass., 1955).

[10] Millicent Todd Bingham, *Ancestors' Brocades* (New York, 1945), p. 402.

[11] A close analysis of the gatherings in any single fascicle makes clear that theme was not an organizing principle. See Appendix I.

[12] Preface, *Poems, First Series* (Boston, 1890).

[13] *Ancestors' Brocades,* pp. 64–65.

[14] *Ancestors' Brocades,* p. 72.

[15] *Ancestors' Brocades,* p. 140.

[16] *Ancestors' Brocades,* p. 142.

[17] Among the poems left by ED there were more than sixty describing her dedication to Jesus, and twenty-five others in which the explicit metaphor of the dedicated bride of Christ appears. Over one hundred poems speak of her

commitment to poetry. And the same interplay of thought and image exists among them all. See Appendix II.

[18] These passages, and those following, are taken from letters that appear in *Ancestors' Brocades,* Chapter IX, "Preparation of *Poems, Second Series."*

[19] There is among the manuscript holdings in the Houghton Library, Harvard University, a packet of poems written by Lavinia. They are in the "Miscellaneous Box" and dated 1898. The following three poems are typical:

Night

The stars kept winking and blinking,
    as if they had secrets to tell;
But as nobody asked any questions,
    Nobody heard any tales.

. . .

The ingenuity of pain
    Groping for tenderest nooks
Then plants its fangs in quivering flesh.

. . .

The pines let drop their needles
    As noiseless as the snow,
They carpet all the woods with plush
    And light the darkest paths.

[20] *The Recognition of Emily Dickinson,* ed. by Caesar R. Blake and Carlton F. Wells (Ann Arbor, 1964) contains reprints of the most caustic attacks made on the poetry, notably those of Andrew Lang in England and Maurice Thompson in America. Their objections are the same as those earlier warnings of Arlo Bates to Thomas Niles. A full documentation of the critical reception of *Poems, First Series* is contained in an as yet unpublished manuscript by Karl Oppens, "Der Literarische Ruhm Emily Dickinsons." He has recovered a multitude of ephemeral reviews as they appeared in newspapers and journals scattered across America and in England.

[21] W. D. Howells, "The Strange Poems of Emily Dickinson," *Harper's New Monthly Magazine,* LXXXII (January, 1891), 318–20.

[22] Esther calls him "Master" and speaks with reverence of his part in bringing her poetic nature to fruition.

[23] Jay Leyda, *The Years and Hours of Emily Dickinson,* II (New Haven, 1960), p. 296.

[24] He approached ED at the suggestion of Helen Hunt Jackson.

[25] Leyda, p. 297.

[26] *Ibid.,* p. 213.

[27] *Ibid.,* p. 239.

[28] T. W. Higginson, "Emily Dickinson's Letters," *Atlantic Monthly,* LXVIII (October, 1891), 453.

[29] *Ancestors' Brocades,* p. 164.

[30] "Introduction to the First Edition," *Letters of Emily Dickinson* (Boston, 1894), 2 Volumes.

[31] This whole legend of the secrecy of the poet's activities may very well have stemmed from this predilection. It cannot be verified, for the one place where one would expect to find the evidence for the truth of the story of Lavinia arriving "shortly after Emily's death . . . trembling with excitement [for] she had discovered a veritable treasure—a box full of Emily's poems which she had had no instructions to destroy," (*Ancestors' Brocades,* p. 16) is silent on this episode. In neither the diary nor the journal which Mrs. Todd kept so faithfully is there a single reference or note to this event, which surely would have provided some excitement for Mrs. Todd.

[32] *Ancestors' Brocades,* p. 310.

Chapter Two: Literary Intrigue

[1] Martha Gilbert Dickinson Bianchi, *The Point of View* (New York, 1918).

[2] Martha Dickinson Bianchi, *The Life and Letters of Emily Dickinson* (Boston, 1924).

[3] In the same year, 1924, Mrs. Bianchi, now in possession of all copyrights, combined *Poems, First Series, Second Series, Third Series* with her own *The Single Hound* and published *The Complete Poems of Emily Dickinson.* No effort was made to change the organization of the book; the poems were still divided according to their subject matter, and as Mrs. Todd had long ago expanded the section on religion to prove the poet had been orthodox, so now Mrs. Bianchi added many love poems to prove the poet had been in love. All the textual emendations, especially the excessive alterations of *Poems, Third Series,* remained in this reprinting. When still another volume, *Further Poems,* appeared, in 1929, the errors there led some reviewers to remark that many poems seemed spurious.

[4] Genevieve Taggard, *The Life and Mind of Emily Dickinson* (New York, 1930).

[5] Josephine Pollitt, *Emily Dickinson: The Human Background of her Poetry* (New York, 1930).

[6] Wadsworth had not died; he had simply gone to California.

[7] Not only were these poems written during the Civil War period, but newspapers and magazines were featuring articles on artillery operations. Higginson himself wrote several.

[8] *Ancestors' Brocades,* p. 384, pp. 389–90.

[9] *Letters of Emily Dickinson,* ed. Mabel Loomis Todd (Boston, 1931), New and Enlarged Edition, pp. 342–357.

[10] *Emily Dickinson: Face to Face,* ed. Martha Dickinson Bianchi (Boston, 1932).

[11] Although *Ancestors' Brocades* was completed in 1935, it was withheld from publication until the death of Mrs. Bianchi, which occurred in 1943.

[12] *Unpublished Poems of Emily Dickinson,* ed. Martha Dickinson Bianchi and Alfred Leete Hampson (Boston, 1935).

[13] *Bolts of Melody: New Poems of Emily Dickinson,* ed. Mabel Loomis Todd and Millicent Todd Bingham (New York, 1945).

[14] Millicent Todd Bingham, *Emily Dickinson: A Revelation* (New York, 1954).

[15] Millicent Todd Bingham, *Emily Dickinson's Home* (New York, 1955).

[16] *Ancestors' Brocades,* p. 111.

[17] As nearly as can be judged, ED continued to create her threaded booklets into the 1870's. Thomas Johnson ascribes the last fascicle to the year 1872. But Packets 86 through 93 contain 240 poems that are neatly transcribed, despite variant words, and seem either to be awaiting the poet's decision, or to have been placed aside as second best, but not so poor that they needed to be discarded.

[18] George F. Whicher, *This Was A Poet* (New York, 1938), p. 138.

[19] I believe that Constance Rourke's influential study of American humor had recently come out of the ground, in 1931: *American Humor: A Study of National Character.* Thereafter no critic wrote on any nineteenth-century American writer without devoting a portion of his study to that writer's comic spirit. *Ibid.,* p. 153.

[20] Henry W. Wells, *Introduction to Emily Dickinson* (Chicago, 1947), p. 276.

[21] Richard Chase, *Emily Dickinson* (New York, 1951), p. 131.

[22] Rebecca Patterson, *The Riddle of Emily Dickinson* (Boston, 1951).

[23] Clark Griffith, *The Long Shadow: Emily Dickinson's Tragic Poetry* (Princeton, 1964).

[24] *Ibid.,* p. 6.

[25] *The Poems of Emily Dickinson,* Including Variant Readings Critically Compared with all Known Manuscripts, ed. Thomas H. Johnson (Cambridge, Mass., 1955).

[26] *The Letters of Emily Dickinson,* eds. Thomas H. Johnson and Theodora Ward (Cambridge, Mass., 1958).

[27] Jay Leyda, *The Years and Hours of Emily Dickinson* (New Haven, 1960).

[28] *Thomas H. Johnson, An Interpretative Biography* (Cambridge, Mass., 1955), p. 214.

[29] The interpretations of Friedrich, Ciardi, Anderson and Hogue are taken from *14 by Emily Dickinson,* ed. T. M. Davis (Chicago, 1964), pp. 65–69.

[30] Griffith, *Long Shadow,* pp. 135–37.

[31] William Howard, "Emily Dickinson's Poetic Vocabulary," *PMLA,* LXXII (1957), 225–48.

[32] "The Private World: Poems of Emily Dickinson," in *Poetry and Experience* (Boston, 1961).

[33] "Poetry and Punctuation," *Saturday Review,* XLVI (March, 1963), 20–27.

[34] *Int. Biog.,* p. 84.

[35] *Int. Biog.,* p. 88.

[36] Charles R. Anderson, *Emily Dickinson's Poetry: Stairway of Surprise* (New York, 1960), p. 24.

[37] R. H. Pearce, "On the Continuity of American Poetry," *Hudson Review* (Winter, 1958), 518–39.

[38] The most disconcerting example of such fragmentation is the recent study by Albert J. Gelpi, *Emily Dickinson: The Mind of the Poet* (Cambridge, 1965). He wrenches lines from any place in the canon in order to document his narrative, whether it be the legend of Wadsworth as the renounced lover, or his survey of nineteenth-century Puritanism, Romanticism, and Transcendentalism.

It is no surprise to find a critic in the 1960's still writing about Wadsworth in this way; once Thomas Johnson had affirmed it, few would question so authoritative a judgment of the matter. But it is surprising to find a critic in the 1960's so freely juxtaposing snippets from widely scattered contexts, disjointing not merely chronology but the poems as discrete entities along the way.

Chapter Three: "Letter to a Young Contributor"

[1] Saints and Their Bodies, I, p. 582.
Mademoiselle's Campaigns, II, p. 193.
Water-Lilies, II, p. 465.
Physical Courage, II, p. 728.
Ought Women to Learn the Alphabet?, III, p. 137.
A Letter to a Dyspeptic, III, p. 464.

A Charge with Prince Rupert, III, p. 725.

The Murder of the Innocents, IV, p. 345.

The Maroons of Jamaica, V, p. 213; The Maroons of Surinam, V, p. 549.

Theodore Parker, VI, p. 449.

Fayal and the Portuguese, VI, p. 526.

Barbarism and Civilization, VII, p. 51.

Gymnastics, VII, p. 283.

April Days, VII, p. 385.

Denmark Vesey, VII, p. 528.

The Ordeal by Battle, VIII, p. 88.

Nat Turner's Insurrection, VIII, p. 173.

My Out Door Study, VIII, p. 302.

A New Counterblast, VIII, p. 696.

Snow, IX, p. 188.

Letter to a Young Contributor, IX, p. 401.

2 "Thomas Wentworth Higginson gives us in 'My Out Door Study' one of his deliciously truthful pictures of rural scenes and diversions . . ." *Spr. Rep.,* Aug. 21, 1861.

3 *Letters,* #260.

4 *Cecil Dreeme* is a novel by Theodore Winthrop, 1862. Cecil Dreeme, an artist living in Washington Square, New York, is torn by spiritual conflict.

5 See, for example, "The Malay—took the Pearl—" " 'Tis little I—could care for Pearls—" "Shells from the Coast mistaking—" and "I play at Riches—to appease."

6 Among those sent to Bowles, the following poems were not copied into any fascicle:

I would distil a cup,

Should you but fail [at] —Sea—

Teach Him—when He makes the *names*—

The Juggler's *Hat* her Country is—

While Asters—

I'll send the feather from my Hat!

"*Speech*"—is a prank of *Parliament*—

Would you like summer? Taste of ours.

If it had no pencil

Title divine—is mine!

Ourselves we do inter with sweet derision.

He is alive, this morning—

As Summer into Autumn slips

I have no Life but this —
Could mortal lip divine
Not that he goes — we love him more

Nor were these transcribed: (to the Hollands)

I have a Bird in spring [also Sue]
The Wind begun to knead the Grass — [also Higginson and Sue]
Count not that far that can be had, [also Sue]

(to Higginson)

Best Gains — must have the Losses' Test —
Not "Revelation" — 'tis — that waits, [also Sue]
Paradise is of the option.

(to Sue)

Whose cheek is this?
Is it true, dear Sue?
Could *I* — then — shut the door —
An Hour is a Sea
Love reckons by itself — alone —
The Dust behind I strove to join

[7] See his Chapter I, *The Art of Emily Dickinson's Early Poetry* (Cambridge, 1966), p. 1.

[8] It is worth noticing that Emily Dickinson wrote the following poem and transcribed it into Fascicle 31:

Wolfe demanded during dying
"Which obtain the Day"?
"General, the British" — "Easy"
Answered Wolfe "to die"

Montcalm, his opposing Spirit
Rendered with a smile
"Sweet" said he "my own Surrender
Liberty's beguile"

[9] Her third letter, June 7, 1862, echoes this phrase: "You think me 'uncontrolled' — I have no Tribunal."

[10] It is impossible to fix with absolute accuracy the date of composition of any poem left in the booklets. Johnson explains that the poems were copied from worksheets that were then discarded. He wisely refrains from any assumption of infallibility in his dating of the poems. But it scarcely matters

that we prove she wrote this in 1862 rather than in 1863, which is Johnson's assigned date. What is relevant is the recurring metaphor. ED very often constructed a poem deliberately out of an image she encountered in her reading. She liked to challenge her thoughts (and skill) by borrowing a fragment out of the newspaper and magazine verse or from the less than elegant books she pored over, and then proceed to improve it. The alteration of the word "distilled" to the far more tortuous "wrung" is a good example of her practice. See Appendix III for examples of the sources of her borrowings.

[11] See Appendix II, G, H, J.

[12] That the metaphors direct us to this meaning may be verified by citing the definition for "disc," in the Webster's 1847 Dictionary that ED used:

Disc: in Botany, the whole surface of a leaf; the central part of a radiate compound flower. A term applied to certain bodies or projections situated between the base of the stamens and the base of the ovary, but forming part with neither.

The minuteness of that part of the flower, and the fact of the specific arrangement of the parts does suggest the design of a snowflake.

[13] There are a great many poems in the canon which render the paradox in just these terms, poems that depict the problem, the irresolution, the insolubility and yet always the challenge of the quest for such knowledge. (See Appendix II, D.)

[14] See Appendix II, D, The Poems That Contemplate the Problem of Knowing.

Chapter Four: Dickinson and Higginson

[1] Jay Leyda's *Years and Hours* recaptures much useful and elusive material. Higginson's letters appear there. II, p. 55.

[2] "Emily Dickinson's Letters," *Atlantic Monthly*, Oct. 1891.

[3] *Letters*, #261 (April 25, 1862).

[4] *Letters*, #153 (January 13, 1854) to E. E. Hale. "Mr. Newton was with my Father two years, before going to Worcester. . . . I was then but a child . . . [he] became to me a gentle, yet grave Preceptor. . . ."

[5] *Spr. Rep.*, Apr. 3, 1860.

[6] Martin Tupper's poetry, *Proverbial Philosophy* (1846), was in the Dickinson library.

[7] *Spr. Rep.*, Aug. 11, 1860.

[8] This question is explored in Appendix III where the material contained in the Dickinson library is discussed in this connection. There was, for example, the well-thumbed volumes *Divine Emblems* by Francis Quarles, *Inscriptions on the Grave Stones in the Grave Yards of Northampton and of*

other towns in the Valley of the Connecticut, compiled by Bridgman, and *Lyra Domestica,* collected by Spitta, works never mentioned anywhere by Emily Dickinson but which provide many instances of her borrowing. Indeed there are as many instances as one has patience to track down in these and in the more obvious sources, the *Springfield Republican,* the *Atlantic* and *Harper's.*

Jack L. Capps refused to accept ED's "professed complete literary independence" and proceeded to make a careful study of the whole matter of her literary influences, tracing allusions in her prose and verse to their sources, usually, in the Dickinson library. When he has no direct allusions as his clue, he works from the other direction, finding marked passages in the books in the library and locating similar passages in the poems. *Emily Dickinson's Reading: 1836–1886* (Cambridge, 1966).

[9] In Fascicle 86 there are two poems transcribed onto a single piece of stationery, an obvious sign that they were related. One is a speculation about poetry, the other is a contemplation of the meaning of death.

> To own the Art within the Soul
> The Soul to entertain
> With Silence as a Company
> And Festival maintain
>
> Is an unfurnished Circumstance
> Possession is to One
> As an Estate perpetual
> Or a reduceless Mine.
>
> . . .
>
> There is a finished feeling
> Experienced at Graves—
> A leisure of the Future—
> A Wilderness of Size.
>
> By Death's bold Exhibition
> Preciser what we are
> And the Eternal function
> Enabled to infer.

[10] "The Errand from My Heart—" *Horizon,* III (July, 1961), 100–105.

[11] *Int. Biog.,* p. 114.

[12] "South Winds jostle them—" has been thought a bagatelle written to accompany a gift of flowers, but it is more plausible to suppose that Emily

Dickinson used this poem as a gift card for her enclosed poems, which do indeed seem to be pluckings from her world of nature:

> South Winds jostle them —
> Bumblebees come —
> Hover — Hesitate — Drink, and are gone —
> Butterflies pause — on their passage Cashmere —
> I, softly plucking,
> Present them — Here —

[13] "There's a certain slant of light" has these lines:

> We can find no scars,
> But internal difference,
> Where the meanings are.

[14] "They are religious — except me — and address an Eclipse . . . whom they call their 'Father.'" In the Lexicon "seal" is a mark of authenticity; it signifies fulfilled and complete.

[15] *Explicator*, XI, December 1952, Item 17.

[16] "Emily Dickinson's Love Poetry," *The University of Kansas City Review*, XXVIII, Winter 1960, p. 96.

[17] *Stairway of Surprise*, p. 11.

[18] James T. Fields was the editor of *Atlantic Monthly*.

[19] *The Long Shadow*, p. 9.

[20] *Ibid.*, p. 169.

[21] *Letters*, #193.

[22] *Letters*, #223.

[23] *Letters*, #187.

[24] *Letters*, #233.

[25] *Int. Biog.*, p. 104.

[26] He formed the first all-Negro company to fight for the North.

[27] *Int. Biog.*, p. 113.

[28] *Victorian Poets*, pp. 262–65.

[29] *Int. Biog.*, p. 110.

[30] *Int. Biog.*, p. 99.

[31] See Appendix II, C, Poems that render the poet's longing to be with someone.

[32] See Appendix II, O, Poems that have the metaphor of a boat or a ship at sea, on the sea.

[33] See Appendix I.

[34] *Letters*, #265.

[35] *Spr. Rep.*, July 7, 1860.

[36] John Berryman, *Stephen Crane,* New York, 1950, p. 58.

[37] *Literary History of the United States,* Eds. Spiller, Thorp, Johnson, Canby. New York, 1957, pp. 1184–1189.

Chapter Five: Dickinson and Bowles

[1] There is a variant poem which combines the image of stooping and the allusion to the Travelling Show and joins these to a metaphor of the mountain and the Daisy, a conception of the relationship between Bowles and herself that appears frequently in the poems of appeal, notably in the "Master Letters" and the verses associated with them.

> The Himmaleh was known to stoop
> Unto the Daisy low —
> Transported with Compassion
> That such a Doll should grow
> Where Tent by Tent — Her Universe
> Hung out it's Flags of Snow —

This poem appears in Fascicle 19, and it is copied onto the same sheet of paper with "Why do I love" You, Sir?

[2] George S. Merriam, *The Life and Times of Samuel Bowles* (New York, 1885), p. 388. It has been erroneously assumed that Franklin Sanborn wrote the literary articles and reviews for the *Republican.* But during the time under discussion here, 1858–1861, Sanborn was in Concord; between 1855 and 1858 he boarded in Mrs. Thoreau's house, walking and talking daily with Henry Thoreau [Joseph Wood Krutch, *Thoreau,* American Men of Letters Series, New York, 1948]. Bronson Alcott's *Journal* has an entry for January 9, 1859: "Sanborn, Henry Thoreau, and Allen take tea and pass the evening with us." In 1859 Sanborn was deeply involved with John Brown and his cause; he helped Brown secure arms and eventually became so entangled in the raid on Harper's Ferry, he had to flee arrest. Thus that line of reasoning which argues for Sanborn as the man responsible for the literary articles and poems that appeared in the *Republican* is false. We have, in addition to Merriam's statement, "At this time, and for a number of years, the literary editor was Mrs. Frances H. Cook . . ." several references to Mrs. Cook in Bowles' own letters to his wife, for example, this written on July 29, 1861: "I wish you would give my love to Mrs. Cook[e], and thank her for her pleasant note."

[3] *Years and Hours,* I, p. 363.

[4] *Years and Hours,* I, p. 366.

[5] Johnson's comment on "Tho' my destiny be Fustian —" reveals how important it is to read Emily Dickinson in context with poems similar in

thought or imagery rather than in terms of conjecture that derives from the obvious and the conventional. His note says "This poem, which may have accompanied the gift of a rose, evidently was sent to Dr. and Mrs. Holland." But the poet says she prefers her Gipsey being, and the word in the fourth stanza, "Roses" derives from the "Rosier" bosom of the second stanza, and not from ED's garden. And what would poor Mrs. Holland make of that Autumn "pencil"? Johnson edited the poem, but perhaps forgot the second stanza of the variant:

> The General Rose—decay—
> But this—in Lady's Drawer
> Make Summer—When the Lady lie
> In Ceaseless Rosemary—

Perhaps Johnson forgot also that Dr. Holland wrote verse.

[6] *Years and Hours,* I, p. 368.

[7] Saturday, April 30, 1859. Collette was a frequent contributor:

Spr. Rep.: February 18, 1860: "Susie"; February 25, 1860: "A Bygone"; March 31, 1860: "Are You Glad?" January 5, 1861: "Fallen Asleep"; March 9, 1861: "Waiting"; March 30, 1861: "The Silent Army"; April 13, 1861: "A Story for Little Nellie"; June 2, 1861: "Mary," "Ho-Hum"; June 9, 1861: "The Deep Sleep." It is a curious coincidence that Collette Loomis was the lamented sister of Eben Jenks Loomis, the father of Mabel Loomis Todd.

[8] *Spr. Rep.,* February 20, 1860.

[9] *Spr. Rep.,* July 14, 1860.

[10] *Letters,* #223.

[11] An advertisement for the printer, Samuel Bowles & Co., announces "*Catalogues of the State Normal School at Westfield.*"

[12] Chase, p. 83.

[13] I leave the full discussion of this article to a later context, the second Master letter.

[14] "He was weak, and I was strong—then—" renders the encounter in much the same way, laying more emphasis on this long passage of time.

[15] Johnson identifies Herschel as the astronomer who discovered the planet Uranus.

[16] Emily Dickinson renders her fantasy of this transcendent reunion in several variant poems noted in the Appendix under the rubric of "Quest" II, P.

[17] We recognize this moat of pearl as a variant image of the belt of poetry that was put around the poet's life in "He put the Belt around my life—" and the baggage strapped with pearl which the poet carried with her on her way to Heaven from "Dropped into the Ether Acre—"

[18] The puzzled inquiry that was sent by a local poet to Samuel Bowles is discussed in Chapter Nine.

Chapter Six: The Master Letters I

[1] *Letters,* #187.

[2] A letter, #252, sent to Samuel Bowles, has this phrase: "When you come to Amherst, please God it were Today—I will tell you about the picture—if I can, I will."

[3] This line has relevance too for that cryptic paragraph written to T. W. Higginson: "You say 'Beyond your knowledge.' You would not jest with me, because I believe you—but Preceptor—you cannot mean it? All men say 'What' to me, but I thought it a fashion." (*Letters,* #271.)

[4] There is a duplication of this thought in *Letters,* #193, to Bowles: "Good Night, Mr. Bowles! This is what they say who come back in the morning, also the closing paragraph on repealed lips. Confidence in Daybreak modifies Dusk."

[5] It is interesting to see that even the word "Postillions" has in addition to the common meaning (the riders on the lead horse, acting as guide), also a relationship to "Postillator: one who expounds Scripture, verse by verse."

[6] *Letters,* #193.

[7] *Letters,* #205.

[8] This poem is in Fascicle 82, where "If recollecting were forgetting," may be found. There are so many poems describing flowers as signs of regeneration in Fascicle 82 one is tempted to characterize that fascicle as a repository for these messages.

[9] See Appendix II F, Poems that personify Nature.

[10] "I never told the buried gold"; "Like her the Saints retire"; "Artists wrestled here!" "If this is 'fading'"; "The Sun kept stooping—stooping—low!" "She sweeps with many-colored Brooms—" and "Blazing in Gold and quenching in Purple."

[11] See Appendix II H, Poems that contemplate the experience of death.

[12] See Appendix II O, Poems that have the metaphor of a ship at sea, or the sea.

[13] See Appendix II D, Poems that contemplate the problem of knowing.

[14] See Appendix II M, Poems rendering quest.

[15] The Lexicon defines "Loom" as "That part of an oar which is within board," quoting the Maritime Dictionary.

Chapter Seven: The Master Letters II

[1] *Letters,* #233.

[2] "That *Bareheaded life*—under the grass—worries one like a Wasp."

[3] *Him* refers back to *Day,* as in the last line *He* means *Day.*

[4] This is a reference to the pious cant that accompanies any sentence of a court, when the sentence is death.

[5] "The first Day's Night had come—" "Sunset at Night—is natural—" "We grow accustomed to the Dark." See Appendix II A, Poems that render an affliction. Every fascicle but two is represented.

[6] This metaphor derives from the event in Scripture when Christ appears to his disciples and announces his identity. All believed except Thomas, who was convinced only after he had put his fingers into the wounds on Christ's body; only then did Thomas cease to doubt the reality of the suffering of Jesus.

[7] This conception Emily Dickinson has of her poetry as a means of release is exactly the same view she expressed to Higginson in the third letter she wrote to him (#265, June 7, 1862): "I felt a palsy, here—the Verses just relieve." The palsy derived from her fear of death.

[8] The Lexicon definition of crescent is "increasing, growing."

[9] The Lexicon has another definition for crescent. It is the very name of the military order "instituted by Renatus, of Anjou, King of Sicily [the Plantagenets] so-called from the symbol of a crescent of gold-enamelled."

[10] Here is the metaphor from which the letter to Bowles derived. Both images echo exactly Byron's "Sonnet on Chillon":

> Eternal Spirit of the chainless Mind!
>   Brightest in dungeons, Liberty! thou art,
>   For there thy habitation is the heart—
> The heart which love of thee alone can bind;
> And when thy sons to fetters are consign'd—
>   To fetters, and the damp vault's dayless gloom,
>   Their country conquers with their martyrdom,
> And Freedom's fame finds wings on every wind.
> Chillon! thy prison is a holy place,
>   And thy sad floor an altar. . . .

One recalls in this literary context Emily Dickinson's poem:

> Talk with prudence to a Beggar
> Of "Potosi," and the mines!
> Reverently, to the Hungry
> Of your viands, and your wines!
>
> Cautious hint to any Captive
> You have passed enfranchized feet!
> Anecdotes of air in Dungeons
> Have sometimes proved deadly sweet!

Here is proof, surely, that Emily Dickinson's protestation to T. W. Higginson that she would never "consciously touch a paint, mixed by another person—" (*Letters*, #271) was mere hyperbole.

[11] This is a reference to Bowles' active support of liberal causes and public events as well as to his departures.

[12] This thought survives the encounter and revives in the poem "I could suffice for Him, I knew—" and its brooding variant, "I cannot live with You—"

[13] Long afterwards, the reason for the decision to "elude" unqualified eyes is given:

> I shall not murmur if at last
> The ones I loved below
> Permission have to understand
> For what I shunned them so—
> Divulging it would rest my Heart
> But it would ravage their's—
> Why, Katie, Treason has a Voice—
> But mine—dispels—in Tears.

The poet says that the withdrawal, the shunning of men and women, had a specific cause, hinting it was some act of treason which had a voice (as that Vesuvius did, as the *Springfield Republican* did). The poem is presumed to have been written in 1877.

[14] Any one of the poems listed in Appendix II C, Poems that render the poet's longing to be with someone or his transfiguring power, may have served as example here.

[15] *Letters*, #249. The brackets here indicate illegible letters.

[16] *Letters*, #248.

[17] That this was also the case with her sister-in-law, Susan, will be amply demonstrated by Professor Richard B. Sewall in his forthcoming biography. He describes the two households with an authority derived from the hard evidence of indisputable documents.

[18] *Letters*, #229.

[19] *Letters*, #241.

[20] See Appendix II I, Poems that contemplate Jesus or God.

[21] *Letters*, #415.

Chapter Eight: The Poetic Manner

[1] See Appendix II C, Poems that render the poet's longing to be with someone or his transfiguring power.

[2] Any one of the poems listed in Appendix II B, Poems that render the solitary self as a conscious choice, may serve as an example.

[3]

Put up my lute!
What of—my Music!
Since the sole ear I cared to charm—
Passive—as Granite—laps my Music—
Sobbing will suit—as well as psalm!

Chapter Nine: The Practice of Poetry

[1] He may have taken his cue from Theodore Spencer's review in *New England Quarterly,* II (July, 1929) p. 498: "Had she lived in the seventeenth century, her position would have been . . . somewhere between Herbert and Donne."

[2] Whicher, pp. 210–11.

[3] Judith Banzer, "Compound Manner: Emily Dickinson and the Metaphysical Poets," *American Literature,* XXXII (Jan. 1961), 417–33.

[4] This column usually had a caption "Gems from . . ." which may have inspired the poet to insist and insist on her own "gems."

[5] Anderson, pp. 298–99.

[6] He must therefore miss such an intriguing borrowing as this line from a letter to Samuel Bowles dated November 1862:

I did not need the little Bat—to enforce your memory—for that can stand alone, like the Best Brocade—

with its variant in a letter to Higginson dated November 1871:

Mrs. Hunt's Poems are stronger than any written by women since Mrs— Browning, with the exception of Mrs Lewes—but truth like Ancestor's Brocades can stand alone—

Johnson's note to both letters (#277, #368) suggests this was a reference to George Eliot's *The Mill on the Floss* and he quotes the line:

Mrs. Glegg . . . had inherited from her grandmother . . . a brocaded gown that would stand up empty, like a suit of armour . . .

But there is also this line that appears in Act Second, Scene One of *The Contrast,* by Royall Tyler (1787), one of our earliest American plays:

His conversation is like a rich old fashioned brocade, it will stand alone;

[7] Capps, p. 145.

[8] *Cyclopaedia of English Literature,* ed. Robert Chambers (Boston, 1847), II, 202.

[9] Chambers', I, pp. 109–10.

[10] On "Oblivion," on "Light the Shadow of God," "Toleration," "Death," "Study of God's Works," "Ghosts," "Of Myself," and "Charity." Nowhere is the word "circumference" mentioned. See Appendix III D.

[11] In Appendix III B are reprinted poems from the *Hymns,* the *Lyra,* the *Inscriptions,* that may just as well have been substituted for those quoted on the pages above. In Appendix III A, the Emily Dickinson Association material lists the titles of books that may be examined as possible sources for the poet's borrowings. Especially significant in this respect is Quarles' entire book of *Divine Emblems,* where glosses may be found for an incalculable number of lines. An Emblem is reprinted in Appendix III C.

Jack Capp's book on Emily Dickinson's reading is rich in examples of the poet's use of literature as flint to her spark. Quarles' book does not even appear in Capps' listing, but he does provide the sources of many perplexing allusions scattered throughout the Poems.

In Appendix II are lists of Emily Dickinson's poems arranged under the rubrics of ideas and metaphors; these may supply variant poems for any ones cited above.

[12] In the Variorum text, Johnson's note says this poem was sent to Samuel Bowles and that it was signed "Emily." But in the *Letters* he seems less certain. His note to Letter #220 tells us that the poem was found among the letters and poems sent to Bowles, that it was in the poet's handwriting, on a folded sheet of paper, but that there was a message written in an unfamiliar hand on the inside of the piece of stationery. He quotes the message:

> Enclosed in this was a sprig of white pine, which I have carefully preserved; I have also laid aside for you a letter of thanks from Clara Pease [a frequent contributor to the Original Poetry column]. You may expect to hear from the children by the next bulletin. I hope you are all well.
>
> F. H. C.

Johnson is puzzled. He speculates:

> "F. H. C." has not been identified, nor is it clear whether "F. H. C." was an intermediary between ED and Bowles, or one of her correspondents. No correspondent with those initials is known, and since the poem is signed "Emily," one suspects it was intended for Bowles.

Mrs. Frances H. Cook was the literary editor of the *Springfield Republican* and she may simply have been opening Bowles' correspondence while he was recovering from an attack of sciatica at Northampton. It is a curious coincidence that the same issue of the *Republican* that printed "The May-Wine" by ED also printed "What Fell with the Flag at Sumter," signed "F. H. C." (May 4, 1861). The newspaper had been publishing poems signed by its literary editor for years and continued to do so well after 1862.

[13] It is this phrase precisely that was the take-off point for all the Browne scholarship.

[14] Considering both Chambers' assessment of Browne and Tyler's summary dismissal of his school of writing, it is no surprise to find the 1847 Lexicon forgoing any examples of usage that derive from such exemplars. Webster chooses Milton whenever he can find occasion for it.

[15] If we miss "circumferentor" there is always Emily Dickinson's compass.

Chapter Ten: The Fascicles

[1] This identifying number derives from the Houghton archives listing [H], the manuscript page assigned [55], and the location of the poem on the piece of stationery [a].

[2] We can see at once how frequently it was the practice of the poet to write variant poems and place them in variant fascicles, by citing another poem written on the same subject, Religious Doubt. It is the perishing and living anew, the annihilation and Immortality of H55c above that is Seesawing in this poem, H213c, Fascicle 24:

> Robbed by Death—but that was easy—
> To the failing Eye
> I could hold the latest Glowing—
> Robbed by Liberty
>
> For Her Jugular Defences—
> This, too, I endured—
> Hint of Glory—it afforded—
> For the Brave Beloved—
>
> Fraud of Distance—Fraud of Danger,
> Fraud of Death—to bear—
> It is Bounty—to Suspense's
> Vague Calamity—
>
> Staking our entire Possession
> On a Hair's result—
> Then—Seesawing—cooly—on it—
> Trying if it split—

[3] If anyone believes e. e. cummings invented the device of disjointed syntax let him study this quatrain. Conventionally the lines would read, The

Summer Grace for Notice strove / her best array to stimulate the Eye / Remote, the Heart Refused too utterly.

[4] Emily Dickinson will never forget to justify silence. Defense of silence is woven into the fibres of her soul.

[5] The imagery used to depict the action of wakeful memory is a modulation of the metaphor of a dramatic enactment from "Drama's Vitallest Expression is the Common Day."

[6] She says fairly the same thing in "I could suffice for Him, I knew—" The imagery of the "piercing Virtue" which puts out her eyes and leaves her with a "Covered Vision" has its variant in "Before I got my eye put out."

[7] Quarles (1592–1644) was urged by Phineas Fletcher to write English poems for these engravings. Mario Praz, *Studies in Seventeenth Century Imagery* (London, 1947), has much that is valuable on the emblematists of the seventeenth century, Quarles among them.

[8] We know that Emily Dickinson did have trouble with her eyes, and for a period of time did fear the loss of her sight, but that is not what she is referring to here, although doubtless it is the memory of this experience she is transforming into the metaphor of this poem.

[9] In another poem ("There came a Day at Summer's Full,") the poet is less timid and allows her soul to pass its solstice immediately.

[10] In "I heard a Fly buzz—when I died—" hearing gives way before sight fails.

A Selected Bibliography

I. Primary Sources

Poems, First Series. Ed. Mabel Loomis Todd and T. W. Higginson. Boston, 1890.

Poems, Second Series. Ed. Mabel Loomis Todd and T. W. Higginson. Boston, 1891.

Poems, Third Series. Ed. Mabel Loomis Todd. Boston, 1896.

The Single Hound: Poems of a Lifetime. Ed. Martha Dickinson Bianchi. Boston, 1914.

The Complete Poems of Emily Dickinson. Ed. Martha Dickinson Bianchi. Boston, 1924.

Selected Poems. Ed. Conrad Aiken. London, 1924.

Emily Dickinson. Ed. Louis Untermeyer. (The Pamphlet Poets) New York, 1927.

Further Poems of Emily Dickinson Withheld From Publication By Her Sister Lavinia. Ed. Martha Dickinson Bianchi and Alfred Leete Hampson. Boston, 1929.

Bolts of Melody: New Poems of Emily Dickinson. Ed. Mabel Loomis Todd and Millicent Todd Bingham. New York, 1945.

Emily Dickinson Love Poems. (The Peter Pauper Press) Mount Vernon, 1950.

Poems of Emily Dickinson. Ed. Louis Untermeyer. New York, 1952.

The Poems of Emily Dickinson, Including Variant Readings Critically Compared with all Known Manuscripts. Ed. Thomas H. Johnson. 3 vols. Cambridge, 1955.

The Complete Poems of Emily Dickinson. Ed. Thomas H. Johnson. Boston, 1960.

Final Harvest: Emily Dickinson's Poems. Ed. Thomas H. Johnson. Boston, 1961. 575 poems taken from *The Poems* . . .

Emily Dickinson. Ed. Alain Bosquet. (Poètes d'Aujourdui, no. 55) Paris, 1957. French and English texts of 100 poems.

A Concordance to the Poems of Emily Dickinson. Ed. S. P. Rosenbaum. Cornell University Concordance Series. Ithaca, 1965.

Letters of Emily Dickinson. Ed. Mabel Loomis Todd. Boston, 1894. Reissued, New York, 1931.

The Life and Letters of Emily Dickinson. Ed. Martha Dickinson Bianchi. Boston, 1924. 5th printing with corrections, 1929.

Emily Dickinson: Face to Face. Unpublished Letters With Notes and Reminiscences. Ed. Martha Dickinson Bianchi. Boston, 1932.

Emily Dickinson's Letters to Dr. and Mrs. Josiah Gilbert Holland. Ed. Theodora Van Wagenen Ward. Cambridge, 1951.

Emily Dickinson: A Revelation. Ed. Millicent Todd Bingham. New York, 1954.

Emily Dickinson's Home: Letters of Edward Dickinson and His Family. Ed. Millicent Todd Bingham. New York, 1955.

The Letters of Emily Dickinson. Ed. Thomas H. Johnson and Theodora Ward. 3 vols. Cambridge, 1958.

The Lyman Letters: New Light on Emily Dickinson and Her Family. Ed. Richard B. Sewall. Amherst, 1965.

II. *Biographical and Critical Works*

Adams, Richard P. "Pure Poetry: Emily Dickinson," *Tulane Studies in English,* VII (1957), 133–152.

Aiken, Conrad. "Emily Dickinson," in *A Reviewer's A B C.* New York, 1935.

Allen, Caroline C. "The Homestead in Amherst," *Horn Book,* XXXIII (February, 1957), 30–34.

Allen, Gay W. "Emily Dickinson," in *American Prosody.* New York, 1935.

Anderson, Charles R. *Emily Dickinson's Poetry: Stairway of Surprise.* New York, 1960.

– – –. "From a Window in Amherst: Emily Dickinson Looks at the American Scene," *New England Quarterly,* XXXI (1958), 147–171.

– – –. "The Conscious Self in Emily Dickinson's Poetry," *American Literature,* XXXI (1959), 290–308.

– – –. "The Trap of Time in Emily Dickinson's Poetry," *Journal of English Literary History,* XXVI (1959), 402–424.

Anthony, Mother Mary. "Emily Dickinson's Scriptural Echoes," *Massachusetts Review,* II (1961), 557–561.

Baldi, Sergio. "The Poetry of Emily Dickinson," *Sewanee Review,* LXVIII (1960), 438–449.

Banzer, Judith. "Compound Manner: Emily Dickinson and the Metaphysical Poets," *American Literature,* XXXII (1961), 417–433.

Barbot, Mary E. "Emily Dickinson Parallels," *New England Quarterly,* XIV (1941), 689–696.

Bingham, Millicent Todd. *Ancestor's Brocades: The Literary Debut of Emily Dickinson.* New York, 1945.

―――. *Emily Dickinson's Home.* New York, 1955.

―――. *Emily Dickinson: A Revelation.* New York, 1954.

―――. "Emily Dickinson's Handwriting: A Master Key," *New England Quarterly*, XXII (1949), 229–234.

Blackmur, R. P. "Emily Dickinson: Notes on Prejudice and Fact," in *The Expense of Greatness.* New York, 1940.

―――. "Emily Dickinson's Notation," *Kenyon Review,* XVIII (1956), 224–237.

Blake, Caesar Robert, and C. F. Wells, eds. *The Recognition of Emily Dickinson, Selected Criticism Since 1890.* Ann Arbor, 1964.

Bogan, Louise. "A Mystical Poet," in *Emily Dickinson: Three Views.* Amherst, 1960.

Bosquet, Alain. "Introduction," *Emily Dickinson.* (Poètes d'Aujourdui, no. 55) Paris, 1957.

Bradford, Gamaliel. "Emily Dickinson," in *Portraits of American Women.* Boston, 1919.

Brenner, Rica. "Emily Dickinson," in *Twelve American Poets Before 1900.* New York, 1933.

Brooks, Van Wyck. "Emily Dickinson," in *New England: Indian Summer.* New York, 1940.

Brown, Winnifred, and Alma Watson, eds. *Guests in Eden.* A collection of testimonial essays to Martha Dickinson Bianchi. New York, 1946.

Cambon, Glauco. "On Translating Dickinson," *Chelsea,* No. 7 (1960), 77–87.

―――. "Violence and Abstraction in Emily Dickinson," *Sewanee Review,* LXVIII (1960), 450–464.

Capps, Jack L. *Emily Dickinson's Reading: 1836–1886.* Cambridge, 1966.

Carpenter, Frederick I. "Emily Dickinson and the Rhymes of Dreams," *University of Kansas City Review,* XX (1953), 113–120.

Catel, Jean. "Emily Dickinson: Essai d'Analyse Psychologique," *Revue Anglo-Amér.,* II (1925), 394–405.

―――. "Emily Dickinson: L'Oeuvre," *Revue Anglo-Amér.,* II (1925), 105–120.

Chase, Richard. *Emily Dickinson.* New York, 1951.

Childs, Herbert Ellsworth. "Emily Dickinson, Spinster," *Western Humanities Review,* III (1949), 303–309.

―――. "Emily Dickinson and Sir Thomas Browne," *American Literature,* XXII (1951), 455–465.

Connors, Donald F. "The Significance of Emily Dickinson," *College English,* III (1942), 624–633.

Copple, Lee B. "Three Related Themes of Hunger and Thirst, Homelessness, and Obscurity as Symbols of Privation, Renunciation, and Compensation in the Poems of Emily Dickinson." Unpubl. Diss., University of Michigan, 1954.

Davidson, James. "Emily Dickinson and Isaac Watts," *Boston Public Library Quarterly,* VI (1954), 141–149.

England, Martha W. "Emily Dickinson and Isaac Watts: Puritan Hymnodists," *Bulletin of the New York Public Library,* 69 (1965), 83–116.

Erskine, John. "The Dickinson Saga," *Yale Review,* XXXV (1945), 74–83.

Ford, Thomas W. "The Theme of Death in the Poetry of Emily Dickinson." Unpubl. Diss., University of Texas, 1959.

Franklin, R. W. *The Editing of Emily Dickinson, A Reconsideration.* Madison, 1967.

Frye, Northrop. "Emily Dickinson," in *Fables of Identity.* New York, 1963.

Garlington, Jack. "Emily Dickinson's Curious Biographers," *College Quarterly,* VI (1957), 170–177.

Gelpi, Albert J. *Emily Dickinson—The Mind of the Poet.* Cambridge, 1965.

Glenn, Eunice. "Emily Dickinson's Poetry: A Revaluation," *Sewanee Review,* LI (1943), 574–588.

Gregor, Norman. "The Luxury of Doubt: A Study of the Relationship Between Imagery and Theme in Emily Dickinson's Poetry," Unpubl. Diss., University of New Mexico, 1955.

Gregory, Horace. "The Real Emily Dickinson," *Commonweal,* LXVIII (August 1, 1958), 449–450.

Griffith, Clark. "Emily Dickinson's Love Poetry," *University of Kansas City Review,* XXVII (1960), 93–100.

– – –. *The Long Shadow: Emily Dickinson's Tragic Poetry.* Princeton, 1964.

Higgins, David J. "Portrait of Emily Dickinson: The Poet and her Prose," Unpubl. Diss., Columbia University, 1961.

Higginson, Thomas Wentworth. *Carlyle's Laugh and Other Surprises.* Boston, 1909.

– – –. "Emily Dickinson's Letters," *Atlantic Monthly,* 68 (1891), 444–456.

– – –. "Letter to a Young Contributor," *Atlantic Monthly,* 9 (1862), 401–411.

Hindus, Milton. "Emily's Prose: A Note," *Kenyon Review,* II (1940), 88–91.

Howard, William. "Emily Dickinson's Poetic Vocabulary," *PMLA,* LXXII (1957), 225–248.

Humiliata, Sister Mary. "Emily Dickinson—Mystic Poet?" *College English,* XII (1950), 144–149.

Jenkins, MacGregor. *Emily Dickinson, Friend and Neighbor.* Boston, 1930.

Jennings, Elizabeth. "Emily Dickinson and the Poetry of the Inner Life," *A Review of English Literature,* III (1962), 78–87.

Johnson, Thomas H. *Emily Dickinson: An Interpretive Biography.* Cambridge, 1955.

– – –. "Emily Dickinson, Creating the Poems," *Harvard Library Bulletin,* VII (1953), 257–270.

– – –. "Establishing a Text: The Emily Dickinson Papers," *Studies in Bibliography,* V (1952–1953), 21–32.

Jones, Rowena R. "Emily Dickinson's 'Flood Subject': Immortality." Unpubl. Diss., Northwestern University, 1960.

Junonen, Helvi. "Emily Dickinson," *Parnasso* (Helsinki) VII (1958), 245–249.

Kazin, Alfred. "Called Back," in *Contemporaries.* Boston, 1962.

Kelcher, Julia. "The Enigma of Emily Dickinson," *New Mexico Quarterly,* II (1932), 326–332.

Leary, Lewis. "The Poems of Emily Dickinson," *Thought,* XXXI (1956), 282–286.

Leyda, Jay. *A House to Be Born In.* Gehenna Press, 1958. (A poem)

– – –. *The Years and Hours of Emily Dickinson.* 2 vols. New Haven, 1960.

Lowell, Amy. *Poetry and Poets.* Boston, 1930.

MacLeish, Archibald. "The Private World," in *Emily Dickinson: Three Views.* Amherst, 1960.

McKay, Margery. "Amazing Sense: The Application of a New Method to the Poetry of Emily Dickinson." Unpubl. Honors Thesis, Swarthmore College, 1936.

McLean, (Miss) Sydney R. "Emily Dickinson at Mount Holyoke," *New England Quarterly,* VII (1934), 25–42.

McNaughton, Ruth Flanders. *The Imagery of Emily Dickinson.* University of Nebraska Studies, New Series, No. 4, 1949.

Manierre, William R. "Emily Dickinson: Visions and Revisions," *Texas Studies in Literature and Language,* V (1963), 5–16.

Marcellino, Ralph. "Emily Dickinson's 'Ablative Estate,'" *Classical Journal,* LIII (1958), 231–232.

Marcus, Mordecai. "Struggle for Integrity and Growth in the Poetry of Emily Dickinson." Unpubl. Master's Thesis, New York University, 1950.

– – –. "Nature Symbolism in the Poetry of Emily Dickinson." Unpubl. Diss., University of Kansas, 1958.

Matthiessen, F. O. "The Problem of the Private Poet," *Kenyon Review,* VII (1945), 584–597.

Maurois, André. "Emily Dickinson, poétesse et recluse," *Revue de Paris,* LX (1954), 1–13.

Meredith, Robert. "Emily Dickinson and the Acquisitive Society," *New England Quarterly,* XXXVII (1964), 435–452.

Miles, Susan. "The Irregularities of Emily Dickinson," *London Mercury,* XIII (1925), 145–158.

Miller, Betty. "Elizabeth and Emily Elizabeth," *Twentieth Century,* XLIX (1956), 578–583.

Miller, James E., Jr. "Emily Dickinson: The Thunderer's Tongue," *Minnesota Review,* II (1962), 289–304.

Monteiro, George. "Emily Dickinson's Merchant God," *Notes and Queries* (1959), 455–456.

– – –. "Traditional Ideas in Dickinson's 'I Felt a Funeral in My Brain,'" *Modern Language Notes,* LXXV (1960), 656–663.

Moore, Marianne. "Emily Dickinson," *Poetry,* XLI (1933), 219–226.

Moseley, Edwin. "The Gambit of Emily Dickinson," *University of Kansas City Review,* XVI (1949), 11–19.

Niemeyer, Carl A. "The Gentleman with the Deep Voice," *Union College Review,* XLVII (1958), 6–8.

Nist, John, "Two American Poets and a Spider," *Walt Whitman Birthplace Bulletin,* IV (1961), 8–11.

Ochshorn, Myron. "In Search of Emily Dickinson," *New Mexico Quarterly,* XXIII (1953), 94–106.

Oppens, Kurt. "Emily Dickinson: Uberlieferung und Prophetie," *Merkur,* XIV (1960), 17–40.

Parkes, E. W. "The Public and the Private Poet," *South Atlantic Quarterly,* LVI (1957), 480–485.

Pattee. F. L. "Gentian, Not Rose: The Real Emily Dickinson," *Sewanee Review,* 45 (1937), 180–197.

Patterson, Rebecca. "Elizabeth Browning and Emily Dickinson," *Education Leader,* XX (1956), 21–48.

– – –. "Emily Dickinson's Palette," *Midwest Quarterly,* V (Summer, 1964), 271–291.

– – –. "Emily Dickinson's Palette," (II), *Midwest Quarterly,* VI (Autumn, 1964), 91–117.

– – –. "Emily Dickinson's Hummingbird," *Education Leader,* XXII (1958), 12–19.

– – –. *The Riddle of Emily Dickinson.* Boston, 1951.

Pearce, R. H. "On the Continuity of American Poetry," *Hudson Review* (1958), 518–539.

Perkinson, Grace E. "Emily Dickinson and Children," *Horn Book,* XXXIII (1957), 19–27.

Pohl, Frederick J. "The Emily Dickinson Controversy," *Sewanee Review,* XLI (1933), 467–482.

Pollitt, Josephine. *Emily Dickinson: The Human Background of Her Poetry.* New York, 1930.

Porter, David T. *The Art of Emily Dickinson's Early Poetry*. Cambridge, 1966.

Powell, Desmond Stevens. *Emily Dickinson*. Colorado, 1934.

Power, Sister Mary James. *In the Name of the Bee: The Significance of Emily Dickinson*. New York, 1943.

Ransom, John Crowe. "Emily Dickinson: A Poet Restored," *Perspectives, USA*, No. 15 (1956), 5–20.

Rourke, Constance. *Amercian Humor: A Study of the National Character*. Garden City, 1931, pp. 209–212.

Schappes, Morris. "Errors in Mrs. Bianchi's Edition of Emily Dickinson's *Letters*," *American Literature*, IV (1933), 369–384.

Scott, Winfield T. " 'The Errand From My Heart,' " *Horizon*, III (1961), 100–105.

Sewall, Richard B., ed. *Emily Dickinson, A Collection of Critical Essays*. New Jersey, 1963.

Shackford, Martha. "Emily Dickinson," in *Talks on Ten Poets, Wordsworth to Moody*. New York, 1958, pp. 98–111.

Sherrer, Grace B. "A Study of Unusual Verb Constructions in the Poems of Emily Dickinson," *American Literature*, VII (1935), 37–46.

Southworth, James. "Emily Dickinson," in *Some Modern American Poets*. Oxford, 1950.

Spicer, John L. "The Poems of Emily Dickinson," *Boston Public Library Quarterly*, VIII (1956), 135–143.

Stamm, Edith Perry. "Emily Dickinson: Poetry and Punctuation," *Saturday Review*, XLVI (March, 1963), 20–27.

Sweetser, Kate Dickinson. "Emily Dickinson, A Girl of Genius," in *Great American Girls*. New York, 1931.

Taggard, Genevieve. *The Life and Mind of Emily Dickinson*. New York, 1930.

Tate, Allen. "Emily Dickinson," *Reactionary Essays on Poetry and Ideas*. New York, 1936.

Thackrey, Donald E. *Emily Dickinson's Approach to Poetry*. University of Nebraska Studies, New Series, No. 13, 1954.

Ward, Theodora Van Wagenen. "Emily Dickinson and T. W. Higginson," *Boston Public Library Quarterly*, V (1953), 3–18.

–––. *The Capsule of the Mind: Chapters in the Life of Emily Dickinson*. Cambridge, 1961.

Warren, Austin. "Emily Dickinson," *Sewanee Review*, LXV (1957), 565–586.

Wells, Anna M. *Dear Preceptor, the Life and Times of Thomas Wentworth Higginson*. Boston, 1963.

———. "Early Criticism of Emily Dickinson," *American Literature,* I (1929), 243–259.

Wells, Henry W. *Introduction to Emily Dickinson.* Chicago, 1947.

Wheatcroft, John S. "Emily Dickinson and the Orthodox Tradition," Unpubl. Diss., Rutgers University, 1960.

———. "Emily Dickinson's Poetry and Jonathan Edwards on the Will," *Bucknell Review,* X (1961), 102–127.

Whicher, George F. "Emily Dickinson's Earliest Friend," *American Literature,* VI (1934), 3–17.

———. "In Emily Dickinson's Garden," *Atlantic Monthly,* 177 (1946), 64–70.

———. *This Was a Poet: A Critical Biography of Emily Dickinson.* New York, 1938.

Wilbur, Richard. "Sumptuous Destitution," in *Emily Dickinson: Three Views.* Amherst, 1960.

Wilder, Thornton. "Emily Dickinson," *Atlantic Monthly,* 190 (1952), 43–48.

Willy, Margaret. "The Poetry of Emily Dickinson," *Essays and Studies,* X (1957), 91–104.

Wilson, Suzanne M. "Structure and Imagery Patterns in the Poetry of Emily Dickinson." Unpubl. Diss., University of Southern California, 1959.

———. "Emily Dickinson and Twentieth-Century Poetry of Sensibility," *American Literature,* XXXVI (1964), 349–358.

Winters, Yvor. "Emily Dickinson and the Limits of Judgment," in *Maule's Curse.* Connecticut, 1938.

Wright, Nathalia. "Emily Dickinson's 'Boanerges' and Thoreau's 'Atropos': Locomotives on the Same Line?" *Modern Language Notes,* LXXII (1957), 101–103.

For a listing of explications of individual poems see *Poetry Explication,* George Arms and Joseph M. Kuntz, eds. New York, 1950. Revised edition, Denver, 1962.

For compact reprints of varying interpretations of individual poems see *14 by Emily Dickinson,* Thomas M. Davis, ed. Chicago, 1964.

A Concordance to the Poems of Emily Dickinson, S. P. Rosenbaum, ed. Ithaca, N. Y., 1964.

Index of Poems by Variorum Number

ONLY THOSE POEMS WHICH WERE PLACED INTO FASCICLES OR PACKETS, or are otherwise significant, have been indexed.

Column one: poem number according to T. H. Johnson, *The Poems of Emily Dickinson,* Variorum edition.

Column two: fascicle or packet number according to the arrangement in the Houghton Library or Frost Library verified or revised by R. W. Franklin.

"X" signifies the poem was not placed into a threaded booklet or packet. "L" signifies "Letter." The number is that assigned by T. H. Johnson, *The Letters of Emily Dickinson.*

Column three: manuscript number.

"H" signifies the manuscript was in the possession of Martha Dickinson Bianchi (inherited from her mother, Susan Dickinson), transferred to Arthur Leete Hampson, sold to Gilbert Montague, who presented the collection to the Houghton Library, Harvard University, Cambridge, Massachusetts.

Column four: manuscript number.

"B" signifies the manuscript remained with Mabel Loomis Todd, was inherited by her daughter Millicent Todd Bingham, who presented the collection to the Frost Library, Amherst College, Amherst, Massachusetts.

INDEX OF POEMS by Variorum Numbers*

| 1 | 98 | B3–4 | 3 | X | SDR | |
| 2 | 95 | B6 | 4 | 82 | | B8 |

* Prepared with the assistance of Matthias Kriesberg.

5	X	L173		46	80	B6
6	82		B1a	47	80	B6
7	82		B5	48	80	B6a
8	80		B1	49	1	H3b
9	80		B1a	50	1	H3c
10	80		B1a	51	1	H3d
11	1	H3a		52	1	H4b
12	1	H4a		53	1	H4c
13	1	H4d		54	1	H4e
14	80		B8a	55	1	H4f
15	80		B2	56	80	B8
16	X	L193		57	80	B8a
17	80		B6a	58	1	H1a
18	82		B1	59	2–3	H5a
19	82		B1a	60	2–3	H7a
20	82		B2	61	2–3	H7b
21	82		B2	62	2–3	H7d
22	82		B2a	63	2–3	H7f
23	82		B3	64	2–3	H8a
24	82		B4	65	2–3	H8c
25	82		B4a	66	83	B1
26	82		B5a	67	83	B1a
27	82		B6	68	83	B2a
28	82		B6	69	83	B3a
29	82		B6a	70	83	B5
30	82		B7	71	83	B7a
31	82		B7	72	83	B8
32	82		B7a	73	2–3	H9a
33	82		B7a	74	2–3	H9b
34	82		B8a	75	2–3	H10b
35	82		B8a	76	2–3	H10d
36	80		B2	77	2–3	H10e
37	80		B2a	78	2–3	H11d
38	80		B2a	79	2–3	H12c
39	80		B3	80	2–3	H12d
40	80		B3a	81	7	H31b
41	80		B4	82	X	HB186
42	80		B4	83	7	H29a
43	80		B4a	84	83	B6a
44	80		B4a	85	7	H30c
45	80		B5a	86	83	B3

169	4	H14c		208	37	H201c
170	4	H14d		209	37	H201d
171	4	H15a		210	37	H201f
172	4	H15b		211	37	H202e
173	4	H15c		212	37	H202f
174	4	H15d		213	98	B3
	34	H184b		214	14?	H72a
175	4	H16a		215	15	H79
176	4	H16c		216	2–3	H11c
177	4	H16d			37	H203c
178	4	H17c		217	20	H110a
179	4	H17d		218	X	L232
180	4	H17e		219	23	H74b
181	14?	H72c		220	X	L239
182	14?	H72d		221	8	H36d
183	14?	H72e		222	X	L208
184	14?	H72f		223	8	H34
185	14?	H72g		224	37	H204d
	37	H201e		225	20	H110e
186	15	H78a		226	X	L249
187	15	H78b		227	X	L(1931)190
188	15	H78c		228	23	H127a
189	15	H80d		229	92	B4a
190	15	H80e		230	37	H200a
191	15	H81a		231	37	H200b
192	15	H81b		232	37	H200c
193	15	H81c		233	37	H200d
194	15	H81d		234	37	H203b
195	15	H82b		235	37	H204a
196	15	H82c		236	37	H204b
197	15	H83b		237	37	H204c
198	15	H83c		238	14?	H71c
199	15	H83d		239	14?	H71d
200	15	H33e		240	8	H36a
201	15	H83f			14?	H69c
202	15	H83g		241	32	H53b
203	15	H84a		242	32	H54c
204	15	H84b		243	8	H32d
205	15	H84c		244	8	H33a
206	15	H84d		245	8	H35b
207	37	H201b		246	8	H36c

247	8	H37		286	8	H33b		
248	8	H38a		287	8	H220		
249	8	H38b		288	8	H35a		
250	8	H38c		289	23	H126a		
251	8	H38d		290	23	H74c		
252	23	H126b		291	23	H129a		
253	23	H46a		292	23	H129c		
254	23	H46b		293	20	H109a		
255	23	H46c		294	20	H110d		
256	23	H46d		295	20	H111		
257	23	H74a		296	20	H112a		
258	23	H74d		297	20	H112b		
259	18	H98d		298	20	H112c		
	23	H127b		299	26	H47a		
260	23	H127c		300	5	H382b		
261	23	H127d		301	13	H63d		
262	23	H128b		302	13	H65b		
263	20	H109b		303	13	H65c		
264	20	H109c		304	16	H86b		
265	20	H110b		305	16	H87b		
266	20	H110c		306	17	H90a		
267	20	H110f	B32	307	21	H113c		
268	102			308	21	H115b		
269	15	H78d		309	25	H139b		
	18	H97c		310	26	H49b		
270	37	H203a		311	29	H155a		
271	14?	H71a		312	84		B7	
272	14?	H71b		313	9	H43a		
273	14?	H75a		314	19	H103b		
274	14?	H75b		315	19	H108c		
275	14?	H76a		316	31	H169b		
276	14?	H76b		317	8	H36b		
277	14?	H69b		318	37	H202a		
278	14?	H69d		319	14?	H69a		
279	32	H53a		320	98	B33		
280	32	H53c		321	14?	H77a		
281	32	H54a		322	23	H128a		
282	32	H54b		323	82		B4a	
283	8	H32a		324	15	H84e		
284	8	H32b		325	23	H129b		
285	8	H32c		326	27	H73c		

327	32	H171a			367	13	H64c	
328	85		B10		368	13	H66a	
329	84		B12		369	13	H66c	
330	X	L(1931)200			370	13	H66d	
331	X	L(1931)198			371	16	H85	
332	26	H47c			372	16	H86d	
333	27	H73a			373	16	H87a	
334	27	H73b			374	16	H87c	
335	25	H134d			375	16	H88a	
336	80		B7		376	16	H88d	
337	27	H23b			377	17	H90c	
338	27	H24a			378	17	H90d	
339	27	H24c			379	5	H93c	
340	6	H26b			380	17	H94a	
341	6	H26c			381	17	H94b	
342	6	H381a			382	17	H94c	
343	6	H381b			383	17	H67a	
	29	H70d			384	17	H68a	
344	6	H381c			385	17	H68c	
345	33	H179b			386	5	H95b	
346	33	H179c			387	5	H96c	
347	33	H179d			388	5	H96d	
348	85		B1		389	21	H113a	
349	85		B3a		390	21	H115a	
350	85		B4a		391	21	H115c	
351	85		B9		392	21	H115d	
352	85		B9a		393	21	H116a	
353	14?	H77c			394	21	H116c	
354	28	H149a			395	21	H117b	
355	28	H149c			396	21	H114a	
356	28	H150a			397	21	H114b	
357	28	H150c			398	21	H114c	
358	28	H150d			399	21	H114d	
359	17	H20b			400	91		
360	17	H20c			401	91		B11
361	17	H20d			402	25	H134b	B12a
362	17	H22c			403	25	H135d–136	
363	17	H22d			404	25	H137b	
364	13	H62a			405	25	H137c	
365	13	H63b			406	25	H137d	
366	13	H64b			407	25	H138d	

408	25	H139c		448	34	H183a	
409	25	H140b		449	34	H183c	
410	26	H141a		450	34	H183d	
411	26	H141b		451	34	H184a	
412	26	H142b		452	34	H184c	
413	26	H143a		453	34	H184d–185	
414	26	H172a		454	34	H186c–187	
415	26	H172c		455	40	H214a	
416	26	H173a		456	40	H214c	
417	26	H173b		457	40	H215a	
418	26	H173c		458	40	H217c	
419	26	H174a		459	40	H217d	
420	26	H174b		460	40	H218a	
421	26	H174c		461	40	H219a	
422	26	H48b		462	40	H219b	
423	26	H48c		463	40	H219c	
424	26	H48d		464	40	H219d	
425	27	H144a		465	84		B2
426	27	H144c		466	84		B5a
427	27	H145a		467	84		B6a
428	27	H145b		468	84		B8
429	27	H145c		469	84		B8a
430	27	H146a		470	84		B10
431	27	H146b		471	84		B12a
432	27	H146c		472	9	H39c	
433	27	H147		473	9	H40b	
	90		B7a	474	9	H42a	
434	28	H151b		475	9	H42c	
435	28	H151d		476	9	H43b–44a	
436	28	H152a		477	9	H44d	
437	28	H152c		478	11	H51b	
438	28	H153b		479	19	H104a	
439	28	H153c		480	19	H104b	
440	28	H154b		481	19	H104c	
441	29	H70b		482	19	H104d	
442	29	H70c		483	19	H106b	
443	29	H19a		484	19	H106d	
444	29	H158b		485	19	H107a	
445	32	H61a		486	19	H107c	
446	32	H61c		487	19	H107d	
447	34	H182b		488	19	H108a	

489	19	H108b		527	13	H64a	
490	88		B6a	528	13	H66b	
491	88		B6	529	17	H92a	
	89		B6	530	16	H92b	
492	89		B4	531	16	H92c	
493	89		B7	532	16	H384	
494	89		B56(?)	533	16	H86a	
	98	H23a	B4A-1	534	16	H88c	
495	27			535	16	H89a	
496	27	H23c		536	16	H89b	
497	27	H24b		537	17	H90b	
498	6	H25a		538	5	H91a	
499	6	H25b		539	5	H91b	
500	6	H26a		540	5	H91c	
501	6	H26d		541	5	H91d	
502	6	H381d		542	5	H93a	
503	6	H27		543	5	H93b	
504	33	H179a		544	5	H93d	
505	85		B2	545	17	H67b	
506	85		B3	546	17	H67c	
507	85		B4	547	17	H67d	
508	85		B5	548	17	H68b	
509	85		B6	549	17	H68d	
510	85		B7	550	5	H95a	
511	85		B8	551	5	H95c	
512	85		B11	552	5	H96a	
513	85		B12	553	5	H96b	
514	14	H77b		554	21	H113b	
515	5	H18a		555	21	H116b	
516	5	H18b		556	21	H116d	
517	5	H18c		557	21	H117a	
518	28	H149b		558	21	H117c	
519	28	H150b		559	21	H117d	
520	5	H382a		560	21	H117e	
521	5	H382c		561	21	H21a	
522	17	H22a		562	21	H21b	
523	17	H22b		563	91		B12
	88		B10a	564	25	H134a	
524	13	H62b		565	25	H134c	
525	13	H63a		566	25	H135a	
526	13	H63c		567	25	H135b	

649	11	H52a			690	11	H132b		
650	11	H52b			691	X	L229		
651	11	H52c			692	22	H118a		
652	19	H103a			693	22	H118b		
653	19	H105a			694	22	H118c		
654	19	H105b			695	22	H119b		
655	19	H105c			696	22	H121a		
656	19	H105d			697	22	H121b		
657	19	H106a			698	22	H121c		
658	19	H106c			699	22	H121d		
659	19	H106e			700	22	H122b		
660	19	H107b			701	22	H122d		
661	88		B5		702	22	H123b		
662	88		B5a		703	22	H123c		
663	89		B8		704	22	H123d–124		
664	98		B3–21		705	12	H55c		
665	18	H101c			706	12	H56b		
666	18	H101d			707	12	H56d		
667	12	H59a			708	12	H58b		
668	22	H119c			709	12	H59b		
669	84		B1a		710	11	H131b		
670	13	H65a			711	11	H133b		
671	18	H99b			712	31	H165a		
672	17	H20a			713	31	H165c		
673	22	H123a			714	31	H168b		
674	84		B2a		715	31	H168c		
675	11	H133d			716	31	H170a		
676	81		B4a		717	31	H170b		
677	81		B3a		718	81		B6	
678	31	H166a			719	81		B7	
679	12	H55a			720	18	H98c		
680	22	H120b			721	18	H99a		
681	30	H164a			722	18	H99c		
682	81		B11		723	18	H99d		
683	16	H88b			724	18	H100a		
684	X	L280			725	18	H100c		
685	X	L280			726	18	H100d		
686	30	H163c			727	18	H101b		
687	X	L(1931)202			728	18	H102b		
688	X	L252			729	18	H102c		
689	22	H122c			730	30	H160b		

731	30	H160c		772	81		B1a	
732	30	H162b		773	81		B2	
733	22	H118d		774	81		B2a	
734	22	H119a		775	81		B2a	
735	22	H119d		776	81		B3	
736	22	H120a		777	81		B4	
737	22	H125a		778	81		B5	
738	22	H125b		779	81		B5a	
739	22	H125c		780	81		B6a	
740	12	H55b		781	81		B7	
741	12	H56a		782	81		B7a	
742	12	H56c		783	81		B8	
743	12	H57a		784	81		B9	
744	12	H57b		785	81		B9a	
745	12	H57c		786	81		B10	
746	12	H58a		787	81		B11a	
747	12	H58c		788	18	H97b		
748	12	H58d		789	18	H98a		
749	12	H59c		790	18	H98b		
750	12	H60a		791	18	H100b		
751	12	H60b		792	18	H101a		
752	12	H60c		793	18	H102a		
753	12	H60d		794	30	H159a		
754	11	H131a		795	30	H159b		
755	11	H131c		796	30	H159c		
756	11	H132a		797	30	H160a		
757	11	H132c		798	30	H161b		
758	11	H133a		799	30	H161c		
759	31	H165b		800	30	H161d		
760	31	H166b		801	30	H163a		
761	31	H166c		802	30	H162c		
762	31	H167a		803	30	H162a		
763	31	H167b		804	30	H163b		
764	31	H167c		805	30	H164b		
765	31	H167d		806	30	H164c		
766	31	H168a		807	30	H164d		
767	31	H168d		808	86		B2	
768	31	H169a		809	86		B9	
769	31	H170c		810	86		B10	
770	31	H170d		811	86		B12a	
771	81		B1	812	86		B13	

813	86		B15	853	86		B12
814	87		B5	854	86		B13a
815	87		B5a	855	86		B16
816	87		B7	856	86		B16a
817	87		B10a	857	87		B1
818	91		B4	858	87		B1a
819	91		B6a	859	87		B3
820	91		B9a	860	87		B3
821	92		B4	861	87		B3a
822	92		B7	862	87		B4
823	33	H176d		863	87		B4
824	106		B8	864	87		B6
825	X	L312		865	87		B6a
826	X	HB163a		866	87		B8
827	24	H130a		867	87		B8a
828	92		B1	868	87		B9
829	92		B8a	869	87		B9a
830	33	H176c		870	87		B10
831	86		B7	871	87		B11
832	91		B2	872	87		B11a
833	87		B4a	873	87		B12
834	86		B8	874	91		B1
835	91		B3	875	91		B2a
836	87		B7	876	30	H161a	
837	91		B3a		86		B1a
838	86		B2	877	91		B3a
839	86		B3	878	91		B4a
840	86		B3a	879	91		B5
841	86		B4	880	91		B5a
842	86		B4a	881	91		B6
843	86		B7a	882	91		B10
844	86		B8	883	91		B13
845	86		B1	884	91		B13
	91		B3	885	91		B13a
846	86		B8a	886	91		B14a
847	86		B9	887	92		B2
848	86	B9a		888	92		B2a
849	86	B9a		889	92		B3
850	86	B10		890	92		B7a
851	86	B10a		891	92		B9a
852	86	B11		892	92		B11

893	92		B13a	933	87		B7a	
894	92		B15	934	87		B9	
895	92		B15a	935	87		B12a	
896	92		B16	936	87		B13	
897	92		B16	937	87		B13a	
898	92		B16a	938	87		B14	
899	92		B17a	939	87		B14a	
900	92		B18	940	91		B1a	
901	3	H177b		941	91		B2	
902	24	H209a		942	91		B4	
903	1	H2h		943	91		**B7**	
	24	H210a		944	91		B7a	
904	24	H210c		945	91		B9	
905	24	H210d		946	91		B10a	
906	24	H211a		947	91		B14	
907	24	H211b		948	92		B1a	
908	24	H211c		949	92		B3a	
909	24	H213b		950	92		B8	
910	33	H175a		951	92		B9	
911	33	H175d		952	92		B10	
912	33	H176b		953	92		B10a	
913	33	H177a		954	92		B12	
914	33	H177d		955	92		B12a	
915	33	H178a		956	92		B13	
916	33	H178b		957	92		B14	
917	33	H178c		958	92		B14a	
918	33	H178d		959	92		B17	
919	33	H178e		960	92		B18a	
920	33	H180c		961	24	H130b	
921	109		B14	962	24	H130c	
922	86		B1	963	24	H209b	
923	86		B2a	964	24	H209c	
924	86		B5	965	24	H209d	
925	86		B5a	966	24	H210b	
926	86		B6a	967	24	H211d	
927	86		B11	968	24	H212a	
928	86		B11a	969	24	H212b	
929	86		B14a	970	24	H213a	
930	86		B15a	971	24	H213c	
931	87		B1	972	24	H213d	
932	87		B2a	973	33	H175b	

974	33	H175c		1014	90		B12
975	33	H176a		1015	90		B12
976	33	H176e		1016	90		B12a
977	33	H177c		1017	90		B12a
978	33	H180a		1018	90		B13
979	33	H180b		1019	90		B13a
980	102		B42	1020	90		B14
981	102		B12	1021	90		B14a
982	18	H97a		1022	90		B15
	90		B2a	1023	90		B15
983	90		B4a	1024	90		B15a
984	90		B8a	1025	90		B16
985	88		B12a	1026	90		B16a
986	88		B13	1027	90		B17a
987	88		B14a	1028	90		B18
988	88		B17a	1029	90		B18
989	88		B18a	1030	88		B1
990	92		B6a	1031	88		B2
991	100		B8	1032	88		B2a
992	X	H331		1033	88		B3
993	11	H133c		1034	88		B4
994	88		B11a	1035	88		B7
995	90		B3a	1036	88		B7a
996	88		B4	1037	88		B7a
997	90		B1	1038	88		B8a
998	90		B2	1039	88		B9
999	90		B3	1040	88		B9a
1000	90		B4	1041	88		B10
1001	90		B5	1042	88		B10
1002	90		B5	1043	88		B10
1003	90		B5a	1044	88		B11a
1004	90		B5a	1045	88		B15
1005	90		B6	1046	88		B15a
1006	90		B6	1047	88		B16a
1007	90		B6a	1048	88		B17a
1008	90		B6a	1049	88		B18
1009	90		B7	1050	92		B6
1010	90		B9a	1051	102		B26
1011	90		B9a	1052	98		B3–14
1012	90		B10a	1053	16	H86c	
1013	90		B11a	1054	90		B1a

1055	90		B9	1099	35	H189b
1056	90		B10	1100	35	H191b
1057	90		B13a	1104	35	H188c
1058	90		B17	1105	86	
1059	88		B1a	1114	33	H176f
1060	88		B3a	1142	22	H122a
1061	88		B11	1177	38	H208d
1062	88		B12		90	
1063	88		B14	1180	93	
1064	88		B15	1181	84	B21b
1065	88		B17	1182	38	H206b
1067	84		B11	1185	38	H205a
1068	X	L314		1187	38	H205b
1069	X	L319		1189	93	
1070	88		B4a	1191	93	
1071	35	H188b		1194	38	H207
1072	X	L250		1195	38	H208b
1073	88		B1	1196	38	H205c
1074	X	L318		1197	38	H206a
1076	19	H108d		1200	38	H206c
1077	35	H189a		1201	38	H208a
1078	35	H189c		1202	93	
1079	35	H189d		1203	38	H208c
1080	35	H190a		1205	93	
1081	35	H190b		1209	36	H199a
1082	35	H190c		1214	93	
1083	35	H190d		1219	89	
1084	35	H191a		1220	89	
1085	35	H191c		1221	93	
1086	35	H192a		1224	36	H195
1087	35	H192b		1225	36	H281
1088	35	H192c		1226	36	H197
1089	35	H192d		1227	36	H198
1090	35	H193a		1228	36	H199b, c
1091	35	H193b		1229	93	
1092	35	H193c		1230	93	
1093	35	H193d		1231	93	
1094	35	H193e		1255	36	H196
1095	35	H193f		1256	93	
1097	35	H188a		1269	36	
1098	35	H188d		1272	93	

Right-hand column B-codes:
B14 (1105), B11 (1177/90), B7 (1180), B4 (1181), B2 (1189), B14 (1191), B1 (1202), B8 (1205), B4 (1214), B2 (1219), B1 (1220), B6 (1221), B3 (1229), B9 (1230), B13 (1231), B10 (1256), B103–8 (1269), B5 (1272)

1274	93		B12		1712	29	″
1280	93		B11		1725	13	″
1282	102		B11		1727	16	″
1344	38	H380c			1729	80	″
1353	38	H380a			1730	80	″
1354	38	H380b			1737	8	″
1540	92		B5		1739	16	″
1710	29	no ms.					

Index of Poems According to First Lines